Elizabeth Wiskemann

Elizabeth Wiskemann

Scholar, Journalist, Secret Agent

GEOFFREY FIELD

OXFORD
UNIVERSITY PRESS

OXFORD
UNIVERSITY PRESS

Great Clarendon Street, Oxford, OX2 6DP,
United Kingdom

Oxford University Press is a department of the University of Oxford.
It furthers the University's objective of excellence in research, scholarship,
and education by publishing worldwide. Oxford is a registered trade mark of
Oxford University Press in the UK and in certain other countries

First Edition published in 2023

Impression: 1

Published in the United States of America by Oxford University Press
198 Madison Avenue, New York, NY 10016, United States of America

British Library Cataloguing in Publication Data
Data available

Library of Congress Control Number: 2022943968

ISBN 978-0-19-287062-9

DOI: 10.1093/oso/9780192870629.001.0001

Printed and bound in the UK by
Clays Ltd, Elcograf S.p.A.

For Linda

Acknowledgments

One of the more agreeable tasks after finishing a book is thanking all the colleagues and friends who have helped along the way. Wiskemann's letters and other documents relevant to my task are dispersed, often in small batches, in many archives and several countries and I owe special thanks to numerous librarians and archivists in Britain, Germany, Switzerland, Italy, Ireland, and the United States who have answered my many queries, sent me copies of documents, and provided help when I could visit archives in person. They are too many to name, but I owe special thanks to Ms Anne Thomson, archivist at Newnham College, Cambridge; Dr. James Peters and Ms Karen Jacques of the John Rylands Library, Manchester; Ms Patricia McGuire, Archivist of King's College Cambridge; Ms Judith Curthoys of the Bodleian Library; Ms Rebecca Hughes of Trinity College, Cambridge Archives; Bill Noblett of the Cambridge University Library (for help with the J.H. Plumb papers); Mr Paul Barnaby, Archivist of the Edinburgh University Archives; Ms Helen Price of Leeds University Library; Ms Lucy McCann of the Bodleian; Mr Malcolm Madden of Chatham House; Mr Jeff Walden of the BBC Archives Caversham; Ms Elena Gallo of the Centro Studi Generazioni e Luoghi Archivi, Biella, Italy; Dr. Ilaria Della Monica, archivist of the I Tatti Berenson papers, Florence, and Dr. Ulrich Weber of the Schweizerisches Literaturarchiv, Bern. Also in Bern, Professor Roger Sidler and his son Leo were of great help with the Arnold Künzli Nachlass. The online finding-aids produced by archivists for these and other documentary collections were invaluable for locating unpublished papers; without them and the possibility of internet searches, my research would have been incomparably more difficult.

Several friends have provided help and encouragement. I owe a special debt to Volker Berghahn and Christoph Kimmich for reading the manuscript and making many suggestions. I am most fortunate to have Eric Foner as a friend, who over many years has read much of what I have written and never ceases to amaze me with his ability to zero in on key points and come up with solutions. Special thanks also to Carole Fink, Andrew Lyons, Isser Woloch, Louise Yelin, Christian Bailey, Seth Schein, Warren and Joanne Bender, and Dolores Obuch, who also read chapters in draft form and offered valuable comments. Jane Caplan, Deirdre David, David Cannadine, Linda Colley, and Vicky de Grazia provided information about Wiskemann or suggested people who could be helpful and pointed me to archives that might contain letters and other documentation. Both Fritz Stern, who years ago supervised my doctoral dissertation, and my former colleague at Purchase College, Jean Herskovits, showed great interest in this project; sadly, neither lived to see its completion. I am also very grateful to Sally Marks and A.J. Nicholls, who not long before their deaths shared with me their memories of Wiskemann. Thanks also to Professor Jomarie Alano, biographer of Ada Gobetti, Dr. Blair Worden (Oxford), Professor Julia Stapleton (Durham), Professor Ian Hall (Brisbane), and Arthur Gore, 9th Earl of Arran, who answered my questions. Very helpful in sorting out my ideas was an invitation from Professor Patricia Owens of Oxford and Dr. Katharina Rietzler of Sussex to contribute a chapter on Wiskemann to their book, *Women's International Thought: A New History* (Cambridge, 2020), which re-writes the standard disciplinary history of International Relations to include neglected women pioneers.

My thanks to the anonymous readers for Oxford University Press for their acute observations and suggestions. I am especially grateful to my editors at Oxford, Stephanie Ireland and Cathryn Steele, and to Vasuki Ravichandran and the whole production team, including a most painstaking and sharp-eyed copyeditor Giles Flitney and indexer Dawn Dobbins, for their expertise and professionalism in guiding this project across the finish line and into print.

I am also deeply grateful to David and Julian Brigstocke for sharing memories of their mother, Lady Brigstocke, the house on Moore Street, and Wiskemann, and especially for their help with photographs. Thanks also to George and Charles Burton, who sent me photographs of Wiskemann's parents and the Ipswich Burton family and copies of family wills. Carol Hartle Field's assistance with records on Ancestry.com was very helpful. As always, my brothers Les and Brian and their families provided support and hospitality during research trips to Britain. Above all, my thanks to my wife Linda, who read the manuscript and offered criticisms, provided tech support at crucial moments, and cheerfully accepted Wiskemann accompanying our European travels.

Contents

List of Abbreviations

BHE	Bund der Heimatvertriebenen und Entrechteten [League of German Expellees and Those Deprived of Their Rights]
CLNAI	Committee of National Liberation for Northern Italy
EW	Elizabeth Wiskemann
FO	Foreign Office
FRG	Federal Republic of Germany
GDR	German Democratic Republic
IfZ	Institut für Zeitgeschichte, Munich
IR	International Relations
LSE	London School of Economics
MI5	Military Intelligence, security service responsible for British territories
MI6	Military Intelligence, security service responsible for non-British territories
MI9	Military Intelligence responsible for assisting escape of British POWS and servicemen stranded behind enemy lines
MOI	Ministry of Information
NA	National Archives, Kew, London
NAAFI	Navy, Army and Air Force recreational institutes in the war years and later
NAWA	National Archives Washington
NATO	North Atlantic Treaty Organization
OSS	Office of Strategic Services
PCO	Passport Control Officer
PID	Political Intelligence Department, Foreign Office
PPE	Politics, Philosophy, and Economics (Oxford University degree course)
PWE	Political Warfare Executive
RAF	Royal Air Force
RIIA	Royal Institute of International Affairs (Chatham House)
SA	Sturmabteilung
SD	Sicherheitsdienst (SS Intelligence Service)
SIS	Secret Intelligence Service (i.e. MI6, gathering foreign intelligence)
SOE	Special Operations Executive
SS	Schutzstaffel
T4	Tiergartenstrasse 4 [abbrev. for the Nazi euthanasia program]
TLS	*Times Literary Supplement*
UNRRA	United Nations Relief and Rehabilitation Administration
WCC	World Council of Churches, Geneva

Captions for Photographs/Illustrations

Chapter 1

Chapter 2

Chapter 3

Chapter 4

Chapter 5

Chapter 6

Introduction

On July 6, 1971, British newspapers announced the suicide of Elizabeth Meta Wiskemann from a drug overdose. She had taken a lethal dose of pills washed down by alcohol. Letters to the *Times* soon appeared praising her as an "outstanding scholar, a sensitive and loyal friend and a brave woman who risked her life for her country."[1] She was well known as a commentator on European politics and her books and articles were once fixtures on the reading lists of students of international affairs and Eastern Europe, as well as undergraduates in the 1960s studying twentieth-century European history. Today she is largely forgotten and—except for a few specialists—her name mostly draws blank looks from those whose intellectual formation came later. The author of ten books, including several of lasting significance, scores of essays and press articles, translations, and innumerable reviews, she was both prolific and remarkable for her breadth of expertise, writing with equal mastery about Germany, France, Italy, Switzerland, and Eastern Europe. Also, few could match her personal acquaintance with so many of the politicians, intellectuals, and officials about whom she wrote. As Leonard Woolf once put it: "You know more people than anyone else in Europe."[2] She liked to describe herself as a scholar-journalist and as a woman was among the very few who achieved distinction in both these male-dominated spheres. She also spent the Second World War as a British intelligence agent in Switzerland, running agents and gathering information about Axis-occupied Europe.

A 'Victorian' born in 1899 a few months before the Boer War, Wiskemann's life spans two World Wars, depression, the reconstruction of post-1945 Europe, and the Sixties—roughly speaking what many historians later dubbed "the short twentieth century." She was a schoolgirl during the First World War, somewhat burdened with her father's German surname. Then came Cambridge where—as a student, researcher, and part-time teacher—she flourished in the microenvironment of Bloomsbury's younger generation. She was not uncritical of Bloomsbury: its insular view of foreign countries precluded real understanding of their cultures and populations, and the arrogant, unpolitical sensibility of some of its members was out of step with the 1930s. But for her generation, growing up in the shadow of the First World War, they were liberators, and Bloomsbury's revolt against Victorian attitudes and sexual morality, its aesthetic vision, openness to modernism in literature and art, and its devotion to friendship had a lasting impact on her.

Elizabeth Wiskemann: Scholar, Journalist, Secret Agent. Geoffrey Field, Oxford University Press.
© Geoffrey Field 2023. DOI: 10.1093/oso/9780192870629.003.0001

Hoping for an academic career, Wiskemann embarked upon a doctorate, but found her ambition thwarted, not least by an unsympathetic male supervisor. Rare exceptions aside—like medievalist Eileen Power, the epitome of a stylish and successful "new woman" academic—prejudice against women in universities was pervasive and very few positions were open to them. Wiskemann's career prospects in Cambridge seemingly blocked, she was especially drawn to Paris and Berlin, fascinated by their avant-garde cultural scene and political turbulence; they seemed more open, freer, less constrained by rules and conventions than British society—places where a self-reliant young woman could test her mettle and "learn about life." She loved travel, which in the interwar years was inherently 'modern' and a little 'daring' for a lone female: "Fairly early I found myself wanting to get inside a country, wanting to stay in its homes, to live with its citizens and if possible speak its language."[3] From 1930 she began spending long periods in Berlin where in the space of a few years she reinvented herself as a successful foreign correspondent for the *New Statesman* and other journals—a remarkable achievement given that most female journalists were confined to the women's pages of papers and very few covered political news, domestic or foreign. Her turn to journalism in Berlin in the early 1930s was propitious in place and time, but it took talent, unrelenting drive to find sources and research stories, and no little courage amid mounting lawlessness and Nazi terror. Her reports were detailed, cogent, and shrewd, capturing brilliantly the frantic pace of political events, even on those occasions when her expectations were mistaken.[4] Like Timothy Garton Ash today, she viewed the crafts of history and journalism as closely related, at their best sharing similar virtues: "exhaustive, scrupulous research, a sophisticated, critical approach to the sources, a strong sense of time and place, imaginative sympathy with all sides, logical argument, clear and vivid prose."[5]

The Thirties was in the eyes of many a golden age of the foreign correspondent, satirized by Evelyn Waugh and celebrated by Hitchcock. Central Europe especially was the arena of an outstanding collection of British and American journalists who chronicled the Weimar Republic's disintegration and the growing danger of Hitler. Among the British contingent were experienced men like Norman Ebbutt, F.A. Voigt, G.R. Gedye, and Marcel Fodor—men who had spent many years in Central Europe, were proficient in local languages, and were knowledgeable about the culture, history, and customs of the lands they covered. The American correspondents included several—James Vincent Sheean, Dorothy Thompson, Edgar Mowrer, William Shirer and John Gunther—who became international celebrities. There were differences between the two groups. In the US, newspapers and broadcasting were booming and it was relatively easy for adventurous, untrained reporters to land jobs and assignments. Their readers were generally less knowledgeable about Europe and their writing was more personal, interpreting events as eyewitnesses. The British press was harder to break into, almost impossible without connections; money was tighter; readers were mostly better informed; and articles tended to be drier, more factual, with less insertion of the reporter's self. The contrast between Martha Gellhorn's brilliant and personal report on Czechoslovakia in 1938, "Obituary of a Democracy," and Wiskemann's more academic dissection of the Sudeten German problem with its complex cultural and historical origin is a striking illustration of this.[6]

Always skillful in networking and acquiring influential contacts, Wiskemann found friends in both groups, but most important in her journalistic training were Ebbutt and Voigt, experienced journalist-activists who were intent on shaping opinion and influencing national policy. She listened carefully, learned quickly, and through shared contacts interviewed many of the key political figures of the day. In addition to the consolidation of the Nazi regime in Germany, Wiskemann also reported in detail on the 12 million Germans living outside the Reich's post-Versailles borders whom Hitler fashioned into a potent foreign policy weapon, and she developed a lasting interest in contested borderlands such as the Saar, the Sudetenland, Switzerland, and the Tyrol. Her sympathies lay with small states, often the victims of international and inter-ethnic conflicts; she studied demographic changes and pondered the problem of how multilingual, multi-ethnic, and multi-confessional populations might construct stable and united polities. By 1939, remarkably for a freelance reporter, she had achieved an international reputation for her articles and two highly praised books on Czechoslovakia and Nazi economic and political penetration of south-east Europe. Convinced already by 1935 that Hitler was intent on provoking another war, Wiskemann became one of the earliest voices admonishing Britain and France to rearm in preparation and a crusader against Chamberlain's policy of Appeasement. As Julie Gottlieb has shown, the "male-centrism" of standard accounts of British debate about Nazism and Appeasement has marginalized or excluded altogether the vociferous and effective role played by numerous women activists, including Wiskemann.[7]

When war broke out, Wiskemann looked for a job in research, propaganda, or some facet of intelligence. The links between the British secret service and foreign correspondents were already considerable in the 1930s and her first-hand knowledge of much of Europe and the skills she had honed gathering information made her an ideal recruit. And yet her war service was also somewhat serendipitous. After German forces occupied much of Western Europe and Mussolini entered the war, what began as a brief and vague semi-official assignment in neutral Switzerland turned into five years working at one of the key "listening posts" for intelligence about Axis Europe. Several sources attest to Wiskemann's success as an intelligence agent. Her experiences, which can be pieced together in some detail, illustrate the day-to-day work of an agent in the field, the contacts and sources she relied upon, her close collaboration with Allen Dulles and the OSS, and, equally interesting, the difficulties she encountered in her own embassy, reflective of both the internecine infighting between Whitehall's covert agencies and prejudice against an assertive female outsider whose position seemed anomalous. Most accounts of Britain's female agents focus on the exploits of those like Violette Szabo, Nora Inayat Khan, and Christine Glanville who were infiltrated into occupied France by SOE; far less recognized are those like Wiskemann in Bern, Elisabeth Pares in Stockholm, and Nancy Lambton in Teheran who were posted to neutral countries and fed intelligence back to London.

The Allied victory in 1945 signaled the end of Wiskemann's personal campaign to defeat Hitler and Nazism; this had been her continual focus for more than a dozen years. She knew that starting over in her mid-forties would be difficult, notwithstanding the reputation she had achieved in the 1930s as an author and foreign correspondent. Initially she moved to Rome where, as a correspondent for the *Economist* and the *Spectator*, she analyzed the birth of the Italian Republic, while also writing the first major study of the Axis alliance between Hitler and Mussolini. Her stay in Italy coincided with a particularly rich and innovative period in cultural life and she got to know not only most of the leading politicians but also writers like Croce, Moravia, and Carlo Levi. For Wiskemann and activists like her friend Ada Gobetti, the Italian partisans' struggle against the German occupation 1943–45 was a "finest hour," a morally transformative movement of purification and rebirth after decades of Fascism. And, while historians have become more divided over its legacy, viewing it as contradictory and ambiguous, Wiskemann never forgot the courage and possibility manifested in the *Resistenza* and she was bitterly disappointed, like most of her circle, at the early Republic's failure to translate its social and political values into a concrete and viable program for postwar reconstruction.

Postwar Wiskemann also remained very much engaged with Eastern Europe but, as Communist regimes took power, the kind of regular journeys she had made earlier became impossible, especially for a freelance reporter; perforce her journalism turned more and more to developments in Germany, Austria, Switzerland, and Italy while employment as a regular book reviewer, especially for the *Times Literary Supplement* and the *Spectator*, and work for Chatham House both paid her bills and burnished her reputation as a contemporary historian, in particular as an expert on the Second World War and Nazi Germany. Her scholarly productivity was prodigious: including four books (effectively five if one counts her contributions to Chatham House's *Survey of International Affairs*) in the dozen years after the war, one of them—*Germany's Eastern Neighbours*—the first English-language account of the postwar expulsion of 12 million ethnic Germans from Eastern Europe. No stranger to controversy, her insistence that West Germany should accept the expulsions and the Oder–Neisse frontier with Poland as irreversible provoked a storm of criticism in West Germany. Famously opinionated and forever marked by the 1930s, she was highly suspicious of Germany and Germans, alert—arguably, overly sensitive—to the possibility of neo-Fascist and neo-Nazi revival; but in this too she shared the mindset of large numbers of British contemporaries, particularly in their antipathy towards Adenauer's Germany, something forgotten or downplayed in later years.

Wiskemann's reputation as a commentator on foreign policy and a scholar of European history was achieved largely outside, or rather on the fringes of, academia. Approaching sixty, she didn't expect to return to university teaching after a gap of more than twenty years. But life took an unexpected turn and she was appointed to a Chair of International Relations at Edinburgh (the first woman to receive a Chair there in any discipline) and later moved to the newly founded University of Sussex. British university life was changing in the early 1960s with the creation of several new universities, a doubling of the numbers of students, and—more slowly—an increase in women faculty. It was also in this period that International Relations and Contemporary History began to gain institutional presence in university curricula. Wiskemann's writing in these years illustrates these changes, including four non-specialist books of contemporary history largely written for undergraduates, while her presence at Edinburgh and Sussex also reflects the importance of journalists in these two fledgling disciplines.

As a journalist, historian, and political commentator, Wiskemann focused on international affairs, and her opinions about British politics occupy little space in this book. Not that she didn't have strong views, but detailed information about them has not survived. Early on she favored the Liberal party, but in the course of the Second World War her politics moved sharply left: the ravages of war and people's sacrifices, she argued, necessitated sweeping social reform and a redistribution of wealth, most of all in countries like Italy where disparities were most extreme. She also supported closer European integration and favored Britain playing a prominent role in this. Above all, her focus on European politics was defined by "the German question" and the threat of German power. Already by the time she went off to Cambridge, the Europe Wiskemann had studied in high school barely existed: the Habsburg, Hohenzollern, and Romanov emperors had been overthrown and the map of Eastern Europe was about to be re-drawn. Much of her later research and writing focused on the consequences of this geopolitical earthquake for the populations of Mitteleuropa and the German borderlands. She had strong political opinions and the issues she focused upon were highly contentious. Examining this epicenter, whether in the 1930s or after the Second World War, "placed her," in Mark Cornwall's words, "in a no-man's land where she was bound to be a target from many quarters."[8] The region, she felt, could or should have acted as an "essential hinge" or a bridge drawing together East and West Europe, facilitating economic and cultural exchange between them. At her death, however, the bipartite division between the West and a Soviet-dominated East seemed greater, more immutable than ever. With the implosion of the Soviet Union two decades later, debate about Mitteleuropa's future was rekindled.[9] Wiskemann would have been suspicious of German conservatives in the 1990s who spoke of 'the lost East' and advanced a thinly veiled revisionist project, and she would have embraced warmly Czech, Hungarian, and Polish liberal intellectuals (Havel, Kundera, Konrád, Milosz) who proclaimed a unifying common cultural heritage. Ultimately, however, she would have been disappointed by NATO and European Union enlargement and the failure of Europe's new center to realize her image of an "essential hinge." And, one might add, many of the disturbing features of today's Europe—rising nationalism, the descent of East European states into illiberalism and authoritarianism, democracy under pressure, and the international free trade regime under attack—would have alarmed her by their familiarity.

*   *   *

This biography focuses primarily upon Wiskemann's individual experiences as journalist, spy, and scholar, but aside from the intrinsic interest of her life and writings, her story should also be viewed as illustrative of a whole cohort of women, born between the late 1890s and the First World War, who graduated from university in the 1920s and early 1930s. They came from upper-middle-class or aristocratic families, belonged to the first large group of women to gain a university education, and—whether or not they identified as feminists—were the legatees of the recent women's struggle for the franchise.[10] Better educated than their mothers, influenced by debate about the "new woman" and the suffrage campaign, they sought greater freedom in many areas of their lives. They wanted careers and were in no rush to marry and have children. They were ambitious and challenged conventional expectations about women's roles. The First World War shaped their early years, and they were attracted by the liberal internationalism of men like Arnold Toynbee, Gilbert Murray, and Alfred Zimmern and shared their enthusiasm for the League of Nations and the prospect of international cooperation. With few opportunities open in universities and the Foreign Service still closed to women, they looked to journalism, the BBC, pressure group organizations, and the agencies of the League to pursue their interests in international politics.

Several accounts in recent years have examined women's engagement in international affairs in the interwar period. As the hopes of the 1920s faded and economic depression and renewed international conflict darkened their horizons in the 1930s, this cohort became active participants in debates about how to prevent another war and in the anti-fascist and anti-Appeasement movements.[11] Some, like the Quaker cousins Jean and Tessa Rowntree, were active in international relief efforts and worked to get socialists and Jews out of Czechoslovakia in 1938–39. The remarkable career of Francesca Wilson has also attracted attention; she took part in relief efforts in two World Wars, famine relief in Soviet Russia, the rescue of Basque children from Civil War Spain, and UNRRA's massive relief efforts in postwar Yugoslavia.[12] Doreen Warriner seemed to be on a fast track towards an academic career; her research focused on peasant societies in Central and Eastern Europe. But in 1938, deeply troubled by the Munich Agreement, she gave up a Rockefeller fellowship, flew to Prague, and, through the British Committee for Refugees, began organizing the emigration of socialists and Jews whose lives were increasingly imperiled.[13] The political activism of others like Elizabeth Monroe, Hester Pinney (later Hester Marsden-Smedley), Shiela Grant Duff, and Wiskemann herself was channeled through their writings as foreign correspondents publicizing the Nazi and Fascist danger.

The careers of a number of these women intersected with Wiskemann's life and activities, although because of a paucity of personal records it is sometimes unclear how well they were acquainted. Aside from their shared political activism in the 1930s, their career trajectories evince several common features. First, the continuing importance of journalism. They wished both to enlighten readers and to influence public policy. Several, like Wiskemann, got their start as foreign correspondents and many remained active as journalists and broadcasters for most of their lives. Indeed, a strong female network of alumnae from Cambridge and Oxford operated within the BBC.[14] Another important formative influence was the Royal Institute for International Affairs or Chatham House, so named because of its location in the London mansion once owned by William Pitt, earl of Chatham. It was founded in 1920 as an independent institute to foster research in international relations and to promote public understanding of global affairs. The Institute was more hospitable to women than many university faculties, playing an important role as a source of research grants and publishing opportunities as well as a forum for meeting scholars and policymakers in their fields. All these women wrote for Chatham House journals, and Wiskemann's early reputation owed much to a book that it commissioned.[15] The same is true of Elizabeth Monroe, who became a leading expert on Middle East affairs, and both Warriner and Monroe seem to have gained considerable influence on its committees.

An equally important (and often neglected) shared experience was government service in the Second World War. The significance of the war for men's careers, including many academics, is well-documented, less so for professional women. The expansion of the wartime state offered unprecedented opportunities for those, like Wiskemann, with expertise in foreign affairs, especially in the propaganda, information, and intelligence agencies. For example, Shiela Grant Duff, author of a bestselling Penguin special, *Europe and the Czechs*, became head of the Czech section of the BBC's European Service; Elisabeth Barker, daughter of the political theorist Sir Ernest Barker and a close friend of Wiskemann, moved from the BBC to Foreign Office Intelligence, eventually becoming head of PWE's South-east Europe Directorate. Margaret Lambert worked for the BBC Austrian Service and then the intelligence service interrogating German prisoners of war, while Ann Lambton occupied a similar post to Wiskemann as press attaché to the British Embassy in Teheran where she was involved in propaganda and SOE activities.[16] Recruited by the Ministry of information, Elizabeth Monroe's organizational talents led to her appointment as head of its Middle East Division, while Warriner moved from the Ministry of Economic Warfare to PWE's Cairo offices, helping to administer shipping and supplies for British forces in the Middle East, and then in 1944 joined UNRRA's mission to supply relief to Yugoslav war victims.[17]

War service played a critical role for this group of women in forging important personal networks and shaping the future direction of their scholarly research. Wiskemann's later writing was largely devoted to the era of the dictators, the consequences of the Second World War, and the contested borderlands resulting from it. Margaret Lambert was editor-in-chief of the British series of *Documents on German Foreign Policy, 1918–45*. As a distinguished correspondent for Reuters and the BBC, Elisabeth Barker wrote two books on Balkan affairs; then, after her retirement in 1970, she published six more, returning to topics she once covered as a journalist now supplemented by recently released files from the national archives.[18] Monroe worked as a foreign correspondent in the Middle East, covering every major story from Britain's withdrawal from Palestine, Suez, the Iraqi and Jordanian revolutions, to the landing of American marines in Beirut in 1982. Her book, *Britain's Moment in the Middle East 1914–1956* (1963) remains a classic. Warriner became Britain's leading expert on peasant societies, under-development, and land reform, publishing a steady stream of books, journalism, and reports for the United Nations and other international agencies.[19] In the postwar years many of these women obtained academic positions, although—as in Wiskemann's case—their contribution to International Relations and Contemporary History often originated from outside or on the margins of the academy.[20] None of these women is well known today. Warriner has recently received more attention but mostly for her heroic rescue work in Prague in 1939 and the fact that she alerted Nicholas Winton, the chief organizer of the *Kindertransport*, to the desperate plight of Jewish children in Czechoslovakia.[21] As scholars begin to recover and re-examine these largely forgotten pioneers, their careers (including Wiskemann's) provide a reminder that they were always there, hidden in plain sight.[22]

A collective biography of these women would be a fascinating project but impossible, I fear, because of the paucity of sources; they were mostly reticent about themselves, and none left much in the way of archival papers. Wiskemann also presents difficulties for a biographer.[23] Her published writings are voluminous, but she left no diaries or formal archive and while she had many friends and acquaintances, she either didn't keep their letters or destroyed them before her death. Also, the memoir she wrote focused on only twenty years of her professional life and is largely silent about her emotions, personal relations, ambition, and self-awareness. It described the Europe she saw as a participant observer, but one who wished to limit the participant's self-exposure. Even photographs of her were hard to find at first. Had I embarked on the task earlier, it would certainly have been easier to fill some of the gaps or silences through interviewing her friends and colleagues. But most had died by the time I began this project, depriving me of valuable first-hand recollections. Fortunately, many of Wiskemann's acquaintances were sufficiently interesting or eminent to have left papers of their own which contain a good deal of her correspondence, now spread across numerous libraries and archives.[24] In addition, files in the archives of newspapers, publishers, private institutions like Chatham House, and official state agencies with which she was involved were also invaluable in piecing together a fuller picture of her travels and activities.

Writing this book has involved a good deal of detective work, searching for documents and unearthing biographical details. Wiskemann was, as her friends made clear, a very private person, "dauntingly discreet," and reticent—about as far from today's confessional mode as can be imagined—and so, unavoidably, gaps remain. I have mostly chosen to acknowledge them rather than substitute speculation. But none of these lacunae, I think, would seriously alter the analysis presented here. As biography widens its scope, focusing less upon high politics, power, and celebrities, and especially as it attempts to recover 'unrecorded lives,' especially of women who were not particularly famous, so these problems of sources and documentation are inevitable.[25] Almost nothing is known, for example, about Wiskemann's brother and sister, while, despite many inquiries, I have been able to find little information about Marchese Francesco Antinori, the Italian diplomat whom she contemplated marrying in 1944. Few subjects attract more curiosity than sex, and the fact that Wiskemann remained unmarried invites speculation. Mark Cornwall has suggested that "her attitude to her gender was…ambiguous" and refers to her "unresolved sexuality,"[26] but he provides no evidence and I found no lesbian relationships, only heterosexual affairs. Her friendships with women were mutually supportive at a time when and in careers where professional women were rare and prejudice and innuendo about spinsters, unmarried "new women", and "business women" was rife. In 1966 when her old friend Martin Wight joked that she was a puritan (he was referring to her unrelenting insistence upon factual accuracy) Wiskemann disagreed: "I'm too fond of pleasure to be called puritan, and, although my lovers admired my purity (isn't that different?) I did have them and felt no shame – nor do." The memoir she had just begun, she assured him, concerned her views about Europe, not her private life: "In my old-fashioned way I abhor the way people now display what should be private."[27] Inevitably, then, my book is both less and more than a conventional biography. I have focused mostly on the public persona in an effort to show how her successes and disappointments, her political engagement, and her experiences as foreign correspondent, secret agent, author, and academic scholar illuminate larger historical issues as well as more individual themes such as this woman's struggle to earn a living, define herself, and protect her independence.

1

Becoming a Journalist

From Cambridge to Berlin

The opening of Elizabeth Wiskemann's memoir is unusual; she was clearly reluctant to provide much information about her family or her early life and shied away from personal exposure. In the first sentence she writes: "I am told that I must begin *The Europe I Saw* by indicating through what kinds of spectacles I looked." Three brief pages follow, providing a few bare details about her parents, her schooling and Cambridge studies, and ending with her second trip to Berlin in 1930. She omits her own birthdate, does not mention her father by name, and not until chapter six, and then only in passing, do we learn that she had two siblings. Clearly uncomfortable revealing personal details, she preferred to restrict her experiences to those encountered after she reached the age of thirty. Friendships were always vitally important to Wiskemann, family far less or so it would seem. As a result, very little is known about her early life or her family: they scarcely appear in her writings, no diaries or letters have survived, and she seems to have lived a life very separate from them.

She was born on August 13, 1899, in the upper-middle-class London suburb of Sidcup, the youngest child of a German businessman, Heinrich Odomar Hugo Wiskemann, and his wife Emily, *née* Burton. Her father's family came from Hesse-Cassel; he was born in 1860, emigrated to London in 1880 to avoid conscription into the Prussian army, and married Emily Burton in 1888. Her mother's family were of Welsh and Huguenot descent and Wiskemann adds that her maternal grandmother was the elder sister of Samuel Savage Lewis, who was for many years the librarian of Corpus Christi College, Cambridge, and bequeathed his very considerable collection of gems to the library there.[1] This maternal grandmother, Mary Bunnell Lewis (1826–1912), also married a very successful Ipswich wholesale grocer, Henry May Burton (1824–1879). Emily Burton was one of six children from that marriage, and two of her brothers, who were very prominent in Ipswich business and community affairs, were knighted.[2] The Burtons were very prosperous, and Elizabeth's Wiskemann's mother grew up in some luxury in a large house with servants.

Elizabeth was sent to Notting Hill High School. This was a private day school (non-boarding) established in 1873 as part of the Girls' Public Day School Trust. Her older sister Eugenia had been expensively educated as a boarder at Bedales in Hampshire and her brother George at Wellington College.[3] Possibly the decision

Elizabeth Wiskemann: Scholar, Journalist, Secret Agent. Geoffrey Field, Oxford University Press.
© Geoffrey Field 2023. DOI: 10.1093/oso/9780192870629.003.0002

to send Elizabeth to Notting Hill was indicative of a decline in the family's fortunes, but her parents may also have decided that this excellent day school was more suited to their youngest child. The school's annual magazine, now online, includes numerous entries for "Betty Wiskemann," as she was called, and records her all-round success. Already in 1911 she was winning academic prizes and continued to do so—for general progress, French, Latin recitation, chemistry, and mathematics. In addition, she was a very active Gurney House member, taking part in the debating society and drama group, helping to raise funds for the Charity Society and aid for Belgian refugees during the war years, playing hockey, and becoming captain of netball and the swimming team. Her mother seems to have donated money for prizes, and in 1913 the recently founded 'Deutsche Klub' was pleased to have found a "sehr gütige Gönnerin" in Mrs Wiskemann. As a young child Elizabeth was taken to see her father's family; otherwise her connections to Germany were few. There is no mention of 'Betty' in the Klub notes; her interests in her final years seem to have focused more on history, French, and Latin literature, and her academic success was crowned by a scholarship to read History at Newnham College, Cambridge. Elizabeth's ties to the school continued throughout her life. Its magazine records that she was a member of the Old Girls' Association [OGA], returned in 1922 to play hockey and tennis for the OGA against the school, and contributed brief notes about Cambridge after she left. Later issues followed her career as teacher, journalist, and author; she also lectured at the school in the 1950s, and her death was recalled with sorrow at the prize-giving ceremonies in 1972.[4]

Her later years at Notting Hill coincided with the First World War when spy mania and anti-German hatred was widespread; shops were looted and wrecked and in parts of London crowds rampaged against people of German and Austrian origin. Elizabeth's comment on this was typically understated: "It was very disagreeable to have a German name then. It was not, however, positively painful at school where I was known; it made one afraid to meet people one did not know, and it made one understand, without really being persecuted, what persecution feels like."[5] Although he had lived in England for thirty-five years, her father was briefly interned as an enemy alien and then released, but as late as November 1917, Conservative MP Sir William Joynson-Hicks, a leading hardliner on internment, raised a question in the Commons specifically complaining that Hugo Wiskemann still had the use of a telephone.[6] None of this could have been good for business. Early in his marriage Hugo Wiskemann appears to have run into financial difficulties, but he recovered and seems to have become quite prosperous trading in chemicals at the London Wool Exchange. During the war and the early postwar slump, however, his situation deteriorated rapidly, so much so that by 1922 he was forced to file for bankruptcy; with liabilities of £20,885, he was forced to liquidate his assets, which included the furniture and his dead wife's jewelry.[7] In addition to the family's more precarious economic situation,

Figure 1.1. "Elizabeth Wiskemann c. 1905, about six years old."

Elizabeth's success in gaining a Cambridge scholarship was overshadowed by the sudden death in March 1918 of her mother, only fifty-five years of age, in the first wave of the influenza pandemic, just seven months before Elizabeth went up to Newnham. This was a shattering blow: she was far closer to her mother than to her father, whom she regarded as weak and rather foolish: "It was my mother who was unusually intelligent and enlightened; my father followed in her wake as best he could."[8]

The Cambridge that she entered was overwhelmingly masculine (about 9% of students were women). The women's colleges, Girton and Newnham, were small and relatively poor. Women students attended lectures by courtesy of the lecturer concerned and some seated them separately and addressed themselves only to the male undergraduates. Women could not use the university library and, while they could sit examinations in many subjects, they were awarded special diplomas rather than formal degrees (this remained the case until 1948). Moreover, unlike in other British universities, women faculty at Cambridge had no share in discussions about degree syllabi or the organization of teaching and were excluded from university posts. In 1897 a campaign was launched to fully integrate the women's colleges into the university and to treat women and men equally, but it produced an angry backlash and the proposal was rejected. At Oxford women got full university membership in May 1920, although a quota was soon imposed to check the growing number of female students. Another campaign for equality got underway at Cambridge in 1920, embraced enthusiastically by many women who recently had been active in the suffrage campaign. After a bitter fight, however, the measure again went down to defeat the following year. Granting equality would have meant not only allowing women to obtain degrees but also bestowing equal status with respect to voting rights and the governance of the university. The vehemence surrounding the issue also reflected a broader backlash that developed in the immediate postwar years, shaped by rising unemployment and economic cuts. On the poll day in October 1921, angry male undergraduates celebrated by rushing to Newnham, where they used a handcart to batter and seriously damage the bronze memorial entry gates to the college.[9] These events, which immediately caught the attention of the national press, ensured that the women's colleges acted cautiously in the following years, anxious not to jeopardize their hard-won but subordinate place in the university.

It had long been Wiskemann's ambition to go to Cambridge and she flourished there, making numerous friends who remained close all her life. Rules about chaperones were still observed, although female students were on a less tight rein than before the Great War: "now two or more students might entertain young men in their rooms to tea, if permission was obtained in writing from the Mistress, the names and colleges of the students present being given."[10] And yet for most female students Cambridge was undoubtedly liberating: they were away from their parents' homes with opportunities to make new friends and unaccustomed freedom to organize their own lives. Socially Wiskemann's Cambridge was what John Lehmann once referred to as "Bloomsbury by the Cam."[11] Some of her connections to Bloomsbury derived from her sister having gone to Bedales, the progressive co-educational public school favored by many liberal intellectuals. While attending Bedales, for example, the children of the aristocratic Hungarian Bekassy family had often stayed with the Wiskemanns in London prior to 1914. The poet Ferenc Bekassy had gone on to King's where his friends included Keynes, James Strachey, and Rupert Brooke. A more important link, however, was Emily Burton's close friend Ivy Gladys Pretious, who married the civil servant and industrialist Charles Tennyson.[12] Ivy was the epitome of the Edwardian "new woman"; she was mostly raised by the barrister and positivist philosopher Frederic Harrison and worked as Emily Hobhouse's private secretary during her campaign against "the methods of barbarism" being employed by the British in South Africa, herding Boer families into concentration camps. Before marrying Tennyson, as a single woman she attracted the attentions of several suitors, including Bertrand Russell and Lloyd George. The Tennysons often visited the Wiskemann home, as did Francis Birrell (stepbrother of Tennyson) and David Garnett, much beloved in Bloomsbury circles. In the months before going up to Cambridge, Wiskemann worked briefly at the bookshop Birrell and Garnett opened opposite the British Museum which was frequented by their friends the Stracheys, Woolfs, Bells, Keynes, Forster, and other denizens of Bloomsbury. "I learnt," Wiskemann wrote, "more about the art of literature and the other arts there than anywhere, even Cambridge or Florence." At Newnham, Pernel Strachey, Lytton's older sister, was a tutor and director of studies in modern languages and in 1923 became the college's Principal. And among Wiskemann's friends and contemporaries at the college were: Frances Marshall (later married to Ralph Partridge), Lettice Baker (who married the mathematician Frank Ramsey), and 'Betty' Norton, all with strong Bloomsbury connections.[13]

As she had at high school, Wiskemann stood out academically and especially enjoyed the special subject paper on the Enlightenment which she chose for part two of the History Tripos. Her sights were set on an academic career, although in the 1920s very few positions were open to women—indeed, finding someone to supervise their postgraduate research was not easy and they were eligible for very few research grants. The decline of her family's finances also became a serious impediment since her father's business was in crisis, leading to his bankruptcy in 1922. Afterwards Hugo seems to have lived on what was left of his wife's money and eventually returned to Germany, where he died in 1932. Elizabeth could expect no financial assistance from home and her relationship to her father seems to have become strained and distant. His failure seems to have reinforced her drive to succeed and to protect her independence.

Wiskemann got a first in History and then taught for a year at a boarding school for girls before embarking on a doctoral dissertation.[14] She chose a topic in diplomatic history (a growing specialty in the wake of the Versailles peace agreements), focusing on the relations between Britain, Louis Napoleon, and the Vatican in the early 1860s, and worked first on Foreign Office documents at the Public Record Office in London, later traveling to archives in Paris and Vienna. Initially Wiskemann made good progress with her doctoral research. She applied successfully for a highly competitive Research Studentship from the Gilchrist Educational Trust in 1923 but had to postpone taking it for one year because of illness. In 1925 she applied for further research funding, but narrowly missed obtaining a Junior Research Fellowship at Newnham. The reports on her progress were good. Harmsworth Professor J. Holland Rose wrote: "She has displayed not only praiseworthy industry but also acuteness of perception to the value of evidence and, in general, good judgment." W.F. Reddaway of King's, while noting "an occasional tendency to be slipshod or arrogant," judged her work to be of permanent value, "conspicuous for energy, lucidity and imagination as well as for learning and research"; he added: "I only wish that more dissertations were as readable." The college Principal, Pernel Strachey, wrote: "I am very sorry that you have been disappointed about the Fellowship but perhaps you will be able to try again next year"; the College also awarded her £100 to help complete her research.[15]

While revising her manuscript, Wiskemann began tutoring undergraduates part-time at Newnham and taught Workers' Educational Association classes. Time passed, and she also seems to have transferred to another doctoral supervisor, H.W.V. Temperley, one of the nation's most distinguished scholars of British foreign policy. This proved a disaster. Temperley was well known for his difficult, misogynistic nature: "From the beginning," his biographer, John Fair, wrote, "Harold seemed far more capable of romantic attachment to artifacts, literature, and ideas than to women." His antagonism towards research students was legendary: "One young lady amongst them," Fair added, indicating in a footnote that it was Wiskemann, "once declared that in a moment of anger he threatened to kick her downstairs."[16] Having received little help or guidance, when she finally submitted her thesis in late 1928 it was awarded an M.Litt. rather than a PhD—a serious setback to her career aspirations, even though most successful male scholars in that era never embarked on a postgraduate degree. Her junior examiner, F.A. Simpson, who became a leading authority on the Second Empire, later told her that he had a higher opinion of the manuscript but was too timid to oppose the senior professor. Like other middle-class women who attended university in the 1920s, Wiskemann understood that they needed especially stellar qualifications; few attempted more than a first degree and most who worked after graduation became schoolteachers.[17] Wiskemann always believed that she was a victim of her supervisor's "serious resentment of an independent woman." This reverse, Mark Cornwall suggests, fueled "a lifelong subconscious quest to prove that her qualities as an historian matched those of any professional male academic."[18]

In these Cambridge years, along with tutoring Newnham undergraduates for their modern European and French Enlightenment exam papers, Wiskemann traveled regularly to the Continent both for research and for pleasure. Europe was cheap, sterling was strong, and she lived very inexpensively, often staying with friends. There was also a "magical holiday" (probably in 1926) with three Newnham friends on a commercial schooner along the Dalmatian coast. It was on this trip that she first encountered the novelist Richard Hughes ('Diccon' as she called him), who had already in his twenties published poems and criticism and had a play performed in the West End. Hughes was on an extended trip to the coastal areas of Slovenia and Croatia. It was Wiskemann's first fascinated glimpse of an area, including Bosnia and Montenegro, which was to figure large in her writings; she also experienced first-hand the mutual hostility of Italian and Yugoslav frontier guards and the two nations' bitter territorial rivalries over the Adriatic.[19]

Wiskemann's social life at Cambridge was also very active, enriched by friendship with a whole new crop of students, some with Bloomsbury connections. She was attracted to a free-thinking, free-living group, including Julian Bell, Julian Trevelyan, Michael Redgrave, Hugh Sykes Davies, Kathleen Raine, Jacob Bronowski,

Humphrey Jennings, and William Empson. Some, like Bell, were elected to the Apostles; others were aspiring poets, artists, critics, and writers. Their first literary efforts were published in *Granta* and the *Cambridge Review*, and they founded two rival publications for their poetry and criticism: *Venture* and the more daring and explicitly modernist *Experiment*.[20] They also put a good deal of effort into resuscitating the left-leaning, anti-clerical Heretics Society, which had been founded in 1909 by the philosopher Charles K. Ogden, along with Keynes and Bertrand Russell, but by the mid-1920s had lost most of its older generation of aesthetes and philosophers. Unlike the Apostles, it was open to women, and it was in a 1924 paper to the Society that Virginia Woolf first made the proverbial assertion that "on or about December 1910 human character changed" (another of the Society's invitees was Marie Stopes, the birth control campaigner and author of *Married Love*, 1918). Another Newnham participant, Margaret Gardiner, later a patron of the arts and left-wing political activist, has described the atmosphere of its meetings:

> The Heretics on Sunday evenings, exempt from chaperons, was a splendid institution for us. It was an occasion for meeting friends and making friends and, of course, listening to distinguished lectures and lively questioning. Among the lecturers, I particularly remember Roger Fry – whom I already knew from my school-days – with his irresistible shaggy charm and enthusiasms. And Boris Anrep with his brilliant – and surely intentional? – misuse of English, and Gertrude Stein, looking and speaking like a disapproving governess, her hair severely scraped back to match her attitude to her audience…We were all, I think, vaguely socialist, but that was about as far as it went. The emphasis was on personal relations and personal morality: we were, indeed, the suburbs of Bloomsbury.[21]

Although they were more focused on avant-garde literature and the arts than politics, Marxism became part of the new Heretics' discussions, along with Surrealism and Freudian psychology. Among Wiskemann's close friends, William Empson, I.A. Richards' prize student, was in many ways the leader of the group. He took over as President of the society in 1928. Flamboyant, brilliant, an incredibly precocious scholar and poet, he was already completing his path-breaking work of criticism, *Seven Types of Ambiguity*, as an undergraduate and was about to take up a prestigious college fellowship. He projected, Kathleen Raine recalled, an "impression of perpetual self-consuming mental intensity" which "spellbound us all."[22] Charming, witty, deeply intellectual, a good conversationalist, and a few years older than most of her student friends in the early 1920s, Wiskemann became Empson's first love affair, aside from his earlier homosexual experimentation. The affair, it seems, lasted for five months or more and Empson went so far as to arrange a lunch party in late February 1929 to formally introduce

Wiskemann to his mentor and tutor I.A. Richards (who had assumed a quasi-paternal role in his life).[23] Empson's biographer, John Haffenden, gives a compelling description of her:

> [S]he had real attractions, most notably a vivacious and even flamboyant personality, coupled with a devouring interest in European culture. An authentic intellectual and exuberant conversationalist, she knew how to charm and had a flair for cultivating distinguished people; equally, she was something of a snob, prone to push herself forward, selective in her attachments. (Among her other enthusiasms, she had a passion for the Bloomsbury circle and all it stood for). She was very kind to the people she collected but could be abrasive and unkind to the less favoured. All the same, if she could sometimes be prickly and quick to take offence, she was essentially a vigorous, ambitious, sensitive and warm-hearted person who strove to meet the highest standards of intellectual endeavour.[24]

Haffenden's description is nuanced and accurate; but if she pushed herself forward, it was because she had to. As for her 'passion' for Bloomsbury, it was closely interwoven with the value she attached to friendship and her dead mother's links to the group. Wiskemann later admitted that she somewhat idealized Bloomsbury. She cherished its equality between men and women, though its notions of emancipation were sometimes too confined to conversation; it was also often arrogant and insular toward foreigners. But she wrote: "Never have I found a purer love of virtue, wisdom, and beauty, a more genuine superiority towards material things…In the rapid confusion of ordinary life it is good to have known once that such candles burn."[25]

For these budding Cambridge aesthetes, one of the major events of October 1928 was the feminist lectures that Virginia Woolf gave at Newnham and Girton which were expanded and published as *A Room of One's Own* the following year. In her diary, Woolf wrote somewhat condescendingly of her audience as "starved but valiant young women…Intelligent, eager, poor; & destined to become schoolmistresses in shoals. I blandly told them to drink wine and have a room of their own." There is no concrete proof that Wiskemann attended, but I am certain she would not have missed this opportunity given her ties to Bloomsbury. Hermione Lee has commented that these "energetic college girls…did not think of themselves as disadvantaged," but for Wiskemann, without money and struggling to build a future, Woolf's message spoke to her reality, especially after the downgrading of her doctoral thesis.[26]

She was also soon caught up in a different crisis when college rules and Bloomsbury freedom collided. Empson and Wiskemann were not overly careful, and disaster intervened in July 1929. A college bedmaker found condoms in Empson's room and reported finding him in bed with a woman. The authorities at

Magdalene College immediately took action against Empson: "The Master (with an air of melancholy conviction) told me that anybody who had ever touched a French letter, no matter when or why, could never be allowed with safety in the company of young men, because he was sure in some subtle way…to pollute their innocence"[27] He was stripped of his fellowship and sent down for sexual misconduct. His mentor, I.A. Richards, was abroad on holiday and unreachable, and by the time he learned of the matter the expulsion was a *fait accompli*. To his friend Julian Trevelyan, Empson wrote: "What happened (since you ask) was the porters found a French letter in my rooms, and the bed-maker had also been very industrious at reading letters and so forth; let it be a warning to you, young man. I had no idea one was so officially spied on. It was high time I got away from the place; I shall do journalism now if I can." Empson took pains to conceal Wiskemann's identity and screened her from exposure, though how effectively is unclear. Cambridge is a small place, full of gossips, and the scandal spread rapidly throughout the colleges. I.A. Richards was incensed and complained to his fellow dons, Empson's friends began holding protests, and, through Julian Bell, reports reached David Garnett and the older generation of Bloomsbury. The whole thing was an absurd tragedy and Empson was justifiably bitter, although he also reflected: "it has all been my own fault, and I ought to have taken decent care of another person's interests, if not my own."[28] The Heretics had lost their leader, although Empson had lined up Wittgenstein as a speaker for the coming year and offered suggestions of others who should be approached. Keeping the Society going fell especially to Wiskemann and Julian Trevelyan ("Sorry to expose you to all the work"[29]); they sent out "a flurry of solicitous" speaker invitations and managed to get Arthur Waley, G.E. Moore, and C.E.M. Joad to address its members.[30]

Julian was the son of the poet, playwright, and translator Robert Trevelyan and nephew of the great historian G.M. Trevelyan; both his father and uncle were elected to the Cambridge Apostles and his father had close ties to Bloomsbury and had accompanied E.M. Forster on his first visit to India. After Bedales, Julian, like his father, became a student at Trinity reading English literature, although his real love was painting. Tall, handsome, with thick unruly hair, Julian cut quite a figure around Cambridge. In his own words, he "affected a great eccentricity": "I would wear large black felt hats such as I imagined artists wore and I bicycled the streets in carpet slippers."[31] He devoted little time to his formal studies, focusing more on student clubs and magazines. "Our thoughts…," he remembered, "were more and more directed towards Paris of which Cambridge seemed a sordid and distant suburb. We refused to eat in our college halls but dined expensively at a very seedy French restaurant, and, as soon as the term was over, we would dash off to Montparnasse and its various gods and goddesses." Unsurprisingly, after two years he abandoned his degree and moved to Paris in 1930. He soon Joined Stanley Hayter's print workshop, *Atelier Dix-Sept*, working alongside Miro, Max Ernst, Giacometti, Angus Calder, Campigli, Vieira da Silva, and others; Picasso was also an occasional visitor. Julian loved the conviviality and the collaborative practice of the *Atelier Dix-Sept* environment and soon his flat/studio at 7 Villa Brune became a crossroads for British and American visitors to Paris, including Cambridge friends like artist George Reavey and novelist Malcolm Lowry.[32]

As for Wiskemann, by 1930 she too was looking beyond Cambridge, although she could not give up teaching undergraduates, her sole source of income. She loved to travel, albeit on a shoestring, and had already visited France, Italy, Austria, and Eastern Europe. When her plans to go to Spain with friends during the Christmas vacation 1928–29 fell through, she accepted a Newnham friend's invitation to visit her in Berlin. This was shortly after her doctoral dissertation was downgraded to an M.Litt. degree when, as she admitted, she was completely *bouleversée*: worried about her future, how she might pay her way and live independently. Her first trip to Germany since being taken to see her grandparents before the First World War, it was crucial in shaping her future. She found Berlin both ugly, repellent in many ways, but also politically fascinating and before long she was returning to Germany as soon as her teaching obligations permitted. Hitherto, Wiskemann's historical and cultural interests focused more on France and Italy than Central Europe. And even as she began spending time in Berlin, her love of art, theatre, and architecture, and her growing relationship to Julian Trevelyan, drew her to Paris.

Only Wiskemann's letters have survived, many of them detailing plans to meet or travel together. Julian's autobiography, written almost thirty years later, mentions her only in passing, and *The Europe I Saw* is equally restrained. She was ten years older than Julian, who was only twenty when he quit Cambridge for Paris. Shortly before a visit to see him in Paris, she writes in late December 1929: "My *tendre amitié* for Paris grows – a refuge from all these Germans, Poles, Communists. And here I must confess that I wronged you at I Tatti and said I thought Cambridge would suck you in for its academic period." She warns: "I shall be very wild in Paris."[33] Her letters are full of comments about art, museums, and the theatre. She eagerly crammed into her schedule in Paris "the new Giradoux put on by Jouvet,"[34] loved the opera and concerts, and was given a tour of the Guimet collection by Gordon Luce, a friend of Arthur Waley and a scholar of Burmese art, which opened her eyes to Asian art and architecture. She was also eager to extend her circle of acquaintances: arriving early in Paris to have lunch with Julian and Cocteau, arranging to see Cartier Bresson, and writing to Julian: "I have Aldous Huxley's address in Paris, so let us go calling upon him."[35] She describes her delight in seeing works by Dérain, Corot, and Picasso and lists what she is reading: Robert Graves's *Goodbye to All That*, Robert Bridges's long philosophical poem, *Testament of Beauty*, and Thomas Mann's novella "Disorder and Early Sorrow." "I got back last night," she writes to Guglielmo Alberti, whom she had met at I Tatti with the Berensons, "after a wild weekend in Paris with Julian Trevelyan and other friends. I enjoyed 'Les criminels' and 'Amphitryon' but rather for the acting than the rest, I think. Piscator's apparatus does mean that one gets the most brilliant production of things like 'Les criminels' in Berlin. I am thinking of the 'Kaufmann von Berlin' which I saw last September. Did you see the 'Dreigroschen Oper' in Munich, I wonder?"[36]*

Anticipating a quick visit to Paris in early April 1930, she tells Julian: "I am happy in our entanglement. But are you a Trevelyan and a Puritan at heart after all? You shook your head with an air of real depreciation at the idea of feelings getting the better of one. Surely it is all a delicate and exquisite juggling of balls, one is called intellect, another emotion and so on, and you must never drop one nor let another monopolise your attention for long."[37] En route to Berlin after one visit, she writes: "Darling Julian...I loved Paris before but not so passionately as now [sic!] to her caresses as to those of my dearest lover. Thank you a thousand times for this week of desire satisfied despite the fanning of the flames in cruel Berlin."[38] In early July 1930 they organized a secret (from his parents) trip, which she let him pay for, to Belgium and Holland to visit art museums. But there were also tensions. She was quick to take offence at perceived slights, especially if she felt she was being taken for granted, making it clear that she was "unwilling to be handed to your parents as a tonic they must swallow for their souls' good." She added: "Perhaps my greater difficulty is that I don't know where you and I are. I suspect one of our differences of opinion here. You may well say does one need to know; it is certainly no epistolary topic."[39] Money and her need to make a living came up fairly often as she struggled to meet her travel and living expenses. Julian, like many of their friends, had the cushion of a private income, which he described as "very modest...but it seemed untold wealth to my friends."[40] When he pressed her to travel to Italy with him in September 1930, she protested, telling him not to sulk: "I always must be fresh in October or I could not get through it all. I suppose this is all very strange to a young man. But to women without £500 a year who want to lead full lives I believe it is essential to think the thing out so."[41]

In fact, she did not return to Cambridge. Instead, she decided to take a leave and settle in Berlin for an extended stay which turned out to be about nine months. "I wanted," she explained to Julian, "a big city out of England where I could improve a language, get a little history written, and be able to earn some money. The last need dictates Berlin...If my pupils melt away, Berlin loses its *raison d'être*."[42] Before she had stayed at a pension on Marburgerstrasse, a lively street full of clubs and restaurants frequented by artists and theatre people. Arriving in the autumn of 1930, she rented a bed-sitting room in a large apartment on Bismarckstrasse in Charlottenburg opposite the opera house. It belonged to a woman of aristocratic family, now in reduced circumstances and highly

---

* "Les criminels" or *Die Verbrecher* by Ferdinand Bruckner (1929). "Amphitryon 38" by Jean Giradoux (premiered in 1929). "Der Kaufmann von Berlin" by Walter Mehring was first staged by Erwin Piscator in 1929 and was highly controversial for its depiction of Berlin in the inflation crisis of 1923 and the lives of Jews in the capital.

indignant over the decline of her fortunes, who blamed the Treaty of Versailles. Like other impecunious English visitors, Wiskemann paid her way by cobbling together work translating official documents for the British Embassy and by giving private lessons in English.[43] She also seems to have continued her historical research, possibly hoping to revise or expand her thesis into articles or a book, and in December 1930 she enjoyed a fares-paid trip to Florence to give some lectures.[44] The Berlin political and social scene had changed dramatically since her first Christmas visit in December 1928. The economy had been shattered by depression and deflationary policies, unemployment had risen rapidly, and politics were polarized, with both the Communists and, even more, the Nazi party making spectacular gains in the Reichstag elections of September 1930. The atmosphere, she wrote, "was one of exaggerated desperation" compared to the preceding period.

Berlin had become a favored destination for many young British intellectuals, who went there in unprecedented numbers in the late 1920s and early 1930s, aided by extremely favorable exchange rates.[45] Some, like Auden and Isherwood, were drawn to the more open homosexual scene of Berlin, its reputation for sensational nightlife, racy cabarets, and aura of sexual permissiveness; many also sought out Germany as the new center of artistic modernism and avant-garde culture; others were eager to experience the defeated enemy in all its social and political turbulence. Wiskemann, of course, had family ties to Germany; but more important was her desire for something new, a test, an adventure, and a need to get away. Years later she had no qualms admitting "that all that fuss about the French letters was on her account,"[46] but at the time she felt wounded and distressed by the uproar in Cambridge over Empson. "Altogether," she reflected "I fancy in the end when some things have stopped hurting it will have been a good thing to have had this change."[47]

Her mood in the first months was very volatile. Sometimes it all seemed a bad mistake. Lonely and discouraged at one point, she even thought of abandoning her plans and returning to England with a few days "to refresh my tired spirit" in Paris. "You are quite right," she confesses to Julian, "that Berlin is a hideous place and Italy exquisite. Perhaps I shall not endure Berlin more than to the end of February...The article I want to write can, I find, be better tackled in London than Berlin."[48] Or again:

In most ways the Berlin experiment has been a rather unpleasant failure. I think I had to make it for I think I should have despised myself if I had not. But things have just happened very unfortunately personally and otherwise, and I have not been very fit. The most obvious piece of work for me to do turns out to be in the Record Office in London and a starving friend here needs the lessons I have acquired so it is rather indicated that I leave them to him. Berlin is grim and hateful this winter and hideous beyond endurance.

She adds:

> I promise not to be melancholic once I'm in Paris. Frenchness and beauty and
> you and all the Cocteaus you can muster (Opium is admirable) will easily exhil-
> arate me to my wildest heights. I've met no-one new of any interest here and it is
> silly to waste my life moldering while I'm still youngish and not naked of other
> attributes…I long, quite childishly, but I think naturally, for parties of all kinds
> and dancing.[49]

At other times, she was much happier. She loved Berlin's museums and especially
the Pergamon altar, opened to the public for the first time since 1908 in a new
museum. She had also managed to acquire some well-paying students, including
"the seven-year-old daughter of the Japanese *chargé d'affaires*" and "a senior official in the German Ministry of Finance, a Jew, to whom Edgar Mowrer had introduced me."[50] "I now teach English to the Permanent Secretary of the [German]
Treasury in Berlin and danced all my last night there with a delightful creature
belonging to the British Embassy."[51] She informed Julian: "I'm having a gay, happy
time and often go a-dancing [the expression of a German friend] which I love. I
have a very delightful mentor in the matter who seems to have relatively bottom-
less pockets."[52] She and Phyllis Dobb, whom she knew from Cambridge, joined
forces to give their own parties, and once summer arrived there were trips to the
nearby woods and lakes, swimming parties, and sailing.[53] Always adept at networking, she was soon introduced to artists, actors, writers, architects, and academics, including Arthur Koestler, already a successful journalist for the Ullstein
press, the architect Erich Mendelsohn, and George Grosz, with whom she danced
at a party in his flat—an experience she described as "daunting rather than agreeable, as he was acidly drunk."[54] But she remained uncertain about her future, confiding to her friend Julian Bell:

> I have lived through some stirring times; on the whole I have been very happy
> and am tempted by an opportunity of remaining abroad. But then two
> Constables of English landscape stabbed me, so I think I shall be back. I want it
> in many ways, but I have many delightful friends in Berlin and there are one or
> two old hostilities in Cambridge which are never allowed to die. I always find it
> so nice of you not to be affected by these…but to treat me (as I think you do) as
> myself and not as a malicious myth. There will be rather few people I shall much
> want to see in Cambridge, but I hope you'll be generous.[55]

A couple of months later she had another change of heart: "Cambridge seems
very drab and flat," she told Julian, and "I now mean to go off to 11 unbroken
months of grim Berlin if the currency situation makes it in the least feasible to
chuck Cambridge and plunge." In fact her finances never allowed it and so,

between 1932 and 1936, she developed a routine, spending term time tutoring undergraduates in Cambridge and the rest of the year in Central Europe.[56]

Berlin was violent, edgy, decadent, and Wiskemann was shocked by people's callousness and the arrogance of many towards the poor and unemployed. She enjoyed the experimental theatre and films, as well as the coffee houses and night-clubs. But she was troubled by the intense passion and ideological divisions of Berlin, whose intellectual life exuded "an almost ferocious destructiveness." It was very different from the Paris cultural scene, to say nothing of the muted tone of compromise so prevalent in British cultural life: "I remember feeling what a blessed thing a British compromise between preserving everything and smashing everything might be." And while sexually liberal herself and used to the homo-sexuality of Bloomsbury and Cambridge, the explicitness of Berlin's gay scene (Auden found the town "a bugger's daydream") left her a little shocked. Her land-lady's son and daughter, both Nazis around twenty years old, were "very willing to sell their bodies for homosexual purposes" (she coolly described the *ménage* as "characteristic of the place and period"), while the militant homosexuality of Klaus and Erika Mann and Pamela Wedekind, whom she had met in Munich, gave her pause: "Like much of what was most attractive in Weimar Germany they caused one to reflect upon the frontiers between liberty and license."[57] Many of her new Berlin friends and acquaintances were liberal Jews, prominent in aca-demic, political, and cultural life, and she feared that their conspicuous success fueled popular anti-Semitism. As she wrote many years later, "the extraordinary prevalence of Jews among the dominant writers, artists and scientists…was bound to provoke a reaction unless those Jews behaved with imaginative restraint in the new circumstances. They failed signally in this respect, many seeming to glory in being outsiders."[58] But she also learned to appreciate Berlin for being so unlike the rest of Prussia: its "wild and perverse young persons were still…roman-tic and hopeful, and the ordinary people…constantly displayed through every catastrophe, that extraordinary common sense which always made Hitler seem ridiculous to a large proportion of their number."[59]

Her relationship with Julian blew hot and cold. Ten years older than him and very determined to control her own life, she never expected their periodic meet-ings and travels to amount to anything permanent. Both embarked on other rela-tionships, but she enjoyed their times together and especially valued meeting his friends and sharing their insights on art. "Something was good. I think still is and that we both want it to be. Do not destroy my wanting."[60] At times she scolded him: "Nor do I wish to play the doormat – once or twice you angered me, wrongly, I think. The incident that sticks in my mind is your declaration that you needed me for a gesture of emancipation, as if my reputation were not threadbare enough without another rent. Not unreasonable but a little crude."[61] Eager to come to Paris for Julian's twenty-first birthday, she found him evasive and difficult. His parents were going to be there, which added to his stress ("herewith wishes for your fortification as against family stress"). In the end she seems to have been disinvited with little warning and felt "disconcerted by the peremptory way in which you forbade me Paris. I wasn't coming only for you, you know." She added: "I must admit that having been cast out as an embarrassment both in February and March I shall feel very timid of staying in Villa Brune unless my timidity is effectively countered."[62] They next saw each other in August 1931 near the shores of Lake Balaton in Hungary, where Wiskemann was staying with the Bekassys, old friends of her family. Julian, along with another Cambridge friend, Ralph Parker, was on his way to explore the remote Byzantine monasteries of Serbia and Greece. It was a journey that had a dramatic transformative effect on his art and led to his first major exhibition at the Bloomsbury Gallery in London. Though friendly, their relationship had changed. In the autumn Wiskemann invited him to stay in Cambridge—"remember I have a particularly comfortable spare bed with Giorgione's Flagellation hanging over it!"[63]—and she returned to the Villa Brune for New Year's but was again angered by his behavior:

> Please do drop the mystery business about staying or traveling with me…It is particularly unpleasant for me to refer naturally to something we have done together only to find that you are making a melodramatic mystery which imme- diately suggests everything or that makes me appear to be wrongly boasting of the conquest of a man much younger than myself – a thing I should never boast of, I hope.

She could, she wrote, be "his friend and lover as the sixteenth century said – but I will not be your plaything… [and] I will not always have my quietism exploited."[64] Four months later in May she writes: "Julian, are we still at DAGGERS DRAWN? I can't remember."[65]

*   *   *

Aside from her mixed and rather mercurial reactions to life in Berlin, Wiskemann's letters to Julian illustrate her growing fascination with German pol- itics and her first steps towards a career in journalism. "Berlin has indeed been exciting," she wrote in July 1931, "I've never lived in such volcanic circumstances. The Hoover proposal [for a moratorium on reparations payments] literally warded off a definite collapse and here we are hanging on again to see if Paris can be persuaded not to seal Germany's doom. I think that sort of language is really applicable!" Two weeks later she notes: "Things here are pretty catastrophic. The currency may collapse."[66] After the Wall Street crash of October 1929, financial crisis spread rapidly across Europe and economic activity declined precipitously; nowhere was the contraction more sudden or severe than in Germany, where industrial production dropped by 40%, share prices collapsed, the agrarian sector suffered increased farm sales and bankruptcies, and public indebtedness spiraled.

Unemployment and under-employment reached unprecedented levels—soup kitchens, poverty, and dole queues were everywhere. With the huge Nazi gains in the Reichstag elections of September 1930, parliamentary government had effectively ceased and henceforth Chancellor Brüning was forced to rely on presidential decrees to implement his program. While Wiskemann's life in Berlin may have begun as a personal adventure, she became riveted by the deepening political crisis of Weimar democracy and the dramatic rise of Nazism, which she was determined to write about, so much so that by 1932 teaching at Cambridge had become a means of financing a new career as a foreign correspondent, a freelance journalist.

The most important influence on Wiskemann's turn towards political journalism was Frederick A. Voigt, the *Manchester Guardian's* correspondent for Germany. The son of German parents brought up and educated in England, he had been reporting from Berlin since 1921. It was Voigt's scoop that revealed in 1926 the secret collaboration between the Reichswehr and the Soviet military to evade the provisions of the Versailles Treaty. A hard-driving, hyperactive investigative reporter, he traveled widely and had excellent contacts not only in Weimar political circles but throughout Eastern Europe, contacts he shared with others. Voigt introduced Wiskemann to his friend George Grosz and many academics, journalists, and politicians, especially Social Democrats like Rudolf Breitscheid, at whose home she often dined.[67] And it was Voigt who in late January 1931 took Wiskemann and Dorothy Thompson to their first big Nazi rally, addressed by Goebbels at the Berlin *Sportpalast*. Horrified by the mass hysteria and atmosphere of violence—what Voigt called "the lynching spirit" ('heads will roll,' 'the November criminals')—all three came away filled with "gloomy foreboding."[68] Voigt, Wiskemann recalled, "was absolutely fearless; a man of erudition to the point of pedantry; and a considerable eccentric. Stiff and prudish in manner, he was by contrast somewhat free in his behavior and his conversation. There was a touch of the macabre and pessimistic about him which made him better than most of his contemporaries to face the stark reality of Hitlerism."[69] He had concluded very early (and soon convinced Wiskemann) that the Nazi revolution, like those of 1789 and 1917 in France and Russia, would have profound consequences far beyond Germany's borders; its anti-communism, he argued, masked extreme expansionist goals.

Encouraged by Voigt and other friends, Wiskemann put aside her academic work and focused on the political crisis that was fast enveloping Germany in 1932. Here she had help from publishing contacts in Britain, especially her Cambridge friend Kingsley Martin, who had recently become editor of the *New Statesman*, the most widely read of the British weeklies in British Labour and left-of-center intellectual circles.[70] After trying her hand at some unsigned reports, she published her first real article in April on the bitterly contested presidential election between Hindenburg and Hitler. To Julian she reported happily, "my first real journalistic success and I am duly gratified." During three weeks in Berlin, she wrote, "I was sheltered within the shadow of various rather great men who urged me on, but at the end I went to Munich in solemn solitude and collected much material which has provided a *Statesman* article and may do more."[71] At the Brown House in Munich she had interviewed 'Putzi' Hanfstaengl, who was then handling Nazi publicity for foreign journalists.

Initially, when the Center party leader Heinrich Brüning became Chancellor, she was critical of his radical deflationary program of tax increases and reduction of government expenditures and his stubborn refusal to compromise and work with the Social Democrats. "A step towards dictatorship has really been taken," she wrote Julian.[72] But by 1932, with spiraling street violence and talk of a possible coup by the SA, her views had changed—influenced perhaps by her friend Norman Ebbutt of the *Times*, a confidant of the Chancellor who had put her in touch with him. Now she argued that while Brüning's might be "at best a plebiscitary dictatorship," in the present circumstances democracy was "beside the point."[73] Hindenburg's victory in the presidential runoff had raised her spirits, even though Hitler had polled over 13 million votes: "Last autumn, with the bank crash behind and the winter ahead, it looked as if extremism must win, despite the Chancellor's determination, 'moderation' must vanish. But now three interesting facts are emerging – Hitlerism cannot stand success, Communism is at best at a standstill, and there is a new patriotism among Moderates."[74] Emergency decrees banning the SA and SS showed, she believed, a renewed will to counteract a possible Nazi putsch. There were signs that Ruhr industrialists were reducing their economic backing for the Nazis, while the threat of a Hitler presidency seemed to have forged a marriage of convenience between the Catholic Center and the Social Democrats, helping to bolster the Republic. "This spring," she concluded, "one has a new feeling of the solidity of the Germans as a political entity, and as fairly sensible creatures, most of them... [E]ven a year ago there was no focus for reasonable patriotism." But now, "for the time," Hindenburg and the Iron Front's victory had created "a new patriotism, standing for conservation, continuity, and no more coercion than is legal."[75] It was, she wrote, "the unexpected crystallization of a commonsense *bloc*...one breathed a sigh of relief." She was, of course, completely wrong: "never was a hope more forlorn."[76]

This article was soon followed by a steady stream: "I found I could generally place at least four review articles after each journey, and in those days they paid for a few weeks abroad lived frugally."[77] During the next two years, she emerged as the *New Statesman*'s lead correspondent in the German capital, albeit on a freelance basis. Before long she was also contributing to the *Contemporary Review*, the *Nineteenth Century*, and the *Scotsman*. She also approached a friend at the BBC about broadcasting but was told that Vernon Bartlett was already covering German politics.[78] Her talents were quickly apparent. She was able to capture in concise, pungent prose both the atmosphere of the time and the complexities of a fast-changing political scene. Always good at networking, she also got interviews with leading figures like Brüning, Kurt von Schleicher, Franz von Papen (later), and many others. Voigt was impressed by her abilities; indeed, in September he wrote to his editor, W.P. Crozier, who needed a Rome correspondent: "If you are still looking out for someone, I can recommend Miss B [Betty] Wiskemann who has been writing about Germany for the 'New Statesman and Nation'. She has considerable knowledge of history, some acquaintance with archaeology, and good political judgment. Her articles have been…very careful and accurate."[79] Nothing came of this, although after the Second World War she did settle in Rome for two years, reporting for several papers.

Wiskemann owed her journalistic training to a remarkable *corps d'elite* of foreign correspondents representing the English-language press in Berlin in the early 1930s. Aside from Voigt, her chief mentors were Norman Ebbutt of the *Times*,[80] a mild-mannered man, generous with his expertise and a close confidant of Brüning and other high officials, and Darsie Gillie, then working for the *Morning Post*. Still in his twenties Gillie, Wiskemann wrote, "had a real purity of judgment that was infallible"; he was an expert on Poland as well as Germany and later became a brilliant commentator on France.[81] Another important figure was Edgar Mowrer of the *Chicago Daily News*; more deeply anti-German and anti-Weimar than the others, his book, *Germany Puts the Clock Back* (1933), became a huge best-seller, exhausting its first print run of 50,000 copies in one week. The correspondent for Reuters was Cecil Sprigge, whom Wiskemann had met earlier in Rome, while Douglas Reed and Donald McLachlan were Ebbutt's assistants and Hugh Carleton Greene reported first from Munich and then Berlin for the *Daily Telegraph*. Another prominent figure was Sefton Delmer of the *Daily Express*, who was somewhat suspect to the others because of his social connections to leading Nazis.[82] The Americans included Hubert Knickerbocker (whom Wiskemann didn't think much of) and William Shirer, while Dorothy Thompson and Sinclair Lewis were also there for a time. Two historians were part of the group: E.J. Passant, a Cambridge don,[83] and John Wheeler-Bennett, a private scholar who knew Franz von Papen, Hjalmar Schacht, and Kurt von Schleicher well and had close ties to the Foreign Office in London.

Many of this stellar cadre met regularly, presided over by Ebbutt, at their corner *Stammtisch* in the Taverne bar and restaurant on Georgenkirchstrasse in the Friedrichshain district, where they drank and thrashed out the news and rumors.[84] "There" wrote Mowrer's wife Lilian, "you could learn more of the true conditions in Germany than anywhere else in the entire country, for even individual Nazis knew little of what was going on outside their own zone of misdeeds."[85] Trying to cover large areas and fast-moving events, reporters saw the advantage of pooling their resources. As John Gunther (whom Wiskemann got to know in Vienna) put it: "The basis of journalism in Europe is friendship…News gathering in Europe is largely a collaboration, whereby men who know and trust

Figure 1.2. "F.A. Voigt in 1935," by Lucia Moholy. Artimage.

one another exchange gossip, background and information."[86] They were a hard-living, fun-loving group. Cecil Sprigge, something of a dandy, was dubbed the Don Juan of Berlin, which—Wiskemann commented—was in those days "a tall-ish order."[87] Voigt, another ardent womanizer, referred to the bed in his Berlin flat "die Sündenwiese" ["meadow or pasture of sin"]; he was, Wiskemann recalled, "eccentric and…in those days lewd and leftist."[88] She became one of the few female 'regulars' at these gatherings and was always conscious of being an independent woman in a male-dominated environment, needing to prove her worth.

In the months after Hindenburg's re-election as President of the Republic the pace of events accelerated. The Nazis made further gains in state elections, Brüning was forced out, replaced as Chancellor by Papen, and intensifying street violence, especially in Prussia, led Papen to oust the Social Democratic Prussian state government as incapable of maintaining order and to appoint a Reich Commissar with full powers over the state. There was no resistance from the deposed ministers, the trade unions, or the Reichsbanner, the socialist paramilitary organization; they seemed too paralyzed to act. Voigt still had some small hope that the Reichsbanner would defend the Republic, but after interviewing its leader, Karl Höltermann, Wiskemann came away disappointed: "If so intelligent a man [Voigt] could nurse so complete an illusion, the illusion of the liberals, I felt the end to be in sight."[89] She had good access to the thinking of the Papen regime through two young officials, Erwin Planck, son of the physicist, who was State Secretary in the Reichschancellery, and his friend Major Marcks, who headed the government's press department. From them she heard the rhetoric of the "conservative revolution"[90]: the idea that a strong authoritarian state above parties could be built by integrating the Nazis into a broad coalition as a subordinate partner. These goals were undermined by the government's disastrous showing in the late July Reichstag elections when the number of Nazi deputies rose from 107 to 230; also, Hitler insisted on being Chancellor of the coalition, something President Hindenburg refused to accept.

The following month, August 1932, an incident took place in the Silesian village of Potempa which shook Wiskemann "to the core." A group of SA brutally murdered an unemployed miner and Communist sympathizer of Polish descent in front of his mother and brother. At first, in the near civil war atmosphere of that summer, this incident, horrific though it was, caused little public comment until a court sentenced five SA men to death and bands of stormtroopers in the area responded by attacking Jewish shops and smashing up liberal and socialist newspaper offices; Goering praised the condemned men and sent money to their families, while Hitler pledged his unswerving solidarity with them by telegram. Papen soon backed down, overruled the court, and commuted the sentences; the murderers were later freed in March 1933. This affair, to which she returned almost obsessively in her later writings ("for me personally of prophetic significance"[91]), was deeply abhorrent to Wiskemann. It was both a glaring illustration of what a Hitler government would mean for the rule of law and an indication of how far the racist corrosion now pervaded public attitudes—she recalled lunching with a seemingly respectable solicitor who called the victim of the SA men a mere nothing, a *Minusmensch*, echoing the *Völkischer Beobachter*'s insistence that "one soul does not equal another."[92] To Julian Trevelyan, she commented: "The Germans are deplorable. The only sympathetic ones are becoming more and more oppressed by the others."[93] It was around this time that Francis Birrell, a close family friend since her childhood, who was returning to England from a trip to the Soviet Union, spent a couple of days with her: "It was like pure sunshine in a darkening corner when he came to Berlin that time." They went to see *Twelfth Night* in German with Helene Thimig, Max Reinhardt's wife, playing Viola. "We began by resenting Shakespeare in German, but Viola was completely disarming: I have never enjoyed her more. Francis was delighted. He would have wept to think of the book-burning that was to come so soon." His death at age forty-six from a brain tumor in early 1935 came as a terrible shock.[94]

By the year's end, all of Papen's initiatives had collapsed and his government failed to achieve public support for its policies in a second Reichstag election in November, even though support for the Nazi party declined by 2 million votes. General Schleicher prevailed upon Hindenburg to sack Papen and took over the

Chancellorship himself. The real losers from Papen's failure, Wiskemann argued, were Alfred Hugenberg and the big industrial interests he represented. They had applauded the effort to turn the clock back to the Bismarckian era with a concerted attack on socialism, workers' wages, and welfare benefits. In little more than six months this had increased support for the Communist party and produced a shift to the left of the Nazi party—as indicated by Nazi support for the Communist-inspired strike of Berlin transport workers.[95] After the November Reichstag elections, Wiskemann wrote, the government feared a general strike and the nation seemed closer to revolution than ever before. "It seems clear," she argued, "that Schleicher must be cautiously welcomed by all but those who wish to provoke a violent revolution in Germany."[96]

Flexible and intelligent, Schleicher abandoned Papen's frontal attack on the trade unions and sought their cooperation for a program of economic stimulus, relief for the unemployed, and a land settlement scheme reminiscent of the Brüning era. He also seemed more open to working with the Reichstag, reviving "the feeling now that Weimar is not ended and can be mended."[97] With Hitler's followers growing impatient at his failure to seize power, Schleicher believed that he could take advantage of these fissiparous tendencies to draw Gregor Strasser and his wing of the party into close collaboration. In Wiskemann's opinion, he "was trying to do the only possible thing...to enroll the support of both trade unionists and Strasser's so-called moderate Nazis, who were not Nazis at all in Hitler's sense."[98] She also speculated, like many others, that support for the Nazis might have reached its zenith and ebbed, noting that the party had offered no coherent solution to the economic depression and "would probably be helpless in office,"[99] while "the mere keeping together of so large and heterogeneous a mass in anything but opposition is clearly out of the question."[100] "Liberalism," she wrote, "has all but vanished in contemporary Germany" and "perhaps Kurt von Schleicher is the most representative figure to be found in Germany in 1932. He is a soldier and his outlook is authoritarian, but the Germans – not only on the Right – applaud the authoritarian conception."[101] Voigt was more pessimistic, writing to his Editor: "The Schleicher regime is an acknowledged transition regime, though transition to what is very dark."[102]

These early attempts to grasp what was happening in Germany were highly intelligent, detailed, and full of astute insights; they also illustrate how fast the situation was changing and how difficult it was to predict the future. For Wiskemann, for all her fear and loathing of Nazism, it was hard to believe Hitler would become Chancellor and govern effectively. But her faith in Schleicher was soon overtaken by events: Gregor Strasser abruptly resigned his party offices and removed himself from the scene, while Papen betrayed Schleicher, reopening negotiations with Hitler. Back in Cambridge in early January 1933 and just about to post off an article, Wiskemann added a hasty reference to these new developments: "The news of the Papen-Hitler interview at Cologne has just come...The incident is sensational, but I do not anticipate that it will greatly facilitate a Nazi participation with Schleicher [i.e. by the left wing of the Nazi movement], nor that it can very seriously destroy the none too steady equilibrium which Schleicher's appointment as Chancellor did so much to restore."[103] Again, she was mistaken, for Schleicher's position was now untenable.

On January 30, 1933, Hitler was appointed German Chancellor. Wiskemann was in Cambridge, where the Lent term had just started, but she quickly returned to Berlin for a few days. "One searches in vain," she wrote, "for any ray of hope."[104] She encountered the euphoria of the SA and SS parading in the streets, all constraints on their behavior now jettisoned. With the Prussian police ordered by Goering to cooperate with right-wing paramilitary groups, a wave of uncontrolled terror was soon unleashed against political enemies and old scores were settled. People were savagely beaten, tortured, and killed with impunity. In February 1933, around the time of the Reichstag Fire, Ebbutt sent her to a working-class flat where a father and son had been beaten up and dragged off by the SA, leaving a terrified family: "He thought that if a woman went to see them it would attract less attention and also that my German was fairly – only fairly – German-sounding. So I went to the address with some sort of password. I found the mother and daughter stunned with fear...the bullet marks were all over the flat...The women had no idea where their men were."[105] Trade union and Communist party offices were broken into and smashed; the liberal and left-wing press was cowed and muzzled; and while Communists and Socialists staged isolated demonstrations, their leaders were incapable of orchestrating a coordinated resistance. In truth, with the police and the army now in support of the stormtroopers, an armed uprising would have been suicidal. Voigt, long a vocal opponent of the Nazis, had been transferred to Paris for his own safety. But he warned against any inclination to downplay or normalize what was happening, writing to his editor:

Very few people in England have the slightest conception of what a Terror is and it is no easy matter to make it understood, but it should be attempted at least. The Brown Terror...is a frightfully dangerous inrush of Barbarism into the civilized world, a profound crisis in German – and therefore our own – civilization, and the biggest historical event since the Great War. It is very near to ourselves – much nearer than people imagine – and it is of the utmost importance that it be understood in all its horror and significance, that the facts should be vividly and boldly stated.[106]

Elections for a new Reichstag had been set for March 5. Germany was soon saturated by a massive campaign of intimidation and propaganda, while on February 27 the burning of the Reichstag building added to Nazi-fomented hysteria about the threat of a Communist putsch and accelerated the systematic suppression of all freedoms. On election day, Wiskemann, who had returned to Berlin a few days earlier, met with other foreign correspondents at Ebbutt's flat. They were joined by John Wheeler-Bennett and by Voigt, who had taken the risk of returning to Berlin. "An Englishman whom [Ebbutt] did not trust and who had turned up unasked" was forcibly kept out.[107] They divided into small groups and drove around the city, observing the polling stations, where stormtroopers were posted, creating in many precincts an atmosphere of palpable terror: "It was in a Wedding public house," she recalled, "that a Storm Trooper snatched a cigarette I was smoking from my mouth, informing me that the Führer disapproved of women smoking." "The people I admired most that day," she added, "were the Socialists one saw standing outside polling booths with a placard displaying only the number of the Socialist Party list – I think it was 2 – because they had been forbidden by Goering to display any party propaganda. They must each have known they would be beaten up terribly. When Germans are politically brave, I thought, they are heroic…The next few days were more and more of a nightmare."[108]

The Nazi party made large gains, but less than expected and it failed to achieve an absolute majority. Although unable to campaign, the Communists had still gained over 12% of the votes, while the Social Democrats managed to get over 18% and the Catholic Center polled about 11%, roughly what it had in the previous election. In the days after the vote, violence reached a new peak as the stormtroopers, feeling completely legitimated by the victory, targeted their enemies for beatings, torture, and murder. Around March 10, Wiskemann accompanied Mowrer, Ebbutt, and Darsie Gillie to meet a Jewish lawyer:

> We took a taxi in the direction of the man's flat, got out, dispersed, and each arrived separately, we hoped unobserved. At last we found ourselves closeted with an ugly little man who showed us the sworn testimony of clients of his, by no means all Jewish, of how they had been tortured by SA men. After a night or two in SA detention they had been allowed to go home though cautioned to remain silent…It was clear to us that no one would have invented these fearful stories. The plain little Jewish *Anwalt* [lawyer] knew that he would be torn limb from limb for letting us see these things but he entreated us to tell the world with no thought for him. We never heard of him again and felt little doubt that he paid a terrible price.[109]

That evening she dined at the home of Gustav Stolper, the economist and editor of the *Deutsche Volkswirt*, along with Theodor Heuss[110] and his wife, whom she met for the first time. Both men were liberal Reichstag deputies. The dinner was tense since there had been threats that Nazis would invade the place. They did their best to eat and talk; all stayed late, not wishing to advertise their fear. In fact, when the Stolpers were out three evenings later, the Nazis came and wrecked the house.[111]

Just before returning to London, on March 21, Wiskemann witnessed Potsdam Day, a propaganda spectacular orchestrated by Goebbels for the opening of the new Reichstag. Hitler and President Hindenburg presided over the ceremony, laying wreaths at the tombs of the Prussian kings and reviewing an endless march-past of the army, SA, SS, and the Stahlhelm. "Tiny children of four and five in SA uniform," Wiskemann recalled, "were collecting money for the Nazis and the women looking after them seemed to quiver with hysterical zeal."[112] Two days later came passage of the Enabling Act giving Hitler extraordinary powers. The left, she wrote, was now "smashed" and "most of the pacifist, intellectual, and aesthetic conceptions, which we are accustomed to regard as the most precious fruits of civilization, are completely discredited in Germany today." Especially horrifying was the enthusiasm of so many Germans for the new order and how easy it was for Goebbels to stoke popular anger—against Marxists yesterday, Jews today and, she warned, foreign enemies tomorrow.[113]

In London she looked for ways to alert people to the savage repression taking place in the Reich and the threat of renewed German militarism, but politicians like the Liberal leader, Sir Herbert Samuel, and her friend the Treasury official David ['Sigi'] Waley had trouble believing things were as bad as she described. She had better luck with the Liberal MP Geoffrey Mander, later a vociferous critic of Chamberlain's Appeasement policy, who was eager for first-hand knowledge of the Nazi Reich and echoed her alarm in the Commons.[114] In the Labour party, she recalled, Hugh Dalton had the best understanding of what was happening. Wiskemann's frustrations at the unwillingness of many in Britain to accept her descriptions of Nazi goals and violence as literal truth echoed Voigt's letters to his *Guardian* editor. "I feel more and more strongly that our own civilization must be defended tooth and nail and that to do so events in Germany must be understood – one of the reasons why the German left went down so ignominiously was that it never understood." The character of Nazism, he added, "will be incomprehensible to papers like the *Times* [and the *Telegraph*]"; they would inevitably try to normalize the regime: "Only the *Guardian* will be left to expose it." "In that fight," he told Crozier, "your part can be and should be a leading part...and it is no exaggeration to say that the civilized world looks to the M.G....for this leadership...its immediate aim the reconquest of liberty in Europe."[115]

Wiskemann returned to Germany in July 1933[116] and again in the autumn. By this time the Nazi consolidation of power was well underway: any opposition that might have come from workers had been pre-empted; the non-Nazi members of the government coalition had been turned into mere ciphers; and Hindenburg had been rendered powerless. Jews were being hounded; state governments had been dissolved and reorganized without elections, losing all their autonomy; the trade unions were also dissolved and replaced by a Nazi-controlled German Labor Front; and by the end of July all other political parties had ceased to exist, leaving only the Nazi party. The Weimar structure had been dismantled at breakneck speed. "The complete control of the press, as well as the wireless, by the Nazi dictatorship," wrote Wiskemann, "has left the ordinary citizen without any means of knowing what is going on in the Brown houses, in the concentration camps, or behind neighbors' doors." And yet it was unclear if the Nazis could solve the problem of mass unemployment or maintain the level of mass enthusiasm they had generated; there were also signs of divisions, strains within the movement, and calls for a "Second Revolution." "The next stage of the revolution," Wiskemann predicted, "will be disappointment and not fulfillment," although she saw little likelihood that Hitler's regime would be overthrown.[117]

At the end of the Nazi regime's first year in power, she also wrote two articles for the *New York Times*, another mark of her growing reputation. In them she detailed the regime's largely successful efforts to expunge the cultural modernism of republican days, although buildings were more durable and Berlin's architectural experimentalism still "reigned in insolent triumph." Racist politics had been injected into literature, the theatre, film, art, and architecture under the aegis of the Goebbels' Reich Chamber of Culture. The impact on women was especially dramatic. The Republic had enfranchised women and propelled them into more public spaces and diverse employment sectors. Nazism prioritized women's roles as homemakers and mothers whose first duty was to the 'race,' while also unifying and politically integrating women's organizations into the *Nationalsozialistische Frauenschaft* led by Gertrud Scholtz-Klink. When Wiskemann inquired if Frau Klink had had an interesting career, she was told: What should she want with a career? She had borne four children. Periods of national decay, like the Weimar years, argued Alfred Rosenberg, Nazism's chief racial ideologue, called forth "the effeminate man and the emancipated woman as symbols of political and cultural decline." As Wiskemann noted, the modern, fashionable urban woman was the main target, especially the highly educated; the lives of female typists and secretaries and even those working in factories had altered little. It was in the law, medicine, the civil service, and teaching that opportunities were shrinking most rapidly. By contrast "girls who joined the Nazi movement in good time have reaped a rich harvest in jobs in the hierarchy of the National Socialist Women's Organization and its subordinate bodies."[118]

* * *

While Berlin and Germany were Wiskemann's chief focus, she soon turned her attention to Nazism's impact on neighboring countries. She had spent time in Vienna some years earlier doing archival research for her ill-fated doctoral dissertation, but in September 1931 traveled there as a reporter. She carried letters of introduction to two leading correspondents: Marcel Fodor of the *Manchester Guardian* and Eric Gedye, who wrote for several papers including the *New York Times*. Both generously provided introductions to other journalists, politicians, and intellectuals, many of whom met regularly at Café Louvre to share leads and stories—just as they did at the Taverne restaurant in Berlin.[119] At the Louvre she also met the Marxist philosopher George Lukacs and Robert Musil, the author of *Der Mann ohne Eigenschaften*.[120]

She returned to Vienna in June 1933, eager to gauge how the economic depression and Nazi success in Germany were impacting the nation's politics. Austrian politics were polarized and deadlocked between the Socialists who controlled Vienna and the right-wing Catholics who dominated the surrounding provinces; Hitler's success had also strengthened the Austrian brand of fascism. Even the League of Nation's financial representative, Rost van Tonningen (later a leading Dutch Nazi) made it clear "that he sympathized with Pan-Germanism, and regarded an independent Austria, for which the League of Nations stood, as nonsense," and she found similar sentiments at a lunch party at the British Legation.[121] Beginning her visit in Salzburg, the first words Wiskemann heard were "Heil Hitler" from a group of boys selling the party's *Völkischer Beobachter* on the streets. From there she moved on to Vienna, where the parliament had recently been dissolved, while Hitler's decision to impose a ban on German tourists visiting Austria had caused great harm to the Austrian economy. A patriotic reaction to this had increased support for the Christian Socialist Chancellor, Engelbert Dollfuss, who had been elected in May 1932, but it was unclear whether he could broker any compromise between the Socialists and Clericals. At this stage Wiskemann was somewhat sympathetic towards Dollfuss ("a tiny cherub-like figure with genuine charm") whom she referred to as "Tom Thumb." Attending a Christian Social Party rally, she was struck by its sensible moderate tone compared to the violence of Nazi meetings and she believed he might rein in growing pro-Nazi terrorism.[122] On this same visit she also met several leading Social Democrats, including Kautsky's economist son, Bendikt, and Otto Bauer, but her most memorable interview was with Karl Seitz, the mayor of Vienna, who had implemented public welfare and educational reforms as well as a huge program of workers' housing which she toured with officials from the *Rathaus*.

By December, however, Dollfuss had begun a systematic assault on "Red Vienna," siphoning off its finances, forcing economic cutbacks and the dismissal of large numbers of municipal officials. Tensions were high, although she expected that the Chancellor's skillful opportunism would contain them. In the *New Statesman* she speculated that "Austrian Fascism will achieve some kind of compromise, and will erect a rather ramshackle structure," although she warned that Austria's future would be determined by external events: "In any international storm this building may well collapse. And when Germany is more completely rearmed, will Italy continue to obstruct her advance?"[123] She wondered whether there was any chance that Catholics and Socialists might work together to safeguard Austrian integrity and freedom from Nazism, but saw little or no hope of this.[124] It was a sad irony, she noted, that Vienna, which was two-thirds Socialist and highly secular, was now being subjected to compulsory Catholicism, while in Catholic Munich, the birthplace of Nazism, the Hitler regime was openly flouting its recent Concordat with the Pope, and imprisoning priests; Dollfuss had installed a right-wing Clerical as mayor of socialist Vienna, while Catholic Munich was administered by a Protestant Nazi.[125]

Wiskemann's next stay in Vienna came in March 1934, a month after Dollfuss had used the army and units of the fascist Heimwehr to smash the workers' movement in Vienna and other big cities. Artillery barrages were launched against the workers' flats, full of women and children, killing 1,500 people and wounding 5,000 others. The municipal housing she had toured a year before was now "heavily scarred by the civil war. Up and down the staircases one found scribbled, between smears of blood and swastikas, 'Murderers of the workers.'"[126] Soon socialists were being hunted down and incarcerated *en masse* and the Socialist Party was outlawed.[127] On an earlier trip to Vienna the previous December, Wiskemann had met Hugh Gaitskell, a recent Oxford graduate and disciple of G.D.H. Cole and Hugh Dalton, who was there studying economics on a Rockefeller fellowship. After the bloodshed, Gaitskell threw himself into aiding socialists: escorting refugees and wanted persons across the border, calling secret meetings, arranging safe houses, and raising money in Britain to relieve the poverty of workers' families and pay for legal defense for those imprisoned. By the time he left, 170 socialists had escaped through Gaitskell's network, using false papers that he obtained or through bribes paid with money from London.[128] Naomi Mitchison, whom Wiskemann had known for several years, also arrived in Vienna, funded by a book advance from Gollancz. She toured workers' housing projects, distributing money sent from London, and worked to publicize their plight with articles in the *Daily Herald* and the *New Statesman*.[129] Gaitskell had urged her to come to Vienna; he also recruited Elwyn Jones, then a law student,[130] to investigate ways in which the rule of law was being undermined and to locate defense lawyers for the accused. They were all in close contact with Eric Gedye, while Voigt also turned up from Paris.[131] The young Gaitskell was deeply marked by his Viennese experiences. He returned home angry and deeply frustrated at socialism's defeat; it shaped his opposition to Appeasement and his insistence that the democracies must rearm quickly. It was a bond he shared with Wiskemann and they remained good friends.

Wiskemann's reporting set the recent bloodshed in larger power-political terms. She contextualized the Viennese street fighting in the shift of influence toward Mussolini, the French left's weakness following the riots of February 1934, and Czech concerns about growing fascist influence in Austria. In tight, economical prose she sketched a complex picture, truly an example of journalism "as the first rough draft of history":[132]

Before the battles of February a precarious balance existed between the influ-ence of Italy in the valley of the Danube and that of the Little Entente,[†] which regarded Italy as an intruder, but relied upon France. Both rivals viewed uneas-ily the new impulse provided by National Socialism to the *Mitteleuropa* idea, the old plan for German hegemony in the Danube newly disguised as a *raciste* demand for Anschluss. Alarmed by this, France decided to resign the initiative in Austria to Italy, and Czechoslovakia unwillingly agreed. But neither France nor Czechoslovakia had abandoned their interest in the survival of the Austrian Social Democrats, who were their allies from several points of view, and who provided a link with Soviet Russia, an old friend of the Czechs and the new friend of France.[‡] Mussolini detested the Socialists as the truest enemies both to his political theories and his Danubian greed, but it was only the collapse of the French left, at the beginning of February, which gave Italy the chance to insist upon the elimination of the Marxist party. Dr. Dollfuss had promised M. Paul-Boncour not to destroy the Socialists, while to M. Barthou he could repudiate the pledge. The news from France, moreover, profoundly affected the morale of the Austrian Socialists; there was a feeling among them that Western democracy had gone to pieces and the time had come for heroic remedies – a great stand, a supreme gesture, must be made in the name of freedom. With the will to fight in both camps, the affair of Linz[§] was more than enough to precipitate the battle.

In June 1934 Wiskemann was once again in Austria,[133] but she was forced to cut short her visit, journeying north to Berlin when news broke of Hitler's purge of the SA and the murder of Röhm, Gregor Strasser, General von Schleicher, and many others in the so-called 'Night of the Long Knives.' A month after Hitler's purge, on July 25, Dollfuss was murdered in an attempted coup by Austrian Nazis, although their goal of *Anschluss* with Germany was frustrated by Mussolini's threats of intervention. By September 1934, when Wiskemann returned to Vienna, the situation was very unstable. Kurt von Schuschnigg had become Chancellor, many socialist workers had gone over to the Nazis, whose rank and file in Austria favored the Otto Strasser wing of the movement, and others had been polarized further left to the Communists. Some groups, it was rumored, even dreamed about restoring the Habsburgs, although this produced strong negative reactions in successor states like Czechoslovakia.[134] The position of the

---

† Refers to the treaty between Czechoslovakia, Yugoslavia and Romania guaranteeing the post-First World War status quo in south-east Europe. Austria and the Habsburg Monarchy, along with Hungary, had been the major territorial losers.

‡ Refers to French efforts, led by Foreign Minister Barthou to re-strengthen French ties with Poland and to bring the USSR into the League of Nations as a counterweight to Hitler. He was assassinated in Marseilles in October 1934.

§ The fighting between the socialists and conservative-fascist forces began in Linz on February 12, 1934, and quickly spread to Vienna, Graz, and other cities.

new Chancellor, Schuschnigg, seemed reasonably secure, particularly since Hitler seemed to have decided upon a course of gradualism. Again, with an acute grasp of the political forces and the personalities involved, she writes:

> Within Austria the new situation is expressed in the substitution of Schuschnigg for Dollfuss. No two men could have presented a greater contrast; indeed, they had nothing in common but their Catholic piety. In the place of Dollfuss's easy charm and flexible opportunism, Schuschnigg offers a quiet cautiousness which conceals clearly defined political conceptions. While Dollfuss played the child-dictator running delightfully from Uncle Pius to Uncle Benito, Schuschnigg, though younger in years, revives the Seipel tradition** and compels a perhaps more serious respect. It would be too ominous to say that this is a less friendly Bruening; the new chancellor is a shy, but not an isolated man. Kurt von Schuschnigg was a General's son; he was born on the old Italian frontier at Riva on Lake Garda, and he studied at Innsbruck. If he cannot rally the peasants of Lower Austria as the peasant Dollfuss could, he is probably on easier terms with his Vice-Chancellor, Prince Starhemberg.†† With a Tyrolese tradition behind him, he will probably wish to be less completely dependent upon Italy, and the changes in international relations may help him to gain a wider measure of support abroad. The Czechs, for instance, may feel able to make economic concessions within a wider Rome agreement. Schuschnigg believes in a German Catholic cultural mission in the old Habsburg tradition...it was he who saved the situation on July 25th.[135]

Initially, Wiskemann's Viennese contacts were mostly Social Democrats, but now she tried to widen her circle of informants by seeking out Pan-Germans, monarchists, and others who were clearly Nazi supporters.[136] Memorable in this respect was a brief trip to Styria in the company of Eugen Kogon, a young Catholic journalist, whom she had met a year before. Kogon, who had studied in Munich, Florence, and Vienna, was originally sympathetic to the political right; his views owed much to the anti-liberal corporate state theories of the Viennese professor Othmar Spann and he was chiefly troubled by the growing influence of Marxism. But the brutality of the Hitler movement and its hostility to the Catholic Church turned him into a vehement anti-Nazi. Kogon and Wiskemann drove to Graz where he introduced her to a group of fiercely pro-Nazi youths who, so soon after Dollfuss's assassination, had no inhibitions about expressing their racism towards Slavs and Jews (and Italians) or their total faith in Hitler. Styria, she reported, was

---

** Ignaz Seipel, a prelate and politician of the conservative Christian Social Party, had been Austrian Chancellor during much of the 1920s.
†† Ernst Rudiger Starhemberg was a conservative nationalist and leader of the Heimwehr paramilitary organization.

comparable to East Prussia, seeing itself as "an outpost of Germanism. Protestantism is stronger there than elsewhere and the Protestant pastors are everywhere notoriously Nazi."[137] In addition, she noted, the area's one giant iron industry firm, the Alpine Montan Company, was half-owned by Thyssen and openly supported the Nazis.[138] They drove back via Steyr and Linz, where again— though officially banned—Nazi supporters had no qualms about expressing their allegiance. She feared that the Austrian government was little better than a hopeless farce if it had so little support in Vienna and so many enemies in the rest of the country. She also interviewed Franz von Papen, who had been appointed German ambassador to Vienna shortly after the Night of the Long Knives. Already in September 1934 she had no illusions about Austria's independence, for it was clear that Hitler could occupy it whenever he chose.[139] When Mussolini invaded Ethiopia in 1935 and moved closer to Hitler, there was nothing to prevent its eventual absorption.

Austria was one example of Nazi tactics of penetration, another that Wiskemann followed closely in 1934–35 was the Saarland. The Versailles Treaty had removed the region from Germany, placing it under the control of the League of Nations for fifteen years, while its coal mining production went as reparations to France. Before 1933, the Saar's German-speaking industrial workers, many of them socialists and communists, favored the return of the area to Germany. But the consolidation of Nazi rule in the Reich generated some resistance to this solution, as did growing evidence of Nazi repression of the Catholic Church in Bavaria and elsewhere. At the end of fifteen years, in January 1935, a plebiscite was to take place in which the Saarlanders would choose between returning to Germany, becoming French, or preserving the status quo. Already by early 1934 pro-Nazis had unleashed a campaign with threats of violence against all "Separatists." "No one dares," Wiskemann wrote, "to advertise in the Socialist press, or be seen in a Jewish café. People visit Jewish doctors and dentists late at night."[140] She toured the region repeatedly, attended mass meetings, interviewed local inhabitants and German industrialists, and gained a thorough knowledge of its economy, sociology, and politics. She also admired the achievements of the League's governing Commission and argued that its policies had been impartial and efficient— especially its economic management, which had produced lower levels of unemployment than in neighboring areas.[141] Free trade with France and a range of economic concessions from Germany had been very beneficial to the territory. Wiskemann also got to know the Commission's British representative and President, Sir Geoffrey Knox, praising him as "the best guarantee for a fair vote," who was waging a "valiant struggle for fair play" in the face of stiff resistance from local mayors, judges, and policemen who were more loyal to Hitler than to him. They got on well: "[Knox] spoke good French and German and was highly intelligent and a great character; he was also a gourmet with a French chef and gave one splendid meals."[142] On more than one occasion, he loaned her his car and driver to visit different parts of the region, including a trip to Volklingen where she interviewed the iron magnate Hermann Röchling, who was leader of the German Front. Asked whether he thought he would be better off under the Third Reich, Röchling answered in the affirmative and then astonished her by declaring that National Socialism was "built upon a basis of love." She passed this on to Knox—or Tyrant Knox as he was known in pro-Nazi circles—who was "enchanted" by the phrase, "he ordered up a special bottle of wine from his cellar and we drank to the basis of love." Shortly thereafter, from Berlin, amid all the talk about the SA and Röhm's homosexuality, she sent Knox "a post-card (by special messenger) to say that I was studying the basis of love afresh in the German capital."[143]

Röchling's German Front was well-funded from Berlin[144] and enjoyed the help of the Trier Gestapo just across the border, whose agents swarmed into the Saar. But Wiskemann took some hope from the signs that Catholic priests were willing to share a platform with Socialist and even Communist advocates of the status quo. She described the applause given to a priest at a workers' meeting when he "spoke of his recent experiences in Germany, how he had been in prison there, how his friends had been afraid to give him shelter when he came out," and how Germany had become "a land thirsting for war."[145] To the Nazis, those who questioned the region's return to the Reich were Rhenish separatists or agents of French intrigue. For Hitler, Wiskemann recognized, overwhelming victory in the plebiscite was crucial to Nazi prestige: "Even a large minority for the status quo would be a humiliating blow";[146] indeed, doubts had been expressed as to "how successfully the Hitler regime could stand a moral defeat of this kind."[147] Having lived close to Hitlerism for two years, the region's inhabitants were about to give their verdict on the regime, "and theirs is the only German judgment which has any immediate opportunity of relatively free expression."[148] "For everyone who finds Hitlerism evil," she warned, "the struggle in the Saar is thus a matter of first-rate importance"; "once the Saar is settled, Hitler is freer to coerce his Catholics and to think about "independent" Austria."[149] She deplored the lack of interest among most of the British public and the League of Nations' weakness in managing the plebiscite or supporting its representatives on the ground, but saw some hope in two areas: among Saar workers, aware of economic discontent in Germany, and Catholics angered by Nazi disregard for the recent Concordat and talk of a renewed *Kulturkampf* against the Church. In the months before the plebiscite, the great unknown was how far Catholic opposition would translate into votes and whether the Catholic Church and left-wing workers could work together.[150] Like Voigt, Wiskemann overestimated the strength of the Catholic resistance. She recognized that the average Sarrois identified as being German, but she also believed that perhaps as many as 30–40% of the population might support a continuance of the League's administration, albeit reformed to make it less authoritarian and more representative—and that, if this were understood as an interim arrangement for, say, five years, the status quo might even win.[151]

In the weeks before the Saar vote, foreign correspondents descended upon the area in droves. This was inevitable and Wiskemann certainly favored as strong a light being thrown on Nazi tactics as possible. But she was also clearly irritated at journalists, unable to speak German, who suddenly appeared, knowing little about the Saar, and expected her to share her expertise.[152] She also feared they were prey to whatever pro-German sources might hand them. She watched the balloting with David Scott, who was sent by the *Times* from Paris; he provided her with transport across the region, she repaid him by supplying the German. Ebbutt and his deputy in Berlin, Douglas Reed, had been told explicitly by their London editor not to go to the Saar; already targets of the regime, their flats had been raided and their movements were being closely monitored.

As the January 13 ballot approached, cheating over voting lists and maneuvering to stack local committees tasked with administering the vote increased dramatically; so did Nazi violence and threats of reprisals against the anti-Nazi 'unity front' [*Einheitsfront*].[153] There was much talk of Nazi 'black lists' and, it was whispered, that ballots were numbered and could be traced. There was also concern that if the status quo prevailed, the Nazis might contemplate a *putsch*, further endangering the peace of Europe. The result was a huge victory for Hitler, with 90% of ballots favoring reintegration with Germany. Returning to England, Wiskemann was troubled to see how many people accepted this "as a perfectly genuine outburst of patriotism" rather than a victory for ferocious repression, weakness on the part of the League powers, and the vast resources of the German Propaganda Ministry "pitted against virtually nothing."[154] The Catholic bishops of Speyer and Trier had also intervened forcefully with a pastoral letter advising all Catholics to support the German Front. In the end the Vatican opted for accommodation, and many Catholics still valued Hitler as a bulwark against Bolshevism. Outside the polling stations, Wiskemann found "frankly Nazi policemen together with *Ordnungsdienst* [pro-Nazi auxiliaries] youths"—reminiscent of the Nazi controlled Reichstag elections of March 1933.[155] She marveled at the bravery of those like the Social Democrat Max Braun and the Catholic opposition leader, Johannes Hoffmann, who became marked men and were forced to escape to France right after the vote.

It was in the Saar that Wiskemann first met Shiela Grant Duff, at the time only twenty-two years old and a novice reporter on assignment from the *Observer*. Grant Duff came from an upper-class family with its roots in banking, Liberal politics, science, and service in India. Her father was killed in the war when she was only five and two uncles also perished; these deaths cast a pall over her early years. Educated at St Paul's and then Oxford, where she read PPE, the new 'modern greats,' she was part of a close-knit group of friends that included Goronwy Rees, Douglas Jay, Isaiah Berlin, Peggy Garnett, and Diana Hubback.[156] She also met and became close friends with Adam von Trott zu Solz, then a Rhodes Scholar and later a prominent figure in the resistance to Hitler. She 'came out,' endured the round of debutante parties, and was presented at Court but was determined to be independent, have a career, and work in some way to prevent another war in Europe.[157]

It was Arnold Toynbee, a relative by marriage, who suggested that she become a foreign correspondent. The foreign editor of the *Times* told her that a girl could not possibly work alongside men but invited her to send in some notes on fashion since she was traveling to Paris anyway. But in Paris she was taken on—as an unpaid trainee—by Edgar Mowrer, whom the Nazi regime had recently expelled from Berlin. She was idealistic, left-wing, and pro-German, and, like most of her friends, regarded Keynes's *Economic Consequences of the Peace* as a Bible. "I left Oxford," she later admitted, "under the influence of Goronwy [Rees] and Miss Headlam Morley, in a haze of pro-German guilt-ridden sentiment."[158] Mowrer soon rebuffed such sentiment and any idea that Allied policy or the Versailles Treaty bore responsibility for Hitler's rise, while first-hand experience of Nazi violence in Berlin and the Saar convinced her that the German regime endangered the peace of Europe.

As the *Observer*'s representative, she met the leading correspondents of the day, who had assembled in Saarbrücken for the plebiscite, including Vernon Bartlett, Kingsley Martin, Alexander Werth, Frederick Voigt, and Wiskemann.[159] Voigt, who had met her friend Goronwy Rees at the *Manchester Guardian*, took Grant Duff "under his wing," escorting her around the mining villages, introducing her to the leaders of the anti-Nazi opposition, and supplying her with background information. This may have irritated Wiskemann, earlier Voigt's protegé, for she tended to disparage Grant Duff—young, inexperienced, full of questions, and engaged on her first real press assignment—as superficial, an amateur. Although Wiskemann was far more established as a journalist, the two women had much in common—political ideas, their crusading anti-Nazism, and determination to alert people to Hitler's expansionist goals—and both came to focus on Eastern Europe. Their paths crossed numerous times and they had many friends, sources, and contacts in common, aside from Mowrer, Werth, and Voigt, including the Czech journalist Hubert Ripka, Ambassador Jan Masaryk, and Adam von Trott zu Solz. They also wrote for many of the same journals. Yet (in print at least) neither had much to say about the other. Perhaps this points to professional rivalry, but on Wiskemann's part there may have been something more. Grant Duff's aristocratic background, her private income, and her extensive social ties to influential people, including her family connection to Clementine Churchill, opened many doors, and this possibly grated on Wiskemann, who had to push hard for every contract and access she got.

In fact, while Grant Duff filed several stories about the Saar, the *Observer* assignment did not lead to something more permanent. Mowrer wrote inviting her back to Paris: "I was sorry about the Observer. The proposition never sounded very concrete to me but I know you counted on it to push you a step further on your zigzag career toward journalism. *Quelle ambition!*...I understand and share your desire to 'earn money' though I never quite understood why you think the worst paid of all the professions a good way to go about it." He added, "Personally I suspect you would do better to marry," and suggested that she and Goronwy would make "a good newspaper team" "if only you would remember that a journalist's first duty (I don't say his only duty) is to find out and describe what is going on and how it goes, and only then why, and shouldn't it be some other-how."[160] Hugh Massingham, the *Observer*'s foreign editor, remarked in a fatherly way: "I really must say how profoundly I disapprove of this desire to go into journalism. It is no life for a nice person."[161] She stayed on for a while in Saarbrücken assisting those (mostly communists) fleeing to France, conveying their belongings across the border, and even providing shelter. It was dangerous activity, especially for an inexperienced twenty-two-year-old. In Paris she covered for Mowrer the anti-fascist Writers Congress for the Defense of Culture, but soon returned to England working as an unpaid assistant to Hugh Dalton, the Labour spokesman for foreign affairs. She and Wiskemann were to meet again two years later in Prague, where they were both deeply engaged in the campaign to protect the independence and integrity of the Czech Republic. But they never became close friends.

In the wake of the Saar vote, events moved quickly. In March Hitler used modest French and British measures to strengthen their militaries as a pretext for proclaiming Germany's reintroduction of conscription, making public the existence of its air force (some 28,000 officers and men were already serving in it), and announcing a huge expansion of the *Wehrmacht* to thirty-six divisions. That Germany had been rearming illegally was well known, but this was a brazen repudiation of the Versailles Treaty. However, it elicited only verbal condemnations from France, Britain, and Italy, not a substantive response. Any hopes Wiskemann had that Hitler's recent moves might galvanize international opposition were dispelled by the signing in June of an Anglo-German Naval Agreement, which assuaged some of the British Admiralty's fears about being overstretched in a dangerous world but permitted increases in German naval spending‡‡ and alienated France, for whom this bilateral pact was an act of supreme treachery. She was appalled that, just one year after the Night of the Long Knives, a British government was willing to come to terms with Hitler, heedless of the damage to its ties with France. Four months later when Mussolini attacked Ethiopia, Britain and France were both reluctant to impose punitive economic sanctions and showed their willingness to reward aggression. A public outcry scuttled the Hoare–Laval pact, which would have granted Mussolini two-thirds of the territory he claimed, but damage to the League as a vehicle for collective security was irreversible.

---

‡‡ Under the Agreement, Germany could construct a navy 35% of the size of the British navy, and a submarine fleet the size of that of Great Britain.

In propelling Hitler and the Italian Duce towards a rapprochement and in further widening divisions among western powers, the crisis created opportunities for bolder German moves both in the demilitarized Rhineland and in Eastern Europe.

By this time Wiskemann was convinced that Hitler was preparing for war. Encouraged by R.W. Seton-Watson, Britain's leading scholar of south-eastern Europe, she decided to spend her Cambridge vacations traveling more outside Germany and Austria. In earlier years she had visited Hungary, staying with old family friends, and had gone briefly to Prague and Poland but more as a tourist "to look at beautiful and interesting things" rather than examine their politics in any depth.[162] She now began to focus more systematically upon Eastern Europe, beginning with Yugoslavia. No country in Eastern Europe had more acute and complicated ethnic divisions; hopes that the new state would foster a roughly equal union of the three main groups—Serbs, Croats, and Slovenes—quickly disappeared; instead, a highly centralized, Serb-dominated kingdom emerged, whose parliamentary politics were violent, deeply corrupt, and dominated by Serb–Croat conflict. In 1928 the Croatian Peasant party leader Radić was assassinated; the following year King Alexander dissolved parliament and created a personal dictatorship, and then in Marseilles, Croatian separatists murdered Alexander in October 1934 along with the French Foreign Minister, Louis Barthou.

Friends of Yugoslavia hoped the King's death and the elections scheduled for May 1935 might bring a change of policy, a return to parliamentarism. Armed with introductions from Seton-Watson, Wiskemann went first to Belgrade and was escorted around by Reuters' correspondent Peter Brown. The most impressive figure she met was the Serbian economist Dragoljub Jovanović, whose goal was to create a united front of the Serb and Croat peasant parties as a prelude to agrarian reform. However, open voting, police intimidation, corruption, and the inveterate hatreds of Croats and Serbs made such an outcome highly unlikely. From Belgrade she went west to Zagreb, whose culture and architecture seemed more familiarly linked to its Habsburg past. She spent time with Radić's widow and his successor as leader of the Croatian peasant party, Vladko Maček, and was welcomed into the intellectual circle of sculptor Ivan Meštrović, a close friend of Seton-Watson. She was also tailed by rather incompetent Serb police agents: "People would come and tell me that my two pursuers were just round the corner…Sometimes I would run quite fast which was most embarrassing…since they ran badly and it drew even more attention to them."[163] It was amusing more than threatening, a contrast to Hitler's Berlin. To Julian Bell she wrote happily: "I have decided that Zagreb (capital of Croatia) is my favorite town, where Meštrović, and a lot of people live. This in spite of discovering that a very beautiful young man who appeared to be normal (and I am an old hand you'd think) was really a nance. However, he had rashly produced a most exquisite boyfriend who was a bi [sexual], so we got very confused."[164] Finally she traveled to

Ljubljana, capital of Slovenia, whose intensely Catholic population strove to remain aloof from the Serb–Croat struggle. There she encountered Fanny Copeland, a formidable traveler and mountaineer, who had adopted this Balkan outpost as her own (rather like Edith Durham in Albania) and expected English visitors to echo her views and disregard other sources.[165] Returning to London, Wiskemann published several insightful articles, testimony to how much she had learned about Yugoslavia's ethnic politics in just a few weeks.[166] Like her friends, Rebecca West and Elisabeth Barker, she found the country fascinating and returned several times in the next years to report on Nazi Germany's growing economic and political penetration of the state.

She returned to Berlin in June 1935, staying at a flat owned by Moritz J. Bonn, a well-known political economist and historian who was Rector of the Berlin Handelshochschule before the Nazis came to power. Recognizing that they were in danger, Bonn, a Jew, and his English wife, Thérèse, had left for London in April 1933.[167] Superficially, Berlin seemed quieter, less violent than before: there were far fewer SA men to be seen and more Jews on the streets, many having fled smaller towns and villages for the greater safety of the large Berlin community, where they could also get help from Jewish charitable organizations. But appearances were deceptive. The churches were attacked more openly and Nazi racism had become even more strident, soon to be codified in the September Nuremberg Laws. Wiskemann was also more conscious of the growing danger for foreign journalists. The group that once frequented the Taverne was much depleted. The *Guardian* transferred Voigt to Paris as soon as Hitler became Chancellor, but the Gestapo pursued him; he narrowly escaped assassination at his Paris flat and the Sûreté Générale detailed an officer to protect him.[168] In December 1933 he was transferred to London but continued to use secret informants in Berlin. W.P. Crozier warned him: "You ought to assume that you are no safer in London than you were in Paris and take precautions accordingly."[169] His successor, Alexander Werth, of Russian-Jewish descent, was also vulnerable and was soon withdrawn. Pressure from his own paper and the Nazi regime forced Edgar Mowrer to leave in August 1933, but he managed to bargain with the regime for the release of an imprisoned Jewish correspondent for the *Neue Freie Presse* in return for his own departure. Hubert Knickerbocker was expelled, so was Dorothy Thompson,[170] while John Wheeler-Bennett, finding the atmosphere increasingly oppressive and dangerous, left immediately after the Röhm putsch; two days before, he had dined on the terrace of the Kaiserhof hotel with two of Papen's young adjutants, neither of whom survived the bloodbath.[171] Sources had to be interviewed in secret; reporters acquired such habits as not talking on the telephone, checking rooms for bugs, and being ever-vigilant for spies and police. Ebbutt remained despite Nazi efforts to have the *Times* recall him, but he was more and more isolated and his reports were sanitized by his editor, Geoffrey Dawson.[172] Undeterred by these dangers, Wiskemann continued her travels in

July 1935, going first to Warsaw and then on to Danzig and Memel, where pro-Nazi groups, inspired by Hitler's victory in the Saar, were intensifying their demands for a return to the Reich.

Many of Wiskemann's articles appeared unsigned or labeled for her protection: "From a Berlin Correspondent" or "From a Correspondent recently in Saarbrücken." But she made no effort to moderate her attacks on the regime, quite the contrary. Early in July she published a hard-hitting essay, titled ironically "A Land Fit for Heroes." Though not untypical of her writing at the time, it was the ostensible grounds for her arrest by the Gestapo in the following year. In it Wiskemann voiced her disgust: "The general line in England to-day is, it seems, to feel that Germany is settling down quite nicely – a few little un-Englishnesses, but then foreigners will be foreigners." "Liberal and intellectual opinion in Germany," she added, "is in despair over the cowardice of England." Dr. Schacht, the finance minister, and other 'reactionaries' were directing the economy, while the purge of the SA had left the Reichswehr in a stronger position to influence Hitler's regime. "But," she wrote, "the price they and their countrymen and Europe must pay for this is to give the wild men their head in other directions,"[173] and Britain's actions only emboldened them:

> In the Germany whose respectability we have now guaranteed with the naval agreement the maltreatment of the Jews is being carried to hitherto unknown lengths, while every genuine Christian and every genuine intellectual or artist is subjected to spasmodic and arbitrary persecution. The reason why there are so many Jews about Berlin is that life in smaller towns or in the country has by now become intolerable for them. Thanks to Statthalter Sprenger, Hessen is probably as bad as Streicher's Franconia but there has been a big press campaign since about March in which the *Westdeutscher Beobachter* (Cologne and Aix) and the *Frankfurter Volksblatt* have been conspicuous too. "You may as well look for virginity in an old whore as for honour and a sense of right in a Jew," is a typically charming *mot* I have received from Munich. Dr. Goebbels' reference to fleas in his speech on July 29th was merely the culmination of the recent offensive. Berlin has become the refuge of the German Jews, but it is by no means a safe refuge. The metropolitan police, presumably out of consideration for foreign susceptibilities, have just forbidden the affixing of notices saying "You are stealing the nation's wealth if you buy from a Jew," but both SA and civilian groups have been mobbing Jews, and since so many ice-cream vendors are Jews the hot weather added to the fun.[174]

The SS and the secret police now wielded terrible power, while the SS's new weekly, *Das Schwarze Korps*, Wiskemann wrote, "makes plain...that the SS is pledged to neo-paganism and every sort of dehumanization. Their ideal is to be hard and simple; indeed, fanatical National Socialism is a kind of 'Back to the

Animal' campaign. And physically anyone is at their mercy; in the last instance, they fear nothing but the Army." And while there were pockets of resistance to this "barbarian yoke" in the bureaucracy and among some groups of workers, none threatened the regime's hold on power.[175] Hitler, in alliance with German heavy industry and the army, was, Wiskemann insisted, intent upon war to create a huge Central European bloc or Mitteleuropa "from the French border and the North Sea down to the Black Sea and the Dvina"—in other words "the territory occupied by the troops of the Central Powers during the years 1917 and 1918."[176] By summer's end, she recalled, she had "abandoned the hopes to which I had been clinging that Hitler and Hitlerism might somehow be deflected by some accident from their own fulfillment."[177]

*   *   *

By 1935, only three years after she first began to publish, Wiskemann had become a well-known foreign correspondent, regularly contributing articles to the *New Statesman* and several other weeklies and monthlies.[178] Her decision to spend time in Berlin originated in a desire for a fresh start and a respite from Cambridge. But by 1932, in the political crisis of Weimar, she discovered her vocation, and in the next years she worked tirelessly to analyze the spread of Nazi power in Germany and the threat it posed to the rest of Europe. Her political assessments were complex and nuanced, and she was not afraid to speculate (and risk being wrong) about the tumultuous events she was witnessing. Attractive, highly intelligent, and personable, she won the respect of seasoned journalists like Voigt, Ebbutt, Gillie, Gedye, and Mowrer. And while her gender may in some respects have been a hindrance in these masculine circles, in others it probably opened doors, facilitating her efforts to get politicians and officials to open up and talk less guardedly.[179] Travel and personal observation were essential to her work, and her often hastily penned notes show her as constantly in motion, arriving or departing from a trip or planning another itinerary across the Continent. Remarkably, as a poorly paid freelancer, she did this on little money and without the fallback of private resources. Tutoring undergraduates was her only predictable source of income, and by 1935 she was hoping to quit teaching altogether, telling a BBC friend in February: "I'm not going to Cambridge after next May term, so the subsistence question will intensify, though it will be marvelous to have time to breathe."[180] And yet Newnham and Cambridge remained an important part of her life, especially the many friendships and social ties she made there.

Thirty-six years of age at the time of the Saar crisis, Wiskemann was deeply ambitious for her career; she was also fiercely independent and self-sufficient, determined to preserve her own freedom of action. Though reticent or oblique in such matters, the circles in which she moved—in Cambridge, Paris, and Berlin— were sexually liberal and feminist. Like many of her friends, she was not looking for marriage or safety and refused to be hemmed in by Victorian morality.

She clearly had a number of affairs, but she was determined to establish the terms of these relationships, and none was allowed to encroach on her own freedom and priorities. She had no intention of subordinating her professional life to the needs or aspirations of another—and this was always the case.

The photograph, Figure 1.3, is possibly the only surviving photograph of Wiskemann from the early 1930s. It was taken at the Ramsey and Muspratt studio

Figure 1.3. "Elizabeth Wiskemann in February 1932," by Ramsey & Muspratt. Permission of Peter Lofts.

in Cambridge. Lettice Ramsey, educated at Bedales and then Newnham, had been the wife of the brilliant mathematician and philosopher Frank Ramsey, who was only twenty-seven when he died of liver disease in 1930. To support her young children, Lettice teamed up with Helen Muspratt and together over the next years they ran a highly successful business and photographed many Bloomsbury and Cambridge luminaries, including Julian Bell and most of Wiskemann's friends. Wiskemann knew Lettice well and her portrait dates from February 1932 (immediately after the studio opened—she may have been their first customer), just as she was about to emerge as a correspondent for the *New Statesman*.

Memoirs about Germany in the early 1930s mention Wiskemann only fleetingly if at all, but I would argue that she does make an appearance—albeit caricatured unfavorably as foreign correspondent Helen Pratt—in Christopher Isherwood's novel *Mr Norris Changes Trains* (1935), the most famous depiction of Weimar Berlin in English. Isherwood first visited Berlin in 1929 and lived there for most of 1930–33. The English coterie in Berlin was small and had many overlapping social connections. Isherwood and Wiskemann moved in the same circles in Cambridge and shared many friends and acquaintances in Berlin. Isherwood modeled many of his fictional characters on friends and acquaintances, changing some details for camouflage, exaggerating others. Helen Pratt, a secondary character in *Mr Norris*, is a foreign correspondent. To the narrator William Bradshaw (Isherwood) she is formidable, a little scary, tough, political, tactless and direct in speech, and someone who doesn't suffer fools gladly. A modern woman, focused, tenacious, and ambitious:

> Helen was Berlin political correspondent to one of the London weeklies and supplemented her income by making translations and giving English lessons. We sometimes passed on pupils to each other. She was a pretty, fair-haired, fragile looking girl, hard as nails, who had been educated at the university of London and took sex seriously. She was accustomed to spending her days and nights in male society and had little use for the company of other girls...Above all else, Helen loathed being reminded that she was a woman, except in bed.[181]

> Not even Goering could silence Helen Pratt. She had decided to investigate the atrocities on her own account. Morning, noon and night she nosed around the city, ferreting out the victims [of violence] or their relations, cross-examining them for details...She bribed, cajoled, pestered...She was out to get the facts.[182]

And later when they meet in London:

> She exuded vitality, success and news. The Nazi Revolution had positively given her a new lease of life. To hear her talk you might have thought she had spent the last two months hiding in Dr. Goebbels' writing desk or under Hitler's bed.

She had the details of every private conversation and the low-down on every scandal. She knew what Schacht had said to Norman, what von Papen had said to Meissner, what Schleicher might shortly be expected to say to the Crown Prince. She knew the amounts of Thyssen's cheques. She had new stories about Röhm, about Heines, about Göring and his uniforms.[183]

It's a rather nasty, spiteful depiction, but he cannot suppress a certain admiration for Helen's bravery and her political engagement. By contrast, he later saw "something youthfully heartless" in his own Bradshaw/Isherwood persona in *Mr Norris*, essentially a tourist preoccupied with boys and sex, and his uninvolved detachment from the poverty, violence, and despair of Berlin. The name game has long been popular with Isherwood readers, but I know of no other woman writing regularly for a London weekly whose circles so overlapped with Isherwood and who so closely fits his Helen Pratt pastiche.[184]

2

Czechoslovakia and the Nazi *'Drang nach Osten'*

From 1935 the "noise of history" was becoming angrier, more urgent, seemingly inexorable. "Like so many contemporaries," John Lehmann recalled, "I was haunted by the feeling that time was running out for a new world war."[1] Within two years, the Saar plebiscite, Mussolini's attack on Ethiopia, German rearmament and the Rhineland crisis, a Civil War in Spain, and growing Nazi pressure on Austria and south-east Europe fractured the European order established in 1919. With the forging of an Axis between Hitler and Mussolini, multilateral pacts like the Locarno accords and the Stresa front were no longer possible, while the League of Nations had become a broken reed. British and French diplomacy, committed to safeguarding the post-1918 system, failed completely to meet the challenge of Nazi and Fascist regimes determined to overthrow it and viewing war as a necessary, even desirable means of achieving their aims. Enfeebled by internal divisions, French foreign policy lacked coherence and became increasingly subservient to London. In Britain, Neville Chamberlain succeeded Stanley Baldwin as Prime Minister in May 1937, replacing a cautious reactive policy with Appeasement, underpinned by the conviction that Hitler's demands could be accommodated without war and accepting changes in Eastern Europe, which was not deemed a vital region for Britain's security. Sustained by a huge Conservative electoral victory in 1935, Chamberlain was largely immune from his critics, both Labour and the small cluster of Tory anti-Appeasers. Failure to grasp Hitler's long-term aims, insistence that Nazi goals were limited in the face of mounting evidence to the contrary, and a predilection for personal bilateral diplomacy further undermined any hope of constructing a broad coalition capable of deterring the dictators in the short term and ensuring better conditions for war when it came.

* * *

Wiskemann watched the crumbling of the postwar European order with horror. It was like witnessing a train crash in slow motion with one's cries of alarm unheard or unheeded. By 1935 she was convinced that Nazism meant war. The Dollfuss murder, the Nazi victory in the Saar, and the unilateral decision to expand the *Wehrmacht* and reintroduce general military service were, in her eyes, clear evidence of Hitler's larger strategy to emasculate the League and undermine

Elizabeth Wiskemann: Scholar, Journalist, Secret Agent. Geoffrey Field, Oxford University Press.
© Geoffrey Field 2023. DOI: 10.1093/oso/9780192870629.003.0003

international solidarity. Britain's willingness to sign a naval agreement with Germany in 1935, which she inveighed against repeatedly in her articles, created a rift between Britain and France, weakening further the Versailles order. This was quickly evident when in October 1935 Mussolini invaded Abyssinia. Britain and France moved first to reward this aggression by giving Italy almost two-thirds of the country, but then backed away amid an international outcry and resorted to half-hearted and ineffective economic sanctions imposed through the League. The crisis had immediate consequences. The League was revealed as powerless to protect the security of smaller nations; British–French relations were further strained; and it convinced the *Duce*, whose standing at home had never been higher, to throw in his lot with Hitler. Hitler now received clear signals that Italy would oppose neither German designs on Austria nor the return of German troops to the demilitarized Rhineland. While she applauded public indignation over the Hoare–Laval pact, Wiskemann always found it sadly ironic that this outcry against international lawlessness worked to Hitler's benefit.

To most Germans, the demilitarization of the Rhineland was an intolerable violation of sovereignty, and a negotiated solution could probably have been arranged within a couple of years anyway. But Hitler saw advantages for his popularity and international prestige in sudden, decisive action. In early March 1936, against the advice of his military commanders, he risked sending German troops across the Rhine bridges into the area, restoring full German sovereignty in flagrant violation of the Versailles and Locarno agreements. It was a small token force and Germany was in no position to withstand a counterattack, but neither France nor Britain was prepared for any riposte and Italy was drawing inexorably closer to Berlin. Since the assassination of Louis Barthou, France's Foreign Minister, in October 1934, Wiskemann had concluded that France had abandoned the leadership of Europe and was merely paying lip service to her treaty obligations. As her reports indicated, the winter months had confronted the Nazi regime with rising prices and food shortages, while unemployment remained stubbornly around 2.5 million; police reports indicated low morale among party members.[2] Hitler had need of a successful gamble and this bold but risky triumph dispelled the problems of the winter, strengthening the regime and enormously enhancing his popularity; it also increased his confidence and made him less ready to listen to military men and diplomats who counseled caution and restraint. Wiskemann immediately understood the larger meaning of the coup: "now if the Germans should come into conflict with Czechs or Austrians, France cannot reply by sending her troops into western Germany."[3] The way was open for further German expansion to the south-east.

Wiskemann returned to Germany in mid-March 1936 to report on the 'election' campaign and the plebiscite staged to ratify Hitler's actions. But first she visited Strasbourg, Metz, Luxembourg, and, for the first time, Switzerland with the aim of gauging public reactions along these western borderlands to Hitler's resort to military force.[4] All along this frontier between France and Germany, areas where people spoke German and Nazi papers and propaganda circulated, she found "dark suspicions of Germany's intentions" and astonishment at British public opinion's apparent *naïf* willingness to "shut its eyes to the danger." While Nazi race theorists viewed these provinces as 'really German' and spoke freely, for example, of *Gau Schweiz*, their populations, she wrote, were deeply shaped by the values of the French Revolution, of individual rights against the state. Even the Alsatians, though not uncritical of French administrative efficiency, recognized how oppressive the "yoke of Hitler" would be: "the whole of this bilingual frontier territory rejects the Pan-German claim which its inhabitants nevertheless seriously fear." "Everyone from Luxembourg to Basle," she reported, "thinks in terms of imminent war" initiated by Germany. "All along the border-country German conceptions are rejected, but Germany's economic hold is strong and her military power is dreaded."[5] As earlier in her reports from the Saar, Wiskemann examined the economic ties between these areas and the Reich. Luxembourg's and Lorraine's steel firms were already linked closely to the Reich and its rearmament program. As her largest customer, Germany had a similar grip on Switzerland, and Swiss bankers had invested large sums in the Reich, but pro-Nazi sentiment had declined since Hitler's June 1934 purge of the SA.

On this first visit she was hugely impressed by Switzerland and its people: their independence and strong democratic traditions, their understanding of and resistance to fascism and National Socialism. Democrats and federalists, they rejected racial, authoritarian, and centralist political theories. And since Hitler's Rhineland coup, all Swiss parties had agreed to additional funds for rearmament and border fortifications—evidence of their determination to defend the nation's neutrality.[6] The Swiss, she argued, were too well informed about Nazism to find it attractive. "To arrive in one of the most beautiful old German towns that exist [Basle]," she recalled, "and to find free discussion going on, even to hear people speak of *Menschenwürde*...was a marvelous luxury, even if the local dialect was at first a little bewildering."[7] She met journalists, League officials, Hans and Emil Oprecht, Ignazio Silone, and Thomas Mann and his family, now in exile, and discovered a lifelong attraction to Swiss cities rather than the mountains: "Wandering through the ancient streets of Strasbourg or Basle, one asks oneself why, if French and German civilization could blend so gloriously in the stones of these cities, is Franco-German cooperation so far to seek."[8]

After brief trips to Cologne and Berlin to see old friends, Wiskemann was in Frankfurt and Mainz on the day of the Rhineland 'election,' although there was only one party on the ballot. Predictably the result showed 98.9% of voters in favor of Hitler and the government's list. Popular euphoria over Hitler's move to remilitarize the Rhineland was immense and undeniable, and the euphoria went far beyond loyal Nazi supporters. As in the Saar, she was astounded at the scale, omnipresence, and "definitely hypnotic" quality of Nazi propaganda:

Everywhere election posters crowded more and more thickly upon one another. In every railway station loudspeakers roared out unceasing slogans about the Leader who is Freedom, Honour, Peace and Bread; if one took a taxi, one was immediately encased with large labels announcing that "The German Taxidriver is for Adolf Hitler"; wherever the road was up, a streamer would appear declaring "Thanks for the Führer, we are building here". Armed though one might be with a skeptical nature and a British passport, one had an uncomfortable feeling of being, not merely exasperated or amused, but also undermined. And the essence of the whole game is to link suggestion with fear; the German citizen is kept constantly aware of what has happened or may happen to dissidents; there is consequently little need for actual violence to-day.[9]

One felt," she wrote, "physically captured, conditioned to behave as Hitler willed; one throbbed with his slogans."[10] Wiskemann was also acutely aware that the Rhineland success marked a change: she noted the infusion of religious symbolism and messianic references into Nazi rhetoric—the "marked advances towards the deification of the Leader, and towards his mystical association, together with the German God and the German people, in a new trinity." "The man who was impelled to become the *suprema lex* and shoot his best friends on June 30th, 1934, had developed alarmingly, for his profound belief in himself – his 'sleep-walking certainty' – has grown from day to day."[11] She added that "the growing plight of the Jews bears witness" to the "barbarization of Germany." "I hear from Jewish acquaintances that old friends, who seemed at first unmoved by the anti-Semitic campaign, have cut them in the streets of late; even rich people without jobs to lose do this, because of the jobs they might someday need. In country towns like Mainz the loathsome *Der Stürmer* is posted up…at regular stations about five minutes' walk from one another." Seeing the token German troops, she was more convinced than ever that France and Britain's failure to call Hitler's bluff had been catastrophic. "Nazi Germany," she wrote, "is governed by terror and hypnotism. It has three obvious characteristics: a falling standard of life, a harsh militaristic and implicitly aggressive flavour, and a deep hostility to the best criteria of civilization…Soon we may have to decide whether a German peace…is better or worse than war."[12]

Wiskemann returned to Cambridge for what turned out to be her last term at Newnham but was soon planning another trip to the Continent and lining up commitments from editors. She hoped to make a study of the Nazi regime's impact on the education system[13] and decided also to revisit Danzig and the Polish border region. She had traveled to Danzig and Memel in the summer of 1935. The ancient German-populated trading city of Danzig (formerly part of Prussia) had been given independent status as a "free city" after the First World War. Situated at the head of the Polish corridor, it provided Poland with an outlet to the Baltic sea but belonged to neither Germany nor Poland; instead, it was self-governed under the supervision of the League of Nations. In 1934, hoping to appease Hitler, Poland had signed a non-aggression pact with Hitler, but the local Nazi party, which controlled Danzig's city government, pushed with growing violence for union with Germany and was much emboldened by events in the Saar. The League's High Commissioner, Sean Lester, like Geoffrey Knox in the Saar, "endured vexation verging on persecution" but had little power at his disposal. A courageous Irishman who became a close friend, he made valiant efforts to protect non-Nazi opposition groups but felt increasingly isolated and powerless in the face of the violence and intimidation unleashed by the Nazi Gauleiter, Albert Forster.[14] The other person who impressed her on this visit was Hermann Rauschning—an "outstanding person…a cultivated and charming man" with a "flexible mind,"[15]—whom Lester arranged for her to meet in secret. A former Nazi President of the Danzig Senate, Rauschning had by 1935 become an outspoken critic of Hitler and an advocate of stronger ties with Poland; he knew his life was in danger and lived in hiding on Polish territory.[16] Having met Hitler several times, he had no doubt that Nazism was a "revolution of nihilism," pursuing total control, committed to waging war in Europe, and prepared to use any means to destroy its enemies. Having come to much the same conclusions, Wiskemann found it extraordinary to have this former Nazi appealing to her to warn the British government of the very things that she feared most.[17] After Danzig, she traveled to the port town of Memel, where the centralizing policies of the Lithuanian government in Kovno, including efforts to suppress the German language, had fostered similarly extreme pro-Nazi feeling among Memel Germans; in German schools, Wiskemann reported, new textbooks "were full of German irredentism, Hitler-worship and the new Nazi distortions of history."[18]

A year later she was apprehensive about returning to Berlin and Danzig. Aside from Ebbutt, most of her journalist friends had left or been expelled. The situation in Danzig had also deteriorated. Having failed to secure a sufficient electoral majority to alter the constitution, local Nazis had turned increasingly to open terror to get their way. Opposition deputies, Nationalists as well as Socialists, were beaten up and newspapers confiscated or suppressed altogether; judges who gave anti-Nazi verdicts were pressured to conform; the police were tightly controlled. Socialists and non-Nazi Nationalists were subject to torture and beatings. The city was also virtually bankrupt and reliant upon German aid, its economy having been undermined by competition from the new Polish port of Gdynia. Sean Lester tried to alert Geneva to the situation in his annual report to the League and by forwarding petitions and protests from Danzigers, but to no avail, while Britain was unwilling to intervene. Thus, when the non-Nazi opposition dispatched representatives to London in January 1936 in hopes of seeing the Foreign Secretary, Sir Anthony Eden, he would not meet with them; instead they put their case before journalists like Wiskemann and Voigt and supporters of the League of Nations Union.[19] By this time Sean Lester was a virtual prisoner, closely watched and his telephones tapped; the Danzig Nazis and the German government were insisting that the League force his resignation.[20]

On July 4, 1936, Wiskemann arrived in the city and spent the next days interviewing people, including Lester who showed her a cupboard full of weapons left behind by Nazi thugs who had attacked a recent Nationalist party meeting: "Stormtroopers from their barracks nearby set upon the Nationalists with hand grenades, with thick wooden clubs with nails knocked into them, and with other weapons of a similarly alarming nature. Elderly men and women, among others, were beaten mercilessly to the ground, and about fifty people had afterwards to be removed to hospital."[21] The true conditions in the town had largely gone unreported in Britain; her accounts in the *New Statesman* and the *Scotsman* (filed immediately after her return to Berlin) captured the desperate situation in graphic detail. The Nazis, she estimated, accounted for about 30% of the population but were rapidly moving towards complete control of the city state. The Polish government (mindful of its non-aggression pact with Germany and wishing to avoid a confrontation) showed little willingness to intervene and guarantee citizens' rights.[22] She saw Lester several times: "I went in and out of his house a good deal and I suppose Gestapo Agents were watching; this could not be helped and had to be faced."[23] It was difficult, she wrote, to praise Lester's courage and resourcefulness enough—and so long as he was there, Danzig's constitution and the League's authority would not be entirely destroyed. But his days were numbered and in 1937 he returned to Geneva, replaced as High Commissioner by the more malleable Swiss diplomat and historian Carl Burckhardt.

After four intensely busy days, Wiskemann returned to Berlin. Her plan was to brief Ebbutt on the situation and then spend a weekend with her friend Count Albrecht von Bernstorff at his family's estate near Hamburg. She had first met Bernstorff when he worked at the German Embassy in London, where he was one of several people, including Ambassador Hoesch and the press attaché, 'Klop' von Ustinov (Peter Ustinov's wildly eccentric father), who were strongly opposed to the Nazi movement. From an aristocratic Mecklenburg family, Bernstorff was a former Rhodes Scholar at Oxford and fervent Anglophile; he left the diplomatic service when Hitler came to power and was by 1936 a board member of Wassermanns, a Jewish bank where he referred to himself as the Court Aryan. Sometimes people viewed him as foolhardy, something of a *Luftmensch*; Wiskemann took him seriously, but in retrospect, she felt, not seriously enough in view of his active involvement in the German resistance and his execution by the SS in April 1945. Later she came to believe that he was careless on principle having concluded that an aristocrat and a Nordic like himself should be as open as possible in his defiance of the Nazis.[24]

Everything was going according to plan, Wiskemann recalled. She went over to Ebbutt's flat for breakfast and even began writing a Danzig article for the *Scotsman* while waiting for Bernstorff: "Then just before midday there was a sharp knock at

Ebbutt's door. His German maid opened it and started back, shaking with fear, into the room we were in, followed by two men in civilian clothes. One of them showed us the words *Geheime Staatspolizei* on something he wore under his coat lapel. I saw that Ebbutt's face was perfectly white – I could not see my own." She was ordered to pack her things and accompany them to headquarters in the Prinz Albrechtstrasse. "I had not slept in the train from Danzig," she recalled, "and my mind was full of Nazi tortures of Socialists and others in Danzig and elsewhere. I knew that a British passport might be ignored or forgotten till afterwards."[25] Ebbutt asked to accompany them but was refused; he then followed part way in a taxi and quickly informed the British Embassy of her arrest.[26] Luckily for his own safety, Bernstorff arrived late at the flat just after she was taken away; Ebbutt told him to make himself scarce and he quickly fled Berlin.

After being taken to an interrogation room, Wiskemann was left alone for a while, then moved to other rooms. "Do for heaven's sake look round," she told herself, "you're in a place of unusual interest." In each room, she recalled, there were large maps of Russia and the neighboring states on the walls, seeming to confirm her expectations of a forthcoming German push to the east. Finally, she was sent for and handed a German translation of a *New Statesman* article, "A Land Fit for Heroes," [see chap. 1, p. 46], that she had published the previous year. It was a fine exposé of conditions in Germany—the maltreatment of Jews, the Nazi crackdown on modern art and culture, the ever-expanding grip of the secret police, and the use of terror and torture to quell worker opposition—but its general themes were ones she had voiced many times (although for the first time it mentioned Himmler's deputy Heydrich, misspelling his name as Heiderich). Asked if she was its author, she showed quick wit, considerable courage, and presence of mind, replying to the police official that she could only tell if she was shown the English original. This seemed to present unexpected difficulties. Her interrogator went off to telephone and then took her to a more senior SS officer, who questioned her about several statements in the essay—specifically, that a new *Kulturkampf* was enveloping Germany, that Jews were being systematically mistreated, and that brutal SS types now dominated Germany. She was now emboldened and defended these sentiments. Finally, the official said that, in view of the upcoming Olympic Games, "he was prepared to let me off lightly." They settled upon a compromise: Wiskemann was released after agreeing to sign a statement that she "could" have written such an essay [*hätte es schreiben können*]. The police had clearly been monitoring her activities for a while and wanted her (and other reporters like her) out of the country during the Berlin Games.[27]

Seen off at the station by Ebbutt and several other British and American acquaintances, she returned to London, where her arrest was already front-page news.[28] Her arrest had only lasted a few hours, but it got wide coverage in the national press and questions were soon put to Foreign Secretary Eden in the Commons, further raising Wiskemann's profile as a journalist.[29] To Julian Bell, by this time living in China but still a close friend, she admitted: "It is extraordinary but an increasing number of people take me seriously which gives one a nice confident feeling. Being arrested by those terrible people was no joke. I wouldn't go through that again for anything, though afterwards I was feted like any queen and enjoyed it, though quite incapable of getting any spontaneous sleep for ten nights."[30] This narrow escape took a psychological toll; she found herself, for the first and only time in her life, sleepwalking. "I woke up more than once in the next week or so," she recalled in her memoir, "to find myself standing in the middle of the night against the wall near my bed, muttering to myself 'I would rather die standing.' What made one feel ashamed was to think how infinitely more people in the Nazi concentration camps were enduring; it was the rarest thing for one of them to escape and to be able to cross a blessed frontier."[31] In London she met with Sir Reginald ('Rex') Leeper, Head of the Foreign Office News Department; she should, he advised, write all she could about the Reich but ought not try to return. It was fourteen years before she saw Germany again.[32]

* * *

Wiskemann's political journalism relied heavily upon travel, personal observation, and numerous interviews. Banned from Germany, she was unable to report first-hand the dramatic developments in the Nazi regime during the next three years. Beginning with the announcement of the Four Year Plan in September 1936, a plan for intensive autarchy to make the nation ready for war, the regime pursued a policy of escalating radicalization in all spheres: intensifying the persecution of Jews, culminating in the nationwide pogrom of *Reichskristallnacht*; reorganizing the armed forces and creating a Supreme Command of trusted Nazis, completely pliant to Hitler's will; and, with the Axis with Mussolini in 1937, accelerating the pace of Hitler's expansionist foreign policy. She followed these developments closely from outside and they informed her writing. But her journalism necessarily shifted to the states of Eastern Europe. In the nine months after her expulsion from Berlin, she traveled to Poland, Austria, Hungary, Czechoslovakia, and Romania. Her essays examined the combined impact of economic depression and German pressure upon their politics. Everywhere the same trends were in evidence: a growth of radical right movements, rising anti-Semitism, loss of legal protections for ethnic minorities, the retreat of democratic parties and a sharp turn toward authoritarianism and 'strong men'—from the rule of the Colonels in Poland to Horthy in Hungary and the royalist dictatorship of King Carol in Romania.[33] The situation in Austria under Schuschnigg seemed stable in early 1937 but, without Mussolini's protection, the state had lost its independence in all but name.[34] Wiskemann's attention turned increasingly to Czechoslovakia. In October 1936 she warned: "As time goes on the menace to Prague grows greater. This is the quickest way to attack Russia; indeed Czechoslovakia seems to be the obvious victim for Hitler's next midday coup and...her leaders...are well aware of it."[35] "I accepted," she wrote, "the *Drang nach Südosten* which Hitler seemed to impose upon me."[36]

Czechoslovakia was allied to France and the Soviet Union; it had a strong industrial base and a large, increasingly disaffected German minority. It occupied a key strategic position in Central Europe and was the last surviving democracy in the region. If a general war was approaching in Europe—and Wiskemann was convinced of this—it could well be unleashed over Czechoslovakia. She soon developed, like many of her British contemporaries, a warm affection for the Czechs, even though she described them as "clumsy and ungracious." Prague seemed a joy after Berlin, "an oasis in a desert of dictatorships." "To the English traveler in Central Europe," she wrote, "sick of censored newspapers, controlled telephones, the fear of spies, the freedom of Prague is as refreshing as its architectural loveliness."[37]

Wiskemann had been to Czechoslovakia three times. In February 1934, just after moving from Cambridge to a flat in London, she was invited to lunch at the home of John Wheeler-Bennett; there she met Jan Masaryk, the Czech Ambassador to Britain, and they became lifelong friends. His social ease and charm, linguistic brilliance, and cultural sophistication made Jan the personification of Czechoslovakia's ties to the West. Learning that she was thinking of visiting Prague, he provided her with letters of introduction and arranged meetings with his father, Thomas Masaryk, the nation's President, and Foreign Minister Edvard Beneš. Her meeting in March 1934 with the President ranged over many topics, philosophical and political, but she was shocked by Masaryk's misunderstanding of Nazi Germany. So accustomed was he to the din of Pan-German agitation in the Habsburg Monarchy that he rejected the notion that Nazism represented something new and unprecedented or that Hitler meant war. She replied that Hitler was "something entirely new" and that pre-1914 figures like Georg von Schönerer and Heinrich Class had never been in a position like the Nazi movement to harness all the power of a modern state.[38] On the same trip she also met Hubert Ripka, Beneš's close confidant and a journalist for *Lidove Noviny*, and his wife, Noemi, who soon became close friends; they had a better appreciation of the dangers facing the state. In general, however, she worried that "these people in Prague seemed altogether too quiet and reasonable to deal with the new masters of Germany."[39]

On her first visit, she acknowledged, she knew little about the Sudeten Germans. When she returned, in December 1935, the internal political situation had grown much darker. Of Czechoslovakia's population of 14 million, roughly half were Czechs; 2.6 million were Slovaks; 3.3 million ethnic Germans; over 700,000 Magyars; and 560,000 Ruthenes, to name only the major groups. The overwhelming majority of Czechs believed that only a unitary framework could control separatist tendencies and ensure the state's future. And in the 1920s, despite friction and discrimination, it seemed possible that a workable *modus vivendi* might be established between the different groups. After 1933, however, the combination of severe economic depression, which fell with particular severity upon the largely German industrial areas, and growing pressure from the Nazi Reich fueled an increasingly radical Sudeten German nationalism that threatened the state's fragile unity. In these circumstances, diverse Sudeten German political groups that had developed since the founding of the republic became increasingly unified into a broad front, led by Konrad Henlein, a gymnastics teacher from Reichenberg in northern Bohemia. Indeed, in the 1935 elections the Sudeten German Party won two-thirds of German votes, becoming the largest political party in the state (ahead of the Czech Agrarians and Social Democrats).

Already by 1935 Henlein was being heavily financed from Berlin, although historians remain somewhat divided over exactly when he threw in his lot with Hitler's expansionist plans. As Keith Robbins argued, Henlein's efforts to keep his movement united and to protect his own leadership position meant that he had to be adroit and flexible in how he presented his aims to different groups. This was also true of his several visits to London between 1935 and 1938, where he spoke at Chatham House and met and impressed many people—including R.W. Seton-Watson, Sir Robert Vansittart, and Harold Nicolson—as a straightforward, decent man who wanted the best for his people. In London, for example, he repeatedly denied any financial connection to the German Nazi party, claimed to be a democrat, rejected anti-Semitism, and argued that he favored autonomy within Czechoslovakia rather than incorporation into the Reich.[40] Wiskemann, while acknowledging Henlein's appeal and persuasiveness, remained deeply suspicious of him as a Nazi agent and viewed his party's goal as being to dismantle the republic.

Both in December 1935 and again in September 1936, she had meetings with Czech and Sudeten politicians, including Beneš, who had just replaced Masaryk as President, and the Slovak Agrarian leader Milan Hodža, who had become Prime Minister. She also met Wenzel Jaksch, a leader of the Sudeten German Socialists and a vehement opponent of Henlein. Her first impression of him was that he was energetic and charming, but she was surprised to find him often in the company of former Nazi Otto Strasser, the founder of the "Black Front" against Hitler who had found refuge in Prague. She soon came to distrust both as more Nazi than socialist. She also dined a couple of times with Sir Joseph Addison, the British Ambassador, who was deeply prejudiced against Czechs and Slavs and did much to cultivate an anti-Czech bias in Foreign Office circles.[41] The feeling was growing in London that Czech inflexibility was at the heart of the Sudeten problem and that putting pressure upon Beneš for talks and concessions was necessary.

Already by 1936, then, Wiskemann was following Czech politics closely, but the determining factor in the direction of her research and writing in the next two years was an invitation from A.J. Toynbee, the Director of the Royal Institute of International Affairs [RIIA], or Chatham House, to write a book about the relationship of Czechs and Germans and its historical roots. By the 1930s Chatham House had become the preeminent center for such studies in the nation and was among the earliest institutions to encourage the writing of contemporary history with a policy-related purpose. Although its board and membership were overwhelmingly male in the interwar period, the institute also played an important formative role in the careers of several women who became pioneers in the field of international relations, offering a stimulating intellectual environment as well as providing employment and opportunities to publish.[42] Statesmen and scholars from all over the world gave lectures there; conferences were organized; and it established working groups to study specific problems. In addition, Chatham House sponsored research projects, beginning with a six-volume *History of the Peace Conference of Paris* (1920–24) under the editorship of Wiskemann's nemesis, her doctoral supervisor Harold Temperley. Its house journal, *International Affairs* (to which Wiskemann contributed regularly for more than three decades), was launched in 1922, and, starting in 1924 and continuing for almost thirty years, A.J. Toynbee supervised the institute's annual *Survey of International Affairs*, an unrivaled global survey that profoundly influenced the development of international studies in Britain. Though independent, the institute had close ties to the Foreign Office, for part of its mission was to provide policymakers with historical insights on contemporary issues, and Toynbee often showed officials unpublished drafts from the *Survey* and its other publications.

The book project that Toynbee offered to Wiskemann was planned as the third volume in a series,[43] aided by a grant from the Rockefeller Fund, on the consequences of the 1919 peace settlement for Eastern Europe. The other two were on Hungary and the German–Polish borderlands. In one sense Toynbee's invitation was predictable since Wiskemann had a reputation as an accomplished journalist and was well acquainted with prominent Chatham House figures like John Wheeler-Bennett and R.W. Seton-Watson. She had also lectured there after returning from her visit to Memel in October 1935.[44] But the offer was also somewhat surprising, perhaps, since Chatham House, including its director Toynbee,[45] was more sympathetic than Wiskemann to the grievances of the German minority in Czechoslovakia. Also, her admiration for Thomas and Jan Masaryk was evident in articles she had already written. Later, Wiskemann enjoyed noting that she was not the first person approached as a possible author and admitted she had been "astonished at being engaged by the institute."[46] In their initial conversation, Toynbee presented the project as a study focusing on the Sudeten Germans and then widening into a broader study of German minorities, but the Chatham House publications committee limited the focus to Czechoslovakia.

To gain a better sense of her academic credentials and reputation, Toynbee consulted his sister Jocelyn, a classical archaeologist and graduate of Newnham, who replied that Wiskemann "would do the job for you excellently."[47] Next, he checked with Miss Josephine Pybus, director of history studies at the college, who answered in some detail, praising Wiskemann's supervision of undergraduates and adding: "She would herself admit, I think, that she is more of a journalist than a research worker. She has never produced anything except articles for newspapers and reviews...apart from a slight thesis which she wrote when she first left college, for which she was awarded an M.Litt." "When I say that she is primarily a journalist," she continued, "I do not mean to suggest that she is superficial and incapable of producing a serious and scholarly book, but she has not actually done so, as yet." She was knowledgeable about the Balkans and Czechoslovakia, "would do the 'field work' excellently and I think she has enough sense to realize the difference between what is required for journalistic articles and a solid book." "She strikes me as being able to select the significant facts, to sift fact from fiction, and to make allowances for any bias in her sources of information."[48]

Wiskemann was delighted at the opportunity: "People have been urging me," she replied to Toynbee, "to do a chatty travel book which I should detest, and I have been wanting to do the sort of thing we outlined without the capital to make it possible to begin."[49] This never ceased to be a problem: the kinds of books that she wanted to write simply didn't pay enough to finance themselves and, lacking a permanent position in academia or journalism, she was reliant on multiple free-lance assignments. She also knew that, if she accepted the offer, it would mean giving up her Cambridge teaching: she agonized over the decision but felt she had little choice but to take the plunge. The terms of the contract were far from lavish (indeed, as D. Cameron Watt noted, while Chatham House gave women a rare opportunity to pursue careers in international affairs, they were also "grossly exploited"[50]). Wiskemann agreed to spend at least three months doing research in Czechoslovakia. A draft manuscript (between 100,000 and 200,000 words) was to be finished by year's end and she would receive £200 for her work. In addition, she was allowed 17 shillings a day expenses, provided she submitted receipts and limited herself to second-class travel. Most importantly, she could continue to write journalistic articles, provided she steered clear of the German minority question. Finally, the completed manuscript was due at the beginning of May 1938. "Of course," Wiskemann wrote to Toynbee, "I appreciate the urgency of the work only too well, more especially since some of the people I take most seriously genuinely expect Germany to move against Czechoslovakia between May and July of this year. I feel rather frightened of shouldering the responsibility of tackling perhaps the essential hinge of European affairs. But in any case, I will try to combine efficiency with a reasonable degree of speed."[51] She was convinced that Europe would soon be confronting the Czech-German crisis and was determined that her book should play a role in the debate this would trigger in Britain.

Prague was a city largely neglected by British newspapers, whose correspondents were mostly based in Vienna and used Czech stringers to monitor developments. One exception was Shiela Grant Duff, who was working for the *Observer*. After leaving the Saar, she had campaigned for Labour in the 1935 election and worked as an unpaid assistant to Hugh Dalton, the Labour party's foreign policy spokesman. But she was eager to return to journalism, especially after the Rhineland crisis, which she correctly recognized would increase the danger for the countries of the 'Little Entente,' especially Czechoslovakia. Encouraged by Voigt and Mowrer, she approached Hugh Massingham, who took her on as a (largely) unpaid stringer. "I think we've got a correspondent in Prague," she remembered him saying. "Oh no, I think he died, but if you should happen to meet him, just say you're a correspondent and not the correspondent of *The Observer*."[52] She arrived in August 1936 armed with letters of introduction and, like Wiskemann, dined with Addison, The British Minister, and was appalled by his condescension towards Czechs: Asked if he had Czech friends, he replied: "Friends! They eat in their kitchens." "There is a ghastly snobbishness against the Czechs and all the English hate them," Grant Duff wrote to her friend Diana Hubback. "I get on very badly with the English. Like all diplomats they are caricatures of themselves... so I stick to the Czechs, who are on the other side."[53] She contacted Hubert Ripka, who rapidly became her new mentor, answering her questions, providing introductions, and taking her to Bratislava for a conference of the 'Little Entente.' She also saw Wenzel Jaksch several times along with Otto Strasser and even arranged a meeting between them and her Oxford friend Adam von Trott.[54]

Aside from her published writings, little has survived of Wiskemann's time in Prague, so Grant Duff's experiences as a woman reporter are illuminating, although she was much younger and far less experienced as a journalist. "Prague," she told Hubback, "is beautiful and everyone is gay by nature somehow."[55] "Elizabeth Wiskemann is here too. Do you know her? She is also nicer than I remembered or perhaps it is Prague that makes everybody nicer and is why I am so happy here."[56] But she soon encountered difficulties: "Nobody quite believes that I am correspondent of the *Observer* and the *Observer* doesn't do much to convince them!"[57] This was in part because the paper's editor, J.L. Garvin, was increasingly supportive of the Sudeten Germans and slanted its coverage in that direction, spiking Grant Duff's critical reports about Henlein and the danger he posed. The Foreign Press Association, she complained, also did not accept her, and some Czechs regarded her with suspicion: "I find the Czechs increasingly difficult to get to know. My novelty value is wearing off and it has somehow got about that I like Germans too much."[58] She learned from her Oxford economist friend, Thomas Balogh, that the Czech authorities kept watch on her visits to Berlin and her meetings with Germans in Prague, where Adam von Trott had visited her. She had also aroused the interest of the Berlin police, who suspected she might be a liaison between Mowrer and left-wing dissidents. At his behest she made a brief visit to Malaga in early 1937, which had just fallen to Franco's forces; her task was to find out about the treatment of Republican prisoners and specifically about Arthur Koestler, who had been captured. Mowrer believed that a young unknown "might slip in unnoticed."[59]

Figure 2.1. "Shiela Grant Duff in 1939," by Howard Coster. National Portrait Gallery Co. Ltd.

Not surprisingly, Grant Duff was hurt and confused by the rumors and suspicions. There was gossip that she might be sleeping with Ripka; she was sure a Czech colleague had spread the calumny that she was in the pay of the Nazis (because she had no regular paying job), and she suspected rival journalists, including 'Betty Wiskemann,' "because of their uncollegial attitude."[60] Wiskemann responded with characteristic bluntness:

"Look anyway – what is the matter? Why wouldn't you even speak to me in a normal way on the phone in London for instance? I thought when I had last seen you we were getting along quite nicely. I do hope you don't think that I have been spreading malicious rumours about you because it wouldn't enter my head to do so – I have contradicted the ones that have come my way. I am awfully sorry a few people have been silly but sillinesses pass. If you could deal with us all a bit more gently, it would put everything right. Forgive this – it seems rather impertinent. But do believe it is nicely meant. I expect to be in Prague etc May to July doing a book for Chatham House so shall hope to see you if you feel like healing the mysterious breach which occurred on the phone that day."[61]

Mowrer's advice was sharp and crude: "The story about you is not that you are Ripka's girl and betraying him, but that you 'slept with a Nazi boy from Germany' – an obviously unpardonable offence. This latter story seems to be current in London. I should worry... I agree with Hyka [head of the Press Department in the Czech Foreign Office]... You ought to behave in a more feminine way, which doesn't necessarily include promiscuity... And you ought to be more malleable in mind but with more will of your own. Paradox? I don't think so. And you ought to learn to keep your mouth shut more and listen better and work systematically... I wonder if your mere presence causes as much mischief as you think, or if it is your tactless tongue."[62] Brutal counsel indeed for twenty-four-year-old female reporter. The intense emotions surrounding the Sudeten German question were a challenge for any journalist who wanted to understand the outlook of both Germans and Czechs; every interview seemed like treachery to one side or the other. And for female reporters, political slurs easily morphed into sexual ones or disparagement on grounds of gender.

Finding herself so completely at odds with J.L. Garvin's pro-Appeasement politics, Grant Duff resigned from the *Observer* on May 1937; Britain, she told him, was shirking its natural obligation to protect weaker nations whose independence was threatened.[63] She continued to write articles, often unsigned, for the *Spectator*, *Manchester Guardian*, and the *Contemporary Review* (venues where Wiskemann also published), and, at Ripka's urging, used her social connections to open channels of communication for Beneš with Churchill, Dalton, Harold MacMillan, Voigt, Attlee, and other influential figures. Once she returned to England, Churchill invited her to Chartwell, and later in June 1938 she arranged for him to meet Ripka.[64] After writing a brief pamphlet for the The New Fabian Research Bureau, *German and Czech: A Threat to European Peace* (1937), she was hired by Allen Lane to author a Penguin Special on the growing crisis.

Wiskemann settled in Prague in early May 1937 and found a small flat in the inner city near the river Vltava. The Henlein party's headquarters were close by and it made sense to use Prague as a home base from which to travel out to the Sudeten German settlements located on the borderlands of Bohemia and Moravia."[65] She traveled extensively and for the next six months worked flat out. The gathering pace of the Czech crisis soon made her suspect that her May 1938 deadline might be too late for the book to have an impact. Having already a detailed understanding of Czechoslovakia's contemporary politics, she needed to study as deeply as possible the earlier history of Bohemia and Moravia, to read newspapers and other publications, and to interview many Czechs and Germans in the time available. Her aim was to provide readers with an understanding of the historical dimensions of the crisis and the way that the past shaped the present perceptions of both sides, and to do so as factually and objectively as possible. Language posed a problem: her German was good but there was insufficient time to learn to read and speak Czech as well as research and write the book. She enlisted the aid of several native speakers who helped with the sources, especially her historian friend Otakar Odlozilik, a professor at Prague's Charles University, who translated key Czech documents for her. With her charwoman "signs were our chief medium," although she did pick up some rudimentary Czech.[66]

Her Chatham House credentials clearly helped open doors but, as was the case in Germany, Wiskemann showed extraordinary skill in building a network of sources and gaining access to prominent politicians and officials. For obvious reasons, she was unable to consult the Nazi legation in Prague, while the British Embassy, very much under the sway of Chamberlain's Appeasement, was "unhelpful, making it clear that its staff…did not care for young women who might get themselves into scrapes."[67] She met with Beneš, who had become the nation's president after Masaryk's resignation in 1935, also Kamil Krofta, the Foreign Minister, and the Slovak Prime Minister, Milan Hodža. Her Czech sources included state officials in Prague, as well as journalists and new friends like Hubert Ripka and the legal philosopher Hans Kelsen, a Jew who had fled from Cologne to Geneva and then, in defiance of stiff Sudeten German opposition, took up a professorship at the German University of Prague. Slovakia was not within the scope of her research, but she had earlier met with a Hlinka [Slovak People's Party] activist as well as Slovak officials who tried to convince her, a little too emphatically, of the harmony between Czechs and Slovaks. She had access to several Sudeten German Party leaders, including Konrad Henlein and his chief lieutenants, Karl Hermann Frank, Walter Brand, and Ernst Kundt.[68] These men seemed to know little about her, not even her recent expulsion from Germany. They appear to have connected her to the British League of Nations Society, which may have encouraged some like Heinrich Rutha (Henlein's 'foreign minister') to view her as possibly an advocate for German minority rights.[69]

Wiskemann continued to have discussions with Wenzel Jaksch, leader of the German Social Democrats, but found a strong undercurrent of anti-Slav and anti-Czech prejudice in his brand of socialism and soon came to believe (as did Shiela Grant Duff) that his efforts to win over Henlein supporters were mistaken and harmful; her dislike for him extended into the war years and after. Her sources also included older German politicians on the right; for example, Franz Spina, a leader of the Agrarian party, and Rudolf Haider, a pro-Nazi nationalist who had been imprisoned by the Czechs but was also a fierce opponent of Henlein. She found Haider personally upright and easy to talk to despite his admiration for Hitler.[70] Her best informant among Germans for the period of the First World War and its immediate aftermath was the liberal nationalist politician and passionate advocate of German-Bohemian self-determination, Rudolf Lodgman von Auen. He also gave her an introduction to Leopold Pölzl, the Social Democratic mayor of Aussig, writing: "I feel it right that she should hear all views and parties so that she herself can form a picture of the Sudeten German situation"; he added: "you will be surprised how well-informed she is, which cannot be said otherwise for the English."[71] Finally, Jan Masaryk had supplied her with introductions to some of the Bohemian aristocracy still living on vast estates, though deeply embittered by the Czech government's land reform which had expropriated some of their property. Offended by their class and racist attitudes, Wiskemann judged most of them "of poor value, full of snobbish jibes at the Czechs, deceived by Hitler and Henlein."[72] "In all but two of those castles," she recalled, "I heard nothing but abuse of the Czechs who had brought in an effective agrarian reform."[73] The enlightened exceptions were Prince Maximilian Lobkowicz and Prince Wilhelm Lichnowsky, who were generally loyal to the Prague government. Most unpleasant, perhaps, was her interview with Count Alfons Clary-Aldrigen in his castle at Teplitz, which went badly even though he favored some kind of ethnic settlement to preserve Czechoslovakia. After a long exchange of views, the Count described Wiskemann in his diary as: "a super intelligent masonic Jewess [:] I am sure that she is in the pay of the great Orient to write what they want and the book will be contaminated."[74]

She worked extremely hard during her months in Czechoslovakia, traveling throughout the Sudeten regions, visiting southern Bohemia, Silesia, the Egerland, and areas bordering Saxony and Poland. At times, rail travel was slow and difficult, and sometimes people offered her car rides back to Prague, but she was very wary when the offers came from strangers, fearful of Gestapo kidnapping operations, which sometimes occurred in those days.[75] She was attuned to contrasts between southern Bohemia and the north, differences reflected in the level of ethnic tension, and she grasped the distinctiveness, compared to Reich Germans, of these populations, shaped by centuries of Austrian and Habsburg cultural influences. In the Egerland (across the border from Bavaria) pro-Nazi feeling was especially virulent, and she felt strongly that the area should never have been forcibly integrated into the Czech state in 1919. There, in 1937 immediately after the funeral of Thomas Masaryk, she saw Germans spit on photographs of the dead president. By contrast, people in Moravia seemed altogether gentler and more friendly and disposed to ethnic harmony. Her detailed eye-witness accounts of these communities included specific, concrete details about economic, political, and cultural life in these geographically separated enclaves. These detailed observations—on unemployment, education, racial attitudes, religion, even opera and theatre—make her study a classic even today, since none of these communities existed a decade later.

By contrast, she carried out little local research in smaller Czech communities and, not being able to speak Czech, lacked a first-hand grasp of grassroots Czech attitudes and local Czech radicalism as distinct from official views from Prague. "There was thus a tendency," Mark Cornwall writes, "to polarize, as liberal versus illiberal, the Czech and German positions, even though they might have been less distinctive than she portrayed them." Given this, Cornwall has argued, the degree of detachment and even-handedness she achieved in the final manuscript was striking.[76] From his research in the Czech archives he recounts in detail one remarkable example of Wiskemann's determination to report the views of both sides and her anger when Czech officials violated the civil rights of one of her informants. In June 1937 Wiskemann interviewed Reinhart Küdlich, a local law-yer in Troppau, who had gained a considerable local reputation as legal defender of German nationalists. Part of German Silesia until 1919, the area had become increasingly radicalized both because of Nazi propaganda from across the border and from persistent governmental efforts to 'Czechify' it and its institutions, including the educational system. Küdlich, pro-Nazi himself, was acting as defense counsel for a group of German teachers from nearby Hlučin who had been arrested and charged with espionage. When Wiskemann met him, Küdlich was compiling a dossier about police malpractice at Ostrava, where the teachers were being held, which he intended to submit to the Justice Ministry in Prague.[77]

A couple of months after Wiskemann's meeting with Küdlich, the Ostrava police raided his flat and seized the evidence that might have incriminated them. A month later, in keeping with a general toughening of police actions under the new National Defense Law, Küdlich was questioned and accused of complicity in the espionage case (later the charges were dropped). Wiskemann was close to departing from Prague and returning to London and she had arranged a last interview with Beneš and Hodža. Believing that the raid and Küdlich's arrest had occurred because he had provided her with information, she took advantage of the meeting to protest what had happened. According to a foreign ministry offi-cial, she angrily compared such action to practices in the Third Reich and "burst into hysterical sobbing. She said that in such circumstances she could not defend Czechoslovakia."[78] There was clearly much more to the lawyer's arrest than his conversations with Wiskemann, but the police had, not surprisingly, questioned him about her. In a later telephone conversation, when he tried to defend the police, the same official reported that she became hysterical, called Czechoslovakia a police state, and almost hung up on him. Whether the official's version can be trusted is hard to say; his disparaging references to hysteria were clearly designed to depreciate Wiskemann as an overwrought woman. She was certainly appalled that someone should encounter harm for speaking to her and was deeply con-cerned that Nazi pressure was producing a spiral of repression and radicalization. Her display of emotion was likely a tactic to pressure Beneš.[79]

Worried that she might be questioning her earlier favorable view of the Republic's leadership, foreign office officials were eager for Beneš to meet her again to smooth things over: "She is spreading extremely pessimistic views about minority questions and in conversations with English publicists she has spoken adversely about Czechoslovakia's minority policy. From many indications we can certainly expect that her book will be partially ill-disposed towards our minority policy."[80] They did meet on October 14, just before she left for London, but no record of the encounter has survived. The Küdlich affair illustrates Wiskemann's growing frustration by the end of her stay. Masaryk's state, which she still admired, was splitting apart under external Nazi pressure and resurgent ethnic nationalism. After months of careful study, she understood why and how this was happening, but could find no feasible solution, no "common political principle" that could pull it back together. And time was running out. She returned to London in mid-October 1937 and immediately began writing. "People used to ask me during that winter why I was in such a hurry," she wrote, "and I can remember saying that it might not be worth publishing the book at all if one delayed."[81] Remarkably, she completed the manuscript (of what became a 300-page book) in four months and handed it to Toynbee two months ahead of schedule on March 1, 1938, exhausted and deeply apprehensive about the future.

Two weeks later Hitler occupied Austria, thereby practically closing the ring around Czechoslovakia. For four years, since the murder of Dollfuss, Chancellor Schuschnigg had managed to preserve Austria's fragile independence, but the German–Italian Axis spelled its doom. Already in early November 1937, at the famous "Hossbach" meeting with his chief military advisors and the Foreign Minister, von Neurath, Hitler had been explicit about his intention to absorb Austria and destroy Czechoslovakia.[82] In February Hitler presented a list of demands essentially taking control of Austrian economic and foreign policy and insisting on the appointment of a Nazi Minister of the Interior in charge of security services. When Schuschnigg (hoping to elicit support from France and Britain) baulked and organized a national referendum on the issue of union with Germany, German troops invaded Austria. Among Wiskemann's journalist friends there, Marcel Fodor escaped Vienna in the car of the American *chargé d'affaires*, Eric Gedye was deported immediately by the Gestapo as an undesirable alien and soon moved to Prague,[83] while Eugen Kogon was imprisoned for more than a year in Vienna and then deported to Buchenwald. There had been so little international resistance to union with Austria that Hitler decided to immediately intensify his campaign against Czechoslovakia. On March 28 he conferred with Henlein, who agreed to put forward extreme demands that Prague was bound to refuse. By May the tension, including rumors of German troop movements, culminated with Beneš mobilizing Czech reserves. Wiskemann returned to Prague just after this with plans for several articles and was invited to visit the Czech frontier fortifications and the young Czech draftees manning them.

Czechs and Germans was a remarkable achievement, all the more for a first book written under such time pressure. To be sure, Wiskemann was not a neutral observer and yet her book was for the most part balanced. It surveyed the long, troubled history of Germans and Slavs in Bohemia and Moravia, focusing especially on the period since the 1848 revolutions. The growth of a modern state and party system and economic and cultural life were all refracted through a growing Slav–German ethnic conflict, with the Czechs as subordinate, culminating in the First World War when Czechs turned increasingly towards the Entente powers. As Wiskemann made clear in her complex analysis of ethnicity, class, demography, and culture, there were no easy solutions, either under the Habsburgs or later. Contrary to their many critics, she argued that the treaty-framers of 1918–19 had made pragmatic economic and strategic border decisions; there were no good alternatives. She was sufficiently impartial to criticize Czech chauvinism in the early republic but saw it as rooted in decades of discrimination, while Prague's growing resort to authoritarian measures in the 1930s was regrettable but also reflected the external dangers it faced. Claims of Czech outrages and brutality were often inflated and, Wiskemann noted, the republic's minorities still had far more rights than those in contemporary Germany, Italy, or Poland. She praised earlier unsuccessful reform proposals to grant greater local autonomy to minority groups and faulted the Czech Republic as overly centralized. But, if the Sudeten Germans were open to negotiations before 1934, this had ceased to be the case in later years. Henlein's demands for German autonomy seemed to her completely unworkable, leaving Czechoslovakia a "helpless prey" to its powerful neighbor; equally, cession of the Sudeten regions would destroy the state's strategic and economic viability and open the whole of south-east Europe to German dominance. Sadly, she wrote, "A wise government can greatly reduce friction; but whatever the government, friction there will be, so long as racialistic nationalism is regarded as an absolute standard of good." She added: "Some common political principle which different races can respect is the cement which is needed to repair the Czech-German structure." She reflected wistfully that while Thomas Masaryk's humanism, given time, might have created the necessary cohesion and reconciled German and Slav, that possibility was long past.[84]

Wiskemann's account of the historical roots of the Czech-Sudeten problem condemned chauvinism and extreme nationalism on both sides, but she also portrayed the contemporary crisis as primarily an outgrowth of Hitler's expansionism. As such, her views were unwelcome and stirred up controversy in parts of Whitehall. Throughout the 1920s the dominant attitude towards Czechoslovakia in the Foreign office was highly sympathetic. Though not uncritical of the Czech land reform, officials generally concluded that Czechs needed to give the new state a strong Czech identity and they argued that relative prosperity was helping ethnic Germans come to terms with their position within it. However, this began to change in the 1930s in the context of economic depression, rising unemployment, and rising national conflict in ethnic German areas. A more negative and pessimistic view of the Czech-German relationship was also shaped by reports from Ambassador Addison and his deputy, Sir Robert Hadow, in Prague, who already in the early 1930s believed Czech treatment of the German minority was unjust and questioned the long-term viability of the republic, suggesting that its frontiers might in future have to be adjusted to preserve peace. Over time this encouraged the view in London that Sudeten nationalism and its radicalization was shaped less by Nazi interference than by Czech suppression of basic rights.[85] On his visits to London, as mentioned, Henlein had favorably impressed politicians and Whitehall officials as genial and mild-mannered, a moderate who wanted nothing beyond autonomy within Czechoslovakia and was being pushed into the Nazi camp by Beneš's police state. Wiskemann also recalled being waylaid by former Air Attaché, Group Captain Christie, who chastised her for being unfair to Henlein, even calling her a hysterical warmonger.[86] It was Christie who made the initial contact that brought Henlein to London; he worked for British intelligence and especially Vansittart who, though deeply anti-German, wished to solve the Sudeten problem peaceably.

Sir Robert Hadow and Wiskemann disliked each other from their early meetings in Prague. After he was posted back to London in October 1937, they locked horns again at a Chatham House meeting when she tried to get the speaker Wenzel Jaksch to admit that British pressure on Prague to make concessions was simply reinforcing Czech chauvinism.[87] A month later, Hadow's displeasure increased significantly when Toynbee sent over some early historical chapters of Wiskemann's draft manuscript for Foreign Office comment. This was not an unusual procedure, but Hadow's reaction to the chapter was extreme.[88] Regarding Wiskemann as hopelessly pro-Czech, he told Toynbee, he had examined the manuscript sections closely, making copious notes. He pounced on her claim that ethnic Czechs were the original inhabitants of Bohemia; this he viewed as a ploy to brand Germans as 'intruders on Slav soil.' In fact, her chief source for the historical prologue was a distinguished Sudeten German historian.[89] Not everyone agreed: F. Ashton-Gwatkin, head of the Foreign Office Economic Section, also consulted by Toynbee, was far less critical. In general, he judged the draft sections "interesting and objective and unobjectionable." He went further: "Opinion in this office is that whereas Miss Wiskemann may be biased in one direction, Hadow certainly is in the other; no doubt you will be able to give his criticisms the value which ought to be attached to them, separating the wheat from the chaff."[90]

Initially Toynbee seemed inclined to agree that the text needed toning down; the last two chapters dealing with the period since 1935 were, he felt, "definitely different in tone." He informed Hadow that he had arranged for Wiskemann to take a brief holiday, after which she could "take in hand a thorough revision of these chapters in the light of your comments and others which take the same line."[91] Toynbee's own views are relevant here. Although he advocated a strong, even military, response to Mussolini's invasion of Ethiopia, he was critical of the Versailles Treaty, arguing that too many ethnic Germans had been excluded from the Reich. Long sympathetic to the idea that the treaty required revision, he came away from interviewing Hitler in early 1936 convinced of his "sincerity in desiring peace in Europe" and in July 1937 in the *Economist* chastised Czech injustice towards Sudeten Germans. However, with the Austrian *Anschluss* and now the Czech crisis, his views about Hitler's intentions had changed, although he still favored Czech concessions as a way of staving off Nazi intervention.[92]

Hadow feared that if the book appeared, "the Czechs are going to use it for all they are worth in an endeavor to refute Henlein's claims and 'stir up opposition in England.'" He went on: "I am afraid it will mean a real setback for the very real effort which – as you will have seen in the press – is being made to bring Mr. Beneš to a sense of the 'realities' of the situation and so to direct negotiations with Henlein by which alone we can hope for some détente." Given that foreigners often viewed Chatham House as "an official mouthpiece of the Foreign Office" he wrote "I genuinely fear the insult of 'throwing a monkey-wrench into the machinery' from so responsible a source at the present time." He urged that the book's early June publication should at least be postponed.[93] While Toynbee acknowledged that publication could be stopped even at this late date if "one were sure that…it would do political harm," he insisted: "I think that this danger, in so far as it may have existed, has been substantially removed"; "a good deal of time has been spent in going through these particular chapters [i.e. the disputed ones] almost sentence by sentence in order to secure that they shall be as free as possible from any charge of being one-sided." And he was now satisfied that "the book will give very timely information to the intelligent public in this country."[94] At the same time, in a letter to Sir Ivison Macadam, first Director-General of Chatham House, Toynbee confessed, "I like Hadow very much but my own impression of him was, and is, that he leans over at least as much on the pro-German side as Miss Wiskemann does on the pro-Czech." "There is," he added, "a touch of something rather wild and unbalanced about him."[95]

Toynbee's correspondence implies that his revisions had "corrected Miss Wiskemann's leaning very substantially."[96] But we have no way of judging how much the original draft was altered; no responses exist from Wiskemann about Toynbee's editing and there is nothing in Chatham House files to indicate her disapproval of the changes. This is surprising: having great confidence in her own opinions, Wiskemann never responded well or quietly to criticism.[97] Certainly, at this early stage in her career she was hardly in a position to veto Toynbee's suggestions. But my guess is that much of her manuscript received only minor revisions aside from the section on the post-1935 Henlein movement (chapter 16 and the Conclusion). Her goal from the start was to show the contemporary German–Czech conflict was rooted in historical development, not to write a political polemic.

Czechs and Germans was published on June 2, 1938, just as the crisis seemed to slide towards war. From a publisher's point of view, its timing was propitious. A fortnight earlier, the Prague government called up its reserves and reinforced manpower at its frontier posts, arguing that a German attack was imminent. This catalyzed action in London and by August 2 Neville Chamberlain dispatched Lord Runciman to Prague to mediate. Wiskemann called it a farcical mission with no chance of success, but while sitting in the train just before he left, Runciman was photographed reading *Czechs and Germans*.[98] It was flattering, but she had no illusions the book would influence him.[99] A month later, in early September, after Runciman's predictable failure and a bellicose speech by Hitler at the Nuremberg rally, Chamberlain began his own 'shuttle diplomacy,' flying to meet Hitler in person and then agreeing to the Munich Conference that forced Beneš to surrender the Sudetenland. On his return to London, Chamberlain was greeted by public rejoicing and palpable relief that war had been avoided. But this soon gave way to a mood of despair; within a month, polls showed that 93% of the public no longer believed Hitler's claim that he had no further demands and few now felt that the slide to war could be prevented.

In light of the fast-moving events of the summer and fall of 1938, Wiskemann's book very quickly became the subject of media discussion and dozens of reviews on both sides of the Atlantic. Most praised its remarkable fairness and impartiality.[100] The *Sunday Times* reflected that the book was "never more needed than at the present moment when public opinion is alarmed and perplexed." Voigt in the *Manchester Guardian* called it "a little masterpiece" and a rejoinder to "those who imagine they have ready-made 'solutions' for the acuter problems of our day."[101] George Glasgow, veteran diplomatic correspondent for the *Observer*, pointed to the author's attention to trade and economics and not simply race and nationalist ideology.[102] The *Times*, undeterred by its own pro-Appeasement position, praised it as "a model of dispassionate inquiry." The Nation called it "a brilliant analysis...indispensable to every student of international affairs," while Seton-Watson predicted it "should explode many of the superficial theories that still linger in certain sections of the British press."[103] And the *Daily Telegraph*, which had become hostile to Appeasement policy, described it as "richly coloured with direct personal observation and abundantly documented and researched"; it was, the reviewer continued, "distinguished throughout by a tone of judicial impartiality which inspires ready confidence in the author as a reliable witness."[104]

Critics, however, found her too pro-Czech or rather too anti-Appeasement. Thus, in November 1938 when Chatham House considered sponsoring research on the German minority in Denmark, E.H. Carr—who was working on his pro-Appeasement polemic, *The Twenty Years' Crisis*—argued strongly that "it should not be entrusted to Elizabeth Wiskemann with her marked and well-known anti-German slant." He added that he was concerned about "Chatham House publications acquiring a reputation for a certain bias...The temptation to follow the current intellectual fashion and turn Chatham House into a high-brow anti-Fascist propaganda bureau is obvious: the undesirability of yielding to it not less obvious."[105] Carr, like Hadow, thought in geo-strategic terms: to preserve peace, Hitler's demands in Eastern Europe should be accommodated; German dominance in that region was inevitable and not necessarily harmful to Britain's vital interests; Munich was an overdue recognition of a change in power balance, a border adjustment that would produce a more stable international order. Aside from moral arguments, Wiskemann was skeptical of such 'realism' and was convinced that Hitler's expansionism would be inflamed, not satisfied, by concessions over the Sudetenland.

For pro-Czech activists like Wiskemann, R.W. Seton-Watson, Shiela Grant Duff, Wickham Steed, and Eleonor Rathbone who belonged to the Czech Association, Munich was an unmitigated disaster.[106] Most painful for Wiskemann was the *volte face* of her longtime friend and editor at the *New Statesman*, Kingsley Martin. Like others on the journal, she recognized Kingsley's weaknesses. C.H. Rolph, his biographer, describes how on Tuesday nights writers, especially Konni Zilliacus and Elizabeth Wiskemann, tried to have the last word with him. They were concerned "not so much to feed him with ideas as to stop him saying something about Central and Eastern Europe that they would think harmful." They knew that Kingsley, influenced by Lloyd George, was desperate to find a compromise that would avoid war. He knew very little about foreign countries and was quick to latch onto "slipshod leftist slogans."[107] Over the Sudetenland he vacillated repeatedly, hoping the Czechs could be pushed into making concessions acceptable to Hitler. Finally, on August 27—a month before the Munich Conference, and without consultation—he made a last-minute insertion into an editorial, arguing that Czechoslovakia would be better off without the Sudetenland and advocating its surrender ("the strategical value of the Bohemian frontier should not be made the occasion of a world war. We should not guarantee the *status quo*"[108]). Ritchie Calder and many of the staff were appalled. Keynes was furious, writing to Martin: "we should bluff to the hilt; and if the bluff is called, back out."[109] As for Wiskemann, she felt deeply betrayed, "desolated" (Rolph's word).[110] "It seemed to me," she wrote, "to undo all my work there. It came much worse from the Left than from the *Times*..." She never forgave Kingsley for this and subsequently wrote less for the *New Statesman*.[111] Much later she declared that one tragedy of the era was that "leftist intellectuals informed themselves no better than Neville Chamberlain."[112]

Shiela Grant Duff's Penguin Special, *Europe and the Czechs*, was published the same day as the Munich Agreement. Addressed more to the general reader than Wiskemann's book, it became a best-seller (sales eventually reached 170,000) and she agreed with Penguin to forego royalties for the first 50,000 copies in return for speeding up publication and sending a free copy to every MP.[113] Like Wiskemann, she had found the British Legation in Prague "intensely suspicious of me" and had sharp disagreements with Hadow, writing in April 1938: "It is not that one of us does not believe in the truth but that we do not see the same truth. You see it as the sufferings of the Germans and I as the sufferings of the Czechs. We are both desperately afraid of war and each blame the policy of the other that things have come to this pass."[114]

*   *   *

With the publication of *Czechs and Germans*, Wiskemann's reputation as an expert on Nazi Germany and Eastern Europe soared. In addition to writing articles and reviews at a furious pace, she now received numerous lecture invitations. She spoke about Central Europe in a lecture series on international affairs at London's Morley College, whose Principal was the feminist social reformer Eva Hubback. Other participants included John Langdon Davies (on Spain), Edward Thompson (on India), and Freda Utley (on Japan).[115] In late July and early August 1938 she took part in the Liberal Party Summer School at Oxford, where her topic was the struggle for domination in south-east Europe.[116]

She also received invitations from North America and set sail in early September on a fourteen-week tour which included New York, Boston, Washington, Toronto, Montreal, and Ottawa.[117] In New York she spent time with Dorothy Thompson, a friend from Berlin days, and Hamilton Fish Armstrong, the managing editor of *Foreign Affairs*; together the three waited for news of the Munich Conference, trying to get through to Voigt on the telephone: "By the next day," Wiskemann recalled, "the subject of my lectures seemed emasculated before they had begun."[118] At Harvard she had lunch with the exiled Gaetano Salvemini (a close friend of Bernard Berenson) and Felix Frankfurter on successive days and she was introduced around Washington as a close friend of Rebecca West.[119] The speaking tour was a big success and for her an eye-opener. In a letter of thanks to Hamilton Fish for his many kindnesses, she wrote: "I know I can't know anything about the U.S. in three months, but I'm sure there is a great deal about them that I like immensely. Anyway, I've met a lot of awfully nice people, intelligent and cultivated and free-minded." Uncharacteristically revealing, she added: "I was never quite English enough for the English (which is another reason besides chance and chasing paintings for my international entanglements)."[120] "In a silly Bloomsbury highbrow way," she added, " I used to despise Americans until I saw exactly my own feelings of horror on Edgar Mowrer's face in Berlin in 1933 – it drew the English and the Americans together wonderfully and rightly, and from then on I used to protest when people at home aired pronunciation prejudices. And now being in the States has confirmed all that. I went to lunch on Friday with Dorothy Thompson and Clarence Streit was talking about his plan for expanding the Union of the U.S.A. to take in other democracies – that's just what I've been fumbling for these last two or three months."[121] Like many contemporaries, she was drawn to the Federal Union's idea that a union of democracies might create a more stable international order.[122]

There were also offers of book contracts and, thinking "it was clearly going to be increasingly difficult to write the truth in Europe as long as the policy of Appeasement lasted," she briefly "began to wonder whether I should look for work in America."[123] Already, before leaving for North America, she had discussed with Duckworth the idea for a study of the Habsburg Empire (indicating perhaps a revival of her aspirations for an academic career), but she was torn: "I am genuinely very keen to do the history of Austria but I don't know whether I'll be right to decide to drop out of contemporary international affairs which is what it would mean." Friends were also "insistent that it is very important to me particularly to be published in America too. You see I half or more want a University job in the States if I could get a good offer." Soon she was writing: "I've had rather a good offer to do another contemporary book (quite short) and everyone advises me not to drop out of contemporary things yet."[124] She felt guilty about Duckworth but in the end accepted a contract from Paul Willert, head of Oxford University Press in New York, for a follow-up book on post-Munich developments. She returned to London in mid-November, days after *Reichskristallnacht*, the pogrom that signaled further radicalization of Nazi anti-Semitism. In early March 1939 she set off on a seven-week journey to Switzerland, then Hungary, Romania, and Yugoslavia to gather material for her new book. As she reached Switzerland, on March 15, news broke that Hitler had occupied Prague, underscoring the accuracy of her earlier predictions. Chamberlain responded with a unilateral guarantee to Poland, followed by similar pledges to Romania and Greece, but not a complete reversal of his Appeasement policy.

In her new book, *Undeclared War*, Wiskemann detailed how Nazi Germany was using economic penetration, political pressure, and the grievances of German and other national minorities to dominate south-east Europe and advance Hitler's goal of racial empire.[125] As with *Czechs and Germans*, she worked with incredible speed: after traveling throughout the region for seven weeks, she wrote the book in a little over three months, beginning in March and submitting the finished manuscript in late July 1939.[126] Most of the book was devoted to detailed analysis of Hungary, Romania, Yugoslavia, and Bulgaria: their politics, economies, demography, and ethnic divisions, and the impact of Nazi policies, ideology, and propaganda in the whole region. A shorter chapter examined the ways that the German *Drang nach Osten* was affecting Poles, Balts, and Ukrainians. The bitter tensions between Poles and Ukrainians, the attractions of German overtures to the latter, but also recognition that Poles and Ukrainians had a common Slav interest in defending themselves against Nazi colonialism, were typical of the complexities she described. Moreover, as she made clear, Nazi penetration of Eastern Europe was but a prelude to a larger goal of *Lebensraum* at the expense of the Soviet Union, as foretold in *Mein Kampf*.

She examined in detail the party politics and minority conflicts of these states, especially since the Nazi takeover of Austria and Czechoslovakia, and the economic dominance of Germany in the region. Inspired by the success of the Prussian *Zollverein* in paving the way for German unification under Bismarck, Germans, she argued, viewed economic power as a prerequisite for political domination. By 1939 Hungary was completely dependent on the Reich economically; in March 1939, days after the bloodless takeover of Prague, a commercial treaty had given Hitler control of most of Romania's economic resources, including its oil; Bulgaria was already an economic vassal, while the Yugoslavs were now at the mercy of German trade and investment policies, Berlin having usurped the earlier dominant position of Prague. The eventual goal, Wiskemann argued, was to eliminate all but specialized sectors of industry, since these satellite states were to provide food and natural resources rather than compete with German manufactures. Throughout Eastern Europe, Nazism had successfully manipulated minority conflicts and stoked ingrained anti-Semitism and fears of communism to consolidate German power. Vilification of Jews and Slavs was particularly widespread in Hungary, while in Yugoslavia Croat nationalists had since her previous visits become much more pro-Nazi in hopes of liberation from Belgrade with Hitler's help. Wherever she traveled, Wiskemann interviewed a wide array of politicians, intellectuals, and officials; this gave her a first-hand sense of their personalities and views—knowledge that also proved useful in the war years when she was tasked with gathering and evaluating intelligence from these states. "Noone has mastered the political and economic entanglements of these countries," wrote Rustem Vambery, then teaching at the New School in New York, "with all their party antagonisms, intrigues and personal ramifications, better than Miss Wiskemann."[127]

Like most other commentators in the 1930s, Wiskemann did not examine Nazi ideas or their origin in any systematic way. And while she emphasized the role of business groups in Nazi rearmament and expansionism, she rejected the Marxist conception of the regime as a tool of capitalist interests. There was nothing new in Nazi ideology, she argued; the regime had radicalized older Pan-Germanism, making it immensely more potent by the addition of race theory and modern propaganda methods. This made it possible to disseminate these ideas among the masses of workers and peasants. In a January 1939 essay, she suggested that all the attention directed at Houston Stewart Chamberlain and other 'founding fathers' of the movement had obscured the Habsburg roots of Nazism; it was, she wrote, the most virulent form of Pan-Germanism, nurtured in the ethnic German borderlands excluded from Bismarck's *kleindeutsch* Germany. Here one could find "an exact reflection of the modern Nazi's state of mind"[128]—in the Jew-hating, anti-Slav, and anti-Catholic ultra-nationalism of Bohemia, Moravia, and Austrian Silesia. Her depiction of Hitlerism was also close to that of Hermann Rauschning: a revolutionary nihilistic doctrine, underpinned by a relentless pursuit of total power and territorial *Lebensraum* in the name of the German *Herrenvolk*. She recognized the centrality of anti-Semitism in Nazi racism, but did not press her analysis deeper and at times seemed to view it instrumentally as a destabilizing weapon in the 'undeclared war,' a way of mobilizing ancient atavistic prejudice, and to some degree as a camouflage for naked, limitless imperialism.

One aspect of the book—its long final section, "West of the Axis Powers"—was surprising and in some ways highly personal. It examined not France but Switzerland, a country to which Wiskemann was increasingly drawn since her first visit at the time of the Rhineland crisis. In 1919 Thomas Masaryk had spoken of creating an east European version of Switzerland; by 1939 Wiskemann concluded that this vision could never become reality in the East. A small, federal, multilingual, religiously divided, and multi-ethnic state, like the countries of Eastern Europe, Switzerland found itself severely tested by economic depression and imperiled by the Nazi Reich. On some Nazi maps it figured as *Gau Schweiz*, and pro-Nazi elements certainly existed in the early 1930s, especially among junior army officers. Nazi agents were also active in the country, and large numbers of German students attended Swiss universities. But Switzerland had remained united, stable, and democratic. The effect of Nazi terror, the Rhineland crisis, and Hitler's undermining of Austrian and Czechoslovak independence had been to harden Swiss determination to protect their nation. She praised the Swiss press for publicizing the true nature of the Nazi regime—ordinary Swiss, she argued, were far better informed than Britons—and pointed to the nation's united support, including the Socialist party, for rearmament and its recent extension of military service. If invaded, she argued, the Swiss would resist. The key was a federal structure and a deeply democratic culture, where political life was built from the bottom up—from commune to canton and confederation—in total contradiction to the *Führerprinzip* and Nazi tribalism. The Swiss constitution, she wrote, built around respect for the individual, provided "probably the least imperfect democracy in the world." She later admitted: "the spectacles through which I saw Switzerland in 1939 were just a shade too rosy."[129]

In places *Undeclared War* shows signs of the speed with which Wiskemann worked; she found herself racing to finish as German demands for Danzig became increasingly threatening. By the time the book appeared in October 1939, Britain was already at war, and to some degree public interest had moved beyond the preconditions for the conflict.[130] It received fewer reviews than *Czechs and Germans*, but all were admiring. Historian Keith Feiling praised "this most informing and wise book" for its "clarity, economy and breadth of treatment." Wickham Steed wrote that its insights and accuracy merited only praise and declared angrily: "I hope that Lord Runciman and some others will have the courage to read this book." It is, wrote Richard Coventry in the *New Statesman*, "not only Miss Wiskemann's best book, it is also the book of the year so far as European politics are concerned."[131] He added: "I beg everyone to read and digest this Baedeker of Balkan politics and, above all, to study the chapter on Switzerland in which Miss Wiskemann rounds off both her journey and her argument." This was echoed by her old friend F.A. Voigt, who noted that her academic training, patient research, and "dispassionate discrimination" contrasted with the "flashiness" that typified so many studies; the result was "a very serious contribution to our knowledge of contemporary Europe and not a sort of 'news reel' like most recent books about foreign affairs."[132]

As these reviews attest, by the outbreak of war Wiskemann had achieved considerable individual prominence as a foreign correspondent, as an expert on Central and Eastern Europe, and as a critic of British Appeasement policy.

But she should also be viewed as part of a cohort of women who began to emerge in the 1930s as pioneers in the field of international affairs.[133] Indeed, when the *Times* listed the best books in international affairs from 1938, three of the top four mentioned were written by women, all non-academics. Two, by Wiskemann and Grant Duff, dealt with Czechoslovakia; the third—*The Mediterranean in Politics*—was by Elizabeth Monroe, later a distinguished Middle East scholar.[134] Born roughly between 1898 and 1913, they came from the upper middle class and, unlike their mothers, had studied at university. Appalled by the slaughter of the First World War, they were drawn to the liberal internationalism of men like Toynbee, Lord Cecil, Gilbert Murray, and Alfred Zimmern and joined campaigns to promote internationalism and collective security. But since the Foreign Service and academia were largely closed to them, they pursued their interests in foreign affairs through journalism, broadcasting, and pressure-group activism or the League's bureaucracies. Several, like Wiskemann, wrote for the weekly *Time and Tide*, whose trajectory reflected the shift toward foreign affairs. Founded in 1920 as an explicitly feminist journal, by the 1930s it turned more to international relations and political journalism, constructing the 'modern woman' as both a national and a global citizen capable of addressing foreign policy issues.[135] However, democracy's retreat throughout Europe in the 1930s and the erosion of League's authority produced different responses in this cohort. Helena Swanwick, a founder of the Women's International League for Peace and Freedom, became a strong supporter of Chamberlain's Appeasement policy as the best means of averting war, while Vera Brittain, after a good deal of soul-searching, reaffirmed her pacifism as a moral absolute and criticized "all the so-called peace lovers" who "are back again preferring war to negotiation."[136] Others, as their hopes for the League became increasingly untenable, switched to advocating rapid rearmament, a strategy of coalition-building, and firm resistance to Hitler's demands. For some the turning-point was Italian aggression against Abyssinia or Spain's Civil War, for others it was the Czechoslovak crisis.[137] First-hand experience of Nazism in its early years had convinced Wiskemann, before most of her contemporaries, that Nazism meant war and that efforts to compromise were likely to fail.

* * *

Little has been said in this chapter about Wiskemann's private life. This is partly because few sources have survived. But it is also a reflection of how little personal life she enjoyed. In the space of about four years she had covered many major stories, researched and written two large books, and published scores of articles and reviews. She also spent lengthy periods working abroad in Prague, visited the United States, and traveled frequently to observe European politics first-hand. Since October 1932 she had been renting a small flat in Pimlico at 42 St. George's Square and she had many friends in London, although only fragmentary evidence survives of these relationships. She enjoyed organizing parties, but here too her professional life took increasing precedence over the private. A hurried invitation to J.G. Crowther, the *Guardian* science correspondent, urges: "You must both come because I'm a bit short of men."[138] To Mary Adams of the BBC, she writes, "Forgive me for having asked you to that frosty party. I had a shouting success on another day but everyone got prevented at the last moment the time you came." Very eager to make the acquaintance of the *Listener*'s literary editor, she comments: "I thought of asking [J.R.] Ackerly to a sherry party but thought it would look so very pointed !!"[139] Obtaining commissions, contacting new sources, and finding new outlets to publicize the threat of Nazi barbarism and the errors of British foreign policy came ahead of private life or, rather, the two were often combined.

Her Bloomsbury and Cambridge networks remained important. Occasional weekends were spent with Adrian and Karin Stephens or at Bradenham Hall with Alec and Frances Penrose—and through her writer and publisher friend David Garnett she got to know the novelist Ivy Compton-Burnett and her circle. She also felt close to Julian Bell and they loved exchanging gossip, although he went to China to teach English in 1935. "You must write again soon," she urges, "and tell me about your Chinese mistresses and Communism in Pekin." Having been away in Central Europe, she had little "Bloomsbury scandal" to relate, but continued:

> I went to a party at Ivy's the other night at which Lettice appeared with a very young rather handsome young man clinging to her, Portia seemed a bit unattached. Trevor, tight as usual, made me go through the discomfort of dancing with him while he remembered the PAST (very unsavoury and not mine anyhow), M. Gardiner did her sort of Botticelli Venus stunt attaching herself to various parties. Hugh played the concertina, of course.* He and I have parted forever, I think. I thought it all rather boring and parochial.[140]

A year later, after Julian had sent her some of his poems, she writes: "Today I got back from a weekend with Alec and Frances [Penrose] to find an enormous envelope from China and inside some exquisitely lovely things. I hope my dear, I shall be dead before I cease to 'have time for such matters.' It was sweet of you to send them, the more since I am sure it is I who owe you some sort of writing or sending...I don't forget you Julian, only as you understand I have become such a slave to international affairs." All Bradenham had been consumed with Wallace

---

* Ivy is novelist Ivy Compton-Burnett; Lettice is the photographer Lettice Ramsey (1898–1985), a lover of Julian Bell, whose mathematician husband, Frank, had died in 1930; Portia is the Australian child psychiatrist Portia Holman (1903–1983), who studied medicine at Newnham and, like Julian Bell, went to Spain to serve as a medical orderly on the Republican side; Trevor is probably the translator and BBC German specialist Trevor Blewitt; M. Gardiner is the artist Margaret Gardiner (1904–2005), who also went to Newnham and was longtime partner of scientist J.D. Bernal; Hugh is English don and old Cambridge friend Hugh Sykes-Davies.

Simpson and the King's abdication a few days earlier and "regarded my (very genuine) detachment as a pose." "Julia and Graham Bell were at Alec's too [the painter Graham Bell and Julia Strachey], but," she went on, "I find her a scrap difficult – she does so very much put me in my place or rather not mine for she hasn't a notion of what I do, but the insignificant place –relative to her – which she feels to be my due. I know I don't look 18 in my thirties as she does, but it's just a little annoying to be treated so."[141] She looked forward to Julian's return to England, but she never saw him again; after returning from China in spring 1937, Julian volunteered as an ambulance driver for the Republican side in Spain. He was killed at the Battle of Brunete in June 1937, little more than a month after his arrival.

Wiskemann finished *Undeclared War* at the end of July 1939. By then Hitler's attention was fully focused upon Danzig. She had watched the pace of Nazi foreign policy accelerate, driven forward by mounting confidence and the growing economic strain imposed by massive rearmament. Like many other contemporaries, she had been uncertain as to what would precipitate a European war, although sooner or later it would involve the conquest of 'living space' in the East, principally at the expense of Poland and the USSR. Earlier in 1939, for example, she believed that Hitler's next move might be expansion in the West, possibly invading strategically important Switzerland. London was full of such rumors, and in early 1939 the secret service [SIS] was busy accumulating false intelligence about an imminent German attack on Holland or Switzerland.[142] But by the summer German demands that Danzig should be returned to Germany and Poland's stubborn refusal had spiraled into crisis. Hitler informed his military chiefs in late May of his decision to attack Poland at the earliest suitable opportunity and the Nazi–Soviet pact in late August cleared the way for an invasion,[143] while Chamberlain's guarantees given five months earlier obligated Britain to come to Poland's aid.

As she sent off her manuscript with its ambiguous title, Wiskemann was convinced that Britain would be at war by early September. What she would do in that event was unclear: One possibility was to work for the BBC, whose information services would obviously be expanding; she had some allies there and had begun to provide copy for programs on the Ukraine and German penetration of the Balkans; but breaking into actual broadcasting was much harder. Another possibility was to follow Toynbee and Chatham House, already making plans to establish a government-funded foreign research and press service. As she wrote to the BBC's Leonard Miall in late August: "I shall mostly be in London for some time now unless war is declared in which case I evacuate as a member of the staff of Chatham House."[144] In fact, the conflict would soon to push her in a completely different direction as an agent of British secret intelligence; of this she had no inkling as the Wehrmacht advanced into Poland.

3

Secret Agent in Wartime Switzerland

Wiskemann finished *Undeclared War* in July 1939.[1] In the weeks that followed, the growing crisis over Danzig and the Nazi–Soviet pact pushed Europe inescapably towards the war that she had feared and predicted for over four years. In anticipation of its outbreak, like many of her friends, she focused increasingly upon what kind of war work she might take up, preferably a form of service that would take advantage of her expertise in European affairs. Leonard Miall, who had recently joined the BBC European Service, had hopes of recruiting her, while Chatham House was another possibility given her earlier research for the institute. A.J. Toynbee had set up with government funds the Foreign Research and Press Service, which he envisioned as a group that would advise government agencies on foreign policy issues.[2] Most of its work, at least initially, involved compiling summaries of the foreign press for the Foreign Office and providing historical and social background, although later in the war its focus shifted to preparing blueprints for postwar planning. Wiskemann joined Toynbee in Oxford at Balliol College but she soon grew restless and after six weeks returned to London in hopes of finding a more active role in the burgeoning intelligence services or the new Ministry of Information.[3]

So much has been written about the wartime successes of the British intelligence community that its pitiful state in 1939 has been largely overshadowed. It was starved of resources and personnel in the 1930s[4] and the chief focus of MI5 and MI6 (or the Secret Intelligence Service, SIS) between the wars had been the Soviet Union. They had little understanding of the Nazi regime's leadership, structure, and ideology or of social and economic conditions in the Reich and little grasp of its intelligence capabilities. During the accelerating sequence of foreign policy crises in the late 1930s, Whitehall had trouble distinguishing rumor from reality, underestimated the ability of the German economy to withstand the strains of war, and misjudged the possibility of a Nazi–Soviet pact. False alarms were common and sound information often disregarded (for example, about Hitler's intentions to occupy Prague). In addition, the structure of British intelligence was antiquated and hopelessly vulnerable. It was well known, for example, that the man in charge of SIS operations in any city was the Passport Control Officer [PCO]. Moreover, the fragmented structure of the intelligence community and the diversity of government departments with which it interacted produced major problems in interpreting the raw intelligence it was able to gather. And, given the parochialism of the service ministries (with their own intelligence

Elizabeth Wiskemann: Scholar, Journalist, Secret Agent. Geoffrey Field, Oxford University Press.
© Geoffrey Field 2023. DOI: 10.1093/oso/9780192870629.003.0004

departments) and the Foreign Office's jealous guarding of its monopoly over political intelligence, only limited coordination was achieved prior to the outbreak of war.

In the event of war, it was clear that dramatic changes would have to be made; indeed, already in the 1930s Colonel Claude Dansey, the pugnacious, decisive, and experienced PCO in Rome, who had only contempt for the existing service, began recruiting his own part-time agents among businessmen and journalists, including the film producer Alexander Korda and Frederick Voigt.[5] After leaving Rome in 1936, Dansey developed in effect a parallel structure of agents (called the Z-Organization), separate from the SIS in Bush House, whose chief function was to gather intelligence about Nazi Germany and, to a lesser extent, Fascist Italy. But it was the Venlo disaster of October–November 1939, compounding earlier failures, that became the catalyst of change. Having made contact with anti-Nazi officers who were allegedly planning a military coup against Hitler, two SIS officers were lured to the Dutch–German border and kidnapped, one of them carrying a list of British agents; in one go, almost all of Britain's SIS intelligence network within Germany was exposed and destroyed. The two agents—Best and Stevens—were convenient scapegoats, but the fiasco could not have happened without incompetence at SIS Headquarters and in Whitehall more generally. Under its new head, Robert Menzies, MI6 had to pretty much start from scratch, while his assistant Dansey merged his Z-Organization with what was left of the PCO network and took over all active foreign espionage operations.[6]

When Wiskemann began looking for a job in the intelligence community, it was still fragmented and largely uncoordinated as different government agencies tried to expand their own sphere of activities. Several of her friends, including the Oxford University Press publisher, Paul Willert, and the *Times* correspondent Thomas Barman, had been recruited by Electra House, or Department EH, an organization set up by the Foreign Office under the Canadian newspaper magnate Sir Campbell Stuart. Its focus was anti-German propaganda.[7] She was interviewed by a security agent, who acknowledged that she was "not nearly such a fool as he had expected a woman would be," and by Christmas 1939 it was arranged that EH would send her to Switzerland, although only in a semi-official capacity.[8] She would travel under the guise of writing a book for Oxford University Press, and the Swiss issued her a six-month *permis de sejour*.[9] In fact, she needed additional employment to cover expenses and contacted the *Manchester Guardian* and several magazines with suggestions for articles.[10] To W.P. Crozier, editor of the *Guardian*, she wrote:

> I expect to establish myself in Zurich immediately after Christmas for upwards of six months. I shall be preparing a small book for Sir Ernest Simon but also doing occasional articles for the *Spectator*, *Scotsman* etc. and hope that Switzerland will prove a very good clearing-house for German and other European news, as well as interesting in itself.[11]

Crozier was happy to take articles: "I am keen about getting news relating to what conditions are in Germany. I don't mean politics so much as more homely things – about rationing, food supplies, the ersatzes, the quality of goods, wages, working conditions and all that sort of thing." He would welcome such contributions to the paper's feature: 'Germany from within.' He added: "You should come across things in the papers and you may hear interesting things coming out of Germany. I know you would be sceptical and cautious."[12] Other reports were arranged for the BBC's European Service.

The close similarity between journalists' information gathering and the work of secret agents made foreign correspondents particularly useful recruits to war-time intelligence and many journalists were already performing both functions. Many correspondents, especially in the 1930s, considered themselves journalist-activists, informing the public, speaking truth to power, and, like Wiskemann, hoping to influence policy. Many lived for long periods in the countries they covered; they had excellent contacts and were experts in local languages, history, and customs. All of this made them valuable informants. Dansey had several newspapermen working for him, while several of those that Wiskemann knew in Eastern Europe and elsewhere combined both functions (some using their jour-nalist cover on behalf of the Soviet Union).[13]

Wiskemann left in early January 1940 for Paris and then traveled to Zurich, which became her base of operation in the first few months. There was still a chance that she might take a job with the BBC, and Leonard Miall pursued her, writing in early February: "I hope that we may be having you as a colleague quite soon."[14] At the month's end, she replied: "Wire offering me that job has just arrived. Of course, now it has come I'm much more tied up here. Must wire back asking for 2 or 3 days to think. Terribly perplexing at this moment. But perhaps then I'll be seeing you soon."[15] In March she was briefly recalled to London for further instructions but, deeply torn, decided to pass up the BBC offer and return to Switzerland.[16]

Switzerland had received large numbers of refugees from Fascist Italy and Nazi Germany in the 1920s and 1930s. More than usual, towns like Zurich, Basel, and Geneva had become international crossroads. Many of these exiles were writers and intellectuals, including Thomas Mann, Ignazio Silone, Ernst Toller, Kurt Tucholsky, and Robert Musil. Others were politicians like Carlo Sforza and Joseph Wirth. There were professors and academics who had been expelled from their jobs and, of course, many Jews who had been driven out by Nazi racism or left Italy after Mussolini's anti-Semitic laws of November 1938. The social circles of these anti-fascist and intellectual exiles overlapped, many knew each other prior to arriving in Switzerland, and by the time the war began they had developed a way of life with its own 'institutions.' In Zurich, for example, these included the bookstore of Emil and Emmie Oprecht and the town's *Schauspielhaus*, which pro-vided work for first-rate actors and producers in exile—to Wiskemann it seemed like the last vestige of a free Germany.[17] Here many anti-fascist works were staged, including the premieres of several of Brecht's plays. Close by were coffee houses such as the Café Odeon, once the birthplace of Dada, which had in its day welcomed many celebrated writers and musicians and was now again a regular haunt of foreign exiles. There was also the private library and smoking rooms of the Museumsgesellschaft and the municipal Central Library where emigrés could meet, talk, read, and write. For some refugees, Switzerland was a place of transit—a station on their way to Britain, France, or the United States—rather than of long asylum; for others, even if unintended, exile extended to a decade or more.

Swiss rules for asylum were harsh and became more restrictive after 1933. Often subject to harassment and police surveillance, refugees were not allowed to work, some never managed to secure residence permits, and they were forbidden to engage in any political activities, although here the authorities were more prepared to turn a blind eye in the later stages of the war. Many refugees were also turned away and, especially from 1938, the Swiss tightened regulations designed to limit immigration and the influx of Jews from Nazi-controlled areas. While many in the Swiss population sympathized with the plight of refugees, police and state authorities strove to insulate the country from the widening crisis presented by the war. Already in March 1940 the Bundesrat authorized the setting up of internment camps, and two years later, in August 1942, just as Nazi roundups of Jews moved into high gear, the nation's borders were effectively closed (except for prisoners of war, 'deserters,' and 'political refugees'—a category that excluded victims of racial persecution).[18]

As a neutral nation, Switzerland traded freely with its Axis neighbors and there was a continual flow of officials, businessmen, and agents back and forth across its borders. That it would be a valuable terrain for gathering wartime intelligence about the Nazi empire and Fascist Italy was always clear. In the First World War it had been a major marketplace for espionage, captured with all its monotonous routine and disappointments in Somerset Maugham's *Ashenden* stories. But in the late 1930s it was always assumed that, in the event of another war with Germany, a good deal of Allied intelligence would come through France and the Low Countries. The rapid deterioration of the military situation in 1940 destroyed these earlier assumptions. With Hitler's occupation of Denmark and Norway, followed by his lightning victory in the West against France, Switzerland's importance—as an island of neutrality, surrounded by Axis-held territory—grew dramatically, becoming a vital window for espionage, monitoring the Nazi empire, and gathering human intelligence about enemy politics, society, and morale. The Swiss government trod a delicate line: it possessed a sophisticated intelligence service of its own and was prepared to allow foreign intelligence gathering but drew the line if this endangered Swiss secrets and economic interests or threatened to trigger a German invasion. Given Switzerland's economic importance to the Reich both for its specialized exports and in enabling trade between

Germany and Italy, the Nazis continually spied on Swiss fortifications and military capability and updated plans for a possible invasion. Mindful of this, Britain was eager to avoid antagonizing the Swiss; demands, for example, by the Ministry of Economic Warfare that Britain's economic blockade be extended to include Swiss goods in retaliation for the nation's trade ties with Germany were vigorously rejected. Any such measure would have meant losing a crucial base of intelligence for meager economic gain.[19]

In the first weeks after her arrival, Wiskemann was based mostly in Geneva and in Zurich, where she quickly renewed her acquaintance with Swiss journalists and politicians whom she had interviewed for articles before the war. She gained access to the exile community through her friends, the publisher Emil Oprecht and his wife Emmie. A Communist in his youth, Emil had belonged to Willi Münzenberg's Youth International, but by this time his left-wing politics were defined by anti-fascism and European federalism; he dreamed of a United States of Europe. He was, Wiskemann wrote, "one of the most splendid characters I have ever met, fearless and selfless, always ready to help those in need, well-informed about Europe and eager to strike every blow against Hitler and all that he stood for."[20] In addition to their bookstore in the *Altstadt*, the Oprechts owned a successful publishing house, the Europa Verlag, which focused on exile authors banned from publishing in their own countries. Ignazio Silone's Abruzzi trilogy appeared first in German under their label, and their list included works by Konrad Heiden, Hermann Rauschning, Arthur Koestler, Ernst Bloch, Heinrich Mann, and many others. They provided money, contacts, and aid to numerous refugees, who had few resources and few legal rights in Switzerland.[21] They were also very active in Zurich's *Schauspielhaus* and introduced Wiskemann, a great lover of the theatre, to its actors, who included touring groups from Germany and Austria. She especially admired and became friends with Maria Becker, then at the beginning of her career, and the German-Jewish actress Thérèse Giehse, who had been a close associate of Brecht and had founded the political cabaret *Die Pfeffermühle* with Erika and Klaus Mann.[22] Giehse's personal integrity, both as an artist and as a person, was inspiring and a model of how to behave; her communist politics were overly simplistic in Wiskemann's opinion, but she strengthened the resolve of those around her in their struggle against Hitler.[23] From the time she arrived in Zurich, Wiskemann made the most of the city's vibrant arts scene, including visits to Cabaret Cornichon, which was founded in 1934 to counteract right-wing pro-Nazi movements that had gained a foothold in Switzerland. Cornichon toured Swiss cities, mixing attacks on Nazism and barbs against smug Swiss petit bourgeois provincialism and prejudice towards refugees. Its resort to *Schweizerdütsch* dialect—which still caused Wiskemann difficulties—made it especially popular with Swiss audiences, although performances close to the border at Basel also attracted Germans, raising Nazi objections and demands that it be banned.

In early May 1940 Wiskemann was ordered to relocate to Bern to help with the growing volume of work ferreting information from the German press. Much of the intelligence obtained about Germany came from published sources, channeled to Toynbee's Foreign Research and Press Service (Oxford) and other agencies by four press reading centers in Stockholm, Bern, Lisbon, and Istanbul. The Stockholm Press Bureau was the largest and by November 1940 it was responsible for the lion's share of the task, but Bern also played a large role, especially once work that had been done in the Low Countries was transferred to it. Wiskemann was reluctant to leave cosmopolitan Zurich for the Swiss capital and she had no desire to spend most of her days translating German press articles into English.[24] The move also meant she would, as a member of the embassy staff, enjoy less independence. On earlier visits to the legation she had encountered some antipathy from the Press Attaché, H.V. Daniels, who disapproved of her ill-defined 'roving commission' and treated her as his underling. Although her cover title was Assistant to the Press Attaché, her main role, as defined by London, was to establish contacts and gather secret intelligence for 'Rex' Leeper at the Foreign office. To add to the confusion, she also worked in a 'vague way' for MOI and the BBC.[25] Wiskemann had met Daniels before the war as the *Times* bureau chief in Paris and had formed a low opinion of his abilities. Not one to mince words, she later described him to Leeper as "senile and a fairly complete disaster."[26] She got along well with the British Minister, Sir David Kelly, and his Belgian wife, even though they disagreed about almost everything except Hitler.[27] Kelly was a deeply conservative Anglo-Irish Catholic who feared most the threat Communism posed to Western civilization; he favored Appeasement in the years before the war and seems to have entertained peace feelers from Berlin in July 1940 until Churchill intervened to stop these discussions. She got little help from the Legation's Military Attaché, Colonel Henry Cartwright, whom she soon concluded was second rate. A gentleman of the old school who had made daring escapes from German prison camps in the First World War, he was obsessed with the Venlo debâcle and driven to extreme caution by the threat of German counterespionage. Cartwright saw Wiskemann as an amateur likely to do something rash; she in turn judged him rather stupid and out of touch.[28] She also viewed his repeated warnings about the need for security as patronizing. Having lived in a police state (which he had not), she was more careful, or so she believed, about what she said on the telephone or put on paper than most of the Legation. "It did become clear to me that, certainly in my own Legation," she later wrote, "I was for the first time perhaps since Temperley up against serious resentment of the independent female."[29] Her one close ally on the staff was Daniels's assistant, Arthur ('Boofy') Gore (Later Lord Arran), with whom she developed a lifelong friendship. Interviewed decades later by Anne Sebba, Arran recalled Wiskemann working with "a smile at the absurdity of her surroundings": "I can see her still with her little pieces of paper on which she took notes in her exquisite handwriting, bustling from one secret rendezvous to the next aided by no one, least of all the legation staff." During the darkest times, when a German invasion seemed likely, he (clearly a little smitten) worried if she were late: "then she would rush in with her pretty legs and her pretty face – she must have been a very pretty girl – and I ask for the latest news. She tells me and we are overcome with solemnity though the laughter is always there."[30]

Wiskemann worked extremely hard for the first six months of 1940. She traveled constantly, trying to obtain new sources of intelligence, but also managed to publish several articles, fulfilling her promise to contribute short essays to several magazines. In them she praised Swiss morale and the steps they were taking to prepare for the eventuality of a German invasion. Here was a small nation which prized its strong grassroots democratic traditions, its ethnic, linguistic, and religious diversity, and was ready, in Gibbon's phrase, to "guard the blessings of peace with the sword of freedom."[31] There were uniforms everywhere and border fortifications were being strengthened. Pro-Nazi views had gained currency in some quarters in the mid-1930s, but they largely disappeared after the Czech crisis and hostility towards German visitors became more apparent.[32] On two successive Sundays in April 1940 she attended and reported on meetings of two Swiss *Landesgemeinden*—Appenzell and Glarus—where direct democracy had survived and, in Rousseau-like assemblies, citizens met to elect magistrates and fix taxes. At the Appenzell meeting, held in the little town of Trögen close to Germany, each male citizen wore his sword, the mark of a freeman. It was here that she first saw General Guisan, leader of the Swiss army, who was in charge of preparations against a possible German invasion: "He had taken the trouble to cross Switzerland to a canton on the frontier of Nazi Germany in order to demonstrate his solidarity with the practice of direct democracy…it made a tremendous impression upon the public to see the little Vaudois officer sitting at a fairly conspicuous window."[33] In the canton of Glarus, boys of the community sat at the center of deliberations to be trained in government. "It was," she reflected, "by no means the thoughts of the foreign visitor alone which strayed frequently across the nearby frontier; beyond that frontier political meetings had for seven years consisted of obedient salutes and standing to attention, and troops were at that moment concentrated upon a thoroughly intimidating scale with an invasion of Switzerland fully prepared."[34]

Pressure from Berlin was intense; there were numerous pro-Nazi German students living in the country, and Gestapo agents, directed from Stuttgart just over the border, were very active. "So systematic," she wrote, "has the [German] press campaign been that it has appeared not altogether unlike the journalistic artillery-fire which is apt to precede a Nazi Invasion." In response to these threats the Swiss authorities strove to police strict neutrality, which included careful monitoring, censorship, and sometimes intimidation of the press.[35] In March 1940 Wiskemann was deeply troubled when the *Manchester Guardian* published information she

Figure 3.1. "Elizabeth Wiskemann in the war years" c. 1940.

had contributed and indicated who provided it. Anything about Germany, she warned editor Crozier, had to be anonymous, adding "the stuff I have now sent you about Munich and Stuttgart is even more dangerous."[36] On May 2, only eight days before Hitler launched his offensive in the West, the *Neue Zürcher Zeitung* ran an article in which she praised Churchill's recent appointment as Chair of Britain's Military Co-Ordinating Committee, welcoming his growing popularity and implying that he should replace Chamberlain. Astonishingly, the newspaper—a frequent target of German complaints—clearly identified her as the author, although fast-moving news from the battlefield soon swept everything else aside and there were no repercussions.[37]

*   *   *

By early May 1940 the combined effect of Hitler's military successes, the obstruction (or so it seemed) that she encountered within the Legation, and sheer overwork and insomnia all began to take a toll on Wiskemann. Her closest confidant was a young German refugee, Harry Bergholz, and her letters to him[38] offer rare and detailed insight into her life at the time. A scholar of German and comparative literature, Bergholz had gained a doctorate in Berlin and taught briefly in a Gymnasium, but left Germany in 1936 and became a language teacher at

Charterhouse school. At the beginning of the war he arrived in Switzerland on vacation, but soon found himself marooned. With his German passport he could neither go to Germany, where he was suspected of anti-Nazi activities, nor return to Britain. Without funds, with a precarious visa status, and officially unable to work, he managed to escape being sent to a Swiss labor camp and scraped by doing some ghostwriting.[39] Wiskemann seems to have learned of him from English friends—possibly Robert Birley, headmaster of Charterhouse, but more likely William Robson Scott, a friend of Elizabeth and Harry in Berlin—and in early January 1940 she brought him not only greetings from them but also warm clothing he had left at Charterhouse: "I have just arrived in Switzerland with something for you…and I hope to get over to Lausanne to see you next month. Tomorrow I hope to post things to you – I thought you would like to know that they should reach you soon." A little later, she wrote, "I am ashamed that I did not bring more of your clothes. It's awful for you, all this."[40]

Stranded in Lausanne, Bergholz had offered his services to British intelligence, but with little success. Wiskemann gave him money and tried to help with his plan to emigrate to the United States by consulting a contact she had at the American Consulate about his visa. She supplied him with British papers like the *Spectator* and the weekly *Guardian* and in one letter suggested: "I meant to ask you if I could do any mending for you! Because you see I'm rather good at it and I love to feel I'm the indispensable woman to a chap provided he doesn't take it for granted that I am."[41] He began helping her with contacts (and collecting material for the essays she was writing for the *Listener* and *Foreign Affairs*) and passed along German and Swiss magazine articles. She frequently traveled to spend weekends with him in Lausanne. They became lovers and their relationship did much to sustain Wiskemann through difficult times in the next years; nine years older than Harry, it was she who set the terms and limits. "I suspect you love me more than I deserve," she writes in early May, adding, "Oh dear, how awful the news is – I can scarcely bear it."[42]

Already at the beginning of March 1940 she was fearful that Switzerland would be attacked suddenly: "I have a superstitious feeling the Germans will arrive next weekend in which case I should greatly prefer to be in *la Suisse romande*" [i.e. French-speaking Switzerland], and so she planned a trip to Lausanne for a few days. By mid-May, with the Wehrmacht overrunning Belgium and breaking through the Ardennes, creating havoc among British and French forces, alarm in the British Legation increased greatly; days off were impossible: "My dear, I am so sorry I fear you may have been to the [railway] station rather often today. I can't say very much but I have been advised to stay near certain facilities at least until tomorrow…I still do not think it a good thing to send you telegrams, so that I am bound to be treating you very badly."[43]

By May 20–25, with a French counterattack now impossible and the port of Calais the only viable escape route for much of the British army, she grew still more alarmed, although some in the Bern legation refused to see how desperate the situation was: "I feel in a cold sweat over this evening's news," she wrote to Bergholz, "but our military chaps say one has to expect 4 bad weeks before the tide can turn. Please God they're not too sanguine."[44] She added: "You were awfully good to me on Sunday. Sometimes I feel a wretch to you because I don't care quite as much as you do, but please don't mind that. I do love you and things are almost always so that one cares a little more than the other. I'm not saying this because I want anything to be different but only (I believe) because I don't want at any time to be suddenly disappointing to you. Perhaps it is just that I don't want to care too much but you are increasingly dear to me anyway."[45] Since the Gestapo already had files on her and Bergholz, they knew that, in the event of a German invasion, they could expect to be sent to concentration camps; indeed, she wrote, Swiss editors had already "hustled away on long leave into obscure rustic retreats" their prominent anti-Nazi journalists.[46] Jokingly, she told Bergholz: "If things go on getting worse, I think we had better stage a little Mayerling affair (have I spelt it right? – don't feel sure) – it would be so pleasant compared to what might otherwise happen to us. Fond love, E."[47] A short time later, in closing the same letter, she wrote: "I have pulled myself together – pro tem anyway.... If it weren't for you and duty and the physical impossibility of getting home at present, I should want to be in London more than I can say. Darling London, I hate to have deserted it."[48] Then came better news: "They say here that a big piece of the French Army has broken through (backwards) so that a front can be reconstituted in the S.W. I only hope devoutly that this is true and tell you in this hurried note for your comfort."[49]

In fact, her own situation was about to become a good deal more complicated. As the evacuation of British and Allied troops from Dunkirk reached its conclusion, she wrote on June 5: "I've heard from London that my telegrams are 'models of their kind'! (I think the man there has got it into his head that I'm useless unless encouraged) but they want me to go on trying to collect other stuff just the same, so that I must try to dash about for half days sometimes. I am awfully sorry not to see you this coming weekend but let's hope for the best for the one after."[50] She continued: "I am suffering the torments of the damned and losing all belief in 'safe periods'; it relieves my feelings to yelp at you. I wish my curse would come. It's only due today so there isn't anything very much to fuss about really. It seems so unimportant whether one's pregnant or not in these ghastly days...but it would be even more awkward than ever before."[51] She was furious at herself: "Although one's troubles seem so absurdly insignificant I feel awfully ashamed of taking irresponsible risks – just because of the times I have no right to do so because I've got to put all possible energies into work. O dear. I've taken a huge dose of castor oil and it hurt me quite nicely and I always felt that it must do it (though I know it needn't) and it hasn't. This is in no way a reproach. It was I who forgot my things. Squeals of misery from M.E."[52]

Possibly as a result of her efforts to abort the pregnancy, she soon became very ill with acute appendicitis and had to be moved to hospital for ten days and then recuperated at the home of Sir David and Lady Kelly.[53] In the meantime, officials at the legation were burning papers in preparation for flight if the Germans invaded. To Bergholz she wrote: "I am feeling more irritable and thoroughly bad tempered than it is possible to describe. And you mustn't talk to me about how nice babies and families can be because it makes my lips curl. Try to remember that my kind of English person is more complicated and sophisticated than your kind of German person." She added: "Anyway nothing matters to me much at the moment except most lovely Paris."[54] She arranged to visit him in Lausanne for a few days' recuperation and it was there, sitting in a restaurant at Ouchy on the edge of Lake Geneva, that they heard the news that Reynaud, the French premier, had resigned and that Marshall Pétain was seeking an armistice. It was a shattering blow, for which she was completely unprepared. Her French friends had always more or less shared her opinions, she reflected, and so she had not known how much defeatism had increased in France since Munich.[55] "I feel as if I can't get around this corner with mind or body," she wrote to Bergholz, "but I suppose I must. Poor bequislinged France. What infamy."[56] It had been betrayed from within by a fifth column. The Oprechts invited her to visit, but she replied to Emmie: "I must admit that I am completely broken [kaputt] because of France; this has all come with my illness and it seems that I cannot fully get over it. So I will not be a very pleasant guest...and warn your husband not to push me too hard otherwise I will cry like a child! Such is my nervous state. I believe that for both of you things are roughly the same."[57]

She remained close to Bergholz and often went to Lausanne; they recognized that they were unsuitable partners for the long run,[58] but helped each other through periods of depression and difficult times when he was in despair or—as she put it much later—"my nervous system did not behave very well."[59] In the summer of 1940 Harry was the more dependent; he had no job and his visa situation remained depressingly unresolved. He was stuck in Lausanne with little to occupy him; she became increasingly busy and overworked, traveling constantly. When he seems to have broached the possibility of marriage, she felt guilty: "I always tried to tell you that it wasn't so terrifically important to me and I wanted you not to let it be to you – which was perhaps absurd of me. You wrote once something about having a lot to give each other...I am awfully grateful for your most true affection and always shall be, but you must know perfectly well that a greedy person like me wants lots and lots of other things"[60] Or again, around the same time in August: "I am awfully sorry to have hurt you. I've tried hard not to. You are a very dear person – and, well, there's no point in discussing anything else any more. We both feel the other doesn't understand very well, but that's inevitable."[61] She was still encountering a lot of hostility at the legation in Bern and trips to Lausanne were a welcome escape: "I enjoyed seeing you last weekend though I wished you had been feeling better poor dear. I do feel bad about you

Harry. Partly because I think I very much allowed you to become the victim of political circumstances. I expect I am an unstable devil. Anyway, it's no good looking backwards and I'll be glad to have you in Switzerland as long as we both are stuck here."[62] Three weeks later, "*nervös* and wretched" and eager to escape Bern, she writes: "Sunday evening. Have been working all day...Sunday has made me feel quite desperate. It seems so silly we should both be lonely and I want to discuss your plans with you so I propose to...come over to Lausanne on Wednesday or Thursday evening...so that we can dine together."[63]

* * *

With France's capitulation, Switzerland was completely surrounded by hostile territory; there was no safe way out. Having recovered her health, Wiskemann traveled constantly to broaden her network of intelligence sources, and her superiors in London were clearly pleased with the results. She moved quickly, for example, to establish relations with anti-Pétainiste sources at the French Embassy in Bern. A good friend from pre-war days in London, Roland de Margerie, provided letters of introduction to several new contacts. Through the Oprecht circle she also got to know novelist and playwright Joseph Breitbach; he was, she wrote, "in effect my French opposite number," and he put her in touch with René Janin, the son of a general who was a great friend of Pétain. René provided her with an entrée into banking and business circles in Zurich; he was at the time acting as a voluntary assistant to the French financial attaché in Bern, Marcel Vaidie. Tall, handsome, intelligent, "infiniment cultivé," and unspoilt by his wealth, Janin was, she told Emmie Oprecht, "My only consolation in Bern" "the only person...with whom I feel I have true friendship." He also "seemed too good to be true," she later recalled, "until the effeminacy shone through him." Increasingly alienated by Pétain's regime and unable to reconcile his own politics and his family's connections to Vichy, he emigrated to Brazil at the end of 1940.[64] Vaidie was very different—a career functionary of the French Ministry of Finance, he had worked in several European capitals, including Berlin. He was, Wiskemann wrote, "at first sight an unprepossessing little man but something between a hero and a saint, also witty and generally amusing." Vehemently anti-Nazi and pro-British, he was outraged when a dispatch from Vichy ordered him to fire his Jewish secretary. He refused and soon after they were both dismissed. When his successor arrived in Bern and sought advice on how to hire a competent secretary, Vaidie strongly recommended his own (omitting that she was a Jew). She was re-engaged; nobody gave her away and she continued working at the embassy for the duration of the war. Vaidie had also received funds, probably from British sources, to start a Gaullist center in Bern, and his former secretary kept him (and Wiskemann) well supplied with secret information.[65]

Wiskemann already had an extensive network of friends and informants from her pre-war travels and she was adept at making new contacts; also, a good many people she had known in Germany, Eastern Europe, and France now lived as exiles in Switzerland. Her official activities and her friendships were often scarcely distinguishable. For example, quick notes to her friend Emmie Oprecht in Zurich which arranged visits or planned the details of getting her hair cut or her clothes retailored (she was losing weight) were sprinkled with comments about appointments with Silone or Breitbach or Caratsch, the correspondent of the *Neue Zürcher Zeitung* who had just been expelled from Berlin.

She renewed her acquaintance with Sean Lester and his successor as High Commissioner in Danzig, Carl J. Burckhardt, enjoying their hospitality in Geneva but also pumping them for information and valuable contacts. The two men were very different. Lester was "blunt, modest, insular with few social graces," while Burckhardt was a mandarin type, a polished diplomat and cosmopolitan professor.[66] After Danzig, Lester had become Deputy to the League of Nations' Secretary-General, Joseph Avenol. And by the summer of 1940 he was engaged in a bitter conflict with his boss, who anticipated a German-dominated Europe and wished to liquidate as much of the League as possible, gain control of its capital assets, and then turn the rest into a pro-Axis organization. Lester played a heroic role, managing to outmaneuver and replace Avenol, keeping the League's offices running and thereby providing some continuity in 1945 between it and the post-war United Nations.[67] After one visit, she wrote: "I hasten to return what has become something like the elixir of life! (soap!). Seeing you and the Hills* did me lots of good, I feel immensely more cheerful in consequence. I'm afraid I was so happy to be with people with my own attitude to life that I made a great deal of noise. By the way my men friends long ago accustomed me to every kind of story … Thank you again and every good wish for your work and your pleasure."[68]

She had known Burckhardt since 1936 when the Swiss Ambassador to London had urged him to meet her—describing her as an "intelligent, personable journalist of value … [who] appears to belong to radical socialist circles."[69] After Danzig he had resumed his post as professor in Geneva and also played a leading role on the board of the International Red Cross.[70] He was deeply anti-communist, which lay behind his efforts to broker some accommodation with the Nazis while High Commissioner in Danzig and later his willingness to act as a conduit for peace feelers in 1939–40; these actions made many British officials suspicious of him, and Whitehall was also critical of his insistence that the Red Cross must be absolutely neutral.[71] For Wiskemann, however, he was a valuable source of information and contacts, and when he was criticized in the New York *Herald Tribune*, she reciprocated by writing to Irita van Doren, the editor, in his support. Through the Red Cross, Burckhardt was able to help her locate and send money to two Jewish friends, the Podachs, who had been interned in France but had not been heard from since the German occupation: "they are very scrupulous people and

* Friends of Lester. William Hill was on the staff of the League's Economic, Financial, and Transit section.

their silence scares me... If I could find them I would send them money (through the Red Cross) at once."[72] She also got him to obtain details about the fate of Captain Michael Fleming, who had been injured in Belgium and died in hospital of his wounds.[73]

In May 1940 some Whitehall officials believed the days of Swiss independence were numbered, but by August the invasion threat had receded and they again stressed Switzerland's potential as a "listening post" for Axis Europe. But Wiskemann's personal situation in the legation remained difficult. Doubtless her lack of official status, the vagueness of her instructions from London, and her rather brash, undeferential demeanor all contributed; but Whitehall's continuing internecine struggle for control over intelligence was also working its way through the bureaucracy and had its counterpart locally for agents in the field. Upon becoming Prime Minister, Churchill reorganized the different intelligence organizations that had proliferated since the war's outbreak, unifying propaganda and political warfare, including guerrilla warfare tactics and sabotage, under the Special Operations Executive [SOE], with Hugh Dalton at the Ministry of Economic Warfare as a single directing authority. This consolidation was a failure. Churchill may have wanted, in his famous phrase, to "set Europe ablaze" but he succeeded in setting Whitehall ablaze and Dalton soon found himself engaged in almost continuous inter-departmental wrangling with the Ministry of Information and the Foreign Office,[74] forcing another major reorganization in the summer of 1941.

Several British intelligence organizations were active in Switzerland: Claude Dansey's MI6 agents (with Frederick 'Fanny' Vanden Heuvel as station chief in Geneva) were busy collecting a variety of economic and military intelligence; the War Office's department MI9 was tasked with aiding British troops and POWs seeking to evade or escape capture—although their numbers were very small until 1943. SOE, the direct action and sabotage organization, was also developing a plan for the sabotage of Swiss transalpine rail traffic in the winter of 1940–41—it never came off and would have had disastrous consequences had it been implemented. Indeed, the Chiefs of Staff directed in November 1940 that SOE was forbidden to launch any clandestine operation that might jeopardize Anglo-Swiss relations. At the legation in Bern, Sir David Kelly was highly sensitive to any actions that might provoke retaliation from the Swiss authorities. Its activities hamstrung, SOE in Switzerland turned increasingly to the goal of gathering social, political, and military intelligence for use in British propaganda and as a basis for policymaking at a later stage of the war. For military intelligence, London also relied upon the Military Attaché, Colonel Cartwright, but he was basically unsuited to his job and so cautious that he did little to construct viable intelligence networks. The output of his office was meager and as late as 1942 the War Office still described his reports as "mostly rubbish."[75] Finally, there was Wiskemann, acting on her own to gather intelligence useful for political, psychological, and propaganda purposes. She was both helped and hindered by continuing tensions. It meant that she had a real opportunity to spread her net wide and develop many kinds of sources; it also made it likely that she would bruise egos and face opposition from rival agencies.

By the end of 1940, despite positive feedback from London about the information she was sending,[76] Wiskemann was becoming increasingly dissatisfied by the vagueness of her instructions and the ambiguity of her status. She also felt increasingly vulnerable as a private citizen with no official diplomatic status, and though she raised the issue in May 1940, nothing had been done. Not far from the British Embassy was its German counterpart, and she was shadowed and watched.[77] Moreover, the Swiss security services had begun to clamp down harder on foreigners in the country. Previously it had been relatively easy to dispatch information via a courier service through France, now everything had to be transmitted by safe telegrams or via the diplomatic bags of friendly neutral nations. Getting her information to London required arguing its priority with other officials at the legation, and she continued to meet resistance within her own legation. To 'Rex' Leeper she complained, "how demoralizing it was not knowing for whom I was working, what was wanted or whether what I sent ever reached anyone. When a supercilious 3rd Secretary told me my organization had probably ceased to exist and virtually refused to send telegrams which would have been important for me, I was helpless, and it seemed best to do a job at home."[78] Her closest ally was 'Boofy' Gore, but she confessed to Harry Bergholz: "It is worse than usual in Bern just at present because my only real friend there is away. Also, I'm frightened he won't stay."[79] She was also homesick for London, now experiencing heavy German air raids. To Emmie Oprecht she admitted: "On Monday evening I was so depressed that I said to myself the war of nerves was winning and I must not permit that. I had just received news direct from London from a Pole, quite cheerful, but the longing to be there was overpowering."[80]

Hearing it might be possible to cross southern France by rail and return home through Spain and Portugal, Wiskemann decided to make this extremely risky journey.[81] Immediately before she left, Hitler's forces smashed through Yugoslavia and began their assault on Greece; within ten days the swastika flag was flying over the Acropolis in Athens. "The war," Wiskemann wrote, "seemed like a 'thirty years' war to me that summer."[82] She managed to get a travel permit from the French Embassy in Bern and set off by train from Geneva across Vichy France on April 18, 1941. Two days later she was in Barcelona and from there went to Madrid where, as she put it, the British embassy "guarded me like a hostage though very kindly." Her next destination was Lisbon, where, like many other people, she was marooned for almost three weeks waiting for a plane.[83] Malcolm Muggeridge, another visitor to the city, remembered: "Lisbon with all its lights, seemed after two years of blackout like a celestial vision...I just wandered about the streets marveling at the shops, the restaurants...the smart women and cafés sprawling over the pavements."[84] Here she could swim in the sea, meals with fish and fruit were again plentiful, and two old friends were on hand to show her around "this exquisite rococo city": 'Boofy' Gore, now attached to the Lisbon embassy, and David Scott (with whom she had toured the Saar in 1935), formerly with the *Times* in Paris and now a correspondent for the *News Chronicle*.[85]

But she was also frustrated by the delays, writing to Bergholz: "I wonder more and more why I left Switzerland...I look back with *tendresse* upon all the time in Switzerland."[86] And to Emmie Oprecht: "I always felt, as you know, very unsure about whether I should stay with you and now I am continually wondering if I made the wrong choice."[87] Lisbon, awash with foreign agents and 'cloak and dagger' stories, was a bottleneck with large numbers of refugees waiting anxiously to escape the Continent by boat or plane.[88] On aircraft to England, high-ranking officers got precedence. But Wiskemann was more fortunate than most, despite her low rank. Colonel Dansey, SOE's Director of Operations, had given instructions that he wanted to see her as soon as she got to London,[89] while Walter Adams, another high-ranking intelligence official, wrote to Brigadier Dallas Brooks of MOI, saying that they needed her services at GHQ Central European section and her return should be facilitated.[90] She flew to Bristol and finally reached London on May 14. There she saw the ruins left by months of German bombing; in fact, only four days before she arrived some 3,000 people had been killed and injured in a devastating raid; the Law Courts, the Tower, and the Mint were hit. Marylebone was the only main line station to remain open; Westminster Hall was set on fire and the House of Commons gutted.[91]

Delighted to be back in London, she spent the first couple of weeks looking up old friends, many now dispersed by the raids into makeshift quarters, and delivering messages from those she knew in Switzerland. To Bergholz, she wrote: "I have been in England for 16 days now and rushed off my feet (messages have really been a great burden in addition to everything else (...) I wrote you a card and a letter from Lisbon and I'd be interested to know whether they reached you as I think the hotel porter stole all my letters...confound him. London is delicious, if gashed. My flat is all right so far. I work partly in the country at present. Have seen lots of people, and am, for the moment, popular and interesting. But that could hardly last. Not very much else that I can write. Do hope you're all right. Remember September. Love"[92] As this letter indicated, she quickly reported to her superiors at the Foreign Office's Political Intelligence Department, which had moved to "The Country," as it was called—in fact, Woburn Abbey, the seat of the Duke of Bedford. Over the next months, while awaiting a decision about her future, she saw Jan Masaryk several times and made contact with Yugoslav and Polish groups now exiled in London; she was also invited by General Sikorski, whom she had visited in 1937 when he was under house arrest in Warsaw, to spend a few days at the Polish armed forces headquarters at Fife in Scotland.[93]

While at Woburn she stayed with the Gaitskells, who were living nearby. Hugh had become *Chef de Cabinet*[94] of Hugh Dalton, the Minister of Economic Warfare and head of SOE, and he was now deeply involved in negotiations over the organization's future. Wiskemann's return to England coincided with a major reorganization of the intelligence agencies. After months of competitive struggle between different ministries, the bureaucratic infighting over SOE came to a head. As indicated above, from its creation a year earlier, SOE had never been a truly unitary organization. There was always competition between those sections concerned with direct operations, sabotage, and subversion, and those engaged in propaganda and political or psychological warfare. MI6, the Foreign Office, and the Ministry of Information all viewed SOE as something of an interloper, trespassing on their spheres of control.

Sharp conflict centered on the administration of propaganda, and in the end Eden at the Foreign Office and Brendan Bracken, now in charge of MOI came away successful. Dalton was forced to agree to the removal of propaganda from under SOE's umbrella and the creation of a new separate Political Warfare Executive [PWE] under the direction of 'Rex' Leeper. Friction continued at least until a government reshuffle which sent Dalton to the Board of Trade, but less than before.[95] Although Gaitskell was at the center of the discussions, it is unclear how much Wiskemann knew about them. Her future seemed somewhat uncertain, although she had known Leeper for several years and he valued her work. Kelly, the ambassador in Bern, had also made it known that her network of informants was of great importance, including close contact with the Swiss Social Democrats (through their leader, Hans Oprecht, Emil's brother), which, he admitted, neither the minister nor ordinary diplomatic personnel could "get away with" without "compromising the Legation"—so ingrained were anti-socialist prejudices in Swiss government and business circles.[96]

By July Wiskemann was eager to return to Bern. The decision to travel to London had been entirely her own and she was "always rather sensitive to the suggestion that it was frivolous to have come home and then wished to go back."[97] But she had originally been sent off for a few months; that had turned into a year and nothing had been done to clarify her role and status. "You cannot imagine," she told Leeper, "what a difference it will have made to me to have come back to the new Churchill England and to know what I'm trying to do...Now if I go back, all that [i.e. her role] should be in order and I do know that the efforts I make in Switzerland are probably the best I can make."[98] She was instructed to gather all possible non-military intelligence about enemy and enemy-occupied Europe. She would be under Kelly's authority with full rights to send out information by telegraph and she would do only a minimal amount of work for the embassy's press bureau to justify her cover to the Swiss authorities. "I am certain," she wrote, "that I ought to be able to do better than before...though I've sometimes wondered how I can possibly do everything that people at GHQ have asked for."[99] However,

Sir Charles Hambro, deputy leader of SOE, tried to prevent her return, believing that his organization should control agents in the field. Leeper refused to give way, replying that she would be working for PWE and would have no role in operations or military intelligence.[100]

Wiskemann also indicated that she did not wish to return to Bern without full diplomatic rank, which would both strengthen her position at the legation and provide some protection from interference by the Swiss police. This was no small request. Whereas the Home Civil Service had been open to women since 1919, the Foreign Service resolutely excluded them until 1946. Feminists in the 1930s had attached great significance to overturning the ban but to no avail. In the war years women were hired for administrative work in London, but only on a temporary basis, and the three women on overseas duty, mentioned by Helen McCarthy in her recent study of female diplomats—Freya Stark in Baghdad, Nancy Lambton in Tehran, and Wiskemann—all occupied very ambiguous positions.[101] With good reason, then, Wiskemann was unsure the Foreign Office would bow to her demand; indeed, she even began to sound out other possible jobs at home, including one at the Ministry of Information.[102] But her superiors at PWE had a high regard for her work and her future potential. Moreover, Hitler's invasion of the Soviet Union in June 1941 had transformed the nature of the war. They expected correctly that Switzerland would become even more important as a hub of foreign intelligence, while Wiskemann's detailed knowledge of Eastern European history and politics would make her still more effective as an agent. In the end, then, her terms were met and she returned to Bern with diplomatic rank, only the second woman, she believed, to be accorded this status.[103]

However, London could only arrange her return journey as far as Lisbon; the rest had to be organized from there and she feared being stranded again for several weeks. Once again, weeks dragged by as her trip was being organized. Understandably, she had some fears. In early September 1941 she admitted to Leeper: "I'm afraid that by now the Vichy visa may be hard to get. I rather dread about what may happen to one there anyway, but if papers are in order and I have official backing from my own authorities it must be faced."[104] On the advice of a friend, she approached the French Consul-General in London, a staunch Gaullist who had stayed at his post under Vichy, and who was willing to issue her a transit visa across Vichy France if she dared use it.[105] Armed with the visa and a simple notation in her passport—"Se rend a son poste à la Legation brittanique à Berne"—she flew to Lisbon on September 30, 1941. From there she traveled across Spain and then across southern France to Geneva, accompanied by an American diplomatic courier, Raymond G. Leddy; the US was still neutral and his presence was probably helpful with the Vichy authorities at the Swiss border.[106] They passed across the border safely and arrived on October 7, 1941. Wiskemann had been away almost six months.[107] A couple of weeks later she wrote jubilantly to Lieutenant-Colonel Sutton, PWE's Regional Director responsible for France: "Here I am with full diplomatic status to the horror of that part of the Legation which is only interested in keeping the rules!"[108] "Now my war work began in earnest," she later recalled.

*   *   *

The military situation had changed dramatically since Wiskemann was last in Bern. Hitler's armies were now driving towards Leningrad, Moscow, and Kiev and within two months Pearl Harbor would bring Japan and the United States into the war. As the vast conflict in the East unfolded, including Nazi plans for racial genocide, Switzerland's significance as a 'window' on Axis Europe increased. In the next two years the flow of secret information rose sharply and with it pressure upon Wiskemann to deliver new intelligence. Her return to England had helped clarify her status within the Bern legation and she tried to steer clear of areas guaranteed to raise the hackles of her SOE and MI6 colleagues, but friction occurred because of her broad remit—to gather non-military information for use by several agencies both for propaganda and for straight factual intelligence. The definition of military and non-military intelligence was sometimes hazy. Morale among German soldiers, for example, or certain data about the production of military supplies fit both definitions. One fairly important Swiss intelligence officer had difficulty grasping the distinction when on several occasions he passed intelligence to Wiskemann and was told that the information had nothing to do with her.[109]

Wiskemann's reports covered social and economic conditions in Axis Europe, political developments, signs of resistance and partisan activity, trends in popular opinion and morale, gossip about Nazi and Fascist elites, foreign labor, and evidence of policy changes. The broad range required that she have a large and diverse group of contacts. She read and reported on Swiss and German press stories, both for information that might be helpful for British propaganda and to justify her 'cover' at the legation. The work also involved a lot of translation, transcribing, composing, and (in an era before copy machines and scanners) re-typing reports for London. Prior to November 1942, when the Germans occupied the southern Vichy portion of France, longer reports could be dispatched to London via friendly diplomatic couriers, mostly representatives of South American states, although often this involved delays. Subsequently the Legation relied upon coded telegrams which required condensation and careful drafting to capture the nuances; here too there were often delays in getting messages through as well as competition within the Legation over the use of the telegraph. Of course, phone conversations everywhere had to be coded or disguised, although when Allen Dulles arrived in Bern he made use of a scrambler device. Her days were often long and tiring: hurried notes to friends and acquaintances, many of them containing only hasty travel details, show her in constant motion between Bern, Zurich, Geneva, Basle, and Lausanne, questioning old sources, acquiring new ones, and checking the reliability of what she learned:

The convenient trains – this was characteristically Swiss – left Berne soon after 6am and I got into the way of waking at 5am in case I had to catch one. Then off to Geneva or Lugano and a long talk over lunch; then if the news seemed urgent – and there was seldom any time to be lost – I returned to Berne, plodded up to the Legation, which was a long way from the station, wrote out my telegram and handed it to the cypher clerks. Then I got home perhaps about 8pm, had some food and fell into bed about 9 o'clock, after 16 fairly strenuous hours. In the trains I read all the non-confidential stuff that I had to read and on my return journeys I often made notes on the conversation I had just had, inconspicuously preparing my telegram. Perhaps only two days a week were like this, but often there were more, and I had to be prepared.[110]

As Wiskemann expanded both her network of regular informants and the countries about which she was reporting, London recognized that she desperately needed an assistant. It was no easy task to find someone already in Switzerland who could get security clearance and who had knowledge of European societies and politics. But Wiskemann was fortunate in gaining as a part-time assistant Elizabeth Scott-Montagu, who had escaped to Switzerland after the defeat of France. The rebellious daughter of Lord John Montagu of Beaulieu, Scott-Montagu belonged to the patrician aristocracy, owners of large landed estates and palatial homes (albeit financially more constrained in the post-1918 era of higher taxes and death duties). She had traveled widely, went to finishing school in Lausanne, was presented at Court, and endured London's debutante season in 1928, although she "disliked all the society rigmarole."[111] She was bored and frustrated by the round of hunt balls and dreary house parties, preferring literary and artistic circles. In the 1930s, after her father's death when she was twenty, she studied acting at the Royal Academy of Dramatic Art (along with Vivien Leigh) and performed in several plays; she also trained for a time as a classical pianist in Switzerland and in 1937–38 worked as Toscanini's personal assistant during his trips to conduct the London Music Festival. She was also hired by F.A. Voigt to write for *The Nineteenth Century*, and Geoffrey Dawson even offered her a temporary position at the *Times*. However, when war was declared she abandoned journalism and joined a volunteer ambulance unit which was sent to France. When French and British forces were overrun in June 1940, her transport unit moved south to Bordeaux and returned to England. But Scott-Montagu, hoping that allied forces would rally, made a last-minute choice to stay and was soon forced to make her own way out of France, traveling first to Nice, where she found departure by boat impossible, and then north, eventually crossing the Swiss border to Geneva in September 1940. She had spent three months in hiding, helped by friends, including the former Swiss Ambassador to London. From pre-war visits, she already knew many people in Switzerland, including Emil and Emmie Oprecht, and it was in their Zurich flat that she first met Wiskemann, her future boss. Like many others, she had to wait for a *permis de séjour* from the authorities, but in early 1941 a letter arrived offering her a part-time job at the British Legation in Bern.[112]

For the legation, Elizabeth Scott-Montagu was an ideal candidate. She was intelligent and courageous, spoke French, German, and Italian fluently, and was not a security risk; her involvement in the theatre was a useful cover and she already had a wide range of social contacts in Switzerland and outside. Oddly enough, despite their age difference (Scott-Montagu was ten years younger) and very different backgrounds, the two women had a number of friends and acquaintances in common. These included journalists Alexander Werth, Shiela Grant Duff, F.A. Voigt (who had proposed marriage to Scott-Montagu on the eve of war), and the diplomat Roland de Margerie, whom Wiskemann had known in pre-war London and who was Scott-Montagu's lover on and off for much of the 1930s.[113] Scott-Montagu lived half the week in the Thurgau countryside and half in Bern, where she either stayed at the YWCA or at Wiskemann's flat on the outskirts of town. Of Wiskemann, she recalled: "She was a generous hostess, and after one of her excellent meals, we would forget the war and talk books. She also loved chatting about men and her ex-lovers, transforming herself into an extremely sexy, almost nymphomaniac character."[114] They got along well and shared a love of music and the theatre. Each had lost her mother in the influenza pandemic of 1918—in Scott-Montagu's case, when she was only nine. And they both enjoyed poking fun at the stuffed shirts among the legation staff, although Scott-Montagu soon found that one of her duties was to assuage the feelings of those "at the receiving end of her [EW's] cutting sarcastic wit."[115] Wiskemann's reports to London, Scott-Montagu wrote later, "were remarkable...and I soon came to appreciate the value of what she was doing."[116] Much of her own work involved translating documents and reading the foreign press, but some of the missions entrusted to her required Le Carré-style tradecraft:

> There was one particularly important contact [Fritz Kramer who worked at the German Embassy, see p. 108] who endangered his life each time he passed a report to us. Every detail that concerned him had to be treated as top secret...To do this I had to learn the basic rituals of espionage, including the use of dead letter boxes, where secret messages could be dropped and picked up. Most importantly I was taught how to avoid being followed: this could involve complicated, circuitous journeys around the city which were always very time-consuming. For instance, I would first take a taxi, then unexpectedly pay it off and jump onto a tram, sometimes repeating this operation several times if I were suspicious. To be absolutely certain I was not being tailed, I would then complete the journey on foot. It was certainly good exercise and occasionally good fun too.[117]

Before long, Jock McCaffery, head of SOE in Bern, tried to recruit Scott-Montagu to join his organization. With Switzerland cut off, he found it difficult to get agents past the vigilant Swiss and proposed that she might make contact with partisans in Chiasso, the border town with Italy. She consulted Silone, who was appalled by the scheme, recognizing that her typical English looks would endanger her and anyone she contacted. Scott-Montagu refused while wondering about her motives: "Was it loyalty to Elizabeth...my unsuitability for the job or perhaps just fear?"[118] If she knew, Wiskemann must have been furious at McCaffery's poaching.

The skills that Wiskemann had honed as a journalist translated well into covert activity, and London quickly grew to value her reports. She was a prodigious worker, a skilled networker, a good listener and interviewer, and was experienced at analyzing and synthesizing information from multiple sources. People also trusted her and were willing to share their contacts. From the second half of 1941, Bletchley Park's cryptanalysts were highly successful in reading a growing volume of diplomatic reports sent by Swiss officials working abroad and by foreign diplomats operating in Bern. But this did not diminish the importance of 'human intelligence,' which, though it could be used to validate or corroborate some of Bletchley's results, often covered whole areas and specific issues unlikely to figure into military, economic, and diplomatic signal traffic.

Because of postwar "weeding" and destruction of intelligence files, only a fraction of Wiskemann's telegrams and reports have survived; yet they illustrate the multiplicity of topics she covered.[119] In early 1942 alone, for example, she sent back lengthy reports on politics and social conditions in Romania, Croatia, Slovenia, and Germany, plus a study of foreign workers in the Reich and a detailed analysis by a leading trade union official of the morale of French industrial workers.[120] These accounts covered multiple topics: political parties, popular anxieties, attacks on Jews, oil production (in the case of Romania), and food and other shortages. Sometimes London had a specific request, asking, for example, about the contacts of the Soviet *Tass* correspondent in Geneva: "Moscow is putting out a good deal of information about the Balkans with a Geneva dateline and we are anxious to discover how much there is likely to be behind it."[121] In October 1942 the Foreign Office got wind of a Swiss medical mission to the eastern front and telegraphed Wiskemann to elicit information about shortages of medical supplies, the names of German doctors, sector casualty rates, and the diversion of wounded soldiers to occupied countries.[122] She replied that she had just forwarded a report put together by a well-known doctor (probably Raymond Gautier) who had interviewed members of the mission.[123] At other times, given growing difficulties with sending bulky documents home, it was Wiskemann who asked for instructions. Was PWE interested in copies of the reports being sent by allies like the Yugoslavs and Dutch back to their exiled governments?

Figure 3.2. "Elizabeth Scott-Montagu in 1928," by Bassano Ltd. National Portrait Gallery Co. Ltd.

[Answer, yes].[124] And, in February and March 1943, did London want "an eye-witness account of a hostage shooting scene at a French prison" or a long description of the clearing and destruction of the old port area of Marseilles, including German army deserters living there and the population's removal to a camp?[125] Illustrative of the information she was gathering about France was a resumé of a conversation she had with a man who had spent nineteen years as chief of commercial services to the French Ambassador in Berlin and was now head of an industrial enterprise in Paris. This account, organized in five sections, began with the man's recent experiences in Berlin and how German officials viewed France's postwar role. The second part focused on the morale of German forces in France; the third dealt with the material circumstances and morale of French civilians; then came a section about industry and the transport problems created by France's partition, and finally, a discussion of French political attitudes, growing criticism of Pétain, and the man's suspicion that Allied support for General Giraud (over De Gaulle) reflected the influence of American business interests.[126] Nazi atrocities towards Jews are repeatedly, if briefly, mentioned in Wiskemann's surviving telegrams and reports, although most of what she passed along no longer exists. She was also told specifically in April 1943 that such information had lower priority except where it might indicate a change in the regime's policy.[†]

London was eager to learn about the impact of Allied air raids, both their destructiveness and their psychological effect; housing, food, and fuel shortages; evidence of black-market trading; industrial accidents and signs of workers' fatigue; cases of sabotage and growing dissatisfaction in the labor force. In June 1942 typhus was spreading among Soviet foreign workers, and PWE began a propaganda campaign to intensify the German public's anxiety about diphtheria, tuberculosis, typhus, and scarlet fever. Wiskemann's informants provided local details of the actual situation and feedback about whether the initiative was working. Her reports frequently mentioned the rapid increase of foreign forced workers in the Reich, their deplorable conditions, and the alarm they provoked—here her sources included Polish workers who escaped to Switzerland from farms near Lake Constance and reported that German villagers: "were defeatist and expressed longing for revenge on the Nazis; they were, of course, irritated by all kinds of requisitioning."[127] She was also encouraged to transmit gossip about elite party circles in Berlin: rumors about the sickness of party dignitaries, shifts in their relative power,[128] talk of sexual scandals and luxurious living[129]—anything, in short, that might be used for 'black propaganda' to feed popular resentment and undermine the regime's appeals for patriotic sacrifice.

Wiskemann had many regular informants, including journalists, bankers, diplomats, businessmen, intellectuals, and clerics. Many moved regularly across the Swiss–German and Swiss–French borders and could bring back detailed accounts of what they saw and heard. Most were located in Geneva, Zurich, Basle, and her home base, Bern, and her days were spent commuting between them. In Geneva she had excellent contacts, some from her pre-war visits. Aside from Sean Lester and Carl Jacob Burckhardt at the International Red Cross, they included officials from agencies of the League and other international organizations. Raymond Gautier, from an old Genevese family, was head of the Health Section of the League (later the World Health Organization); he had access to valuable information from doctors of several nationalities, which he passed on to her.[130] Several officials, like Greek diplomat Thanassis Aghnides and the Czech Jaromir Kopecky, were delegates who found ways to stay on after their nations were conquered. A former Slovenian representative to the League retained reliable contacts in Ljubljana after the Italians occupied it in spring 1941, while Yugoslav exiles in London alerted her to several people, including a young Croat, previously part of the Yugoslav delegation, who was well-informed about northern Italy as well as the Balkans. Another occasional source was Romania's former Foreign Minister

---

† Her comments about Jews, genocide, and German and Italian resistance movements are examined in chapter 4.

and Ambassador to the Soviet Union, Grigore Gafencu, who arrived in Geneva in late 1941 and worked with *Journal de Genève*, which had excellent press contacts all over Europe. She also profited from the insights of exiled economist Wilhelm Röpke, who taught at the Rappard Graduate Institute of International Studies, while William Rappard himself was always ready to meet and talk.

Just outside Geneva, she sometimes stayed with a Hungarian couple, Szever and Emmy de Charmant, to whom journalist Paul Ignotus had introduced her. Emmy came from the Jewish Hatvany-Deutsch family, which had vast banking, insurance, and industrial holdings in Hungary, including a virtual monopoly of sugar exports. Szever was a Catholic royalist and very well-informed about Horthy's Hungary, if one discounted his biases.[131] Pierre Dubois (head of the Swiss watch company Pierre DeRoche), was another frequent contact with close ties to the French resistance, and it was in Geneva that Wiskemann met with Odette, the wife of René Massigli, De Gaulle's leading expert on foreign affairs in London, as well as the circle around Léon Blum's daughter-in-law, who came from a Genevan-Jewish family.[132] Renée Blum's husband, Robert, was in a German prisoner-of-war camp, while Léon Blum, whom she visited regularly, was incarcerated at Bourrasol for many months awaiting his trial at Riom. Finally, Dutch theologian W.A. Visser 't Hooft's apartment in Geneva was a meeting place for those seeking information about the anti-Nazi resistance. As General Secretary of the World Council of Churches [WCC][133] Visser 't Hooft was well well-informed about Protestant opposition groups and conditions in Germany and had close ties to the Dutch and French resistance.[134] Visser 't Hooft also organized the "Swiss Road," a secret network connecting Switzerland, resistance in the Netherlands, and the Dutch exile government in London. A highly success-ful courier system was developed dispatching documents and microfilms to Holland and London. At one point in 1943, clearly having difficulties in transmit-ting information via her own legation, Wiskemann sought his help. He asked whether the famous British secret service could not take care of it; laughing, she replied "that the service was so secret that she had no contact with it."[135]

Through Visser 't Hooft, Wiskemann also met two German pastors: Dr. Hans Schoenfeld and Adolf Freudenberg. Schoenfeld [Q4 in London's documents], a staff member of the WCC, traveled widely in Germany, Sweden, and Holland on behalf of prisoners of war; this gave him access to a wide range of useful intelli-gence. He was also trusted by Ernst von Weizsäcker, State Secretary in the Foreign Office in Berlin, and had access to the German diplomatic bag, smuggling infor-mation to Geneva and also to Holland. Pastor Freudenberg had worked for the German foreign service until 1934, when he was dismissed because of his wife's Jewish ancestry. He then studied theology, joined the Confessing Church, and became a pastor in London for a while, and then moved to Geneva to become head of the WCC Secretariat concerned with refugee relief, funding rescue oper-ations for Jews and others from Germany and southern France into Switzerland.

He was a close friend of both Dietrich Bonhoeffer and Bishop Bell of Chichester, the Confessing Church's most important ally in Britain. In addition, shortly after returning to Switzerland in October 1941, Wiskemann was introduced to the theologian Karl Barth. Having resigned his professorship in Bonn in 1935 after refusing to swear allegiance to Hitler, he was living and teaching in Basle. "I thought him admirable," she wrote, "keen, alert, upright, someone who always hit the nail on the head."[136] He was in direct contact with members of the Confessing Church in Germany and used her to send information from these sources to Bishop Bell.

In Zurich, as we have seen, Wiskemann forged close ties to the anti-fascist circles around Emil and Emmie Oprecht and their bookstore. As leading figures in the Zurich *Schauspielhaus*, they also brought Wiskemann into contact with visiting theatre troupes from Berlin, Munich, and Vienna, many of them anti-Nazi and willing to provide information about politics and social conditions in Germany.[137] Emil's brother Hans was the leader of the Social Democrats, the largest party in the Swiss lower house, although it still had no representation on the conservative Federal Council.[138] He was a conduit for information about clandestine Social Democratic groups and trade unionists throughout occupied Europe, while his close friend Walther Bringolf, the socialist mayor of Schaffhausen, was also a mine of information about neighboring Baden-Württemberg and Bavaria. These personal ties were particularly welcome to Ambassador Kelly since Bern's sensitivity to any kind of left-wing politics meant that it was only through Wiskemann's unofficial contacts that he could maintain any links to this important political group.[139] Wiskemann also cultivated close relationships with Swiss and foreign journalists in several cities, but her most important contacts were at the offices of the *Neue Zürcher Zeitung*, including its editor, Willy Bretscher, its foreign editor, Albert Müller,[140] and the paper's Berlin correspondents: Reto Caratsch, who reported from the German capital throughout the 1930s until 1940 and was then posted to Rome, and his successor, Eduard Geilinger.[141] They were among the most astute observers of developments within Axis Europe and were happy to keep her well-informed.

London officials were very interested in economic news, and Wiskemann's banking contacts in Basle were particularly helpful. They included Swedish banker Per Jacobsson, Economic Advisor to the Bank for International Settlements, whom she saw regularly when she visited the town.[142] From another banker she learned of the Nazi euthanasia program in February 1941.[143] She also saw several Swiss and German businessmen in Basle who regularly traveled to Axis territory and could report on conditions in Hungary, Czechoslovakia, and Yugoslavia, as well as Germany. One of these introduced Wiskemann to a man identified simply as Y in her memoir, who became a most important source of economic and other information. Y's wife was Jewish and for that reason they lived in Basle but, as a director of the huge chemical firm Hoffmann La Roche, he traveled to Germany frequently and was closely linked to the liberal German industrialist Robert Bosch, who lived just across the German frontier, in Stuttgart.[144] The Bosch firm made armaments and used forced laborers, as did Hoffmann La Roche, which operated factories in Germany and Poland. Y also turned out to be close to Wiskemann's old Berlin friend Albrecht Bernstorff. She had to be very careful to protect this source, and their meetings were usually at night in his house, close to the border. Sometimes these encounters were nerve-racking; more than once she missed the last train back and had to walk about four miles along a snowy road which ran close to the frontier. Scared of losing her way and encountering a German border guard, she walked doggedly along the tram-lines although theirs was not the most direct route.[145] Walter Laqueur and Richard Breitman have suggested that Y may have been Georg Ernst Veiel, a director of Hoffmann La Roche, and that he could have informed her of plans for the 'Final Solution.' But Wiskemann never disclosed his identity, and she may, like Allen Dulles, have been in contact with the German industrialist Edward Schulte, who was one of the first to warn the Allies of the Holocaust. For sure she also relied on another informant connected to Hoffmann La Roche: the distinguished engineer Waldemar Hellmich (codename Q2 in Whitehall), who in 1933 took over the leadership of the firm in Lörrach, South Baden. He came to Switzerland frequently and was particularly helpful, since he talked to many people and could report on material conditions, morale, and class relations in cities like Stuttgart, Cologne, and Tübingen that he visited frequently.[146]

Bern, Wiskemann's home base, was a less fruitful terrain for her intelligence gathering, partly, perhaps, because of rival agents within the legation.[147] She worked closely, of course, with Vaidie,[148] from whom she learned a lot about Vichy and occupied France, as well as the situation within the French Embassy in Bern. She also became reacquainted with "a good pal of mine," Charles de Jenner, who had been a Swiss councilor in London for many years before the war. Returning home in July 1943, he became employed "at the Political Department [and] gives (or not) all visas asked for by foreigners"; he passed along information about who was entering the country.[149] Another interesting source was a young Montenegrin communist, ostensibly studying theology in Bern, who brought her family letters describing outrages committed against Serbs by the Ustase and Mihailović's Chetniks. In general, Wiskemann supplied Whitehall with some of its best early intelligence on the partisan struggle in Yugoslavia, warning that Mihailović had long ago come to terms with Pavelic, Nedić, and the Italian occu-piers and that true partisans—by no means all communists—were joining Tito, seeing that as the only true course for patriots.[150]

Her most productive and continuous informant in Bern was a German Catholic journalist, Franz Albert Kramer. Shortly after settling there she was visited by the well-known Catholic historian and philosopher Karl Thieme (son of the Protestant theologian of the same name), whom she already knew. Thieme arranged to introduce her to Kramer (codename Q3 in Whitehall and referred to as X in her memoir), who had easy access to the German Legation in Bern and vouched for his genuine wish to work for the British. "I asked him," Wiskemann wrote, "whether he was clear about the risks he was taking, warned him that I could pay him nothing but promised him that I would be completely discreet."[151] Kramer had grown up in Münster, became a journalist, and spent two-year stints (1928–32) working for the Catholic *Germania* and the *Kölnische Zeitung*, first in Paris and then in London. In 1932 he traveled to the Soviet Union and wrote a book about his experiences, which was banned by the Gestapo. He was then hired as a correspondent in Rome for the *Vossische Zeitung* and later the *Berliner Tageblatt* and settled in Switzerland in 1935, where he got a job working for the press department of the German Legation in Bern. Deeply opposed to the Nazi regime, throughout the war years, at least every other week, he supplied Wiskemann with useful intelligence; he met visitors to the legation from Germany and Italy, attended social functions there, and the staff spoke unguardedly in front of him—at least until early 1944, when they began to suspect his reliability.[152]

* * *

The intelligence Wiskemann gathered found its way to several government agencies. Her basic function was to provide information that could be used for British propaganda, or what was referred to as political or psychological warfare. Some was used in BBC broadcasts, or what was known as 'white propaganda' this aimed to be as truthful as possible, building trust and depicting events accurately, albeit from an Allied perspective; it also made no secret of its British origin. She also supplied content for PWE's 'black propaganda' campaign, which expanded dramatically in the second half of the war. To be effective it had to be grounded in a detailed flow of information about conditions within enemy territory. 'Black' or 'subversive' propaganda purported to originate from clandestine resistance groups within Axis Europe; its purpose was to spread false information, erode enemy morale, and fuel suspicion, and ultimately to induce resistance. By 1943 the scale of this program was enormous, infiltrating millions of leaflets into occupied Europe (either dropped by RAF bombers or smuggled in through neutral states) and broadcasting from forty-eight so-called 'freedom stations', called RUs or Research Units, most of them beaming disinformation from the heart of southern England.[153] To have any chance of success, these activities depended upon a constant flow of detailed intelligence—both hard factual information and gossip, rumor and news of scandals, profiteering and corruption. Lastly, once the end of the war came in sight, Wiskemann's reports informed the planning and political assessments being made by PWE's regional directorates, especially those responsible for Italy and south-east Europe.

Working largely alone, except for at best part-time help, she ran a highly effective operation and her superiors in Whitehall were happy. "Not only," they noted, "is she ideally placed to reach the most influential persons connected with Vichy France in Switzerland, not only has she developed suitable channels to get material into occupied France, but we know that whenever she has received material, she has been able to dispatch it to Eastern and Central Europe as well."[154] Already in 1942 PWE's Italian directorate affirmed that "her contributions are among the most useful pieces of information we receive from secret sources and in view of the dearth of reliable intelligence about Italy, her work may be considered invaluable to the section."[155] Similarly, Elisabeth Barker, assistant director of the Balkan section of PWE, wrote: "In the first half of 1942 Miss Wiskemann's material on Yugoslavia was of great value to us since she gave us, through her Croat sources, some of the first indications of the extent and character of the partisan movement in northern Yugoslavia."[156]

Inevitably, perhaps, turf wars and infighting quickly emerged among PWE's departments and they were never fully resolved. Officials in MOI and at the BBC were intent upon protecting their independence and the BBC's credibility from efforts to distort the news for purposes of propaganda. Noel Newsome, Director of the European Service, had, in David Garnett's phrase, "an almost mystical belief" in straightforward news, good or bad, told simply with a punch."[157] This directly contradicted the views of Dalton, 'Rex' Leeper, Richard Crossman, and others who placed more emphasis upon subversive propaganda. Crossman's star was ascendant in 1941–42. At least in the early years of the war, he believed there were significant numbers of working-class anti-Nazis in Germany open to radical appeals. To reach this "alternate Reich," he established a secret station, Research Unit G2 [Sender der europäischen Revolution], which broadcast from November 1940 until June 1942. Staffed mostly by left-wing German refugees, it called for Hitler's overthrow and the establishment of a socialist federal Europe. Other, more conservative figures in PWE, including Leeper and Sir Robert Bruce Lockhart, had no patience with this approach, viewing it as a misguided exercise in political idealism, rooted in too positive a view of Germans, and incapable of damaging the Nazi war machine. Instead, they advocated a more robust, interventionist strategy of deception and lies, calculated to sow discord and subvert the enemy's will to fight. These methods found their chief advocate in Denis Sefton Delmer. Born and partly educated in Germany, he had become a successful journalist after Oxford, working first as Daily Express correspondent in Berlin—where his colleagues, including Wiskemann and Voigt, were suspicious of his friendly relations with Nazi leaders—and then in France and in Spain during its Civil War. While it was clear immediately that Crossman (the titular superior) and Delmer were incompatible in character and in their approach to propaganda, they managed to coexist, and it was only in spring 1943, after Crossman's posting to North Africa, that Delmer took complete charge of black propaganda. Under him, black stations, posing as the voice of dissident Germans, became much more strident, spreading scurrilous tales of Nazi leaders' corruption and immorality, using foulmouthed language and pornography as a bait for listeners. But as Delmer well understood, lies, rumors, and exaggerations were more believable when mixed in with the fruits of press stories and a kernel of hard intelligence.[158]

Intrigues and conflicts within PWE usually figure in historical accounts as a series of Whitehall power struggles. But in Wiskemann's telegrams and correspondence they surface from the perspective of an agent in the field, trying to satisfy a variety of sometimes contradictory claims. Because she delivered information on so many topics and regions, her reports were in demand by the BBC and several of the seven regional directorates of PWE. Matters were further complicated by the fact that—because her official title was Assistant Press Attaché—MOI paid her salary, although her real superiors were at PWE and the Foreign Office. Early in the war, for example, 'Rex' Leeper refused to share information about Wiskemann's activities with MOI. In late summer 1942 inter-agency dispute erupted again. Her reports were being sent to Frank Roberts at the Foreign Office and then on to sections of PWE, but MOI and the BBC insisted that they should see more of this material. At this the Foreign Office balked, arguing that it alone should monitor secret intelligence; there was certain information that must be retained for the FO's exclusive use, to which MOI should not have access.[159] In addition, Wiskemann had to cope with rival claims to her time: if she satisfied Foreign Office enquiries for information about northern Italy, she risked alienating Sefton Delmer, who was adamant that he needed more feedback on conditions in the Reich for black propaganda broadcasts.[160] No wonder she wrote to Colonel Kerr in Whitehall: "I need more instructions about black lists and white lists. Without assistance I cannot make more than sporadic attempts at such things."[161] As the next chapter shows, the last two years of the war, exciting though they were, saw a sharp increase in her workload, while she still faced intrigues and non-cooperation within the Bern legation. Colonel Cartwright, the Military Attaché, for example, complained to Bruce Lockhart, the Director-General of PWE, that Wiskemann was "no good – defeatist, hysterical, amateurish – too many agents."[162] Yet Cartwright was so cautious himself that he rebuffed arguably the most valuable German agent that Allen Dulles ever recruited, who first offered his services to the British Legation. In all this, two things brightened Wiskemann's situation: a growing friendship and collaboration with Allen Dulles, head of the OSS in Switzerland and—after German troops occupied Italy—the arrival of numerous Italian refugees, who were more exuberant and fun-loving than the Swiss, a breath of fresh air.

4

"Dear Mr. Dulles"

A Special Relationship

On Sunday November 8, 1942, Allen Dulles reached the French–Swiss frontier near Annemasse by train, the same day that the Allied 'Torch' landings—the first commitment of US ground forces to a non-Pacific battlefield—took place in North Africa. Although Pétain had ordered French forces to oppose the Allied invasion, he had refused a German directive to declare war on the Allies. All those holding British and American passports were being detained at the border, but after an hour's delay a friendly Vichy official motioned Dulles back onto the train. The following day German forces occupied southern France and the border was completely sealed. Initially, William Donovan, head of the newly created Office of Strategic Service [OSS], had wanted Dulles to work from London, but he insisted that he could be more effective in Switzerland where "I felt my past experience would serve me in good stead." His official title was Special Assistant to the US Minister in Bern, but the Swiss press soon described him as Roosevelt's 'personal representative,' and his true position, thinly disguised at best, was OSS station chief in the country.[1]

Dulles was no stranger to Bern. During the First World War he had worked as a political officer at the American Legation, where he had recruited Czech and Yugoslav dissidents for a spy network in Austria. His diplomatic career flourished: promoted to Second Secretary at the embassy at the age of twenty-five, he was assigned to the American delegation at the Paris peace conference, and by the early 1920s served in a variety of posts, including stints in Berlin and Constantinople. In 1926 he resigned from the Foreign Service, gained a law degree, and joined his brother, John Foster, at the New York law firm of Sullivan and Cromwell, where he was quickly promoted to partner. In the next decade he traveled frequently to Europe on behalf of the firm's corporate clients, meeting in the course of these journeys numerous European leaders, including Hitler and Mussolini. He also served as a legal advisor at arms limitation talks in Geneva. For years John Foster had done richly rewarding business in Berlin, steering investment to Germany regardless of political conditions. Allen was convinced by 1935 that Sullivan and Cromwell should get out of Nazi Germany and succeeded in having the firm's Berlin office closed despite his brother's strong objection. Contrary to John Foster, who was a staunch isolationist, Allen, like his Princeton friend Hamilton Fish Armstrong, became a strong advocate of American

Elizabeth Wiskemann: Scholar, Journalist, Secret Agent. Geoffrey Field, Oxford University Press.
© Geoffrey Field 2023. DOI: 10.1093/oso/9780192870629.003.0005

intervention in the European war.[2] In the period from June 1941 to June 1942 when the United States took steps to create a secret intelligence service, Dulles was perfectly qualified to assume a leading role.

By late 1942 Switzerland had become a vital gateway for intelligence about Axis Europe. Germany absorbed nearly a third of all Swiss exports, hundreds of German firms had subsidiaries there, and Swiss banks played a huge role in Nazi financial and currency operations. It was also a haven for rival espionage operations: the Nazi regime employed many agents in the country (over a hundred were prosecuted by the Swiss), the British were pushing to expand their intelligence gathering capabilities, the Soviet Union operated several highly successful spy rings, and the Swiss had built up their own very well-informed secret service. As Christof Mauch argues, the myth that Dulles "conjured up a network of agents out of thin air within a matter of weeks" is far from the truth,[3] for the groundwork had been laid by Leland Harrison, the US envoy in Bern. But Dulles had a solid network of former acquaintances in finance, business, and the law upon which to build, and very quickly after his arrival he began pulling together a team of helpers and informants. They included Gerald Mayer of the Office of War Information; the Standard oil executive Fred Loufbourow, tasked with locating synthetic gasoline production facilities; and Max Shoop, an old Sullivan and Cromwell colleague, responsible for coordinating with the French resistance.

Dulles also established contacts with his British SIS and SOE counterparts, and quickly made friends with Wiskemann, whom he had met before when she lectured in New York in 1938. They also had a number of mutual friends, especially John Wheeler-Bennett and Rebecca West.[4] For Wiskemann, Dulles's arrival was propitious, for she was once again feeling depressed, isolated, and beleaguered in her own legation. To their surprise and disappointment, Ambassador Kelly and his wife, with whom she had become friendly, were transferred to Buenos Aires in early 1942 and the new ambassador, Sir Clifford Norton, was less supportive. For much of the 1930s Norton had acted as private secretary to Sir Robert Vansittart; even more than Kelly, he was insistent that the activities of SOE and the other intelligence services should in no way jeopardize the good standing of the legation in Bern and thereby undermine cooperation with the Swiss. Wiskemann soon found that she did "not get anything like the support she got from Kelly,"[5] especially when it came to the turf wars that continued to undermine her efforts to do her job. She complained to Sir Bruce Lockhart (now head of PWE): "Briefly, the position is that the new Press Attaché [Evans] refuses in practice to accept me as Assistant Press Attaché. This is not only personally unpleasant but leaves me without the minimum cover which I need. If David Kelly were still here I do not think I should need to appeal to London, but the new Minister wishes me to do so because he says that my position has never been made clear to him."[6] She asked if Lockhart could do something, perhaps have a word with Brendan Bracken (Minister of Information), adding, "it would seem to me a pity to be defeated by what I can only interpret as a fresh outburst of misogyny."[7] A few days later, Michael Balfour, who distributed a good deal of Wiskemann's intelligence, commented that inter-agency tensions were unduly complicating her anomalous position: "Evans is extremely hostile and is trying to take over some of her work and dictate how she shall do the rest."[8] After some weeks, a memo from MOI acknowledged: "It appears that Evans…does not completely realise Miss Wiskemann's status"; he needed to be told that her title "does not mean that he has any lein on her service."[9]

In addition to Evans, she was also under pressure from those running the Low Countries Directorate in PWE, who complained that Wiskemann was relying too much on "a Belgian friend called Helène Hroys [sic!]" and they were "unfavorably impressed by the information quoted from that source."[10] Instead they praised the material provided by another source, Frank Saxe, "whom she dismisses as more or less useless."[11] There seems to have a been another objective of this lobbying for Wiskemann to hire Saxe, a former journalist and League of Nations official who was stranded with his family in Switzerland and was practically penniless; he was apparently the son of someone in the Low Countries Directorate. Wiskemann was sympathetic to his plight, pointing out that he was largely dependent on "the private charity of me and my friends," but he had no network of sources and lacked judgment: "His help can only be in Geneva and slight and, while he is in his present state of hectic anxiety (combined with naturally bad health) it is very difficult to know how reliable his stuff really is."[12] She probably felt that, while something ought to be done for Saxe, there were remedies other than attaching him to her staff. What seems apparent in both the Evans and Saxe cases is that Wiskemann was beginning to recognize that her telegrams and reports were valued by many of her superiors in Whitehall and this leverage strengthened her independence.*

With Dulles's arrival in Bern, Wiskemann's life there improved considerably. He was highly intelligent, well-traveled and knowledgeable about Europe, collegial, shrewd, handsome, and attractive to women. They got along from the start. She soon began sharing her notes and information with him and, a month after his arrival, admitted: "It has been the greatest pleasure I have had in Switzerland to come into touch again with a friend with whom I have so many friends in common."[13] Dulles rented a spacious ground-floor apartment in a large eighteenth-century house at 23 Herrengasse, overlooking the river Aare with the Oberland mountain range as a backdrop. Located in the medieval section of Bern, there was

---

* Helene du Coudray/*née* Helene Heroys (1906–) was not Belgian. She was born in Kiev and spent her childhood in St. Petersburg. She arrived in England (via exile in Finland and Sweden) at the age of thirteen. While an undergraduate at Oxford, she wrote a prize-winning novel, *Another Country* (1928); she wrote three other novels and a well-received biography of Metternich (1935). Fluent in several languages, she settled in Geneva and worked as a translator and interpreter. It appears that she was still working with EW in June 1943.

a good deal of street traffic in the area, while the apartment was also accessible through a more discreet rear entrance, which allowed his numerous visitors to come and go relatively unnoticed. This was to be his base of operations for the next two-and-three-quarter years. Wiskemann was a frequent visitor: they dined together, exchanged information, and discussed politics and the war. He was also generally buoyant and optimistic, in contrast to Bergholz, who sometimes exacerbated her gloomier moments.[14] Six years older than her, she clearly felt Dulles was someone she could confide in and approach for advice: "Though all my friends are delightful to me, things here are almost more difficult than I can face at times. It was a grand job until the change of chief and I was so keen and London seemed really pleased with what I sent...I need some very good advice. If you have an hour to spare? I hope this isn't presuming upon your kindness."[15] Over the next weeks there was some improvement: "Am feeling a bit cheered by further signs of encouragement from London."[16]

Dulles's access to money was useful for some of Wiskemann's sources (and a welcome contrast to the penny-pinching ways of Whitehall); she also enjoyed the flowers he sent and the good food and wine that he somehow obtained and was happy to share—evidently markedly different from her usual boring rations:

Dear Mr. Dulles, I really can't tell you how much I have enjoyed seeing you this week and how much I have appreciated your delightful hospitality...If it were not that I hoped to be fortunate enough to entertain you myself fairly soon, I should be enclosing little *coupons de repas*, since I know to my cost that double cards[†] don't go very far in a *ménage à une personne*. Yours very sincerely, Elizabeth Wiskemann.

A couple of months later she writes:

Dear Mr. Dulles, I'm suffering from a slightly guilty conscience about all the nice meals I have had in your house. Even the extra rations of a diplomat cannot be treated as the widow's cruse. As it undoubtedly is more practical for me to accept your princely hospitality (although I hope to entice you to my 'cloud-cuckooland' some time again), and as I shall probably not hesitate to do so, may I herewith send you a few little yellow coupons which I can perfectly well spare? Even if you do not need them, it makes me feel better! The only things I have not got are *coupons de repas* which I cannot therefore offer to you. Looking forward to seeing you when we are both back from Geneva, Yours ever, Elizabeth Wiskemann.[17]

---

† In Switzerland both food consumed at home and meals in restaurants were rationed. Since it was assumed that they must entertain, diplomats got double rations. Wiskemann also gave coupons to Swiss friends who entertained her.

Figure 4.1. "Allen Dulles," Getty Images.

Douglas Waller has characterized their friendship as an exercise in cunning manipulation or seduction on Dulles's part: the "temperamental" Wiskemann had a "trove" of German intelligence sources and Dulles "charmed their reports out of her with flowers, flirty notes and fancy meals his cook prepared."[18] In fact, their relationship was more of a two-way, mutually beneficial exchange than this suggests. Wiskemann had no qualms about all this—Dulles was an ally working for the same cause, a friend, and someone who was routinely more helpful than her own compatriots in the legation.

Her enthusiasm for Dulles was not universal at the British Legation, although it's difficult to be certain of officials' attitudes. Claude Dansey in London was rather dubious, while Frederick ('Fanny') Vanden Heuvel, the SIS chief in Geneva, was more favorable and sent an aide every week to swap reports with Dulles.[19] Vanden Heuvel recognized that they perceived their mission differently: "We went after a lot of military intelligence, order of battle things, and we weren't too occupied with what would happen after the war, just what we had to do to win the war at the moment, whereas Allen saw his mission as much more encompassing."[20] In general, they wanted to work with OSS, but also to keep an eye on Dulles, who was viewed as being out for himself, competing for agents and spreading money everywhere; the Americans were in general deemed too uncritical of their sources. How much Vanden Heuvel or 'Jock' McCaffery (the head of SOE in Bern) or Ambassador Norton, for that matter, knew about the extent of Wiskemann's contacts with Dulles is unclear—and they might not have been overjoyed to find out. Appended to one report sent to him, she writes: "Am not showing this to my people, only to you."[21] On another she writes: "If Van [Vanden Heuvel] should show it to you later, I think I'd better ask you to look innocent."[22] As Vanden Heuvel indicated, SIS was mostly focused on military rather than social, economic, and political information or what a postwar order might look like; but Dulles's wide-ranging purview overlapped with many areas of interest to Wiskemann. "As I said to you," she wrote to Dulles, "I always try to keep as clear of military information as I possibly can because the military specialists are rather 'touchy'. But actually, as you said, there isn't a line of demarcation."[23]

As surviving documents in the OSS files show, Wiskemann and Dulles were in constant, close contact. She introduced him to many sources, including journalists like Albert Müller, Berlin correspondent of the *Neue Zürcher Zeitung*, the theologian Karl Barth, former French financial attaché Marcel Vaidie, and many others. She shared notes of her conversations with him and passed along documents she had obtained and copies of telegrams she was sending to London. She also disclosed to Dulles things she was learning from two of her best sources, Fritz Kramer and her contact in Hoffmann La Roche.[24] Their exchanges covered a very wide range of topics, including political and social conditions in Germany, France, and Italy; resistance movements in the Reich and occupied Europe; and what was happening closer to home in the German Embassy in Bern. Within three weeks of his arrival Dulles dispatched to Washington a comprehensive telegram describing the situation in Italy, Germany, and the Balkans—his conversations with Wiskemann probably informed parts of it.[25] She had developed a particularly rich array of sources for Yugoslavia, and they spent a lot of time discussing the shifting balance of power within the resistance there; similarly, in 1943 she gained good intelligence on Italy and was ready to share it. Both were also approached by growing numbers of prospective informers and were constantly on their guard against fake sources, *provocateurs*, and Nazi counterintelligence agents trying to entrap them. Several of Wiskemann's letters include warnings about unreliable people. "Kopecky,"‡ she writes, "said we should all be warned that 2 Slovaks have arrived in this country who may try to make out that they are pro-Ally, but they are both Slovak Nazi agents!" She added both their names.[26] On another occasion she writes: "I saw Jean Hussar the other day and it was indicated to me that he would be seeing you. I faintly know some not too good things about him in the past in Belgrade or Prague – can't remember accurately, but I believe Kopecky knows precisely as at some time it was his job to know

---

‡ Jaromir Kopecky, diplomatic representative in Switzerland of the Czech exile government in London.

foreign journalists. Perhaps you could ask K."[27] Franz Kramer alerted her to another man, Ullmann in Geneva, who worked as a correspondent for the *Berliner Börsenzeitung*; the Red Cross and the *Conseil oecuménique des églises* trusted him as an anti-fascist, but he was working for the Nazis.[28]

In Geneva, Wiskemann got to know the daughter-in-law of Léon Blum, who came from a Genevese Jewish family. Blum was imprisoned and then tried at Riom in February 1942, along with Daladier and General Gamelin. After his splendid self-defense at the trial, he remained incarcerated at Bourrasol for many months, where his daughter-in-law, Renée, visited him regularly (her husband, Robert, was a prisoner of war in German hands). Whenever she returned to Switzerland, Wiskemann saw her. In early March 1943, fearing that Blum's deportation was imminent, she urged Dulles to meet with the family:

> Blum is obviously in the greatest danger and apparently a plan for his rescue was made some little time ago and should now be put in action. As he was in touch with your President up to November, I feel that perhaps it is a situation for an American to handle and, as you can get into immediate touch – as I imagine – with either Washington or London, I am presuming to ask you to consider the position. Apart from feelings of humanity, I myself am indebted to this circle for valuable information and should feel ashamed to make no effort on their behalf. Further, it would be politically worthwhile to snatch away the prisoners of [the castle of] Bourrasol.[29]

It was, in fact, too late; on March 31 the SS flew Léon Blum to Buchenwald and he remained there for the rest of the war. Because the British records are so incomplete, it is difficult to know—apart from her occasional requests for information—what intelligence Dulles supplied in return from his own growing network.[30] He had, for example, very good ties to the Swiss secret service and Buro Hä, and in Fritz Kolbe [alias George Wood] he had an especially valuable agent at the center of power in Berlin. They shared information usable in their respective media and black propaganda campaigns, but Dulles was also eager to get military intelligence, for example about German research for what became the V1 and V2 weapons. This was not part of Wiskemann's remit.

In the Dulles–Wiskemann correspondence for 1943 the situation in the Balkans understandably occupied much of their attention. By the spring, the Red Army's victory at Stalingrad signaled a decisive shift in the war, while the British and Americans had defeated Axis forces in North Africa. At the same time, resistance movements in the Balkans and Greece posed an increasing threat on the Nazis' southern flank. SOE was eager to expand its operations there and British policy was in the process of changing horses, abandoning Mihailović's royalist nationalists and backing Tito's communist partisans. Previously the government had oscillated between the two, hoping to get them to cooperate or at least remain independent but focus on the Germans. Wiskemann had numerous sources of detailed intelligence for the area, several of them Croats affiliated with Maček's Peasant party and others who were Tito supporters. They produced convincing evidence that Mihailović was doing little to oppose the Nazis.[31] She was in some doubt over what to send to London about the conflict, especially since she had been warned to avoid military matters, but in the end passed along the pro-Tito information, arguing that there were many non-communists, including army officers, who had joined the partisans as the only true course of action for patriots. She consulted Dulles over this, but they disagreed: a staunch anticommunist, he insisted that the Allies must stick to Mihailović and not fall into a trap laid by communist propagandists.[32] In fact, Whitehall was receiving other, similar reports—from SOE Cairo, for example—as well as Soviet protests that Mihailović was little better than a collaborator. Elisabeth Barker at the Balkan Directorate in London noted that Wiskemann's intelligence agreed in "its general trend" with their other findings, adding "we have by now a fairly good idea of her sources and can evaluate her material accordingly."[33] In May 1943 William Deakin parachuted as a liaison into Tito's headquarters in the Montenegrin highlands, and by the year's end Churchill had committed fully to arming Tito's partisans.[34]

From the summer of 1943, Italy became a major focus for Whitehall and Wiskemann. Having driven Rommel from North Africa, Allied forces crossed the Mediterranean, landing in Sicily in mid-July, while the intensification of Allied bombing of northern industrial cities caused mass evacuations and helped spark the first mass strikes in twenty years. The Fascist regime had grown increasingly weak and shaky; finally, a palace coup toppled Mussolini from power on July 25. This raised high hopes for an armistice between Italy and the Allies. By announcing that Italy would remain in the war, the King and his new chief minister, Badoglio, hoped to deceive the Germans while an armistice was being negotiated. But talks became deadlocked as Hitler poured additional divisions over the Brenner Pass. Italians' early euphoria at Mussolini's fall gave way to despair. Badoglio had taken no steps to organize military resistance against German intervention; indeed, his only decisive action was to send troops to fire on crowds celebrating 'unconditional peace.' And while the Allies had occupied Sicily with relative ease, they were unprepared for a full-scale invasion of the mainland, since the bulk of their forces were needed for the anticipated landings in France. Further territorial gains in Italy would have required the assistance of the Italian army, but in the absence of orders, Italian troops throughout the country had dispersed in confusion or were soon taken prisoner by the Germans. On September 8 an armistice was finally announced, but within days German forces were in complete control of Italy as far south as Salerno, while a daring commando raid rescued Mussolini from captivity at Gran Sasso, high in the Abruzzi mountains. Italy now became the terrain of a bloody, protracted series of concurrent conflicts—German against Allied forces; the Italian partisan resistance against the Nazi occupation; fascists and anti-fascists.

Before the war, Wiskemann admitted in her memoir, her relationship to Italy had been cultural rather than political. She had traveled there several times and felt deep repulsion at the trucks full of blackshirted fascists hurtling through the streets of Florence during the election campaign of 1924. But her focus was Italy's beautiful landscape and cities, its magnificent painting and architecture. In Rome she first met Cecil Sprigge, then working for the *Manchester Guardian*, and in Florence, introduced by Robert Trevelyan (Julian's father), she was welcomed into Bernard Berenson's circle at I Tatti. On the first of several visits, probably in 1930, she arrived in a downpour "soaked to the skin" so that Nicky Mariano, Berenson's secretary, had to lend her dry clothes. She described herself "sitting on the floor in my bedroom gaping deliriously out of the window" at the Tuscan landscape; "A Baldovinetti, I think, hung over my bed and I wondered whether I was dreaming that I was sleeping in the Uffizi."[35] She also met Lina Waterfield, "a marvelously beautiful creature" who lived in a large palazzo nearby; the author of several books, she was also the *Observer*'s correspondent in Italy, whose hard-hitting critiques of the Fascist regime brought her into increasing conflict with her pro-Appeasement editor, J.L. Garvin. Two other regular members of the Berenson circle, with whom Wiskemann became friends, were the journalist Umberto Morra, a close associate of Piero Gobetti, and the writer and literary critic Guglielmo Alberti. She reconnected with them as exiles in Switzerland during the war. At I Tatti the conversation was deeply anti-fascist, but, for Wiskemann in the 1930s, Italy was an intellectual and cultural feast and she chose not to write about its politics—except for the South Tyrol and Trieste, former parts of the Habsburg Empire, or circumstances where Mussolini's foreign policy intersected with that of Hitler. Following events in Germany and most of Central and South-eastern Europe was quite enough, she wrote, while also admitting that after her expulsion from Berlin in 1936 she had no wish to risk being banished from Italy.[36]

In the early war years, she had few reliable informants about Italy.[37] A small group of Italian anti-fascist exiles had been living in Switzerland since the late 1920s. They included Egidio Reale, one of the founders of *Giustizia e Libertà*, who fled to Switzerland in 1926 and taught at the Rappard Institute of International Studies in Geneva while also publishing liberal tracts and books which were infiltrated into Italy. Other early arrivals with whom Wiskemann became friendly were Giuseppe Delogu, art historian and expert on Venetian painting, and Fernando Schiavetti, a journalist who ran the Italian free school in Zurich established by anti-fascists. She also met Ignazio Silone through the Oprechts. One of the founders of the Italian Communist Party in 1921, Silone left Italy in 1927 for a mission to Moscow and then settled in Zurich in 1929, remaining there until 1944. Already by the late 1920s he had become disillusioned with the party and Stalinism. Drawn to communism by its humanistic ideals rather than Marxist economic theory, he now saw in the party's iron discipline: "a new version of the inhuman reality against which, in declaring ourselves socialists, we had rebelled."[38] Impoverished and struggling with ill health, Silone had worked at first as a typist and translator and taught Italian to get by. It was in Zurich—in the Museumsgesellschaft reading rooms where she worked—that he met his Irish wife, Darina Laracy. There too he explored the roots of his political disillusionment and worked towards a new synthesis of socialism and Christian values in his Abruzzo trilogy of novels that made him world famous in the early postwar years.[39] Published first in German by the Oprechts, the books circulated in clandestine translations in Fascist Italy.

Eventually Wiskemann got to know Silone well, although he was a notoriously complicated and sometimes difficult person. But in the early war years he provided her with little useful intelligence; he was, she wrote, "highly intelligent and fairly well-informed but had lived too long in exile."[40] In fact, Silone had developed a large network of contacts both in Italy and within the Italian Swiss exile community, and in 1940 they established in Zurich the Centro Estero, or foreign office of the Italian Socialist Party [PSI], which developed ties to dissidents within Italy as well as socialist and labor movements overseas. But Silone had to be careful not to flout openly the Swiss ban on political activity among foreign exiles. In December 1942, encouraged by growing unrest in Italy, he issued a Manifesto calling upon Italians to accomplish their own liberation through civil disobedience. After Moscow publicized his cell's existence, the Swiss police felt obliged to act. Silone was arrested and spent Christmas 1942 in prison but was released soon after suffering from high fever and a pulmonary hemorrhage; he then moved to Davos and was placed under house arrest. Dulles, who arrived in Bern just before this, was soon in contact with Silone and he became his Socialist group's chief source of funds, although Silone insisted that the money must come via a socialist organization in the US or labor unions, "as they wanted to keep the record clean." He passed along information about Italy's political and social situation and gave advice about Allied propaganda directed at the country.[41]

Wiskemann saw Silone frequently in 1943. Like him, for some months before the actual coup against Mussolini she believed that a change of regime was close at hand. London pressed her constantly for information. In early July she wrote Dulles: "Please forgive me if I have been telephoning you at awkward moments. I had particularly on my conscience...that I was able to see our friend at Baden [A small town near Zurich; Silone had moved there from Davos] on Thursday and got a good deal from him dated July 10. It kept me there half the night and on Friday and Saturday morning London peppered me with telegrams so that I had really no moment." About to rush off to Zurich, she added: "I expect his material will have reached you – if not, I can let you have my records of it first thing Wednesday."[42] Ten days later she was asking Dulles if he could arrange for her to interview Egidio Reale about the situation in Rome, since "London is very keen on his stuff."[43] Later they wanted detailed information about strikes and demonstrations that were spreading across cities in the north, forcing her to ask Dulles if he had anything from Silone that "you don't want or can spare to me."[44] With Dulles's help she was also able to furnish London with copies of anti-fascist leaflets and appeals circulating in Italy. In October, when Silone had fallen ill and missed a meeting, she asks: "If you have any recent stuff from him might I see it?"[45]

Politically the period from September 1943 to D-Day, Wiskemann wrote, was "in some ways the hardest to bear. The Allies seemed unable to use their opportunity in Italy, and the other satellite powers, on tiptoe to follow Italy's example, fell back into something like a coma of indifference."[46] With Mussolini's overthrow and the Badoglio interregnum, many opponents of the regime in Italy no longer felt the need to operate in secret, while some exiles in Switzerland who hurried back to Rome were soon caught in acute danger between Nazi and neo-Fascist forces. Hitler's swift response to the coup produced a renewed flood of refugees across the Swiss border: Italian anti-fascists, escaped Allied POWs, and Jews, now being hunted down in Italy and deported to death camps. Some had harrowing escapes; all hoped to return home again by Christmas at the latest, and "as the prospect of this receded, they, like many other people, succumbed to exaggerated gloom."[47] Among this fresh wave of exiles were old friends of Wiskemann like Guglielmo Alberti, Umberto Morra, and the economist, journalist, and advocate of European federalism Professor Luigi Einaudi and his wife, who struggled through the snow for three days to escape across the Alps.[48] Republican leader Cipriano Facchinetti, who had been in the parliament with Matteotti, also settled in Bern; he had been arrested by the Germans in 1943, sent to Rome and imprisoned there, but liberated after the July coup and then forced to flee. Finally, two others who contacted Wiskemann in efforts to press their views on London were Count Stefano Jacini and Duke Tommaso Gallarati-Scotti, originally followers of Don Sturzo's Popolari party and now close to the Christian Democratic resistance. Many of these exiles settled in Lugano, where they gathered at the villa of the Marchesa De Nobili; others congregated in Locarno, where the mayor, Giovanni Battista Rusca, was very welcoming. Closer to Bern, Guglielmo Alberti settled in the medieval city of Fribourg, where he was the central figure in a group at the "Hotel Suisse," strongly influenced by the Dominican priest and neo-Thomist theologian Jean de Menasce. His aim was to integrate his dead friend Piero Gobetti's radicalism and reformed social Catholicism. Wiskemann was often highly critical of Catholicism, but Alberti opened her eyes to the fact that many devout Italian Catholics were critical of the Church hierarchy and advocates of social change.[49]

Soon dissident Fascists also sought asylum in Switzerland. They included Mussolini's daughter, Edda, whose husband, Count Ciano, was imprisoned at Salò and would be executed in January 1944; Dino Alfieri, a former member of the Fascist Grand Council and participant in the July coup; and the industrialist Franco Marinotti. Also, many Italian soldiers, fearing capture by the Germans, escaped into Switzerland, although many soon returned, trekking across the mountains to join the partisan bands.[50]

Ironically, this Italian influx, which resulted from the failures and disappointments of the 1943 summer months, did much to enrich and make more enjoyable Wiskemann's social life: "[They] were certainly like a breath of fresh, warm air in Switzerland towards the end of 1943 and right on until the end of the war. The Swiss Confederation became much noisier and more disorderly but much more fun."[51] She enjoyed watching the Italians' impact upon the stolid Swiss and was soon a constant presence in all these circles, relaying to London the information which they received regularly from Italy, and acting as a channel to pass along their views to Whitehall. She mixed with diplomats, politicians, journalists, and cultural celebrities—many of whom went on to important positions in postwar Italy—and began to develop an insider's understanding of Italian politics. Representatives of the anti-Fascist parties coalesced to establish their own branch of the Committee of National Liberation for Northern Italy [CLNAI], which the Swiss authorities quietly tolerated. Mussolini's fall had also brought changes in the Italian Legation in Bern, which aligned itself with Badoglio. Among its staff as press attaché was Marchese Francesco Antinori, a good friend of Frederick Voigt. As press officer in Berlin until 1940, he had acted as liaison for the meetings between Hitler and Mussolini in Venice and Berlin and saw how Mussolini fell increasingly under the spell of Hitler's Germany. Long critical of the Fascist regime, he watched with greater horror the terror unleashed by the Nazi regime. Writing to his editor from Paris in 1937, Voigt described Antinori as a liberal, Roman Catholic, and Italian patriot, appalled by the atmosphere of Berlin: "When he arrived in Paris he felt that he had come out of prison. When he had to go back again there were tears in his eyes."[52] Already before the war Antinori was passing information to the British and soon he became a source for Wiskemann; she was strongly attracted to this quiet, modest, Anglophile diplomat and before long a serious romance developed between them.

As the Italian campaign and the partisan struggle in the North intensified, so did London's demand for intelligence. Wiskemann's superiors in Whitehall were especially eager for information about the growing unpopularity of the Savoy monarchy. When she quoted one source, a friend of Salvemini, they fired back for elaboration "and give details supporting his statement that the monarchy is discredited."[53] They also asked which leaders the anti-fascist groups saw as possibly replacing the King. Sharing one of these telegrams with Dulles, she added: "Please destroy after perusal." Her informants in the exile community argued that the monarchy's role in the fascist regime, further compounded by its failures during the forty-five days of Badoglio and the King's unheroic flight from Rome after the armistice, all made its continuation impossible. It made no sense to rid Italy of

Fascism but keep the King. Both Sforza and Croce refused to join a Badoglio government and insisted it be replaced. Churchill was deeply suspicious of the anti-fascist resistance. He was contemptuous of Sforza ("a foolish and played out old man" who wanted to become king[54]) and Croce and wanted the monarchy and Badoglio to continue but, under American pressure, was forced to accept that the King should step down in favor of his son Prince Umberto, until such time as the Italian people could settle the 'institutional question' once and for all.[55] Wiskemann, like the majority of her informants, favored a republic and thought Churchill completely wrong on this issue; Dulles took the same position as Churchill, convinced that the Crown offered the best insurance against the far left and a communist takeover.[56]

In October 1943 Wiskemann got a stroke of luck. Croat friends introduced her to a businessman in textiles [she called him source Z in her memoir; Whitehall knew him as Q1], a Slovak Jew by origin but with an Italian passport. Deeply anti-Nazi, he traveled frequently to the towns of northern Italy, especially Milan, and volunteered to gather intelligence for her. She was at first ambivalent because of the terrible dangers to a Jew if he were discovered by the Nazis or neo-Fascists [i.e. Salò Republic fascists], but he proved to be a valuable and dedicated informant about social conditions in the North, roundups of Jews, the partisan struggle, and the Salò Republic.[57] Her reports on Italy were already highly praised in 1942, but now her well-crafted telegrams were regarded as even more important. After the liberation of France, when longer documents (not only 'flimsies' or telegrams) could once again be sent home, PWE's Italian Directorate commented: "now when we see an original, we can appreciate the care and accuracy with which Miss W. has previously succeeded in conveying the tone of her information, even within the restricted limits of a cable after translation into another tongue. It is considered that no praise is too high for the ability with which these vivid impressions have been composed in the past by the informant and for the intelligence and discrimination which Miss W. has used in conveying their gist when restricted to a minimum of words."[58] The intelligence she was providing was all the more valuable because SOE's unit at Bern was performing poorly. Ambassador Norton kept them on a tight rein, 'Jock' McCaffery, the station head, lacked the stamina and resourcefulness required for the job, and at the crucial moment of the Italian armistice and the German invasion, "he suffered a complete breakdown, from which it took him a full six weeks to recover."[59]

By the end of 1943 the British government was increasingly concerned about the postwar order in lands occupied by Axis forces. The strength of communist forces in Yugoslavia had been evident for some time and Churchill pragmatically was prepared to back them. Greece was a different matter and so was Italy. The problem in Italy seemed partly resolved in March 1944 when the Communist leader Togliatti returned from Moscow and, under Stalin's instructions, opted to join Badoglio's government. But by June a new government was formed, essentially by leaders of the Committee of National Liberation. Preoccupation with the ultimate aims of communist partisans in the North (and their ties to Tito) was also an increasing worry for Silone and several of Wiskemann's liberal informants in Switzerland. In January 1944 Tommaso Gallarati Scotti met with her to express his fears that left extremists might seize power in the North before Allied troops ever got there, entrenching the country's division and producing anarchy or fratricidal conflict. What was needed, he argued, was a clear Allied statement that only after reunification could the nation's political future be determined by the Italian people. He also put forward people, including Croce, Bonomi, Sforza, and de Gasperi, for a government to be named as soon as the Allies entered Rome. In late September 1944 he had another long conversation with Wiskemann urging her to convey to London his fears of a Russian takeover directly to Eden, "who is more open to these international problems."[60] In fact, not only did Churchill disapprove of several of those mentioned, describing Italian politics as "an endless series of intrigues among the six or seven leftish parties," but Eden's hatred for Italians was so extreme at this point that even his own officials were said to describe him as "almost psychopathic."[61]

By the spring and summer of 1944, aided by British and American equipment and assistance, Italian partisan groups were doing considerable damage to German lines of communication and, while hard-pressed by regular Allied forces, Kesselring was stretched for troops to deploy against them. In early September 1944 they executed a plan to seize a large mountainous area around Domodossola, between Lake Maggiore and the Swiss frontier, expelling German and Fascist forces. There they established a short-lived Republic of 85,000 population.[62] The partisans began building up local self-government from below, issued their own postage stamps and currency, and recruited many workers and peasants to take an active part. Schools were reopened, the Fascist curriculum replaced, and ideas advanced for social and economic reforms.[63] The Swiss government recognized the Republic and sent in food and medical supplies. But the British and the Americans were unhappy about these developments and the prevalence of communists there. SOE in Bern had standing instructions to use partisans solely for minor sabotage and guerrilla actions and to discourage political activity or armed risings; they were already looking ahead to the issue of how to disarm the partisans and organize a peaceful transition once peace came. Thus, McCaffery and Dulles were half-hearted in their promises of aid and warned that a German counterattack would soon occur. It came in mid-October when Kesselring launched a major offensive, causing many casualties, retaking the area, and scattering the partisans—many of them escaping into Switzerland. Finally, in November 1944, after the Allied offensive against the German Gothic Line foundered, General Alexander, in a radio address, postponed further attacks and ordered the partisan brigades to stand down (i.e. go on the defensive instead of initiating attacks) until the spring. With Allied campaigning suspended, German forces and Salò fascists went on the offensive, using the next months to wipe out large numbers of resistance fighters.

The Domodossola Republic lasted only six weeks, but to Wiskemann it was a spectacular moral gesture, a courageous replay of Mazzini's Roman Republic of 1849: "a symbolic, if temporary regime, one that should express the national aspiration independently of all Allied political influence."[64] She was eager to go there (which could be done by rail) and informed Bruce Lockhart that an eyewitness report might be of value to PWE, but Ambassador Clifford Norton refused permission.[65] In early September at Brissago she was able, through field glasses, to observe partisans driving out fascist and German troops from Campione on the Italian side.[66] For Domodossola she had to rely on reports brought back by Gigino Battisti, son of the socialist leader in the pre-1914 Trentino; Wiskemann was also close to his widowed mother, Ernesta, a militant socialist who had fled to Lugano in September 1943. It was Gigino who also passed to her the story of Corinda Mengussato, a twenty-year-old courier for the Garibaldi brigades operating in the Trentino, who was savagely tortured then executed by the Germans but refused to betray the names of her comrades. Wiskemann was deeply moved by the activist role of many women in the resistance, including Ada Gobetti and Joyce Lussu, with whom she became friends after the war. The story of the Italian Resistance, she wrote, "was one of the most moving that I have ever lived close to,"[67] while the death of so many young partisan leaders was "acutely felt in the following years."[68] "The Italians," she wrote, "were now at their best; their anarchistic ingenuity was an excellent weapon for clandestine activity. After the despair of mid-September 1943 [i.e. the King's flight to Brindisi and German occupation] a wave of enthusiasm for justice and liberty welled up and brought with it an exaltation reminiscent of the days of Garibaldi, an exaltation which inspired astonishing bravery, especially among the many and diverse victims of the Gestapo."[69] With parts of the Swiss–Italian frontier now much more permeable and resistance fighters moving back and forth across the border, sometimes staying on the Swiss side to recuperate from wounds, it was much easier to obtain information on the resistance, including clandestine newssheets, fliers, and bulletins from the Committee of National Liberation.[70] London asked for information on opinion among the clergy, students, industrialists, and peasants and estimates of the strength of different political parties. Officials in PWE's Italian section admitted: "For the past eighteen months the bulk of the latest news from German-occupied Italy has been dependent upon the valuable evidence provided by eyewitnesses transmitted to us in a more or less weekly Pilot telegram from Bern."[71]

Inspired by the youth and courage of the resistance, Wiskemann's politics moved further left. She greatly admired men like Salvemini, the Rosselli brothers, Piero Gobetti, and Gramsci (whom she regarded as the 'liberal conscience of communism') and identified closely with the Action party [Partito d'Azione] and its hopes for "a second Risorgimento," this time embracing the whole population, including peasants, workers, and women. Action was committed to a fusion of liberal and socialist ideas, protecting individual freedom but advocating radical social reforms. It also consistently portrayed the Italian conflict in ideological terms as part of a European civil war between fascist and anti-fascist values and civilizations. Wartime resistance called for broad coalitions that subsumed older party rivalries, offering the possibility of a unifying progressive politics. Wiskemann recognized that nations would develop their own singular solutions to the problems of reconstruction, but she was convinced that the scale of the war's destruction meant that socialist 'collectivist methods' had become essential and, in places like Italy, were long overdue.[72] Victory would be drained of its meaning if the pre-war order and its inequities were reproduced. In international affairs too, she was briefly swept along by the Russomania generated by Stalingrad and the Red Army's success; like Beneš, she wondered whether Eastern Europe might become a bridge between the West and the Soviet Union, although events in Poland and elsewhere quickly destroyed her euphoria.[73]

While they cooperated closely on matters of intelligence, Dulles and Wiskemann were politically far apart and increasingly so. Over Tito, the Italian monarchy, the German resistance, and European partisans they disagreed. Dulles's outlook was defined more and more by his anti-communism and concern to limit Soviet gains in Europe. This underpinned his positive assessment of the German resistance, his interest in Nazi peace overtures, his willingness in the last months of the war to deal with SS General Karl Wolff, and his later efforts to quash prosecutions against German business leaders and bankers strongly implicated in Nazi crimes. But Dulles and Wiskemann both opposed the Allies' declaration at Casablanca that they would seek "unconditional surrender," believing it a straitjacket that would bolster Nazi propaganda and lengthen the war. Dulles was primarily fearful that it would throw the German masses into the arms of Moscow. Wiskemann focused more on the enormous death toll it would entail. Sending off a bag of intelligence about Germany to London, she added: "I do wish we could do something to make Germans not prefer death, for it seems to me that lots of Allied lives might then be saved."[74] Her sources in Berlin also argued that, in the absence of clear signals, the German resistance was having greater trouble recruiting waverers: "now is the moment to tell Germans exactly what we mean to do with them."[75] However, she was more doubtful than Dulles that the German resistance would strike decisively against Hitler.

*   *   *

By the summer of 1943, not only had the flow in intelligence from Italy increased dramatically, but the growing success of the Allies in the East and the West had also re-energized the German resistance to Hitler, producing a growing flow of secret intelligence to Switzerland and more 'peace feelers' and efforts to make contact with Allied agents. Dulles had developed a large network of sources and he was convinced that a large anti-Nazi opposition existed in the Reich, capable of taking action and shortening the war. London was much more skeptical and cautious. The Venlo debâcle of 1939, when a German sting operation had decimated British spy networks, was an ever-present nightmare. London was deeply worried that German counterespionage could repeat their earlier success, while Nazi *agents provocateurs* and fake 'peace feelers' could heighten Stalin's suspicions of his Western Allies. Indeed, procedures for dealing with German contacts were tightened up in early 1943. As a result, the Bern legation was instructed to avoid contacts with enemy subjects. The only exceptions were SIS officers and—over the opposition of Ambassador Sir Clifford Norton—Wiskemann, whose intelligence gathering was impossible without such meetings.[76]

She had critics within her own legation, including the Military Attaché Colonel Cartwright, who regarded Wiskemann as a rank amateur.[77] In fact she was extremely prudent and cautious. Sending reports that came from within the German legation to Dulles, she referred to her informant Kramer: "I have been trying to keep him very quiet for a bit and discouraging him from trying to see any of us until things have 'subsided' a bit. I think it's wiser, isn't it?"[78] Cartwright himself took suspicion and caution to extremes. When the German diplomat Fritz Kolbe approached him, he was rebuffed and quickly shown the door.[79] Fortunately, Kolbe took a further gamble and made contact with Allen Dulles in August 1943, becoming one of his most important agents. Kolbe (Dulles gave him the code name George Wood), an unprepossessing bureaucrat who seemed least likely to risk betraying his government, was a former member of the *Wandervögel* youth and a passionate anti-Nazi. He had never joined the Nazi party but had nonetheless worked his way up to become an assistant to Karl Ritter, who was the Foreign Office liaison with the German military. In this job Kolbe oversaw a huge flow of reports and cable traffic. He had already engaged in espionage on a small scale when, in 1943, he was promoted to be a courier and sent to Bern entrusted with the diplomatic bag (an additional justification was that he had recently instituted divorce proceedings against his Swiss wife, who had refused to return to Germany with him in 1939). At their first meeting Kolbe handed over a large stack of cables (or 'flimsies' in the jargon of the day). At first Dulles had doubts about their authenticity, but he soon realized their significance. He shared some with Vanden Heuvel, who passed them to Dansey in London; Dansey suspected a campaign of disinformation, but Kim Philby shared them with Bletchley cryptanalysts, who found them not only genuine but valuable in their code-breaking efforts. Unpaid and motivated by hatred of the Hitler regime, over the next twenty months Kolbe made five trips to Bern, bringing over 1,600 secret documents.[80] How much Wiskemann knew about Kolbe's identity is unclear, but in her frequent conversations with Dulles she would certainly have learned some of what he had to report.

Knowing that she had enemies within the legation who would be quick to react to any mistakes on her part, Wiskemann was especially cautious. On one occasion, she was accosted on the street by someone who claimed to have been sent by Carl Goerdeler, the former mayor of Leipzig and a leader of the Conservative resistance. Fearful of being set up, she immediately sent him away. "Later," she wrote in her memoir, "when I knew how wildly indiscreet Goerdeler had been, I changed my mind; I now believe that Goerdeler had really sent him to me, incredible though it seemed at the time."[81] Afraid of Nazi counterespionage traps, she was always wary of Germans hoping to use her to contact London.[82] In a different category were two old friends from Berlin, whose appearance aroused concerns for their safety. Richard Kuenzer, the son of an industrialist, was a liberal originally from Baden whose south German traditions he always contrasted to those of Prussia. It was Voigt who had first introduced them. A lawyer and diplomat, Kuenzer was from the beginning appalled by the rise of the Nazis. "He was," Wiskemann recalled, "really rather alarming since his sense of fun so easily got the better of him...After Hitler was in power [he] used to give big dinner parties in Berlin with hilarious mimicry of the *Fuehrer*. I enjoyed going to his house but shared the obvious anxiety of his delightful wife lest someone present were a Nazi spy."[83] Kuenzer was in contact with various German resistance groups, including the circle which gathered around Johanna Solf, wife of a former German Ambassador to Tokyo. Acting as a courier for the German Foreign Office, he began traveling to Switzerland in 1940–41, although Wiskemann seems not to have encountered him until somewhat later. She met him at the home of the Oprechts in Zurich, but took every precaution, since he had always been reckless and she was astonished that he was allowed to travel to Switzerland at all, and maybe it was only to entrap him.[84] Kuenzer used these trips as a cover for maintaining contact with former Center Party Chancellor Joseph Wirth (another acquaintance of Wiskemann[85]), now living in Lucerne, and to organize escape opportunities for Jews.

The second old friend who contacted Wiskemann in 1943 was Count Albrecht von Bernstorff. He moved in the same resistance circles as Kuenzer and Adam von Trott zu Solz, although some regarded him as too talkative and indiscreet and therefore a security risk. He owned property at Vevey near Lausanne and suggested that Wiskemann meet him there, She thought it unsafe but felt she couldn't refuse since he was the one most at risk.[86] Like Kuenzer, he was courageous in helping Jews escape from the Reich, but the full extent of his activities is unknown.[87] They had a long talk; he told her a good deal about the situation in Berlin and brought news that two of Admiral Canaris's people had been arrested: "General Oster and some name like Donani" [in fact Hans von Dohnanyi]; he also "referred to Goerdeler as still the most practical possibility as an anti-Nazi political leader"[88] She insisted that they leave separately. But at Lausanne station she saw, to her horror, that he got into the same train compartment; she hid behind her newspapers since she couldn't rely on him to avoid speaking to her in that public place.[89] She never saw him again.

Both Kuenzer and Bernstorff were arrested in July 1943 after returning from Switzerland and two months later the Solf circle was infiltrated by a Gestapo spy, implicating both men as members of the group. They ended up in Ravensbrück and were murdered in April 1945, two weeks before the German surrender.

The Oprechts lived close to the German Consulate in Zurich and it was through them, and possibly through the aristocratic German-American financier Gero von Schulze-Gaevernitz,[90] whom she also knew, that Wiskemann received messages from Hans Bernd Gisevius suggesting that they should meet. Deeply distrustful and fearful that he was an SD plant, she refused to see him but wrote later "perhaps I was wrong."[91] Her anxiety was understandable. Gisevius had begun his career as a protégé of Arthur Nebe working for the Gestapo.[§] Later he transferred to the Ministry of Interior but formed close ties to German opposition figures like Hjalmar Schacht and Hans Oster. When the war began, he again moved into intelligence, working for the Abwehr under Admiral Canaris. It was Canaris and Oster who sent him to Zurich as Vice-Consul. There his real work included shielding members of the German underground who had established connections to Allied and Swiss secret networks and were in danger of being exposed by the numerous SD and Gestapo agents operating throughout Switzerland. He was also instructed to make contact with the Allies, and to keep an eye on Canaris's close acquaintance, Halina Szymańska, who was also a British agent working at the Polish legation in Bern. "In this way," as Peter Hoffmann has written, "Gisevius was aware of and in some way a participant in most opposition activities that were channeled via Switzerland."[92] His first meeting with Dulles in January 1943 was brokered by Schulze-Gaevernitz, a friend of Gisevius and essentially Dulles's right-hand man, whom he had known for many years. In later meetings Dulles's confidence in Gisevius increased, especially when the latter pointed out an American code that had been cracked by German counterintelligence and breaches of security in the Herrengasse household itself.

Gisevius's main goal was to convince Dulles that the Allies should focus on the rapid advance of Bolshevism into Europe and to consider a cease-fire arrangement that would allow for a continuation of the war in the East. Schulze-Gaevernitz had indicated to Gisevius that Dulles was open to talks on a purely political level and not only secret intelligence. Dulles was convinced that eliminating Hitler would hasten a German collapse and shorten the war, although it was not until 1944 that he believed the German opposition capable of a serious coup.

§ Arthur Nebe (1894–1945) became head of the *Kriminalpolizei* in 1936 and then a high official in the *Reichssicherheitshauptamt*. In 1941 he volunteered to serve as commanding officer of *Einsatzgruppe B*, responsible for mass killings in the Minsk area. In his memoir, Gisevius sanitized this part of Nebe's career as a "brief command at the front." Wiskemann knew of the Minsk operations through a Swiss medical mission to the eastern front. Nebe later became involved in the July plot against Hitler, although his motives are highly suspect. He was executed for his connection to the plotters in March 1945.

He urged Washington to step up its propaganda campaign to separate Germans from their Nazi leaders, but he remained clear in his talks with Gisevius that a separate cease-fire was out of the question—although Gisevius either was unconvinced of the inflexibility of the American position or failed to convey it to his co-conspirators in Berlin. Over the next year he became Dulles's most important source on the German resistance to Hitler.

In addition to everything else, Gisevius was also busy working on a self-justificatory memoir about the Third Reich, which he wanted to have ready for publication as soon as the war ended. Eager to get help editing and translating the voluminous manuscript, he accepted Dulles's recommendation of Mary Bancroft as a suitable helper. Bancroft, an American socialite and close friend of Carl Jung, had been living in Switzerland since 1934. Officially a journalist, she worked for OSS and was Dulles's lover. She was instructed to charm and flatter Gisevius, who was very much open to feminine wiles, and to extract as much information as possible. She soon recruited Elizabeth Scott-Montagu, who had been working part-time with Wiskemann at the Bern legation, to help as translator and amanuensis. Gisevius was flattered to have an English noblewoman working on his book, and the two women proved an effective team: they would work together for a while in the afternoons, then loosen things up with a few drinks, flirting and teasing information out of their German author.[93] Scott-Montagu had been looking to change her work, but her departure angered Wiskemann, who obviously felt hurt and betrayed. More than twenty years passed, Scott-Montagu recalled, before the rift was patched up and they could again meet as friends.[94] There is no mention of this in Wiskemann's correspondence with Dulles—perhaps she was unaware of his role.

Another prominent figure in German resistance circles who was eager to meet with Wiskemann was Adam von Trott zu Solz. From an aristocratic Hessian family, Trott was a Foreign Office official and among the most active members of the Kreisau Circle, so named after Count Helmuth von Moltke's estate in Silesia. They included a diversity of viewpoints (over, for example, whether Hitler should be killed) but were mostly Christian conservatives, deeply suspicious of liberal democracy. As a Rhodes Scholar at Balliol, Trott had made many British and American friends—including Maurice Bowra, Isaiah Berlin, David Astor, Shiela Grant Duff, and A.L. Rowse—but some of these friendships soured after he wrote a letter to the *Manchester Guardian* in 1934 rebutting an article about discrimination against Jews in the German courts. There is no doubt that Trott was a determined, fearless—and sometimes carelessly indiscreet—anti-Nazi, but his defensive nationalism and fierce criticism of the Versailles Treaty, combined with the ease with which he was able to journey abroad, and his approaches to Appeasers like Lord Halifax and the so-called 'Cliveden set', made people suspicious. On the one hand, he encouraged determined opposition to Nazi foreign policy and tried to rally foreign support for internal opponents of the regime; on the other, in 1939 he urged further accommodation, to save the peace (long enough, in his defenders' view, to allow time for the German opposition to bring off a coup against Hitler). Trott's contorted maneuvers in personal diplomacy almost inevitably aroused concern among former friends and in Whitehall that he might be a Nazi agent. Even those who loved and admired him were severely tested; this is most evident in his long exchange of letters with Shiela Grant Duff, whom Trott met at Oxford and to whom he once proposed marriage. Spread over seven years, the correspondence charts the fragmentation of a close friendship, driven apart by events and passionate differences over how to confront the menace of Nazism.[95] By the outbreak of war their correspondence had ended; Grant Duff, like Wiskemann, joined Toynbee's Foreign Research and Press Service and later the BBC European Service, while Trott took a job in the German Foreign Office, under whose cover he worked for the resistance.

It was Harry Bergholz who arranged the first meeting between Trott and Wiskemann, at his room in Lausanne in early 1942. After this they met whenever Trott came to Switzerland. "Once when he left her house, his attention was caught by a Swiss policeman who had obviously been standing there during the whole of his meeting. It worried him temporarily, although in itself there was no need to connect it to danger."[96] Like many others, Wiskemann found the tall, handsome, aristocratic Trott a magnetic personality: "a bewilderingly brilliant creature, infinitely German in the intellectual complexity in which he loved to indulge." She also found him unrealistic and anxiety-producing in his reckless disregard for secrecy—identifying himself by name, for example, on the telephone, despite her attempts to get him to adopt a pseudonym.[97]

Trott was eager to use her as a way of making contact with the British government, and in the course of this first meeting he outlined a program which he imagined would be acceptable to London: The Germans would evacuate all occupied territories in the west, including Alsace and also all of Czechoslovakia; Austria would remain within the Reich, Poland would re-emerge as independent, but otherwise Germany would get 'a free hand' in the east and hostilities against Russia would only be suspended. Believing that Germans were not ready for democracy, he anticipated an interim military government in the Reich, to be replaced later by a civilian corporative government of chosen experts. Wiskemann was asked to forward these ideas to officials in London and the leaders of the Anglican Church.[98] There was little or no chance that Churchill or Eden would respond to such ideas and enter into a dialogue. In terms of specific usable intelligence—about conditions, morale, and public opinion in Hitler's Germany—Wiskemann did not learn much from Trott; she received, for example, far more news from Franz Kramer about troop morale on the Russian front, although Trott's brother was fighting there. Like Grant Duff, she found his political outlook full of contradictions that a rather murky but passionate Hegelianism did nothing to resolve; she also disliked what she saw as his lingering sympathy with

Germany's eastern expansionism and the idea of a German national mission to rule Slavs. His conversation reminded her of earlier talks with Schleicher's *protégés* before Hitler became Chancellor. Trott was already in contact with Visser 't Hooft, who in April 1942 conveyed a lengthy memorandum to Stafford Cripps and Churchill in London; his goal was to get assurances about the future of Germany from London which might then get the military to commit to a coup. Shortly after, a further approach was made by Dietrich Bonhoeffer in Stockholm to Bishop Bell of Chichester, who was then lecturing in neutral Sweden.[99]

Trott was well-known to Foreign Office officials in London since the late 1930s, and by 1942 the most forceful among them had concluded that the German resistance was not capable of doing anything that would shorten the war. Those groups that existed were judged to be neither large nor well-organized and lacking in popular support. Some of these civilian approaches, officials suspected, were German government efforts to sow dissension between the Western Allies and the Soviets; even genuine ones were viewed as unable to mount effective action against Hitler. And while German military leaders were in theory capable of action, they would expect negotiations and assurances for the future which were not feasible. Informed of Wiskemann's meetings, Geoffrey W. Harrison at the FO's German desk minuted on June 12, 1942:

> I understand that Sir S[tafford]. Cripps suggested that Miss Wiskemann should be told to 'cool off' Adam von Trott on the grounds that he is too valuable. It seems to me regrettable that it would be known that Herr von Trott is in contact at all with Miss Wiskemann and I am very doubtful about asking her to 'cool him off'. In fact, I do not think it is in our interest to do so since his value to us as a 'martyr' is likely to exceed his value to us in post-war Germany.[100]

Wiskemann's last meeting with Trott was on April 14, 1944: Only thirty-five years old, he looked old and exhausted, a broken man who knew he was doomed. Appalled by Allied terror bombings of German cities, he brought her photographs of rows of corpses, many of them children, and tried to persuade her to make an appeal to London, which she knew would have no effect on RAF strategy. She hated the indiscriminate bombing of cities, viewing it as not only immoral but also bad policy, but told him that nothing she might say would have any effect. She admitted: "In my own mind I was also saying to myself, as I was often obliged to, 'they will say you are squeamish because you are a woman'." She urged him not to return to the Reich, but he insisted that he had to. After leaving he telephoned once more, again using his own name, and she told him he had left behind his fine pair of gloves: "He said 'keep them as a gauge,' for his safety he meant."[101] Moltke, Bonhoeffer, and Dohnányi, and Bernstorff and Kuenzer were already in prison and Trott knew that his time was running out. He was arrested days after Stauffenberg's failed attempt to assassinate Hitler, tried, and barbarously executed in August 1944.[102] At his trial, Wiskemann was grateful that his journeys to Switzerland were not mentioned and that only Sweden came up; she took solace from the fact that no careless slip of hers had a role in his death. She gave the gloves to people collecting clothes for the Italian partisans: "After all that the SS had done in Italy, I felt glad that the Italians should have a good pair of German gloves with a German mark of origin."[103]

On the afternoon of July 20, 1944, when news of the plot against Hitler's life came through on the telephone, Wiskemann was in conversation with Dulles at his office in the Herrengasse. At that moment they had no idea whether it had succeeded.[104] Later Wiskemann was deeply troubled by the BBC's and the British press's unsympathetic tone in reporting the plot (to the effect that "this was the selfish plot of a group of Prussian aristocrats"[105] or a last-ditch effort to protect Prussian militarism). Had she known, she would have been even more distressed at her friend Wheeler-Bennett's *Realpolitik* verdict on the failed conspiracy and the hunting down of those involved. In a memorandum of July 25, a few days after the failed coup attempt, he wrote:

> It may now be said with all definiteness that we are better off with things as they are today than if the plot of July 20th had succeeded and Hitler had been assassinated... By the failure of the plot we have been spared the embarrassments, both at home and in the United States, which might have resulted from such a move and, moreover, the present purge is presumably removing from the scene numerous individuals who might have caused us difficulty... the Gestapo and the S.S. have done us an appreciable service in removing a selection of those who would undoubtedly have posed as 'good' Germans after the war, while preparing for a third World War. It is our advantage therefore that the purge should continue, since the killing of Germans by Germans will save us from future embarrassments of many kinds.[106]

Adam von Trott's life and the attitude of the British government to the German opposition resurfaced in the late 1960s in a debate in which Wiskemann played a minor role. It was triggered by the publication of a biography of Trott by Christopher Sykes, *Troubled Loyalty* (1968).[107] Although sympathetic studies of the German resistance were appearing in West Germany, in Britain the dominant view remained highly critical of figures like Trott as ambivalent, romantic, and impractical, while German generals were condemned for their failure to stand up to Hitler. David Astor, owner of the *Observer* and a close Oxford friend of Trott, got Trott's widow and relatives of the Kreisau Circle to agree to a biography that would vindicate Trott, and recruited Sykes, a highly competent biographer, for the task. But Sykes—though promised complete freedom—quickly found himself embattled with Trott's "adorers" who "won't look at any facts that leave him [Adam] as anything but perfect. Which he wasn't." Among his many sources,

Sykes met several times with Wiskemann and drew upon her memories of Trott. The result was a fine, nuanced portrayal of Trott: his complexity and confusions, his courage, his abhorrence of Nazism and torments as an ardent nationalist and patriot at war with his own country. Reviews were overwhelmingly favorable and the book's depiction of Trott was both sympathetic and largely congruent with Wiskemann's assessment and that of Sheila Grant Duff's later memoir.[108] However, Trott's devotees were incensed—at his depiction as a Hamlet-like figure—and a heated debate ensued in *Encounter* lasting several months between Astor, Sykes, Trevor-Roper, Wheeler-Bennett, and others. These exchanges quickly revealed deeper disagreement over whether the British government had been unreasonably hostile, belittling, and unresponsive towards the German opposition and, as a result, bore a share of responsibility for the failure to prevent and later to shorten the war.[109]

Aside from arguing that Sykes had depicted Trott as too conservative and conflicted in his politics, David Astor essentially restated Bishop Bell's wartime critique that the British government should have embraced the German opposition; firm commitment might have produced a coup against Hitler at the time of the Czech crisis, while clear assurances later about the future of Germany could have persuaded German generals to abandon their allegiance to the *Führer*, thereby greatly enhancing the opposition's chance of success. In particular, Astor's wrath fell upon John Wheeler-Bennett, an erstwhile friend of Trott, who had once favored responding to the opposition's overtures, but turned into a fierce critic of the military's moral abdication in his book *Nemesis of Power* (London,1953), a study of the army's political role since 1918.[110] Most of those involved in the *Encounter* debate rejected Astor's position, although Visser 't Hooft faulted British policy, as he had during the war. In general, British views were little changed. Opening negotiations with the German resistance, it was argued, threatened to drive a wedge between the Western allies and Stalin; the opposition seemed too fragmented and too divorced from the mass of Germans to be credible; also, its proposals for a settlement were vague, contradictory, and unacceptable in the context of 1944. The risks, in other words, were excessive given the chance of success. Early in the war Chamberlain had believed that significant anti-Nazi factions existed, and he was prepared to contact them. This had facilitated the Venlo debâcle. But by 1943 the mood in governing circles was very different; so-called 'Vansittartism'—the view that one could not differentiate between Nazis and Germans—had become dominant. To prevent a repeat of the "stab in the back" mythology, it was also deemed essential that Germany be purged by complete military defeat. There was also a feeling that the liberal recipe tried in 1918, of leaving Germans to reform their politics, was unacceptable. The German opposition's assumption that after a coup they would be allowed to decide their governmental structure ran counter to Allied ideas about the need for occupation and a program of "denazification" and "re-education."

The claim that Britain's indifference to the German *Widerstand* undermined the chances of a successful coup against Hitler's regime downplays this larger context and the many reasons why it was highly unlikely that the kind of assurances Trott and others were seeking could be given. That said, Churchill's insistence on "absolute silence" towards such overtures, strongly endorsed by Eden and senior officials in Whitehall, encouraged, as P.R.J. King has argued, a kind of bureaucratic "group think" which meant that information about conflicts within the Nazi state, gathered by SIS and intelligence agents like Wiskemann, were discounted, blocked, hamstrung.[111] The divisions between the Abwehr and Himmler were, for example, brilliantly evaluated by Trevor-Roper in 1942, who presented his findings directly to Churchill's advisor, Lord Cherwell, while in May and June of 1944 SIS was getting reports from Lisbon of an imminent coup attempt. And yet when the ill-fated July 20 assassination plot occurred, the British government was unprepared and largely uninformed. The government's conviction and that of Whitehall was that Air Marshal Harris's area bombing and black propaganda was the way to break German morale and shorten the war, not by pinning one's hopes upon a military–civilian coup orchestrated from above.

By contrast, as we have seen, Allen Dulles was much more open to intelligence about the German opposition. Deeply worried about the advance of Soviet forces and the threat that large parts of Europe would go communist, by 1944 he believed that a coup was likely and that it could hasten peace. And yet, Dulles too was in no position to provide Germans with any assurances for the future: as a result, he often left Washington in the dark about details of his contacts with the German resistance. In the wake of the July plot, massive roundups shattered the resistance in Germany.[**] Dulles's fears increased that Germany would descend into social chaos while Soviet forces would soon reach Yugoslavia and then seal off Trieste and northern Italy, where communist partisan activity was already prevalent. By early 1945 feelers for talks were coming to him from Italy, especially from SS General Karl Wolff, Himmler's police leader and effectively military governor in Italy.[112] Dulles began negotiations (code name "Operation Sunrise") and met with Wolff secretly with the aim of hastening the war's end, saving many lives, and protecting northern Italian industries from scorched-earth destruction. Hearing of these conversations, Stalin immediately made angry and insulting protests to Roosevelt in Washington. Roosevelt demanded that the negotiations be broken off, but Dulles continued without authorization. After numerous delays a cease-fire was arranged, but only five days before the general unconditional surrender of all German forces. Wolff's goal in all this was clearly to save his own skin; Dulles insisted Sunrise involved no *quid pro quo*, but two Swiss intermediaries later admitted that it did, and recent research has shown convincingly that Dulles

---

[**] Gisevius returned to Berlin in advance of the attempted coup. After its failure he went into hiding and, with Dulles's help, he finally managed to escape on false papers to Switzerland in late January 1945. He was one of the few to escape execution. He later appeared as a witness at Nuremberg.

went to enormous lengths to shield Wolff and Himmler's representative in Rome, Eugen Dollmann, from war crimes prosecution.[113] Dulles published his own account of Sunrise which did much to burnish his reputation as a master of the clandestine arts.[114]

Wiskemann was far more skeptical than Dulles about the potential of the German resistance. And while revering the physical and moral courage of individuals like Hans and Inge Scholl, Bernstorff, Trott, and many others, she found it difficult to believe that German military leaders would break their oath of allegiance and join a conspiracy. She always believed that Nazi ideology had a far stronger hold on Germans than Fascism had established in Italy; as a result, while opposition to the Hitler regime increased, only a small minority moved from criticism to active resistance. As for "Operation Sunrise," through her Italian friends and informants (especially the Slovak, codenamed Z or Q1), Wiskemann knew a great deal about General Wolff, whom she viewed as "the man primarily responsible for the reign of terror" launched against Italian civilians and partisans in the North. He was, she wrote, "a man with a record as evil as that of Heydrich or Himmler himself."[115] As to Dulles's negotiation: In her memoir she was characteristically unforthcoming: "I personally would not have thought it safe to deal with him (This, however, was a military matter and nothing whatever to do with me)."[116]

*　*　*

As a journalist in Berlin during the early years of the Nazi regime, Wiskemann described the escalating violence towards Jews, and immediately before the war she had experienced first-hand the growing ant-Semitism sweeping through Eastern Europe and its political manipulation. In the war years, news of racial violence, mass killings, deportations, and death camps flowed into Switzerland from numerous sources, and Wiskemann reported to London whatever she learned. Exactly how much she knew is unclear since much of what she conveyed to Whitehall has been destroyed and at times she was specifically told "not to send too much information about concentration camp horrors."[117] Within Switzerland, her Zurich friends the Oprechts and Dübys[118] helped Jews fleeing from France, Italy, and Germany, while Count Bernstorff and Richard Kuenzer, working for the Solf group, helped organize money and lines of escape into the country. Whether Wiskemann played any role in these efforts will probably never be known; she was tight-lipped about such things. But towards war's end her friends the Wertheimers, Jewish art dealers who had escaped from Germany first to Paris and then to Basle, presented her with a Piranesi drawing in recognition of the help she had given to Jews; it became a prize possession, bequeathed at her death to the Fitzwilliam Museum in Cambridge.[119]

Within the Reich, the most radical new racial policy that began with the outbreak of war was the gassing of "incurables" and psychiatric patients in Germany's asylums. The euthanasia program began in August 1939 with the killing of about

5,000 children; it then expanded to adult patients unlikely to contribute to society, focusing upon a quota of 70,000 patients deemed 'unworthy of life.' It continued until the end of the regime and accounted for some 216,400 deaths (considerably more than the number of German Jews killed by the regime). Code-named T-4 after the address of its headquarters at Tiergartenstrasse 4, Berlin, the program was shrouded in secrecy, but inevitably information leaked and efforts to conceal what was happening from families, including careless errors in explaining these deaths, created many rumors and public alarm. The first reports about euthanasia reached London in September 1940 from a source in the Vatican, while American intelligence also picked up information from journalists and from questioning refugees arriving in North America.

Early reports were vague, but soon more factual details reached the legation in Switzerland. In December 1940 Ambassador David Kelly wrote to 'Rex' Leeper at the Foreign Office explaining that, while he had ignored earlier claims that came from anonymous or unknown sources, he had now received more concrete evidence about killing centers at Grafeneck and Linz, where several thousand had been gassed and their cremated remains returned to their relatives.[120] Some of this information seems to have come from Lörrach in south Baden, where Wiskemann had a well-informed source in Waldemar Hellmich. A Swiss woman returning from a sojourn with relatives in Munich also provided details about specific victims. Around this time, before being transferred from Bern to Lisbon, 'Boofy' Gore returned shaken from a visit to friends: "On returning from Basle at the beginning of the year…I remember him saying, 'Elizabeth, do you think it possible that in Germany they are just killing off incurables?' I replied 'Yes, Boofy, it is perfectly possible'."[121]

In March 1941 Wiskemann received "fresh evidence supplied by an Austrian-born Swiss who had just returned from visiting Vienna to the effect that all elderly people in Vienna were in terror."[122] She also informed her journalist friend Thomas Barman in Whitehall, now working in black propaganda. Kelly transmitted the details by telegram and urged London to go public with the information.[123] The BBC broadcast that 100,000 were said to have been killed already and that there were plans to extend the program to badly invalided veterans at the war's end. Goebbels quickly responded with a radio address denying that veterans were involved. The Foreign Office (and the American State Department) were more reluctant to use T4 in their propaganda, although by the summer of 1941, PWE leaflets dropped over north Germany provided details. In September it was American journalist William Shirer in *Life* magazine and *Readers' Digest* who alerted the wider American and British public to the mass killing techniques employed in the program, soon to be used against Jews. At the time, Wiskemann was waiting in London for transport back to Bern; she immediately wrote to Leeper: "I am interested to see that the stuff I sent home about euthanasia over 6 months ago is now coming from Shirer with the same places, Grafeneck and Sonnenstein, mentioned."[124]

Only fragments of the intelligence she sent to London about Jews can be identified; much was probably 'weeded' out from the files and much was dispersed to multiple agencies. Information was continually being passed to the World Jewish Congress, the World Council of Churches, representatives of East European governments, the League of Nations, the International Red Cross, and many other groups. Wiskemann was, then, well situated to obtain a great deal of information about the implementation of Nazi racial policy. Elizabeth Scott-Montagu recalled translating documents they had received on what was happening at Treblinka. In April 1942, on information recently supplied by a Swiss commercial representative, Wiskemann reported on racial violence in Antonescu's Romania—he "confirms that the most horrible things have undoubtedly occurred – this is not just talk...there is no doubt that Jews were literally butchered around December." At the port city of Braila her source observed how Jews "were without notice and without provision packed into goods trucks and transported to Transnistria"[††]; many never survived the four days' journey.[125] Another telegram, in March 1943, noted: "a usually reliable source reports an SS official in S.W. Germany stated the end of February in casual conversation that during the second half of 1942 about 30,000 Polish Jews had been killed by gas. He confirmed that this is the usual fate of Jews who cannot work."[126] The figure she cited was, of course, too low; but, as a good agent, she was accurately relaying the information that she had received. The same month she passed to Dulles information from Visser 't Hooft about the latest wave of Jewish persecution in Berlin and the roundups of *Mischlinge*.[127] Dulles's own reports contain little relating to the fate of European Jews, and his reticence is one of the most controversial and least understandable aspects of his performance in Bern.[128] Clearly Dulles learned a great deal and knew that information was reaching Washington via the US Legation, but the paucity of information in OSS archives, it has been speculated, may reflect the priority given to other covert projects and other aspects of the Nazi regime.[129] Max Hastings pointed out that Dulles provided little traffic on the Holocaust and that he failed to grasp that Nazi genocide of Jews transcended other mass murders underway.[130] This was certainly not the case with Wiskemann, who well understood the centrality and singularity of the regime's anti-Jewish policies.

In the circles in which Wiskemann moved there was constant discussion of the murder of Jews by the Nazi regime. Information about the mass slaughter carried out by *Einsatzgruppen* in the wake of the invasion of the Soviet Union, the roundups and deportations of Jews from Western and Central Europe, and the gassing of victims in Operation Reinhard, all were known in Switzerland, at least in part. Operations on such a scale could not be kept secret; many thousands of people

†† Transnistria was conquered by the Germans and Romanians in the summer of 1941 and was transferred to Romanian control. Some 300,000 Jews lived there pre-1939; tens of thousands were massacred by *Einsatzgruppen D* and the area was then used to deport Jews from elsewhere in Romania to ghettos and camps in the region.

were involved and still more were witnesses. Reports circulated in Geneva and Bern which pointed unambiguously to the genocidal intent of German policy. Wiskemann recalled later that "the Jewish banker with the German wife in Basle who had first brought us news...of the 'liquidation' of incurables" had "by the end of 1941" reported the 'final solution' to her.[131] Certainly, she grasped early on the continental scale of the regime's Jewish policy and in early August 1942 would have been aware of the famous telegram that Gerhart Riegner, Secretary of the World Jewish Congress in Geneva, sent to London (via Ambassador Norton) and Washington about a plan for the "extermination" after deportation of 3.5–4 million Jews in German-controlled and -occupied Europe.[132]

It was through her contact with Gerhart Riegner and Czech diplomat Jaromir Kopecky that Wiskemann's name—albeit tangentially—has entered scholarly debate about two issues of Holocaust historiography: First, when did the Western allies have knowledge of the location and true function of Auschwitz-Birkenau as the principal killing center of Jews? And second, should the allies have bombed Auschwitz or the Budapest–Birkenau railway? Both issues relate to the arrival in Switzerland from Bratislava of two reports about the death camp; the first by two escaped Slovaks, Vrba and Wetzler, who described the camp and the gassing procedure in detail, and the second, some weeks later, by two other escapees, Mordowicz and Rosin, who brought news that the deportation of Hungarian Jews was underway and that 90% of these recent transports were gassed and burned immediately. Until now the lives of most Hungarian Jews were not directly in danger. Regent Horthy, while certainly anti-Semitic, had so far rebuffed German pressure to deport Hungarian Jews. But in March 1944, antagonized by his efforts to open negotiations with the Allies and secede from the war, Hitler sent in German troops and Adolf Eichmann arrived to supervise the deportation of the country's Jews.[133] With the takeover in Hungary, Europe's largest remaining Jewish community—over 750,000 people—was in dire peril. Almost all the 600,000 Jews killed by the Germans in 1944 died at Auschwitz, most of them from Hungary.

The two reports provided the first detailed analysis of Auschwitz to reach Switzerland. As Richard Lichtheim, Geneva representative of the Jewish Agency for Palestine, wrote to his executive board: "We now know exactly what has happened and where it happened." There are conflicting accounts of how the reports reached Switzerland. One of the earliest informed was Jaromir Kopecky; other accounts were soon circulating and were reported by the Swiss press. Kopecky received from Bratislava on June 13 a report that combined the Vrba–Wetzler and Mordowicz-Rosin accounts and at once showed it to Gerhart Riegner. Reading the report, Riegner fixed upon a section which described a group of Czechs who were sent from Theresienstadt to Auschwitz, quarantined there for six months, and then killed; this was the first he had heard of quarantining. The document also referred to a second group of Czechs, transported in December 1943. In his words: "Six months, I thought to myself, what does it mean? In only seven days' time the second quarantine expires." He alerted Kopecky and they decided to immediately send a telegram to London in hopes of getting the BBC and US broadcasters to mount a campaign to avert the killing.[134]

Kopecky, Riegner recalled, knew a way: "He goes to the BBC representative at the British embassy, a lady –Wiskemann. I knew her too. And he sends it to her, and said, 'You should do this,' and it was done."[135] "Here," wrote Kopecky to Wiskemann on June 13, "are the details of the urgent message about the group of Jews in danger in Birkenau. Please do what you can so that the details are sent back as quickly as possible and are broadcast at once over the BBC etc. But it will be necessary to avoid mentioning the source. One could say simply over the radio: 'We have received this from a reliable source.' "[136] Drafted by Riegner, the telegram read:

According to report made by two Slovakian Jews who escaped from Birkenau to Bratislava and whose reliability is assured by Jewish leaders there 3,000 Czechoslovakian Jews who were brought from Terezin [Czech for Theresienstadt] to Birkenau on December 20, 1943 will be gassed after six months quarantine on about June 20, 1944. Appealing most urgently that this news may be broadcasted immediately through BBC and American radio in order to prevent at last moment this new massacre. Report which contains horrible detailed description of massacres in gas chambers Auschwitz Birkenau of hundreds of thousands Jews all nationalities occupied Europe states that already first group of about 4,000 Czechoslovakian Jews who arrived from Terezin [Teresienstadt] in Birkenau beginning September 1943 were after six months quarantine gassed on March 7, 1944. Report reveals that treatment both Czechoslovakian transports called SB Transports – Sonderbehandlungstransporte – was strikingly different from usual transports. Families were not separated, even children, school was allowed and prescription 6 months quarantine absolutely unusual. View fact that first group was entirely exterminated danger of imminent extermination second group most serious. Please issue without delay most impressive warning to German butchers who directing slaughter Upper Silesia. Do not mention Bratislava as source. Further reports following. Please inform immediately also the Czechoslovakian government.[137]

Wiskemann also passed on the telegram to Allen Dulles on June 14: "I have just wired this – could you also? EW 14/6."[138] On June 15 the BBC began broadcasting warnings in Czech and German. Dulles passed the message to Roswell McClelland of the War Refugee Board in Switzerland, who cabled it to Washington.

Additional information reached Switzerland in the next days. Lichtheim made his own detailed summary for the Jewish Agency executive in Jerusalem in which he wrote that 1.5 million Jews had been gassed at Birkenau since the spring of 1942. He had no doubt that the Vrba–Wetzler report was true and warned the Zionist leaders of the extreme danger now facing the Jews of Hungary as well as those in Theresienstadt. Soon appeals were made to bomb the railway lines leading to Auschwitz, thus preventing traffic between Hungary and Poland, but these ran into stiff opposition both in London and in Washington, where, at this crucial juncture with the intense battle underway in northern France, the air commands had other strategic priorities. The deportations had been underway for over a month at a rate of 10,000–12,000 people per day; nearly half of Hungarian Jews had already been deported.

Lichtheim contacted Ambassador Norton at the Bern Legation urging him to forward a telegram he had written to the Foreign Office calling for immediate action. The cable, whose dispatch Wiskemann supported, went out on June 26. In addition to laying out facts about the numbers of Jews killed at Auschwitz and that they had already been eliminated from rural Hungary, it contained six points: The first was to give the acts 'the widest publicity.' The second was a warning to the Hungarian government that its members would be held responsible for the fate of the Jews being deported from Hungary. The third was that reprisals be carried out against Germans being held in Allied hands. The fourth was a request for 'the bombing of railway lines' from Hungary to Auschwitz. The fifth was for the precision bombing of the death camp installations. The sixth and final request was for the bombing of government buildings in the Hungarian capital: "the target bombing of all collaborating Hungarian and German agencies in Budapest." The telegram gave the names and addresses of seventy Hungarian and German individuals who were stated to be most directly involved in sending Jews from Hungary to Auschwitz.[139] A week later the Foreign Office in London also received an eight-page summary of the Vrba–Wetzler report from Hubert Ripka, now Foreign Minister in the Czech exile government in London. On July 7 Churchill gave his personal support for bombing the railway lines, but on that day the deportations had halted, temporarily saving 150,000 Jews, although many Budapest Jews were killed later when the Ferenc Szálasi and the Arrow Cross seized power in mid-October 1944.

According to Sir Martin Gilbert, it was Wiskemann who decided "in a stroke of genius" to send Lichtheim's telegram unenciphered—so that Hungarian Intelligence could read it. It was intercepted and shown to Prime Minister Dome Sztójay, who passed it to Regent Horthy. Quite separately, six days later on July 2, as if carrying out the telegram's request, an American bombing raid on Budapest ran into thick cloud cover, missed their target, and did heavy damage to government buildings, including those listed in the Lichtheim telegram. Gilbert has argued that this pushed Horthy, who was still hesitating to confront Eichmann and the Germans, to block further deportations. Indeed, in a letter to the *Times* in 2005 he wrote: "Wallenberg and the other diplomats have all received recognition for their work. Now, Wiskemann, a Briton, deserves hers, as we commemorate the 60th anniversary of the liberation of Auschwitz."[140]

Wiskemann would have regarded this as an embarrassing inflation of what she had done. Her memoir made no reference to her role, and Gilbert's assessment of the Lichtheim telegram's role is too simplistic, for multiple pressures influenced Horthy's decision. He had wanted to stop the deportations in late June, and by early July faced both the threat of a coup from extreme pro-Nazi units within the police (which was successfully countered) and mounting pressure on the other side from Allied governments and appeals to halt the deportations from King Gustav V of Sweden, Pope Pius XII, and President Roosevelt. With the Axis military situation deteriorating rapidly (Soviet troops were only a hundred miles away), Horthy was desperately looking for a way to appease the Allies and he feared severe air attacks on Budapest and severe postwar retribution against Hungary.[141] However, an exchange between Prime Minister Sztójay and Edmund Veesenmeyer, the Reich's plenipotentiary in Hungary, on July 6 suggests that the Lichtheim telegram and subsequent American air raid played some part. When Sztójay explained Horthy's decision to halt deportations, he also revealed in detail the contents of the telegrams sent to the British and US governments from Bern. These, with their threats of retaliatory bombing and warnings of individual retribution, as Veesenmeyer reported to his boss, Foreign Minister Ribbentrop, had made a big impact on Sztójay and the council of ministers. In the end it is impossible to reconstitute in detail Wiskemann's role in this chain of events in the spring and summer of 1944 in Hungary. What does seem clear is that with official diplomatic circles responding slowly and cautiously to the deportations, an 'unofficial' network of people took shape which aimed to break through the silence, publicize the genocide, and generate pressure for action. This group included Riegner, Lichtheim, Visser 't Hooft, Adolf Freudenberg, Kopecky, George Mantello[‡‡], and Wiskemann, who seems to have been in regular contact with these men and part of this concerted effort.[142]

In 1981 when Gilbert analyzed Allied responses to the Holocaust, he was convinced that it was only with the Vrba–Wetzler report that they grasped the true function of Auschwitz. More recent research has demonstrated that, through Polish intelligence, signals intercepts, and other documents, credible knowledge reached them much earlier.[143] Michael Fleming has suggested that the "continued traction" of the argument about "the elusiveness of Auschwitz" stems from the support it gives to the notion that there was a genuine moral debate in London in summer 1944 over the possibility of intervention to save Hungarian Jews, a debate

---

[‡‡] A Jew of Hungarian descent, Mantello (1901–92) worked as First Secretary for the Salvadorean consulate in Geneva. He and Walter Garrett of the Exchange Telegraph Company (a British news service) released news of the Vrba–Wetzler report to the Swiss press. Mantello also saved many Jews by issuing them false Salvadorean citizenship documents. David Kranzler, *The Man Who Stopped The Trains To Auschwitz* (Syracuse: Syracuse University Press, 2000).

in which senior politicians like Churchill and Eden were willing to act but were held back by senior Whitehall officials and the military.[144]

Had it wished to devise a response to Auschwitz, Fleming suggests, the government could have done so much earlier. There was little difference in the official response between the summer of 1944 and earlier debate. Officials insisted that winning the war was the first priority and the only way to save Jews; fears were raised that rescue efforts might produce a flood of unwelcome refugees to Palestine; targeted bombing of the camp was viewed as impracticable and anyway opposed by the Americans. From early in the war, senior officials (including people whom Wiskemann knew well like 'Rex' Leeper, Frank Roberts, and Frank Savery of the FO's Polish section) were inclined to view Jewish atrocity news as exaggerated and, even after the vast scale of the killing was indisputable, they doubted whether there was "a plan" for total extermination.[145] They were also determined to maintain control over the flow of information and restrain public pressure for action and rescue efforts. Far more information circulated, for example, in the Swiss than the British press. In the weeks following Vrba–Wetzler, however, a wider variety of people learned of the camp, with detailed articles appearing in, for example, the *Manchester Guardian* and other papers. Even so, PWE's Weekly Political Intelligence Summary (distributed to about 500 'notables') mentioned the slaughter of Jews and the gas chambers only once prior to July 1944, while BBC broadcasts to Hungary failed to issue warnings to Jews.[146]

As an agent in the field Wiskemann had little idea about discussions taking place in London. As a journalist pre-war she had experienced officials' spirit of disbelief when it came to analysis of Nazi policies or accounts of Jewish suffering. In Bern she was more than once discouraged from sending material on racial atrocities: in April 1943, for example, she was advised: "German information should omit (repeat omit) the following items: i) Material on Jews except when this shows changes in policy by authority, ii) Details of numbers and conditions of foreign workers, iii) Statistics or statements on health of population which are presumably obtainable from public sources."[147] And again in August 1944 she was informed: "We are not interested at this stage in the war in German atrocities in the occupied territories or in the shootings of Jews in Poland and Hungary."[148] Soon after, undeterred, she reported on a meeting that her source Q1 had with a talkative and boastful German named Bernsen, who was a director of the Trieste office of the Hamburg-Bremen shipping and logistics firm Kühne & Nagel, which was heavily involved in the handling of dispossessed Jewish property. Bernsen, she wrote, "had been charged with packing and transporting Jewish possessions in Trieste. He described German military and other authorities as completely corrupt. He is theoretically in Switzerland to discuss with the Red Cross transmission of food arrangements for Greek children but said frankly that the chief object of his journey was to arrange to smuggle all that he had stolen in Italy into Switzerland. Such action had been urgently recommended to him by high

German authorities who had also provided him with all the facilities." She continued: "This individual is also engaged, he says, in blackmailing Jews who escaped to Geneva by offering to rescue valuable possessions left by Jews in Italy, if the Jew pays up; having been paid Bernsen keeps the stuff. He thinks he will find room for activity in Hungary and Roumania after the Germans have abandoned Italy." These confessions, she believed, "were fairly certainly genuine if slightly exaggerated."[149]

By spring 1945, however, as Allied armies invaded Germany and public outcry grew over the liberated concentration camps, instructions from London changed. As Wiskemann wrote later: "In the past I had had messages not to send too much information about concentration camp horrors; I had even destroyed some of my material in some bitterness. Now, suddenly I was to send all I could, now when they could see with their own eyes."[150] Among her last actions before leaving Switzerland was to send to London, now preparing for war crime tribunals, "material on concentration camps and the S.S. which may be immediately relevant and should therefore not wait for me."[151]

*   *   *

On August 23, 1944, as she cycled past the French Embassy, Wiskemann saw that the tricolor flag was again flying there, for the first time since 1940.[152] She quickly telephoned her friend Marcel Vaidie, who confirmed that the Vichy Ambassador, Paul Morand, had fled "à la montagne" and the Gaullists had taken over. Vaidie himself was moving back into his old office, and his close friend Jean Vergé, who Wiskemann knew well, had taken over as chargé d'affaires. With Allied advances since D-Day, Paris was liberated and the frontier was open again. Switzerland was no longer encircled, and travel was theoretically possible to Paris and on to London. It was almost three years since she had been to England; she was longing to at least get some leave and felt an urgent need to make plans for her future. In the next weeks other civilians were beginning to go home on leave,[153] but her workload was heavy, even increasing, and somebody had to be found to fill in. She advised: "With regard, by the way, to someone coming here to 'hold the fort' in my brief absence and possibly stay and work with me, may I say that it would be most unfortunate if another woman should be chosen, as I have already had sufficient disadvantage from being female and it would substantially facilitate things to have some masculine support."[154] After receiving a telegram instructing her to focus upon the cessation of hostilities rather than Germany's future, she wrote to Lieutenant-Colonel Kerr, "This causes me to beg you more insistently to facilitate a short visit to London at the earliest opportunity," adding, "The Minister [Norton] has already suggested to Mr. Lockhart that if I am not to be further officially employed, it is an almost life and death question for me to get back to free-lance political writing and fix certain things with my editors before it is too late. I have to earn my living and having been cut off here has already constituted a serious handicap."[155] But London dragged its feet in finding a replacement, causing Kerr to observe tartly: "Should he [the Director General – i.e. Bruce Lockhart] refuse her request I think she will be a very disgruntled lady, and to do good intelligence work I think you need to be at least moderately 'gruntled'."[156]

Wiskemann was working under intense pressure during this last phase of the war. Demands for information from PWE's different regional directorates increased. Whitehall demanded information about the Salò Republic, Italian attitudes towards the Savoy monarchy, morale in German cities after Allied raids, conditions on the eastern front, and much more. Overworked and understaffed, she found it difficult if not impossible to meet all London's demands. As Brigadier Eric Sachs, Director of Political Warfare Intelligence, recognized in an October 1944 memo: "Miss Wiskemann has been particularly successful in servicing the Italian region, but this has understandably to some extent been at the expense of her servicing the German and Austrian region. Similarly, if the latter is improved, the former will suffer, and the Italian region would be most averse to any diminution of their information concerning north Italy, of which Miss Wiskemann is the chief provider."[157] The Italian section of PWE, now led by the refugee philosopher Raymond Klibansky, had nothing but praise for her work, and those, like Elisabeth Barker, responsible for propaganda aimed at Yugoslavia were equally happy.[158] But her success in these areas provoked attacks from those directing black propaganda against Germany. Clifton Child, a Foreign Office official and close ally of Sefton Delmer, complained to Kerr: "Most of the information which we have received from Bern in the past few months has been of no earthly use to us. We are not interested at this stage in the war in German atrocities, or the shootings of Jews in Poland and Hungary." Instead, he wanted specifics on the breakdown of police and SS authority, the hardships experienced by German civilians, and information about German deserters fleeing into Switzerland.[159] Kerr replied that other departments at Bern (presumably SOE) were already supplying some of this information and he had advised Wiskemann that it would cause "friction and confusion" if she reported on these matters too.[160]

Wiskemann seems to have made a powerful enemy in Sefton Delmer. She had first met him in the early 1930s in Berlin, where he had been a star correspondent for the *Daily Express* but was regarded suspiciously by his peers for having too cozy ties with the Nazi leadership, including Ernst Röhm and Goebbels. Tireless, notoriously combative, and contemptuous of the BBC and people like Crossman and Voigt who had opposed his ideas, Delmer had been appointed Director of PWE's Special Operations in June 1944, although he was effectively that long before. He was convinced that black propaganda, in conjunction with Bomber Command's terror bombings of German cities, could accelerate a German surrender, and he insisted that his needs be given priority. To Kerr he wrote angrily: "Miss Wiskemann herself gave me a thoroughly uncollaborative impression and

I do not think we shall ever get any value for Black out of her. She is infinitely more interested in the hot-blooded Italian angle than the German, and it is quite clear that single-handed she is unable to cover more than one field at a time; and as her preference is Italy, Lugano is the field she has most at heart. That, at any rate, was my impression from what she said." He continued: "[She] gave me the impression of being much too Scarlet Pimpernel-minded for the humdrum needs of mere Black propaganda. She said, for instance, that it was quite impossible for any of the people she sends into Germany to cover such stories as we need as this would blow them completely. I do not know, of course, what valuable secrets these prized agents of Miss Wiskemann's bring back with them, but certainly we are the last to demand that there should be any secret agents going into Germany at all for our purposes. All we want is ordinary, common, decent reporting on the spot on matters of interest to this Unit not secret, hush hush Scarlet Pimpernel nonsense."[161] Kerr passed the letter to his boss, Brigadier Sachs, noting with his usual insouciance: "the attached rather childish effusion from Delmer. Do you think it could be the result of an old and unsuccessful 'pass'?"[162]

It was clear to just about everyone that, on her own, Wiskemann could not cope with all the demands for black and white propaganda for Germany, Italy, Austria, Hungary, and Yugoslavia.[163] But nothing was done to rectify the situation; indeed, Whitehall tried to add to her tasks. Thus, Clifton Child wanted to know why she wasn't supplying information about the activities of prominent Germans in Switzerland (for example, Fieldmarshal Kesselring's efforts to contact his Swiss relatives to safeguard himself postwar).[164] Another telegram pressed her for details about German visitors to Swiss hotels. Clearly infuriated and not one to be pushed around, she shot back that this was not her area of responsibility: "Further I am literally single-handed to dash round from frontier to frontier and cannot possibly watch hotels for German visitors into the bargain. As it is, I have been overworking for three years, practically without leave."[165] Ironically, amid these criticisms, the issue of her salary arose. Wiskemann's pay was £600 p.a. plus traveling expenses (including taxis), which had to be carefully noted and were reviewed by Whitehall accountants. Partly, perhaps, because of the odd way that her position had evolved, this was dramatically less than others (i.e. men) in comparable posts (about £1,300). Norton, the Minister at Bern, called for "an appreciable increase in Miss Wiskemann's salary," suggesting a raise of £250, £150 of which might be designated a rent allowance.[166] MOI had some objections, but the Treasury settled on an increase of £200.[167]

She finally received permission to travel and set off on November 14, 1944, driving to Lyon, where she hoped to get a flight to London. Lyon itself was grim: in their retreat the Germans had destroyed the bridges across the Rhone and only an improvised bridge was in use. Food was scarce and she ate in the US army mess, while waiting for two days to get a plane and then only to Paris. Her days in London were hectic, seeing many old friends for the first time in four years, trying to pull together the threads of her pre-war journalistic life and thinking hard about her future.[168] After the fuel and water shortages of Switzerland she found London warm and hot water more plentiful: "it seemed extraordinary to me... to see brightly burning coal fires and the doors left open – in Switzerland we rushed to close everything round anything that gave out heat. I did not mind a shallow bath provided I could have it and it was hot." Feeling more affluent than usual, she spent one weekend at the Savoy with her oldest friend, "cousin Jane," who had been employed by the BBC pre-war but was now doing censorship work.[169] The rest of time she raced round London seeing British and Allied colleagues and old friends. These included the Kellys, now back in Britain, her old mentor in Berlin, Ernest Rowe-Dutton (working with Keynes on plans for the postwar financial structure), Jan Masaryk, 'Boofy' Gore, and her old friend Moura Budberg, who was working for the Free French. She addressed a group of Foreign Office officials on how the war looked from Switzerland and met with Bruce Lockhart, Frank Roberts, and John Wheeler-Bennett. She also seems to have had a rather hostile encounter with Sefton Delmer. Her last two nights in London were spent with the physicist P.M.S. Blackett and his wife, whom she knew well from her undergraduate years at Cambridge. Her leave lasted only two weeks; then, having agreed to finish out the war, she returned to Bern.[170]

In Bern, where no replacement had been found during her leave, there was plenty to do. Requests for information concerned all manner of things: Italian attitudes towards the Savoy monarchy, the views of the Catholic clergy, Czech deserters from the German army, Hungarian politics and the activities of the churches there. Friends and loyal informants sought news of relatives caught in air raids; she was also swamped with questions about Jews, escaped POWs, refugees, notable Nazis and Quislings now seeking refuge on Swiss soil, German deserters, and the transfer of Nazi party and state funds to Switzerland. Waldemar Hellmich, the director of Hoffmann La Roche in Lörrach, Baden [her source Q2], sought news of his airman son, reported missing from a raid over England; his son had written "an indiscreet letter" which had passed through German censorship and could have attracted the Gestapo's attention. Wiskemann checked with London, which stated definitely that he was neither a POW nor had his body been identified. Kerr authorized enquiries "because she feels he will be useless as a source of information until his present anxiety is relieved."[171] She asked London to respond to a request from her agent, the textile manufacturer Q1, who worried that his former secretary in Como might be accused as a collaborator when, in fact, she had been working for him and the Allies.[172] By contrast, when the powerful Italian industrialist Franco Marinotti applied for a British visa to see his friends at Courtaulds, she pointed out that the partisans viewed him as a fascist enemy who had eagerly cooperated with the Germans: "it will cause more than unnecessary bitterness if he gets a British visa."[173] In general, she worried that Allied occupation authorities in Italy were too quick to reinstate fascists rather than assist those who had supported the Allied cause.

With the end of the war in sight, notwithstanding Hitler's last and briefly successful offensive in the Ardennes, Wiskemann was very worried for her best informants, whom she feared might become overconfident and less prudent now that victory seemed so close. For example, Franz Kramer [Q3], her source within the German Legation at Bern, seemed to be under increasing suspicion when a new press attaché arrived in June 1944 charged with tightening up security. Consequently, she wrote, "he was not quite so helpful towards the end, though he brought me quite entertaining stories about Eva Braun and other German court favorites."[174] The new attaché, Prince Albrecht von Urach, came from a morganatic branch of the Württemberg royal family and had previously served as Foreign Office liaison between the German and Italian press in Rome. He launched a purge of those considered 'unreliable' but luckily his zest for this task soon waned; he also seems to have been engaged in smuggling Nazi capital out of Switzerland to the USA via "Banque Charles" in Monaco, where his second cousin, Louis II, reigned. Summoned to Berlin after questions were raised about his "defeatism," Kramer refused to go and had to break with the legation.[175] Wiskemann was also anxious about Q1, her valuable source on northern Italy, who regularly traveled there. He had been providing intelligence for over a year but was now having difficulty in crossing the frontier.[176] He had managed to get close to Count Thun in Como, who ran a German *Nachrichtenstelle*, and, "In return for a little trivial information cooked up with me," Wiskemann wrote, "Thun gives him the necessary permits to travel to Como and Milan."[177] He was not yet under arrest, but it might happen at any moment and, compounding his troubles, the Swiss were trying to expel him.[178]

Worried that Germany might descend into chaos, creating opportunities for Soviet-sponsored communism, Dulles had for some time argued that Washington needed to identify anti-Nazi Germans whose help could be enlisted once the war ended. Britain was more hesitant in doing this. Indeed, Visser 't Hooft complained to Wiskemann in December 1944: "I tried to make it clear that we would like to pass on information and suggestions to the British Government but that, so far, we had not met with much response." The Americans were more responsive, he added, but "we do not want to deal only with the American Government...which is further away from the realities of the European Continent." She transmitted his letter to London, where Richard Law and Arnold Toynbee welcomed his help, but Eden and Geoffrey Harrison of the Foreign Office German department seem to have dismissed his offer. Noting Visser 't Hooft's connections to the German opposition and the July 20 plotters, Harrison concluded: "I should be very reluctant to see our own official contacts with him extended."[179]

While Visser 't Hooft's offer of help was rebuffed, Whitehall began preparing for the future and Wiskemann was asked to assist in compiling lists of persons in Germany and Austria who may usefully occupy responsible positions after the defeat of the Nazis, "specifically of judges, civil servants, and people of local importance."[180] In late September 1944, trying to get some clarification,

Wiskemann asked: "Am I right in supposing that, as military warfare ends, political warfare is rather likely to expand? If so, I need directives and assistance here. People flood me with suggestions about the future organization of Germany and I am helpless as to how to respond...Innumerable people offer themselves to help re-educate the Germans and so on. Ought I not sometime to have at least a policy about all this? I have next to no idea as to what views are held in London nowadays on such points. There are various people here with more or less solid contacts with West and South Germany of which it might be wise to make use." She adds: "Or is the S.I.S. taking over? They tell me their instructions are increasingly political." A note was penciled onto this (presumably from Director of Plans) advising "a suitably evasive answer" since everyone was in the dark and no policy had been announced as to the future of occupied Germany.[181]

Wiskemann was also anxious to plan her own life, given that she had no job to return to. Anticipating her return to England, Trevor Blewitt, an old friend at the BBC, wrote: "We are on the lookout for suitable experts on Europe to join our panel of Foreign Affairs commentators and I shall be very glad to get in touch with you sometime about it."[182] Another possibility was continuing in government service. But the future of different intelligence agencies was very much up in the air and it was difficult to get answers from her superiors. In April 1945 she asked Kerr if PID would continue to exist, adding that when she was in London the previous November everyone said it would be wound up, but now that seemed uncertain. She needed answers to be able to make her own decisions. An official sent over to Bern by Richard Crossman had spoken of the extensive postwar programs that would be needed during the coming period; she indicated: "It would interest me extremely if there were any possibility of my being 'in' on this."[183] Three weeks later, she wrote: "Would I be useable to help re-educate Germans? It sounds to me a horrible job, but I've had a lot of teaching experience, school...and university."[184] Her preference was to serve PID in Italy, where she had many useful contacts in Rome and the North; she would, she wrote, also consider seriously going to Prague, Vienna, or Germany "but should be grateful to have nothing more to do with Germany for a long time."[185] Raymond Klibansky, head of PWE's Italian Directorate, felt very strongly that a position should be found for her in either the Central Europe or Italian section. Another officer commented: "I feel under some sort of obligation to help her in her struggle for existence as she has done excellent work for us and has suffered, from the point of view of making plans for her future, by being marooned so long in Switzerland."[186] Whether Wiskemann continued to work for British intelligence once peace returned is unclear. Her wide-ranging experience made her highly qualified for the task, but planning for what was called 'the re-education' of Germany had been underway since 1943 while she was fully occupied in Bern. She was, it seems, being considered for something in either Italy or the occupation services of the British zone in Germany.[187] But, not for the first or the last time, one senses reluctance in these overwhelmingly male circles. She was fiercely intelligent and productive, but not pliable and not always a 'team player' ; indeed, she was strongly independent and outspoken—'high maintenance' in today's parlance—a characteristic not viewed as a virtue in bureaucratic circles.[188]

Wiskemann's life in the last two years of the war was overwhelmingly work-focused. They were years of concentrated living: travel, meetings, reports, excitement, and intense activity. There were pleasant dinners and weekends with friends, but she was often lonely, depressed, and homesick. Squabbles with legation officials like Evans, the press attaché, and turf battles with SOE and military intelligence took their toll, as did her worries about sources who traveled to Axis Europe and might be in danger. At Christmas 1943 she wrote to her friend Guglielmo Alberti: "I hope you will have a tolerable Christmas. I'm so childishly homesick that I mostly want to cry in a dark corner." To Allen Dulles she sent: "All my very best wishes for Christmas and for our liberation next year." He replied with roses: "The roses are lovely and give me pleasure and consolation, thank you."[189]

Lack of surviving sources and Wiskemann's own reticence and penchant for privacy mean that her private life is recoverable only in fragments; the rest remains a mystery. Sometimes romantic relationships seem to have blossomed, but if they didn't work out, she turned to Harry Bergholz for solace—even though his pessimism sometimes made matters worse.[190] Bergholz recalled how they relied on each other in difficult times: "Her position in Switzerland, her important, exciting and difficult work, put a nervous strain on her that she sometimes found difficult to endure and she sought a break with a reliable and confidential friend... it was especially good to have a friend in each another when the political storm was at its worst in the outside world... better to be near one another in such moments, instead of alone." He added, "Probably it became clearer earlier to Elizabeth than to I that I was not for her, and she not for me, the ideal life-partner. As a result, there was no anger and no jealousy later when she and I entered into other relationships."[191] Stood up by the international public health expert Raymond Gautier, she wrote Bergholz in March 1943: "My dear, you helped me such a lot – thank you again. I shall come as usual on Wed. 24th unless the skies fall... Have just had an immense telegram from Raymond, full of LOVE but he will not be coming. I would prefer it the other way round! I am cutting him out. I would even rather be quite alone than this kind of messing about. I suppose I was a fool and let myself be fascinated by being adored, whereas the sort of understanding there is between you and me is much more important, au fond. Life still seems VERY BLOODY; my nerve-controls are working again but you can still help me a great deal... Love E."[192] Making plans to visit her friends, the Szilasis, at Brissago, she writes: "I do hope you will be able to come chéri. I enjoyed last weekend very much. It is a curious but lovely relationship between us, I think. I am so glad it has come right."[193]

Two weeks later her mood was much darker: "I hope you are very happy, whether alone or not. I'm not, but that is an old story and a bore. I do miss not being able to drop into supper with you in Lausanne... The feeling of utter desolation from which I suffer is uppermost again, so I had better stop. Anyway, I look forward a great deal to seeing you soon. Hélène [Heroys, see p.114 footnote] tries hard but you are really the only person who helps... thank you again so much, my dear, and I only hope I give as much as I get. After all, *au fond*, although I'm so perplexing, we do understand and trust each other pretty well and that makes me feel – when we're together – as if I were living my normal good life at home. The Greek 'Good Life'? Yes, it was in some ways, even allowing for the enchantment lent by distance. Love E."[194] In August 1943, with "the flat full of food and no one else invited," she invites him for the weekend: "I hesitate a bit because I'm tired and rushed and feel I shall be bad company, but you are very patient with me and it may be quite nice for you to come and I may not be free again – oughtn't to be – am neglecting all my social obligations."[195]

By spring 1944 Wiskemann's letters and quick notes to Bergholz—as always, the recipient of her intimate thoughts and worries—contained more and more references to "F" or Marchese Francesco Antinori, to whom she had become increasingly attached. "F and I are to meet on Monday," she writes, "and after that it may be even worse! Or if Monday doesn't happen, I feel I shall go mad. Should like to have a word with you tonight as to how you and I can keep me organized and on my feet. Can't sleep or eat much."[196] A couple of weeks later: "a quite lovely time with F last weekend, really reciprocal," and at the end of May 1944: "I don't think I'm deceiving myself that things are fairly near perfection between us."[197]

Antinori's situation was precarious; his anti-fascism had impeded his diplomatic career over the years and now his job at the Italian Legation in Bern had ended and he was without means of support. Also, in May 1945 Wiskemann explained to Guglielmo Alberti: "I am in a torment about F for we are devoted to one another. I am terrified that wicked people are trying to get him accused in Rome to make him a victim of the *epurazione*. And you know the more I know him the better I know how good he is." She was organizing her friends in the press to combat such accusations: "Could you not write a protest to the *Sentinelle* – they ought to be bombarded. I have, I think, got the Socialist leader in the Swiss parliament to reprove them. You know Braun von Stumm[§§] would not have F in the house."[198] She also seems to have arranged through Gerald Mayer, Bern head of the US Office of War Information, some translation jobs for Alberti, Antinori, and Bergholz. But she could also be irked at Antinori's passivity, confiding to Alberti: "Francesco came to lunch today and I scolded him. He said he didn't like

---

[§§] A cousin of Francesco, Maria Giuseppina Antinori (1897–1943), married Gustav Braun von Stumm, a fervent Nazi official in the press section of the German Foreign Office. She committed suicide in 1943.

to say anything especially as he had got the impression that it was too late anyway. But he is really very keen and will go to see Mottironi in Geneva whenever we tell him to. I know your mind is naturally full of other things but <u>please help him as much as you can.</u> You will be helping me too."[199] Wiskemann was also requesting help from London. Couldn't something be done for him, she asked Klibansky: "I shall feel horribly ashamed if he is left to starve in a garret after all he has done to help our section" [he was Q6 in her correspondence with London]. She pointed to the numerous meetings he had arranged for her which led to good intelligence and mentioned that Dulles regarded him highly. But, she added, Antinori's cultural and intellectual roots were more in the British tradition and he would be happy to go to England if work could be found for him there.[200]

In May 1945, when Bergholz was deeply worried about his own future since neither a US visa nor a job in Britain had materialized, Wiskemann felt guilty about her preoccupation with Antinori: "In the train: I am terribly sorry that I can't be more help to you and I wish I could have been nicer this evening. I wanted to be because you are a very nice person and it is imperative that you recover yourself after holding out all these years so extraordinarily well. I'm a little bit too much taken up with my own problem, I fear. For the first time in our respective lives he [Francesco] and I would wish to marry, but I dare not give up my passport. Thank you for all your goodness to me and forgive me my irritability sometimes – my fault, not yours. Best love and best luck, Elizabeth"[201] Probably around the same time, she again wrote: "Wednesday morning: Please may I come to you next Sunday at 15.30 till the evening. The worst possible thing has happened to me and I believe you will be good to me won't you? It was one reason why I was in a state. A difficulty, perhaps very grave with Francesco. Je souffre terriblement. Love & gratitude. E"[202]

Antinori returned to Italy in early June 1945: "You do understand," she explained to Bergholz, "I believe, that I had to put F before everything until he goes. It sounds absurd but I know it's true when he says he cares about nothing else in life but me. And I adore him."[203] They did not marry, but remained close for a number of years, especially immediately after the war when Wiskemann was living in Rome.[204] Perhaps her friends were right: that the commitment scared her and she feared losing her independence. As she told Guglielmo Alberti: "We may get married some day when we are VERY old; it all depends upon the promised British law*** which would allow me to keep my British passport without which we should be condemned quite literally to starve."[205] She was in her mid-forties and enjoyed her freedom and her financial independence; also, her career

***

*** This refers to the Labour government's promised British Nationality Act of 1948. Until 1948, women were assumed to renounce their citizenship upon marriage to a foreigner (even if their husband's country did not automatically grant citizenship). It is unclear that Wiskemann's journalistic earnings would have been affected by such a marriage; possibly her connection with Chatham House required citizenship and the same if she were still working for British Intelligence.

in journalism required frequent travel and was not easily adaptable to marriage. Her future was uncertain, but it was hard for her to contemplate subordinating it to another's needs.

Wiskemann herself was making preparations to return to London. First came "a week's pure holiday" at Brissago on Lake Maggiore, where her friends Wilhelm and Lili Szilasi lived; he was a philosopher, a disciple of Husserl and Heidegger, who had left Germany in 1933. Then she packed up and sent off her files to the Foreign Office and finally left Switzerland on June 26. Altogether she had spent five years there. Most of her Italian friends had already left Bern; so had Dulles— her last scribbled note to him asked: "Will I ever see you again?" Just before her departure she received a message from her old friend from Vienna, Eugen Kogon, who had survived six years in Buchenwald and was now recording his experiences for the Allied authorities in what became *Der S.S. Staat*, the first major study of the camps.[206]

In August, not long after Wiskemann left, her source in the German embassy in Bern, Franz Kramer, returned to Germany. He settled in Koblenz, founded a publishing company, and got a license from the Allies to begin publishing as chief editor of the liberal Catholic weekly *Rheinische Merkur*. He died of a heart attack in 1950 aged only forty-nine years. Harry Bergholz was still stranded in Lausanne, supporting himself by ghost-writing and working for an interpreters' training academy. Wiskemann tried to get Robert Birley to hire him back to Charterhouse school, but nothing came of that. In 1947 he emigrated to the US, teaching for ten years in the German department at the University of Michigan and then North Carolina. He and Wiskemann continued to correspond until her death.

Elizabeth Scott-Montagu returned to London, where she began a successful career working on film scripts for several directors, especially Alexander Korda (among the films she worked on was Carol Reed's *The Third Man*, 1949). Later, in the 1960s, she founded a company that produced advertising for TV. Two other women should also be mentioned, whose lives before and after wartime intersected with that of Wiskemann. Elisabeth Barker first came into contact with Wiskemann in the mid-1930s when she worked as BBC Foreign Talks sub-editor; in the war she migrated to Foreign Office intelligence and then PWE, where she became Director of the South-east Europe section.[207] There she was a strong champion of Wiskemann's reports and defended her against occasional criticism from SOE and other quarters.[208] After the war, like Wiskemann, Barker chose to go abroad and wrote brilliantly as a foreign correspondent for Reuters in Tito's Yugoslavia. She and Wiskemann remained good friends, especially in the 1950s when Barker returned to the BBC, eventually becoming head of European Talks.[209] Finally, Shiela Grant Duff, whose journalistic life pre-war had crossed paths with Wiskemann in the Saar and Czechoslovakia, was from May 1941 to September 1943 head of the Czech section of the BBC's European Service. Initially, like Wiskemann, she had joined Toynbee's Foreign Research and Press

Service at Oxford, but soon left, complaining to her 'cousin' Clementine Churchill that the organization was chaotic and amateurish, morale was low, and the group was fast hemorrhaging talent as people resigned hoping to join something more like a central intelligence agency.[210] She was highly successful at the Czech Service of the BBC, working with a remarkable group of exiles, including Hubert Ripka, Jan Masaryk, Josef Korbel (father of Madeleine Albright), and Prokop Drtina.[211] She also married, in 1942, Noel Newsome, who founded the BBC's European Service and was frequently embroiled in turf battles with "Rex' Leeper of the Foreign Office, including over access to the intelligence that Wiskemann was providing. Grant Duff continued to be deeply involved in Czech affairs after the war, but later turned away from politics and professional journalism, devoting herself to farming in Ireland.

While Wiskemann was finalizing her preparations to return home, Britain was in the throes of a general election campaign, which resulted in a landslide victory for the Labour party on July 26. Her politics had moved sharply left in the last phase of the war. Many of her friends and her sources of intelligence were socialists and she admired the role of communists in the European resistance; her enthusiasm for the Action party derived from the hope that it might reconcile the pressing need for sweeping social reform while preserving liberal freedoms. She welcomed the new Labour government; the "central problem of our lives today," she believed, was "the search after *liberal-socialismo*: social justice without sacrifice of individual liberty."[212] She also had hopes that Labour might bring changes in British foreign policy and a modernization of the diplomatic corps, which, she argued, had let the country down between the wars (and whose representatives had often been her antagonists).[213]

Wiskemann had long regarded politics from the standpoint of Europe rather than Britain, and five years in Switzerland strengthened that focus. More than most commentators, she saw things from the perspective of Eastern Europe or Italy. The war, she reflected in August 1945, had "widened the psychological distance between Britain and the rest of Europe." Since Britain was never occupied, Continentals assumed British daily life was hardly affected by the war, while Britons had "no conception of the cost, moral and physical, of a Nazi occupation." And yet Labour's victory indicated to Europeans that the British "realize that collectivist methods have become essential... This is not a matter of party dogma in Europe today, it is a matter of bare, bitter necessity, because no individuals can grapple with the poverty to which Europe is reduced." Americans did not understand this since they lived "in a different economic epoch"; their anti-socialism and efforts to prevent the "over-due socialization of North Italian industry" were causing "popular sympathy even in Western Europe to turn fitfully eastwards."[214]

She had a 'good' war but not an easy one. Successful as an intelligence agent, she bore a lot of responsibility, worried constantly about the risks being taken by those who supplied her with information, but found few allies within her own legation. Bureaucratic slights and rivalries—to which she refused to submit—wore her down, and the strain is evident in her correspondence. She was justifiably proud of her service, although nobody thought to put her name forward for a war decoration and she received none. Now forty-six years old, she had spent the last fifteen years in the fight against Nazism and Fascism. She knew it would be a challenge to begin again—indeed, years later in her memoir, she mused, perhaps, I never have.[215] Her hope was to continue as a freelance European correspondent and also to devote herself to writing history—the history of her own time, which hardly existed as an academic subject. The final war years had rekindled her love of Italy and immersed her in Italian politics; her work in Switzerland with Italian exiles provided her with a wide range of contacts, many of them about to become key figures in the nation's political and cultural life. And so, for professional and personal reasons—including her love for Francesco—she decided to "devote my chief attention to Italy in the next few years, to see what would emerge."[216] In October 1945 she settled in Rome.

5

Starting Over in Postwar Europe

Italy emerged from the war devastated. Much of the country's housing stock was destroyed or severely damaged; 1.5 million deportees and POWs were not finally repatriated until 1947; industrial output was about a quarter of the 1941 figure; unemployment and hunger were widespread, with food shortages especially severe in the cities; and inflation was rampant, with 1945 prices twenty-four times the 1938 level, even after attempts to control rents and electricity and fuel prices. The nation was also deeply divided politically and regionally. Since the coup against Mussolini in September 1943 and German occupation of much of the peninsula, the South had experienced the Badoglio government, but in reality the rule of the Allied Military Government. Apart from the "four days of Naples" in September 1943 just before the Allies arrived, there were no popular insurrections in the South. The armed *Resistenza* was restricted to Northern and Central Italy, where a bitter, protracted conflict was waged against fascism and Nazi occupation, leading to the death of over 44,000 partisans and some 10,000 civilians in reprisal raids, and an unknown number of Italian fascists.

In June 1944, aided by Washington and against Churchill's wishes, Badoglio was finally replaced in Rome by a coalition of resistance parties led by the reformist Socialist Ivanoe Bonomi, who had led a government prior to Mussolini in 1922. By April 1945, as German forces retreated swiftly towards the alpine valleys of the north-east, the Italian resistance called for a general insurrection. The Salò Republic collapsed, Mussolini was captured and killed, and the partisan bands came down from the hills, liberating northern cities like Genoa, Turin, and Milan prior to the Allies' arrival. Local Committees of National Liberation (CNLs), mostly far left in their politics, began establishing local administrations, while the Allied Military Government moved swiftly to stabilize the situation, disarm the partisans, and contain the authority of the CNLs. Eventually, after two months of negotiations among the parties of the national resistance movement, Bonomi was pushed aside, replaced by a more radical interim coalition government with Ferruccio Parri, deputy commander of the resistance and a leader of the Action party as Prime Minister. Its task was to govern until a Constituent Assembly could be elected, which in turn would draft a new constitution, decide the fate of the Savoy monarchy, and undertake sweeping reforms. Parri's government, strongly supported by the local resistance committees, was the most radical that Italy had ever had, and hopes ran high that Italians were about to experience a radical reorganization of politics and society. But the power of the resistance was

Elizabeth Wiskemann: Scholar, Journalist, Secret Agent. Geoffrey Field, Oxford University Press.
© Geoffrey Field 2023. DOI: 10.1093/oso/9780192870629.003.0006

already ebbing; it had limited resonance in the South, while in the North the actions of some liberation committees, purges of former officials and police, and the numerous assassinations of fascists by vigilantes left a legacy of division and bitterness.

Wiskemann arrived in Italy in October 1945 and spent much of the next two years there. Shortly after returning to London, she had arranged to act as a fairly regular Rome correspondent for the *Economist* and also to contribute occasional articles to the *Observer* and the *Spectator*. She also contracted to write a short book for Oxford University Press titled *Italy* – part of a series, aimed at general readers, about European nations as they emerged from the war.[1] And she began planning a larger and more complex project: a scholarly book on the Rome–Berlin Axis and the changing relationship of Mussolini and Hitler. A good deal of German documentation for this was already available in a huge cache of captured files taken to the Foreign Office in London, while the Nuremberg trials soon provided a mass of additional evidence. But the material on Italy was more meager and official documents for Italian policy were unavailable. Here she planned to make good use of her skills as an investigative journalist, and through friends, especially Antinori, who had been Italian Press Attaché in Berlin from 1929 to 1940, she hoped to gain access to former fascist diplomats and officials.

The country was under military occupation, and she had initially to gain accreditation as an officer-journalist from the Allied military authorities and to wear a uniform. This also enabled her to draw rations from the NAAFI in Rome, where food was scarce and market prices were exorbitant. Transport was still in shambles; much of the rail network had been destroyed, bridges were down, and roads in deplorable condition. Travel even over short distances was difficult, slow, and exhausting. She was able to fly to Naples and from there get a ride to Rome, probably on a military vehicle. She soon rented a flat and announced her presence to Guglielmo Alberti: "I should perhaps tell you that I have gone back to writing and am here as a journalist (sometimes even in uniform!) but with the main object of collecting material for two books."[2] A fortnight later she took a hair-raising flight on a military plane to Milan, continued on to friends in Turin, and returned to Rome once train service was restored by means of "all sorts of tentatively restored bridges."[3] "I shall ask Sylvia Sprigge, the Manchester Guardian correspondent, for some introductions," she confessed to Alberti, "and I shall have to be civil to our press officials, but otherwise I should like to rely on you and your friends. My Italian hasn't improved as much as I could wish but it does all right provided no one talks French to me."[4] Before long he was introducing her to his literary circle and providing an introduction to Manlio Brosio, the defense minister. In advance of a visit to his family in Florence, she wrote: "I want to drink in all I can of the Tuscan air in the week with you."[5]

Her first impressions of Rome were deeply troubling. She was shocked by the social inequalities there: the terrible contrast between rich and poor and between Allied soldiers, especially American GIs, and Italian civilians, many of whom were severely undernourished. Inflation was rampant; black market trading was everywhere, so was street theft and prostitution. Fuel was scarce, homes went unheated in the winter months, and power cuts were frequent, but the military government's offices blazed with electric light, even after working hours. Wiskemann's earliest reports publicized the population's distress. At the NAAFI in Rome "one found heaps of tea, ground coffee, powdered milk and sugar on the floor" and yet the streets were full of ragged, hungry children hawking goods; "American soldiers threw away half-full tins of food persistently, but starving Italians were punished if they took these tins from the military dustbins."[6] As Christmas approached and the electrical grid was increasingly burdened, she found that "British soldiers with whom I have spoken did not know that most of the city was without light except for about two days a week during December. When they left lights burning brightly in requisitioned buildings where it was allowed, they did not notice if the houses nearby were in darkness; but it is not surprising that the Italian press has reacted acidly."[7]

Since the early days of liberation, disillusionment had set in, exacerbated by the short-sightedness of the Allied occupiers, who Wiskemann described as "Metternichian legitimists" bent upon re-imposing upon the population a Piedmontese constitution, which never enjoyed national support. Repeatedly during the first six months, her reports for the *Economist* deplored their lack of understanding for what Italians had endured, their prejudice against the left, and accommodation of monarchists, industrialists, and large landowners. She was frustrated by the inaction of Britain's new Labour government: "A little more interest, a greater readiness to treat Italy as an equal, some signs of a desire to end the anomalies of armistice and occupation could create a new mood in Italy, undo the disillusions of Churchillian diplomacy and lay the foundations of lasting Anglo-Italian understanding."[8] Particularly troubling was the behavior of Polish forces under General Anders' command who had fought so valiantly for the liberation of Italy. Over 100,000 of them were stationed in Puglia, the Marches, and further afield in the Venetian provinces. Italians often liked the Poles as individuals, but they increasingly feared the actions of Anders' forces and their interference in Italian politics. Vehemently anti-communist and often anti-Semitic, they came to be seen by many Italian workers as 'mercenaries of the right.' "The reactionary fanaticism of the Polish soldiers," she wrote,

goes so far that when the Socialists of the town of Macerata attempted a peaceful demonstration to celebrate the Labour success in the British elections last summer, members of the Polish Army attacked the demonstrators and burnt the flags which had been hung out; and there is no possible doubt that a number of similar incidents have taken place with dead and wounded among the unarmed Italian Socialists. As for the Communists, while the Poles have requisitioned about 50 of their party offices in the province of Macerata, in Ascoli Piceno, another province in the Marches, one Communist centre has had to be transferred sixteen times because Polish soldiers have regularly requisitioned or burnt it down…the progressive Italian parties can no longer hold meetings where there are Polish troops, and this on the eve of the first free elections to be held in Italy since 1921.[9]

Despite the daily hardships, the poverty, and the atmosphere of political uncertainty, it was an exciting time to be a journalist in Italy, and Wiskemann's many personal contacts helped propel her into the center of a vibrant political and intellectual scene, one in which a host of new cultural and political journals hotly debated the major issues of the day.[10] Two of the most important were Elio Vittorini's Communist *Il Politechnico* and the left liberal Florentine journal *Il Ponte*, edited by Piero Calamandrei; both viewed themselves as guardians of Italian renewal, advancing the vision of a post-fascist culture inspired by the "wind from the North," the *Resistenza*. They also linked Italian cultural debate to similar ideas in France, Germany, and elsewhere, advancing a broad humanism, insisting that culture must be an active force in social reform and that intellectuals must find new ways to eliminate the gulf between themselves and the mass of the population. By contrast, Benedetto Croce's *Quaderni della Critica* espoused a more elitist liberalism, aligning itself with the propertied classes and the continuation of the monarchy. Croce viewed fascism as a European disease and his courageous opposition to it was underpinned by a belief in Italy's pre-1914 evolution towards a more liberal society. For him the intellectual's role in the era of reconstruction was to defend liberty, and this was best achieved by supporting the Liberal party.[11] Writers on the left, supporters of *Giustizia è Libertà* and the *Partito d'Azione*, while deeply influenced by Croce, found his proposals too conservative and elitist and viewed Mussolini's regime, not as an aberration, a catastrophic break in Italian development, but as deeply rooted in the deficiencies of the *Risorgimento* and the flaws of the liberal state. The challenge, they argued, was to forge a new national identity and a genuine democratic culture out of the values of the Resistance. These views, including the necessity for sweeping social and economic reforms and a genuine purge of leading fascists, were also advanced in a host of editorials by Carlo Levi as editor of *L'Italia libera*. Wherever one turned, Wiskemann wrote, the intellectuals of the 1920s were still active, seemingly more eloquent after the long period of enforced silence.[12]

The chief focus of her life and work was Rome, where she soon developed a large network of contacts and informants, many of them acquaintances from her years in Switzerland. "Literary and artistic society in Italy," she wrote, "had a fluidity that I have not met elsewhere"; journalism, the arts, and literature seemed intertwined and "through journalism writers rubbed shoulders with other artists and professionals. Indeed, I had the feeling that everyone articulate in Italy was prepared to have a shot at anything." This lack of professional barriers could, she reflected, sometimes lead to superficiality, but for a foreign observer it opened doors: "one kind of contact produced another more readily than elsewhere. On the other hand, a social gathering became such an avalanche of conversation that it sometimes swept past one." She was welcomed into the circle of Raimondo Craveri, "who knew everyone," and his wife, Elena, Croce's eldest daughter, "a rather gaunt figure, more in the Anglo-Saxon blue-stocking tradition than Neapolitan." Their flat was "an intellectual salon...frequented by historians and followers of Croce."[13] Another gathering place for Rome's politicians and writers was the apartment of Cecil and Sylvia Sprigge, friends for many years who were now correspondents for Reuters and the *Manchester Guardian*. She also saw a good deal of Silone and his Irish wife, Darina, and met Alberto Moravia, spending the evening of the referendum on the monarchy with him and his painter friend Renato Guttuso. She admired Moravia but found him rather melancholy.[14] More to her taste was Carlo Levi—"Solare" as Moravia called him because of his sunny disposition—whose *Christo si è fermato a Eboli* (1945), depicting his experience of *confino* under the fascist regime, was a runaway success. "Written without tendentiousness or lamentation but with profound comprehension," his book, "about an utterly wretched village in Lucania," was the most influential depiction of rural poverty in the South and "far more illuminating than a library of political and academic tomes."[15] She herself went as far south as Naples, eagerly accepting Elena Croce's suggestion that she visit her father: the great man, she wrote, was "very likeable" but "gruff and surly in manner, one of those South Italians who flies in the face of all legend about liquid southern charm."[16]

Aside from Rome, Wiskemann went as often as she could to the industrial North, collecting material for her articles and interviewing people for her Rome–Berlin Axis book. In Turin she visited the Fiat car factories, interviewed workers there, and reconnected with Giulio De Benedetti, again editor of the liberal newspaper *La Stampa*, who had been among the Italian exiles who flooded into Switzerland in 1943. Not far away, in the foothills of the Alps, she went to the Olivetti factories at Ivrea, where Adriano Olivetti was busy transforming a small provincial town into a modern planned city for workers of his typewriter factories. She also became good friends with Ada Gobetti, widow of the anti-fascist leader Piero, who had died tragically young in 1926 after a fascist beating. During the war Ada had been an active resister, smuggling arms and Allied propaganda and providing refuge to those sought by the fascists through a network of safe houses. She was close to many *Giustizia è Libertà* activists, including Georgio Agosti, the political commissar of the Piedmont section with whom Wiskemann discussed the liberation of Turin in April 1945. After the war, as Jomarie Alano has detailed, Ada was for twenty months vice-mayor of Turin (the first woman vice-mayor in Italy) and worked to combat poverty and the severe housing shortage and to promote family welfare, education, and women's rights.[17] In Milan, Wiskemann toured the steel and chemical works of Sesto San Giovanni, interviewing its heavily communist workforce, and also got to know a group of radical bankers, mostly former *Azionisti*, associated with the *Banca Commerciale Italiana*, especially the bank's managing director, Raffaele Matteoli, who played a major role in Italy's postwar economic reconstruction and was also a patron of the arts. One of his junior colleagues was the philosopher Franco Rodano, a leading figure in the effort to mediate between Catholicism and communism; deeply anti-clerical in these early postwar years, Wiskemann respected these leftist Catholics but saw no prospect of their success and was not surprised by Rodano's excommunication in 1947. She also returned several times to Villa I Tatti and introduced Francesco Antinori.[18] While in Switzerland, she received no news of Berenson and had feared the worst; but he had escaped the roundups of Jews and deportations and, thanks to protection by the German Consul in Florence, Gerhard Wolf, he and his art collection survived intact. It "seemed to be the only place in Europe that had not changed... [and] seemed more of a hot-house than before, but one was glad of its warmth, warmth of so special a quality."[19] However, given the privations and misery of so many Italians, the obsessive anti-communism of the conversation there could be grating: "It was very nice at BB's [Bernard Berenson]," she told Alberti after one visit, "but I got very tired of the Red Peril."[20]

*   *   *

Wiskemann's articles for the *Economist* and other publications traced the birth of the Italian Republic and the fast-moving party politics of the early years of peace. As in Berlin in the 1930s, she demonstrated remarkable ability to gain access to leading politicians. She disliked the word 'interview' associating it with a journalist's quoting or summarizing someone's statements; she rarely used quotations, viewing her meetings as exchanges of information which she then integrated into her own analysis. Some of her informants, like Silone, Carlo Sforza, and Ugo La Malfa, a close associate of Parri, she already knew from Switzerland. Others were new. She met Ferruccio Parri and the Christian Democratic leader, Alcide de Gasperi, several times; she visited Don Sturzo, leader of the Catholic *Popolari* party in the early 1920s, who had returned from exile and was living in a convent. She gained audiences with Socialist leader Pietro Nenni and Silone's friend Giuseppe Saragat, who split from the party, opposed to its alliance with the Communists. She attended the Communist party congress at the end of 1945 and 'interviewed' many of the party's leaders, including Palmiro Togliatti, describing him as "sternly disciplined by some ecumenical authority, the ideal cardinal." Three of her sources became Presidents of the Republic and numerous others achieved high office in postwar governments.

Her opinions about what was happening in Italian politics were clear from the beginning and her journalism advanced them forcefully. She arrived in Rome as a firm supporter of the *Partito d'Azione*; she had met several of its leaders in

Switzerland and, with very few exceptions, her friends and the circles in which she now moved largely echoed her enthusiasm for the party. There must, she argued, be a new constitution to replace the essentially Piedmontese structure which had been imposed on Italy in 1861 and a more decentralized government in place of the rigid centralization under Mussolini. She was also a convinced Republican, believing that the House of Savoy's actions during the fascist years and its "moral abdication" in fleeing from Rome in September 1943 had disqualified the monarchy from any future role in the state. She rejected the liberal politics of Benedetto Croce and Luigi Einaudi—two men she otherwise admired—whose idea of liberty recalled that of Adam Smith or Jeremy Bentham. They failed to see that "no starving man is free," and their fear of any redistribution of property pointed to their preference for the Giolittian pre-fascist past.[21] Echoing Action party spokesmen, she insisted that the major task in these years was to reconcile protection of liberal values and individual rights with socialist reforms; sweeping social and economic measures (and foreign, especially American, aid) were essential if Italy was to surmount the crisis. Local CLN committees had every right to expect a 'new deal' after their heroic resistance, and redistribution of wealth was essential and justified.

But the Action party, whose positions she echoed, was small compared to the mass parties—the Socialists, Communists, and Christian Democrats—and for all its significance during the armed resistance, its decline was swift. Parri, who became head of the interim government in June 1945, was a man of great integrity, personally attractive, hardworking, and courageous, but he was also inexperienced, unable to establish clear priorities, and "incapable of making the essential compromises." By November 1945 when the Liberals withdrew their support from the coalition, Parri was forced to resign, replaced by the Christian Democrat de Gasperi.[22] He had symbolized the hopes of the resistance for a radical transformation of society but was unable to make a start; the torch now passed to cautious professional politicians. Wiskemann saw Parri as a romantic figure; he personified "the idealism of Italy's second Risorgimento," exuding "something of the unpractical selflessness of Garibaldi and Mazzini, combined with a detestation of all meretricious oratory which he owed to the fascist era."[23] She distrusted De Gasperi and the machinations of the Vatican, but also blamed the Allies for bolstering the traditional state structure and social elites:

If De Gasperi has thus contributed to the restoration of the political jobbery of the age of Giolitti and the protection of the inordinately rich landowners and industrialists who preferred Fascism to a juster distribution of wealth, his responsibility will be heavy, for social unrest will have been perpetuated. But it is impossible to deny that Allied influence has sometimes worked in the same direction. Misreading the situation with the best possible intentions, Allied military authorities have protected industrialists who flourished under Fascism from the sacrifices a new Italy had a right to demand…By what fatality do British and American officers so often contrive, in Italy as in Germany, to help to recreate the obsolete conditions out of which Fascism, National Socialism and the last war were born?[24]

But if Allied occupiers were culpable, so was the Action party, which soon faded from view: "the saddest thing that happened in Italy in the first winter after the war was the collapse of *Partito d'Azione*."[25] Paralyzed by internal division, it was unable to formulate a clear policy—the moderate or right wing of the party led by Ugo La Malfa envisioned itself as a "democratic republican party, liberal in the English sense," while the Emilio Lussu's left wing "wish[ed] to become a third socialist party." Translating the party's 1943 program, with its rhetoric about reconciling liberal individualism and socialism into concrete policies, was extremely difficult. At the party's congress in February 1946, which Wiskemann attended, members were ill-prepared, resulting in "a chaotic confusion of overlapping resolutions."[26] "There was," she wrote, "something very sad in watching these brilliant people subside into political insignificance and isolation, and to realize that their party had been only an idealistic dream dreamt in war-time. It was all the more painful because they were naturally mocked by many former Fascists."[27] "It was not…a political party at all," she concluded, "but a collection of splendid individuals, of highly educated people, politically inexperienced intellectuals. For this reason, it could have no appeal to wider, less educated, less upright circles. Its tenets, a loose combination of liberalism with socialism and strongly anti-clerical, were too complicated for the general public. Indeed, they turned out to be too complicated for the party's own survival…"[28]

During the next months, in numerous articles Wiskemann analyzed the twists and turns of Italian party politics. By March 1946, as became evident in the municipal commune elections, the Christian Democrats, Communists, and Socialists dominated. These were also the first elections in which Italian women could vote. While arguing that it was hard for an intelligent person to be anything other than a socialist given the huge social and economic inequalities in the nation, Wiskemann was critical of Pietro Nenni's leadership of the Socialist party. His strategy of fusion with Togliatti's much more disciplined and Moscow-directed Communist party led to subservience and angered those like Silone and Saragat on the party's right. Greater independence from the Communists, Wiskemann asserted, would have made Socialism more appealing to neglected middle-class voters, especially teachers and state officials, enabling it to develop into a non-Marxist British-style Labour party with a strong emphasis upon social justice and individual liberty.[29] "To insist," she wrote, "as the Italian Socialists are trying to do, upon revolutionary Marxism and also on love of constitutional liberty is a contradiction in terms, and it divides rather than reconciles opposing wings of the Party."[30] Their failure meant that the Communists, thanks to

Togliatti's skillful maneuvering, had emerged as the only feasible leaders of a left republican bloc.

Three months later, on June 2, 1946, elections were held for a Constituent Assembly that would write a new constitution, and on the same day a referendum took place to decide between continuing the monarchy and establishing a republic. In the first vote the Action party, the locus of so many hopes, suffered a complete rout. It had failed to create a base of popular support, although its intellectual legacy proved more lasting. Some 89% of eligible voters went to the polls, returning 207 Christian Democrats (35% of the vote), 115 Socialists (20%), and 104 Communists (19%).[31] The demise of the Action party was complete, polling barely 1% of the vote and gaining a mere seven seats. Particularly interesting to Wiskemann was the performance of a new, outsider party, the *Fronte dell'Uomo Qualunque* [the Front of the Average Man], organized by a Neapolitan journalist and playwright, Guglielmo Giannini, which got over 5% of the votes. Deeply critical of professional politicians and politics, the Front was a haven for discontented middle-class voters and unrepentant fascists alike. *Qualunquismo* was really a vehicle of protest, more cynical, anti-politics than fascist, although Giannini's tirades often pilloried the left and anti-fascists. In local elections in November 1946 the movement did extremely well in the South and even won over 20% of the vote in Rome itself. Ever watchful for signs of resurgent fascism, Wiskemann viewed it as reproducing "the principles and emotions upon which Fascism was based." She worried that the combination of rampant inflation, high unemployment, and parliamentary dysfunction might fuel neo-fascism and came to believe that Italy's future stability depended on the willingness of the Christian Democrats to play a progressive and conciliatory role in government coalitions.

The referendum on the future form of the state—republic or monarchy—underscored the deep social, cultural, and political fissures within the nation. Wiskemann viewed the vote as a colossal mistake: the new Constituent Assembly, she believed, with the backing of the Allied Military Government, should have abolished the monarchy and declared a Republic. "Unfortunately, people with vested interests now took fright; they decided that the Republic would be a 'red' one and so they intrigued in favour of the Monarchy."[32] Traveling to different regions as an observer, she reported: "At monarchist meetings insolent youths chanting Sa-voi-a as insolent youths used to chant Du-ce are conspicuous, and there is unquestionably more evidence of violence from this side than from the Left." In Apulia, for example, "monarchist meetings frequently end up with a raid on the local Communist or Socialist committee room."[33] The result was an increasingly bitter and divisive campaign that both widened the geographical division between the North and the South and forged stronger ties between propertied interests, former fascists, the Vatican, and a monarchy. "It was a strange experience," she wrote, "to travel through Italy in May 1946 and having found Lombardy and Tuscany clearly Republican and Rome divided, to arrive in the atmosphere of Naples…the old Bourbon capital which had once so bitterly resisted the claims of the House of Savoy, to find the walls covered with *Viva la Casa di Savoia*."[34] Here, she notes, the votes of the poor, illiterate, and unemployed were controlled by the elites and the Camorra; ferocious, well-funded propaganda represented the choice as between the House of Savoy and godless Bolshevism. Wiskemann also criticized the Vatican's active role in the referendum. Catholic Action (in a flagrant breach of the electoral law) put huge pressure upon parishioners, threatening them with the torments of hell and Communism should they vote for a Republic. This pressure, she argued, made the margin of victory narrower, although the National Conference of Christian Democrats—itself split between North and South—finally rejected the monarchy, going against both the Vatican and their own leader, De Gasperi, who had called for neutrality.[35]

In the end the Republic won, but the vote had been close—12.7 to 10.7 million votes. "I'm glad about the Republic," Wiskemann wrote to Alberti, "and think the Italians behaved exceedingly well. And how intolerably the world behaves to them!"[36] The North was solidly republican while monarchy achieved a clear majority in Rome (54%) and the impoverished South (80% in Naples), precisely where a republic was far more likely to improve the people's lot. Ironically, defeat for the monarchy which the Vatican had worked so hard to preserve, left the Catholic Church stronger than ever, as the major institutional support of the status quo in the country. Christian Democracy, Wiskemann noted, was twice as strong as Don Sturzo's *Populari* party ever achieved and this would affect the Republic's ability to deal with issues like renewal of the Concordat, divorce, birth control, and other matters involving the Vatican.[37] Overpopulation in Italy was, she reminded her readers, "a painful actuality, not a matter of specious propaganda as it was in [Hitler's] Germany."[38] Indeed, in an interview with Togliatti, "he appeared as shocked as any Catholic colleague" when she asked point blank whether Italy's high birth rate "did not require the encouragement of birth control if the standard of living was to be raised."[39]

Between November 1946 and February 1947 Wiskemann wrote a four-part analysis of the "Problems of Italian Reconstruction" for the *Economist*. The articles combined political commentary and detailed economic analysis, influenced almost certainly by her discussions with Matteoli and other economists.[40] By early 1947 Italy had made considerable economic progress: agricultural production was increasing and industry was reviving, although still at 65% of the average pre-war production levels, and the transportation system had been largely restored. But further growth was checked by the shortage of capital and the brake imposed by conservative interests on efforts to modernize. The gap between government expenditures and income had grown rapidly; there was little possibility of raising more funds through taxation or left-wing proposals for a capital levy, while the capital shortage limited the import of raw materials and especially coal and fuel, badly needed to stimulate further industrial growth and absorb over

2 million unemployed.[41] Only British and American loans, she argued, could lessen the problem of poverty by facilitating integration of more Italians into the industrial sector.[42] UNRRA was trying to combat poverty and undernourishment, but when its operations ceased, as expected, the situation would be critical.

The Christian Democrats had promised an agrarian reform program that would redistribute land, renegotiate *mezzadria* sharecropping contracts, and improve "the status and the lot of thousands of landless workers who are fortunate if they are employed 150 days in the year."[43] However, the obstacles to such reform, especially in the South, remained formidable and the pace of change was too slow to avoid a crisis.[44] She examined in some detail recent land occupations and rural unrest, especially in Emilia and the South. The regional complexity of Italy's agrarian problems, she recognized, was daunting, and so was the range of measures required—land reclamation, mechanization, the breakup of *latifundi* estates, the formation of cooperatives, and a reversal of Mussolini's policy of requiring grain cultivation on unsuitable land (the 'Battle of Grain'), all of these were necessary. But the regional and political cleavages in Italian society suggested that the political will would not be forthcoming. At one point she thought that Don Sturzo's return to Italy (in the 1920s he had advanced an agrarian reform program) might rally the more progressive wing of the Christian Democrats and forge bonds with the Socialists. But such hopes soon evaporated.

In 1945 it had seemed as if Italy would experience a radical transformation: hopes were high that the left might remake the social structure of Italy. But the next two years represented more of a restoration. The momentum gained from the Resistance was lost; Italy's new constitution replicated many facets of the old; hopes for greater political decentralization and proposals for workers' committees and power-sharing in factories had achieved only limited results;[45] and the northern industrialists and southern landlords had largely recovered their pre-war social power. The process of punishing fascist crimes ground to a halt, the judicial and administrative cadres of the Mussolini era mostly remained in place, and many fascist laws remained on the statute books.[46] Most blame for this, Wiskemann argued, went to the Christian Democrats and the Vatican. But Nenni and the Socialist strategy were also culpable, the party's cooperation or subordination to the Communists had weakened it, forcing many Italians into a stark choice between a left bloc dominated by the Communists or Christian Democracy. This was the "The Situation in Italy" that Wiskemann described to an audience at Chatham House in May 1947, soon after returning to London.[47] The same month, de Gasperi formed a new government excluding the Communists and Socialists.

The national elections of April 1948, the first under Italy's new constitution, are rightly seen as a political benchmark. The campaign that followed was tumultuous and bitterly fought, marked by unprecedented American interference and funding, and portrayed by the Vatican and the right as an apocalyptic choice between Christ or Antichrist, liberty or totalitarianism. Held in the wake of the

Communist seizure of power in Prague two months before, the vote became a crusade in the Cold War which increasingly permeated internal politics. The result was a decisive victory for Christian Democracy as the indispensable alternative to the hard left. Busy writing her book in London, Wiskemann did not cover the election as a journalist; its outcome was depressing but hardly surprising to her.[48] By 1947 she had predicted the trajectory of Italian politics, although she had not foreseen how swiftly and completely the wartime alliance against Hitler would fracture and polarize into western and eastern blocs or how deeply the Cold War would reach into Italian domestic politics. As for De Gasperi, while she had been highly critical of him, over the next years she came to appreciate his moderation, seeing him less as a Vatican agent and more as a relatively liberal-minded conservative, a moderate reformer who inaugurated a needed period of democratic stability and embraced NATO and the 'European Idea.'[49]

Wiskemann's articles paid close attention to Italy's South, its distinctive culture, "its abject and hopeless poverty," and the roots of the nation's North–South division in the *Risorgimento*.[50] The war, followed by the referendum on the monarchy and widespread agrarian unrest, had pushed the *Mezzogiorno* to the forefront of political and intellectual debate. Ignazio Silone had published *Fontamara* and *Bread and Wine*, his powerful evocation of the peasantry of the Abruzzi, while in exile in Switzerland, but many Italians first read them in the early postwar years. Other Italian intellectuals from the North had hidden from fascist police in the South or, like Cesare Pavese and Carlo Levi, were exiled by the fascist regime to poor remote villages. The influence on Wiskemann of Carlo Levi's *Cristo si è fermato a Eboli* (1945), a memoir of his year-long confinement in Lucania (now Basilicata), has already been mentioned.[51] But while she had read a great deal, she had never been south of Naples and her first-hand knowledge of the agrarian population came mostly from touring Piedmont and the Lombardy plain.[52]

It was not until March 1949, after returning to live in London and completing her book about the Axis between Mussolini and Hitler, that she could "at last set out to study *la miseria* of Southern Italy for several weeks more systematically." She wrote later: "Anything I have written on Italy since then has been flavoured by that experience."[53] Her traveling companion was an old friend, Christopher Seton-Watson, the son of R.W. Seton-Watson, Britain's most distinguished scholar of south-east Europe. After schooling at Winchester, Christopher had entered New College, Oxford, in 1937 to read PPE [Philosophy, Politics, and Economics]; he didn't finish his degree, but enlisted in the Royal Artillery at the outbreak of war in 1939, seeing combat in France and Belgium before being evacuated from Dunkirk; later he fought in Greece, Egypt, and across North Africa, and finally in Italy from Naples all the way north to Bologna. Few served in as many campaigns—as his friend and fellow historian Michael Howard wrote: "statistically his chances of surviving those six years with a whole skin must have been very small."[54]

Service in Italy, where he was often appalled by what he saw, pointed Christopher towards his later career as a historian of modern Italy. Already prior to the Allied invasion he had begun to learn Italian, and during the campaign he read local Italian newspapers at every opportunity and studied the politics of the local population. Letters to his family indicate that his political sympathies in these years lay with the Italian communists. His response to what was happening in Italy after 1945 was close to Wiskemann's: he hated the way that Polish troops clashed with Italian communists and tore down posters and insignia praising the Red Army whenever they liberated a town or village. He was deeply disappointed at the failure of the Action party and deplored the Vatican's growing influence and the huge disparity between wealth and poverty: "From one or two people who know Rome I heard stories that made me sick. Roman society with its beautiful manners, its snobbism and contempt for the lower classes – especially for the 'Africans' of Southern Italy – its perfect mastery of the English language and its shameless trimming, seems to be pretty despicable."[55] "I see little future for this impoverished and demoralized and divided country," he wrote, "but I do pray that whoever comes to power will liquidate the parasites who grew rich under fascism and now look to protect their ill-gotten gains from the wrath of their own countrymen."[56] By 1949 he had returned to Oriel College, Oxford, received a 'war degree,' and was teaching history.[57]

It would not have been easy for Wiskemann to travel alone through remote areas of the South. Hotels were few and very basic and travel through this impoverished and ravaged landscape was slow and difficult. As she put it: "This was just before any post-war improvement had time to take effect, so that we saw the *Mezzogiorno* of the first half of the twentieth century." She and Seton-Watson were well-matched traveling companions. "He was efficient, fair-minded, accurate; I think we enjoyed the same lines of thought and the same jokes: we liked our food and drink when they were good – often they were not."[58] They first used Naples as a base and then traveled through Apulia, Lucania (Basilicata), and Calabria; they did not go to Sicily or Sardinia, which would have required considerably more time. They brought introductions for local officials and scholars from various friends and academics—most useful were those from Professor Manlio Rossi-Doria, the leading expert on the agrarian problem in the South. A staunch anti-fascist, he had been confined by the fascist regime in Basilicata and later became a leading figure in the Action party. Reviewing Rossi-Doria's major book on the topic, Wiskemann described it as "the scientific foundation for Carlo Levi's aesthetic interpretation of the south Italian peasantry, the canvas for Levi's paint."[59]

Rossi-Doria believed that the South had great potentiality if it could attract a huge injection of capital. The Italian government had plans for the redistribution of about 1.3 million hectares from the large estates to the peasantry and there were proposals for land reclamation and instruction in more efficient farming methods. But to Wiskemann the problems of overpopulation, low investment, soil erosion, and neglect seemed insuperable.[60] The Marshall Aid allotted to the area was inadequate for the task and the Italian state was essentially insolvent, while the big landowners blocked proposals for reform. Just outside Cosenza, they discovered a Milanese businessman who had sunk all his capital into a farm and a tobacco factory; he had built some decent houses for laborers but, as the news spread, he was overwhelmed by jobseekers from far afield—far more than he could employ, many of them camping out in hopes of work. Soon he was losing money, the dwellings had turned into a slum, and the experiment seemed doomed to fail: "It is easy to guess," wrote Wiskemann, "how foolish the big landowners consider him"; they who took their profits and put little back into this sea of desperate poverty.[61] Equally tragic was their visit to a school in a cave: "There was no money to build a school-house, so a heroic woman-teacher was struggling in the half-light to instruct a few miserable-looking children in this dark, windowless hole in the rock of a hill."[62] In 1944–46, before Wiskemann and Seton-Watson traveled to the South, mass protests and spontaneous land occupations had engulfed the area, while in October 1949, months after they left, another wave of protests and *jacqueries* against property swept through Calabria and spread across the South, including Sicily.

*   *   *

Somehow in these years, in addition to a prodigious output of journalistic articles and a busy social life, Wiskemann also managed to work on two books. The first, *Italy,* was a brief but perceptive introduction to the politics and culture of contemporary Italy, aimed at the general reader. After living in Rome for six months, she returned to London in March 1946, wrote it in two months flat, and was back in Rome by May to cover the Constituent Assembly elections and the referendum on the Savoy monarchy. It surveyed the main themes of Italian history from the early nineteenth century but focused primarily upon the nature of the Fascist regime and the war years, especially the German occupation and the Italian Resistance, whose role, Wiskemann insisted, was little known in Britain but central to understanding contemporary Italy.

Most British readers would have known G.M. Trevelyan's epic depiction of the Risorgimento as a heroic struggle, the triumph of good over evil, and a leap towards liberal democracy; however, it left readers ill-equipped to explain the failure of Italian liberalism and Fascism's rise. Like Gramsci and the Action party, Wiskemann portrayed Italian unification as a flawed process, involving only a small minority of Italians, where the idealists were soon marginalized by Piedmontese power. The result was a virtual conquest of the South by the North, over-centralized administration, and a parliamentary system riddled with corruption and, under Giolitti, one that relied on buying southern votes to produce political majorities. The First World War had exacerbated the nation's social and ideological divisions, encouraging the growth of urban and rural socialism, so that the King, the army, propertied interests, and the Vatican looked to Mussolini to rescue the state and deliver some form of stability. Brief sections of the book examined the Fascist regime's policies and structural development, but more emphasis was placed on the resistance struggle from the 1920s in which many, like Gramsci, Giovanni Amendola, Gobetti, and the Rosselli brothers, paid with their lives, while others, like Salvemini, were forced into exile. "The mind of Italy," she wrote, "had been fettered but not strangled"; most Italians remained hostile to Fascism, opposed the regime's racial legislation, and hated their German allies, who sacrificed their soldiers in North Africa and Russia.[63]

The final third of the book was a passionate defense of Italians and the "Second Risorgimento," the Resistance, which brought together workers, peasants, and intellectuals, men and women, in one national movement. Wiskemann pointed to the heroism of striking Fiat workers in Turin and Milan, the actions of Italian women who joined the armed resistance in their thousands, and the peasant families who risked their lives to aid and shelter escaped British POWs—all contradicting the "usual assumption that the Italians never stirred until the Allies were in Sicily."[64] The British public, she believed, had little inkling of the savagery, torture, and mass executions that marked the two-year German occupation in which over 44,000 patriots were killed. And while attitudes had softened since June 1940 when Mussolini declared war, Italians were still widely condemned or caricatured, and official British policy remained unsympathetic and punitive. Her survey closed with an account of the first year of peace, leading up to the June 1945 elections. The themes were those already explored in her articles: hopes for a new Italy, North–South division, the fissures that weakened progressive groups, and the resurgent power of traditional property interests and the Vatican. While clearly pessimistic about the immediate outcome, she refused to end on a despairing note, pointing to the democratic engagement of ordinary Italians in the *comizietti*, or local political gatherings, she had attended: "The new Constitution may be a failure and there may be fresh convulsion and tumult to come, but... there is so much vitality in ferment that it seems possible that at one moment or another something superlative will be conceived." Nothing she later wrote equaled this fusion of advocacy, exuberant hopes, and sheer delight, and reviewers welcomed the book as a perceptive, popular survey.[65] From her depiction of the flawed liberal state, partly responsible for Fascism, to her effusive account of the Action party's program, its depiction of Italian political culture was effectively *Azionisti* history.

Wiskemann's second book, *The Rome-Berlin Axis* (1949), was a more substantial and pioneering investigation of the Hitler–Mussolini relationship. It drew upon her work as a journalist and a British agent in Switzerland, and she was among the first scholars to gain access to German foreign policy documents captured by the Allies.[66] The Italian archives were closed (the first Italian diplomatic documents for the period were not published until 1953), but she benefited greatly from her unusual access to public figures, in part with Francesco Antinori's help,[67] and from an array of memoirs that appeared soon after the war, including Count Ciano's diaries, smuggled into Switzerland by his widow.[68] Having completed her research, she resigned from the *Economist* in March 1947 to devote herself full-time to her book. Working full throttle, she finished the manuscript by the summer of 1948.[69] It was the first major study of the Hitler–Mussolini relationship and remained for many years the standard account in English. The book examined the relationship between Nazism and Fascism, the forging of the Axis alliance, and the personal relationship between the two dictators, quoting and summarizing for the first time the many letters between them. Each leader, Wiskemann wrote, "was like a malicious caricature of his own people": Hitler, fanatical, resolute, unswerving in his goals, and always knowing what he wanted; Mussolini, more volatile, theatrical, opportunistic, aware of Italy's unpreparedness for war, more fluid in his goals, and prone to compromise.[70]

The book is written from the perspective of Mussolini and Fascist officials looking outwards. For the first time it revealed in detail the shifting balance between the two men: from the early days when Hitler saw Mussolini as a model, although a rival for influence over Austria and south-east Europe, to the *Duce*'s growing subordination to German power and his efforts to check and frustrate his ally's designs. As the asymmetry of their relationship increased, Mussolini was forced to submit to successive humiliations—an increasingly subservient vassal in the Nazi New Order, acquiescing to Hitler's decisions, requiring German assistance in Greece and the Balkans, and ending up a virtual prisoner at Gargnano on Lake Garda. The war and Italy's weakness rendered him subservient, increasingly resentful of Nazi leadership, but unable to escape its embrace.

Historians have long debated the nature of Fascist foreign policy and whether Mussolini had a consistent, coherent set of goals. Wiskemann's interpretation— dominant in the 1950s and, arguably, until much later among leading British scholars—was strongly influenced by her friend Salvemini's view that Fascist policy was more bluster than a set of clearly formulated objectives.[71] With the opening of Italian archives in the late 1960s, however, this consensus began to be challenged. Alan Cassels, for example, argued that the aggressive Mussolini of the 1930s was already present in his revisionist goals a decade earlier, but that domestic constraints prevented him from pursuing a more forceful, dynamic foreign policy. Esmonde Robertson's study of Fascist imperialism outlined a coherent program for territorial revisionism, colonial expansion, and the enlargement of Italian power in the Mediterranean at the expense of France and Britain. And MacGregor Knox went still further, arguing that from 1925 to 1926 Fascist foreign policy was set in its essential details and committed to war and imperial expansion as a means of radicalizing Italian political culture and creating Fascist man.[72] At the time, however, most reviewers were persuaded by Wiskemann's portrayal of Mussolini and his policies; certainly, to have reconstructed the tangled history of the Axis alliance in some detail—only three years after the war's end and before Italian documents were available—was a remarkable feat, and her portrayal of the personal chemistry between the two dictators remains fresh and perceptive even today.

The Rome-Berlin Axis confirmed Wiskemann's status as a leading authority on Fascism and Nazism. "*Czechs and Germans*, published in 1938," wrote G.P. Gooch, "established Miss Wiskemann as one of our leading authorities on international affairs and her latest volume is even more remarkable."[73] In Martin Wight's opinion it ranked "with Namier, Beloff, and Wheeler-Bennett among the half-dozen definitive secondary works on the diplomatic history of Hitler's age."[74] Hugh Trevor-Roper called it "that rare thing, a definitive work of contemporary history,"[75] while for Alan Bullock it was a book "which certainly joins that small group…of first-class, serious historical studies of the contemporary Age of the Tyrants."[76] The least persuasive aspect of the book was Wiskemann's characterization of the two dictators as "pupils of Nietzsche" influenced by his concept of the "superman" and "The Will to Power." Nietzsche, the prophet and poet of decay, seemed in a terrifying way, she argued, to have "projected and facilitated the agony of Europe forty years after his death."[77] Nietzsche, she wrote, inspired the words of Mussolini, but supplied the doctrines that nourished Hitler's deeds; indeed, Hitler's 'new order' "can most nearly be explained as Hitler's interpretation of the aspirations of Nietzsche."[78] The *TLS* reviewer (J.M.D. Pringle, foreign affairs writer for the *Times*) praised it as: "an admirable study which shows great knowledge of the available sources as well as scholarship in the use of them," but added, "there is altogether far too much about Nietzsche."[79] James Joll, a figure of growing importance in the field of contemporary history, also saw the Nietzsche references as an exaggerated attempt to give the story unity given the sharply contrasted character of the two dictators.[80] He also questioned Wiskemann's unconcealed sympathy for Italians, as did another Oxford historian, A.J.P. Taylor (for whom Wiskemann soon developed a deep dislike). While agreeing with the book's main arguments, Taylor dismissed her "soft-heartedness for all Italians" and inclination "to give the Italians too much credit for their brief, though heroic, period of resistance." "It was not," he wrote, "that Fascism was less barbaric and brutal than Nazism, merely that it was less efficient."[81] Few would have gone that far but, as historians have recently shown, the image of *Italiani brava gente*, the claim that Italians behaved well and were, above all, victims, which became so pervasive postwar, served to marginalize or erase collective memory of the worst violence and crimes of the Fascist era while aiding the construction of democratic republican identity.[82]

* * *

While the success of *The Rome-Berlin Axis* increased demand for Wiskemann as a commentator and reviewer for the *Times Literary Supplement*, the *Spectator*, and other journals, none of this work paid well. As she wrote to Alfred Wadsworth, editor of the *Manchester Guardian*, in November 1950: "I have just practically finished a big bit of work for Chatham House and am getting anxious about the ever more acute problem of how to earn my living. I dare not start another book because people can't afford [in Austerity Britain] to buy the sort of book I write, and the printers' [job actions and strikes] have been playing havoc with various journals to which I have habitually contributed."[83] Research projects for Chatham House, especially work on Toynbee's *Survey of International Affairs*, suspended during the war, filled the place of a secure job. Pre-war the annual *Survey* had provided an immediate record of what had happened in the previous year; the catch-up volumes on the Second World War were somewhat different, more like exercises in contemporary history, and Wiskemann contributed sections on Czechoslovakia, Yugoslavia, Hungary, Romania, Bulgaria, and the Italian Resistance.[84]

In 1945 she hoped to continue her career as a freelance journalist as well as a historian of recent history, and in Italy she had been able to do this. But it required constant petitioning of editors with suggestions for articles and trying not to trespass upon the turf of full-time correspondents. As she wrote to Wadsworth, after he declined a proposal for a piece on the Saar: "Of course I understand the difficulty and only hope that you do not mind if I occasionally act upon the old adage that there is no harm in asking."[85] She usually traveled to the Continent a couple of times a year, reporting on Italian, Austrian, and Swiss politics but also writing about contested borderlands like the Saar, Trieste, and the Tyrol, where fewer staff reporters were based. Before the war she had been one of a small coterie of journalists with wide-ranging expertise about Central and Eastern Europe, but by 1948 the tightening grip of Stalinism over Eastern Europe made it increasingly difficult to obtain entry visas, and the hostility between East and West made impossible the kind of individual, unconstrained access that she had enjoyed pre-war to officials and politicians in many of these countries. She also felt that the Cold War somehow lowered public interest in East Europeans and their diverse cultures as opposed to the quarrels about them between the Great Powers.[86]

In the first years of peace, witnessing the devastation of so much of Europe, Wiskemann hoped for a period of peaceful coexistence in which social and economic reconstruction could be the priority of all nations. Her French diplomat friend Marcel Vaidie was doubtful, saying well before the armistice that "this alliance will scarcely survive a combined victory." Wiskemann later confessed: "this was one of the few periods when, unlike Marcel, I rather shirked the disagreeable truth."[87] She had no illusions about Stalinism, but in the afterglow of victory she did not expect the swift Sovietization of Eastern Europe. Beneš talked of countries like Czechoslovakia providing bridges between the West and the USSR, and Togliatti's policies in Italy, joining Badoglio's government, for example, seemed indicative of a desire for cooperation. The USSR's losses in the war, both human and material, were staggering and Stalin needed time, loans, and reparations from defeated Germany to rebuild and to consolidate the territories he had gained. Haunted by the possibility of a resurgent, revanchist Germany, he also wanted a protective *glacis* of friendly states on his western borders, but, with the exception of Czechoslovakia and Yugoslavia, none of these largely agrarian countries had large Communist parties; there was also no guarantee that an effort to impose replica Soviet regimes would be successful or that Communist and Socialist party leaders in Poland, Yugoslavia, or Czechoslovakia would acquiesce. All this pointed, Wiskemann believed, towards Stalin's tolerance of some diversity within a Soviet sphere of influence and accommodation with his Western Allies.

Moreover, in the first two years of peace Stalin's actions seemed more flexible and *ad hoc* rather than elements of the preconceived, three-stage 'master plan' for achieving monolithic Soviet-style regimes that Wiskemann's friend Hugh Seton-Watson described retrospectively.[88] At the time, like Doreen Warriner, she was more focused on the social revolution underway in Eastern Europe than on signs of secret police activities and Soviet control.[89] Her only direct experience of Eastern Europe, however, was in Budapest in September 1948, months after the Communist seizure of control in Prague and the mysterious death/murder (officially a suicide) of her old friend Jan Masaryk. Chatham House was planning a book about postwar Central and south-east Europe, and the editor, Reginald Betts, had asked her to contribute a chapter.[90] She had known pre-war Hungary well, having stayed several times with family friends, the aristocratic Bekassys, at their mansion at Sennye. Her early visits were mostly to Transdanubia, the region lying west of the Danube, which in the interwar years, she wrote, was "like stepping back into the eighteenth century. The villages looked dismally poverty-stricken, the peasants were poor beast-like creatures living in one-story huts along one long miserable village street."[91] Her hosts on these visits were "humanly nice" within their narrow code of social conventions, but she was shocked by their idle, feudal lifestyle and the subservience of their peasant retainers, who seemed little better than serfs; equally jarring were the opinions of the Magyar ruling class: their arrogance ("stupendous"), their ingrained anti-Slav prejudice and anti-Semitism, and their disdain for modernity and urban life. Budapest they viewed "as a sink of iniquity, as a center of Jewish money-lenders and 'intellectuals.'"[92]

Returning for several weeks after nine years' absence, Wiskemann found everything changed, "turned inside out" by the war and the German and Russian occupations. Soviet soldiers had wrecked the library at Sennye and peasants had ransacked the castle, "taken down the curtains, taken up the flooring and so on" (she adds: "and who could blame them"), while its former owners were now living in a summerhouse in the garden. She was mostly afraid of contacting her former hosts lest she cause them political trouble, but in Budapest she was approached by one of the cousins who was employed at the American Legation and was trying to leave the country: she "had become so suspect by the end of 1948...[that] she always arranged to meet me after dark." Aside from government officials, Wiskemann's contacts were mostly with liberal or leftist university people and writers like Tibor Déry (her friend Lili Szilasi's cousin), Gyula Illyés, and the journalist and novelist Lajos Hatvany. The feeling in these moderate leftist circles was mostly one of bewilderment: "No one seemed to know where Hungary was going, but they all said that the one thing of which they were sure was that they did not want to go back to the past."[93]

Many positive things had happened and Wiskemann's chapter described them in some detail. The governing coalition had embarked on a reconstruction drive that included expropriation of large estates and redistribution of land to the peasants, nationalization of major industries and banking, a huge expansion of secular education, and increased health and social benefits for workers. Thus far, she wrote, the coalition government seemed to be working, albeit increasingly dominated by the Communist leaders Gerö and Rákosi, and policy seemed driven by the nation's crisis situation rather than Moscow's directives. But she also found signs of growing uncertainty about the future: peasants were scared that collectivized state farms would soon appropriate the land they had recently acquired, while the escalating Cold War between East and West made many fear increased police repression and intimidation. As the title of one of her articles put it, it was a time of "rough justice in Hungary"—long overdue reforms constituted a social revolution, while the regime's administrative and police methods seemed "much the same in reverse as it had been in the Horthy period," although officials were more industrious and favored the workers and peasants.[94] Full-scale Stalinism, she wrote, did not take hold in Hungary until May 1949; in fact, Rákosi's so called 'salami' tactics to eliminate political opposition were already well advanced by then. Upon returning to London, she quickly finished her chapter for Betts, but by 1950 when the book was published her contribution was outdated. By then then leaders of the Peasant party (the largest by far in terms of public support) had been tried and shot and the Communist party was undergoing a massive purge.[95] When Wiskemann was in Budapest, Laszlo Rajk, a veteran of the Spanish Civil War, was Minister of the Interior and then became Foreign Minister; when her chapter appeared, he had been tried and executed as a "paid agent of a foreign power."[96]

While Wiskemann was in Budapest, the Western powers were engaged in a colossal airlift to supply blockaded Berlin with food, fuel, and other vital materials. This was the final crisis in the breakdown of joint occupation of Germany by the victor powers. It was always clear that policies towards Germany would determine the emergent structure of international relations. After a brief period of cooperation, the ideological incompatibility and conflicting national interests of the wartime allies, their contrasting views about Germany's future role, and spiraling mutual distrust led inexorably to partition of the occupation zones into two German states, each integrated into rival Cold War camps, with Berlin as a 'powder keg' in the center of Europe. The Western Allies were determined to reconstruct Germany, prevent its domination by Stalin, and reintegrate its economy with Western Europe; Stalin was forced to settle for communist control of his occupation zone, which also provided a reliable buffer separating Poland and from West; and the border agreements negotiated at Potsdam remained in place in the absence of a final peace treaty. Today we see the Cold War in global terms; the lens through which Wiskemann saw it was Europe and "the German Question," and for her this could be summed up in three questions: Would the FRG become a prosperous, politically stable, liberal democratic state? Would it accept its existing frontiers, give up claims to lost territories, and abandon expansionist goals in the East? Could a renascent Germany, which had done so much to divide Europe, ever become a "hinge" drawing West and East (especially the Eastern European states within the Soviet bloc) closer together?

It was not until the summer of 1950 that she returned to Germany, fourteen years after her expulsion by the Nazi regime. She stayed about a month, confining her travel to West Germany, visiting Stuttgart, Freiburg, Frankfurt, Bonn, and other cities, seeing old friends, and gathering material for several articles. She saw Theodor Heuss again, whom she had known as a Reichstag member in the last years of the Weimar Republic; he was now President of West Germany and had played a major part in drafting the Republic's Basic Law, or constitution. She also stayed with the Szilasis in Freiburg, where Wilhelm had been appointed to the Chair of Philosophy that Heidegger once occupied. After surviving seven years in Buchenwald, another old friend, Eugen Kogon, had testified at Nuremberg and published *Der S.S. Staat* (1946), a chilling account of Nazi terror in the camps. He and Walter Dirks were now the founders and driving force behind the liberal Catholic *Frankfurter Hefte*. Her friends were mostly "engaged democrats," as Sean Forner has called them. They insisted that Germans could only rebuild their collective identity by confronting their collective guilt and they spent the occupation years advocating grass roots democracy where citizens actively participated in political life and self-rule.[97] By the early 1950s many of them were feeling marginalized or alienated in Chancellor Adenauer's new Germany. An Amnesty law had allowed tens of thousands of former Nazis to escape justice unscathed; government pressure secured early release for numerous others, while Article 131 of the Basic Law reinstated and restored the pensions of hundreds of thousands of civil servants, judges, and career soldiers, including Gestapo members. Offering incentives to quickly rejoin national life, Adenauer was convinced, was a precondition to creating a stable, socially conservative, and economically successful state. The focus was on putting the past aside rather than allocating responsibility, and those, like philosopher Karl Jaspers, who emphasized the importance of confronting Nazi crimes met with considerable public criticism. People were preoccupied with their own personal grief rather than their moral complicity, Wiskemann wrote, and they regarded themselves as victims and the Nuremberg trials as inevitable 'victor's justice'.[98] To Harry Bergholz she confided: "Germany was extremely interesting but, of course, pretty shattering – I think there are probably more Nazis than ever, nor can one be surprised."[99]

Back in London, Wiskemann told *Observer* editor William Clark that she was "bursting with things I want to say but don't see as many possibilities as I would like…I wonder if there is any periodical you can suggest which pays a living wage?"[100] She managed to place several articles, mostly impressionistic efforts to capture the cultural and political mood in the new republic. Her observations were predominantly critical and bleak. Like Eugen Kogon, Walter Dirks, and others, she argued that postwar hopes for democratization and denazification had given way to a mood of passivity and a "Restoration atmosphere."[101] "The keynote in the life of the Federal Republic," she wrote, "is *Restauration*, back to the old men and old ideas, with more than a suggestion of 1815 and Metternich"; "back to legitimacy, however outworn." There was a nostalgia for the Bismarckian system; the new administration was "staffed, not with outspoken Nazis, but with *deutschnationale alte Herren* or 'old boys' of the traditional *Studenten Corps*."[102] It was the same trend she had described in Italy, where the creative possibilities of peace were stifled by a return to old habits, prejudices, and institutions.

In one article she contrasted this postwar cultural life with the violent but fiercely creative aftermath of 1918, when artists and intellectuals tried to fathom the meaning of the conflict, experimenting with new ideas and forms of expression: "Kathe Kollwitz's drawings…spoke the anguish of poverty, Georg Grosz derided vulgarity and vice…Bertolt Brecht's *Dreigroschenoper* reproached society for its outcasts," and the new architecture inspired by Gropius and Bauhaus "searched and found forms to express the aspirations of a socialist industrial society." If Spengler foretold the West's decline, much hope had been placed in the East: "in those days Paris and Moscow met in Berlin. If the political revolution in Germany was a sham, that in the arts, in literature, the theatre and cinema was not. New vistas had opened; possibilities were great." By contrast, "today the Germans seem like crippled shadows flitting among the ruins of their cities." People, she argued, wished only to escape, a mood that precluded genuine experimentation. The latest architecture seemed uninspired; little of interest was happening in the film studios; and philosophy was still centered upon Heidegger, notwithstanding his Nazi associations. As for the theatre, American and French plays, especially those of Sartre, dominated; the Wagner family were planning to re-start the Bayreuth festival and the Passion Play was revived at Oberammergau, although, she added, "it is often whispered in one's ear that the only member of the cast who was not a Nazi in Hitler's day has been given the part of Judas."[103]

With respect to foreign policy, Germans were "full of their European mission," whether it was "a Western Europe following the French lead and depending on America, or something predominantly German but neutral between West and

East, or basically a reunited Germany which will undermine the power of Russia and in the end perhaps control it."[104] Elements of the Social Democratic party pushed the neutral option, but most West Germans had become, seemingly over-night, pro-French and supported the turn to the West. But in foreign policy too, she remarked, the mood was labile and contradictory. Gallup polls indicated that most Germans opposed rearmament, an issue that had become more pressing with the outbreak of the Korean War; but most were also resentful that the Allies had disarmed the nation. There was enthusiastic support for federalism and Schuman's proposal in May 1950 for a European Coal and Steel Community, and yet German nationalism remained strong and revisionist memoirs were linking European integration and the Nazi 'New Order.' She was especially interested in the *Brüderschaft*, a semi-secret organization with neo-Nazi connections, whose propaganda had changed, claiming that the *Wehrmacht* had been defending Europe's *Ostfront* against Bolshevism, while "all nationalities met in the *Waffen S.S.*, that vanguard of the army of Europe."[105] Former Nazis were only too happy to commit themselves to the Cold War campaign against communism. Wiskemann's letters to her Swiss journalist friend Arnold Künzli repeatedly asked for details about these groups and the re-emergence of chauvinist student organizations.[106]

One positive idea that Wiskemann found in the new West Germany, and that she discussed in several essays, was plans for the spread of *Mitbestimmung*, or joint consultation in German industry–worker representation on managerial committees. This was already being tried in parts of the Ruhr under the aegis of the British occupation authorities and it enjoyed considerable support across the political spectrum, despite opposition from Adenauer and some business groups. However, it was unclear whether the worker representatives would be independ-ent or outmaneuvered and co-opted. Her enthusiasm for this form of industrial democracy was reminiscent of her earlier hopes that works councils might achieve a permanent place within Italian industry, although this prospect had been nullified by the success of De Gasperi's Christian democracy. Wiskemann believed that economic democracy in factories could act as a powerful bolster to parliamentary democracy, especially where traditions of democratic politics were weak.[107]

Her preoccupation with a possible revival of Nazism and German chauvinism was also evident in several articles she wrote after visits to the Saar when the province again surfaced as a factor in Franco-German relations in the 1950s. She knew the region well and had reported extensively on the referendum campaign that resulted in its absorption by Nazi Germany in 1935. Since the war's end France had administered the Saar separately from the rest of its occupation zone in hopes of annexing it. This was totally unacceptable to most Germans, and Adenauer recognized this, although, in the interests of European integration and good relations with France, he agreed to a statute which bound the region economically to France, subject to a referendum of the population.[108] Parliamentary elections in the area at the end of 1952 had shown a comfortable majority in favor of the status quo, but by the time of the plebiscite the political atmosphere had changed. Saarlanders had grown more critical of French economic controls and were increasingly attracted by accelerating West German economic prosperity. A major industrial region and rich in coal, the Saarland was central to European federalist plans, and Wiskemann argued that an autonomous Saar with the status of a European territory would be a nucleus for European integration.[109] "France," she wrote, "needs the Saar economically, Germany needs it emotionally."[110] She followed the campaign closely in 1955, attending meetings of the *Deutscher Heimatbund* and the *Landsmannschaften* [Homeland Societies], which voiced the grievances of Germans expelled from Eastern Europe. There, not surprisingly, she encountered strident nationalist language reminiscent of the 1930s; her alarm was also fueled by research she was conducting into the impact of refugee and expellee organizations on West German politics more generally. In cooler moments, however, she recognized how different the postwar situation was: Adenauer wanted the problem resolved amicably, and French interest in the region had also declined by the mid-1950s with the consolidation of the European Coal and Steel Community. Compared to the 1930s, Saarlanders were less afraid, more cynical, and motivated less by nationalism than economic priorities, and in October 1957 they voted to return to Germany by 67% to 32%.[111]

There is no doubt that deep distrust of Germans colored Wiskemann's judgment about the early Federal Republic, but her views were not uncommon. While admiration for the courage of Berliners was high during the Allied airlift of 1947, it was soon eclipsed by a wave of Germanophobia in the British media, fueled by anger over the occupation's excessive costs, claims of resurgent nationalist extremism, and journalists' exposés of the Nazi pasts of prominent figures in the new Germany.[112] Journalists like Drew Middleton of the *New York Times* and Wiskemann's old enemy, Sefton Delmer, who had returned to the *Daily Express*, sharply criticized the Republic's failure to confront its past.[113] "Only four years after Germany's defeat and the suicide of Hitler," Delmer warned in December 1949, "only three years after the Nuremberg trials, in a Germany which is still in ruins, the Nazis are once more coming out into the open. And they are once more coming out on top."[114] But Bonn was not Weimar. Unlike in 1918, Germans did not blame politicians for their hardships, but rather Hitler or the occupying powers. Fear of the left and of Communism focused much more on the Red Army and Stalin's satellite, the GDR. The Basic Law provided a solid foundation for a parliamentary democracy, and Adenauer met with growing support as the economy revived, while his consistent pro-Western policies and support for European integration received strong backing from Washington and inaugurated a closer relationship with France. To be sure, he had no qualms about reinstating former Nazis or making overtures to nationalist and refugee organizations, but

Wiskemann underestimated the difficulties he faced in forging a new national identity, which required integrating not only former Nazis but vast numbers of German expellees from Eastern Europe. Wiskemann emphasized the threat they posed to a stable German democracy, but arguably Adenauer's tolerance defused a potentially dangerous opposition, although it encouraged Germans to forget the past or to see themselves as victims.[115]

∗   ∗   ∗

While following events in the Saar, Wiskemann began thinking about another book, one that would examine Franco-German relations since the war. Their cooperation, she believed, was the most important theme in the new Western Europe, a gauge of the Germany's efforts to become democratic, and potentially a foundation for European federalism. She followed the negotiations for the Schuman Plan closely as the first tentative economic steps towards greater European unity and hoped that Britain would eventually join. Encouraged by her friend Darsie Gillie, the *Manchester Guardian*'s Paris correspondent, she sent a draft proposal to Margaret Cleeve, Secretary of the Research Committee at Chatham House, early in 1953. But nothing came of it and it's unclear

Figure 5.1 "Elizabeth Wiskemann in the 1950s."

why—possibly because other scholars were already working on the topic or perhaps because she had previously published little about France.

Instead, it was another offer from Chatham House that determined her next major project, and this drew her back to the relationship between Germany and Eastern Europe. Financed by a grant from the Rockefeller Foundation, the project focused on Germany's eastern borderlands and the consequences of the Potsdam settlement. Between the wars, Chatham House had commissioned a study of the consequences of the border changes resulting from the First World War, and this was to be a sequel. More directly, however, pressure for the project came from Hugh Seton-Watson, Christopher's brother, a leading scholar of Russia and Eastern Europe and a Chatham House board member. In 1952 Stalin had put forward a proposal for a reunited, neutral, and demilitarized Germany which both Adenauer and the West firmly rejected, although it was not unattractive to sections of the Social Democratic party and some West German intellectuals. Stalin's death the following March brought further uncertainty as his acolytes began to struggle over the spoils of power. If a final peace with Germany and the issue of reunification were ever taken up, Seton-Watson wrote to Cleeve in July 1953, the social situation in these frontier lands would be central to all discussions:

> The proposed study is not of German reunification, but of Germany's eastern frontier. It is conceivable – I certainly wouldn't put it higher – that the unification of the Soviet zone with the Federal Republic may become a practical possibility in the next six months or year. But, if so, the problem of united Germany's eastern border will become not less, but more important. It is simply fantastic that so little is known of this subject in this country & [the] U.S. There is hardly a problem in world affairs today of greater basic importance – and I say this after some thought.[116]

There was Board resistance to taking up the idea in view of the political sensitivity of German reunification, the Potsdam frontiers, and the politics of the German expulsions from Eastern Europe. To these concerns Seton-Watson responded: "As for the political aspect predominating, this was always the case. I have stressed the need to study the social and economic development of Polish-annexed and Czech-held ex-German territories because they form a very large part of the essence of the political problem."[117] Some members thought that an edited book of essays might be preferable, others expressed doubts about Wiskemann.[118] But Seton-Watson was unpersuaded and (supported by Doreen Warriner) pushed for her as sole author. Whoever was chosen, he insisted, must:

> 1) have personal experience of all three countries; 2) know well the 20th century history of all three; 3) know all three languages; 4) fully appreciate the interdependence of political and economic questions in this region. Miss Wiskemann

possesses most of these qualifications – first class under 1) and 2), at least fair under 4), I am not sure how good under 3)... Personally I hope that she will consent to handle it all.[119]

In truth, there were few candidates better qualified for the task, for in some respects the proposed book constituted a sequel to her pre-war research on German–Slav conflicts in Eastern Europe. From the outset the book was envisioned as a contribution to ongoing policy discussions, so speed was essential, and in accepting the job Wiskemann agreed to finish the manuscript in 1954, ready for publication the following spring.[120] As usual Chatham House's terms were anything but lavish. The fee for an estimated year's work was £500, plus £200 for travel, £100 for Polish and Czech experts, and another £100 for contingencies, adding up to £900. Difficulties soon arose, however, when the Communist regimes of Poland and Czechoslovakia ignored her visa requests for travel in the contested areas; consequently, the project had to be reshaped, focusing less on the situation in the borderlands themselves and more on West Germany's integration of expellees from the East. The economic repercussions for the areas from which refugees had come and the circumstances of ethnic Germans who remained in Poland and Czechoslovakia received less attention than originally envisioned. She spent about a month in West Germany, including Berlin, in early 1954 and again in the following year, but most of her research was carried out in London.[121] The book, she later admitted, "presented more difficulties" than anything she had written before and it provoked more controversy; it did not appear until 1956, the only time, I believe, that she missed a publishing deadline.

In August 1948 the International Red Cross estimated that over 12 million eth-nic Germans had been forcibly removed from Central and Eastern Europe since the end of the war. The speed and scale of this population transfer was unprece-dented and many hundreds of thousands of innocent civilians died in the process. Many had fled west ahead of the Soviet advance, while the Czech and Polish governments-in-exile had long voiced their intention of expelling Germans from their territories at the war's end and had received the blessing of the Allies. After the First World War, recognizing that the new map of Eastern Europe had created large national minorities within Poland, Czechoslovakia, Yugoslavia, and other states, the Allied powers tried to impose treaties protecting minority rights as part of the settlement. However, these protections guaranteed by the League of Nations had largely failed. The League had little desire and few sanctions to enforce them, Britain and France increasingly saw them as hindering the process of national assimilation, and in the 1930s, they were often blamed for exacerbat-ing ethnic antagonisms. By the Second World War many British officials, viewing ethnically homogeneous states as inherently more stable and unified, had in prin-ciple come to accept the radical alternative of forced 'transfer' of populations as a way of resolving intractable national conflicts. They often mentioned the 1923

Greek–Turkish population exchange as a successful example, and some in the late 1930s suggested that mass transfer or resettlement was the only way to resolve the Czech-German dispute. During the war Eastern European demography had already been dramatically transformed by the brutal Nazi racial project and it was widely assumed that Hitler's defeat would inevitably lead to mass expulsions of ethnic Germans.

Already in August 1942 the British Cabinet had given Beneš and the exiled Czech government approval for a postwar 'transfer' of the German minority, and the Teheran conference in 1943 had endorsed transfers from the Polish lands. At the time it was argued that the long-term benefits for postwar stabilization outweighed the potential risks. Disagreements focused less on the principle than on the practical difficulty of managing such a vast migration in an orderly manner. In February 1942 Toynbee's Oxford-based Foreign Research and Press Service commissioned a study by philosopher John Mabbott which warned that widespread mistreatment of Germans by Poles and Czechs would result unless the Allies supervised such a transfer; he also estimated that five to ten years would be required to complete the operation.[122] This advice was not wanted or heeded. In November 1943 the British government conducted another survey, which foretold immense suffering and dislocation, no matter what steps were taken, and warned that the government "might be unable, even if they wished, to disclaim responsibility for the human suffering and economic dislocation involved."[123] Responsibility for the transfers, it was suggested, should be handled by the expelling governments and resettlement costs should be borne by the Germans themselves, not the Allies or UNRRA. At Potsdam there was talk of "orderly and humane" transfers between the East and Allied occupation zones, but nothing was done to ensure this and in the chaotic closing phases of the war a massive and violent process of ethnic cleansing—much larger than British officials had ever envisioned—got underway. Germans, most of them women and children, were killed and brutalized at will, driven from their homes, maltreated in makeshift internment camps, and crammed into cattle cars for deportation. The devastated occupation zones of Germany were ill-equipped to receive such a vast inflow of people: many were sick, malnourished, penniless, and traumatized, while allied bombing had severely diminished housing stock, so that many were dumped in refugee camps or billeted in rural areas on families that were already suffering.[124]

Most analyses of these events distinguish between the so-called 'wild' expulsions that began in spring 1945, viewed as spontaneous eruptions of revenge-taking by Czech and Polish civilians, and the supposedly 'organized' expulsions of 1946–47 supervised by the Allies. But, as R.M. Douglas has shown, the first 'wild' wave of forced migration was also executed by police, troops, and militia, with the complicity of the authorities, who wished to stampede Germans across the frontiers. And later deportations also quickly degenerated into a chaos of mismanagement, hunger, disease, criminality, and violence, although transfers from Czechoslovakia were said to be somewhat improved in this phase. None of this was hidden from sight: British officials, UNRRA workers, journalists, and soldiers witnessed these scenes, and the expulsions received extensive coverage in the press. Some protested: Bishop Bell of Chichester, for example, tried to rally the churches, and left-wing publisher Victor Gollanz's "Save Europe Now" campaign called upon the Labour government to intervene. Largely excluded from the Soviet zone and the violence in Poland, the press focused more on what was happening in the Czech lands where Beneš had promised an orderly process. Eric Gedye, whom Wiskemann had known well in pre-war Vienna, shocked readers of the *Daily Herald* with exposés about the grizzly conditions in the Hagibor holding camp in Prague, and F.A. Voigt, once a staunch defender of Czechoslovakia, attacked its 'cleansing' of Sudeten Germans using "methods hardly distinguishable from those of Fascism." "Are mass deportations," asked philosopher Bertrand Russell, "crimes when committed by our enemies during war and justifiable measures of social adjustment when carried out by our allies in time of peace?"[125]

However, the prevailing opinion in British official and political circles was punitively anti-German, unwilling to pressure the Poles and Czechs, downplaying the level of violence or explaining it as the unavoidable consequence of the speed of events and an understandable popular thirst for revenge after years of brutal occupation—a situation that, despite their efforts, neither the Polish nor the Czech government could be expected to control. There was also a strong pro-Czech lobby in Britain which had championed Czech democracy pre-war and campaigned against Appeasement and the betrayal of Munich. Shiela Grant Duff, wartime head of the BBC's Czech section and, as we have seen, a staunch defender of Beneš and Ripka, visited Czech camps shortly after Gedye and argued that humanitarian demands for slowing down or suspending the expulsions were causing added misery by lengthening internment periods and increasing over-crowding.[126] Author and former president of International PEN Storm Jameson visited Prague and downplayed criticism of camp conditions, exonerating the central government and placing any blame on local actors, while Labour MP Tom Williamson found nothing to substantiate press claims of inhuman treatment and slave camps.[127] When the expulsions took place Wiskemann was in Italy and did not publish anything on the subject at the time. Like Grant Duff, she probably viewed the expulsion of Sudeten Germans as tragic but inevitable, justified in the light of the Nazi past. In a book review in January 1946, she wrote: "Indignation has been expressed against the Czechs, since the recent liberation of their country, because they have carried out their accepted intention of expelling a considerable portion of their German minority. It seems that people have already forgotten the vastly greater sufferings gratuitously inflicted on the Czechs by the Germans."[128] Her words were harsh but not uncommon and seven years later when she began her new research—in part, perhaps, because it was an academic project—she seemed little aware of just how sensitive, polarizing, and incendiary the topic remained.

Germany's Eastern Neighbours: Problems Relating to the Oder-Neisse Line and the Czech Frontier Region (1956) was the first major study in English of the post-war expulsion of Germans from Eastern Europe and for a long time it remained unrivalled. It is packed with information and statistics, testimony to Wiskemann's extensive reading of secondary monographs, official reports, press and periodical articles (in German, English, Czech, and Polish), even obscure sources like the *Arbeiterstimme*, published in Wrocław, and the Prague trade union paper, *Aufbau und Frieden*, used to illuminate the social conditions of Germans workers still living in the East. The result was remarkable, especially since she had only two years to do the research. The book wove together multiple interconnecting themes: the war's chaotic final stages; the refugee crisis and the expulsions of ethnic Germans; Allied diplomacy at Teheran, Yalta, and Potsdam; and the integration of millions of refugees into West Germany's economy and their impact on its politics. Brief economic sections also considered the areas from which the expellees came and the situation of the small German minority still living in Poland and Czechoslovakia.

Wiskemann tried to be detached and impartial in her analysis of the expulsions, to strike a balance between the suffering of the expellees and the craving for revenge of occupied populations that had endured forced labor, concentration camps, and mass murder. Her book includes detailed description of the violence to which German expellees were subjected: the vengeance of Soviet troops, the notorious cruelty of Polish militia forces, and indiscriminate Czech reprisals against women and children, including specific outrages like the massacre at Aussig (Ústí) in July 1945 after Germans were blamed for an explosion. And she depicted the chaos, the Belsen-level rations, and the mistreatment that occurred in Czech and Polish holding camps where Germans awaited deportation and herding into cattle cars. "Poles and Czechs," she was clear, "inflicted great and unnecessary suffering upon the Germans they expelled, suffering which had nothing to do with the political principles expressed by transfers of alien population…"[129]

Some of the anger that her book aroused in West Germany undoubtedly resulted from the dispassionate, academic tone of her writing; even positive British reviews remarked on how "with the cold, smooth skill of a surgeon…she has shut her ears to the sounds of horror."[130] But more infuriating were the caustic remarks she injected as asides into pages of factual detail, making clear that she sympathized more with the victims of Nazism. While admitting that there were innocent victims on all sides, Wiskemann rebuked the tendency of many Germans to disclaim "not only all responsibility, but all knowledge of what was done in their name." To West German claims that the Potsdam agreements were provisional until a peace treaty was signed and that the nation's legal frontiers were those of 1937, she commented "it is difficult for Germany's neighbours not to smile sourly over this post-1945 legalism." Or again, in words guaranteed to anger Bonn, she noted that territorial concessions in the past had fortified "the worst elements" in Germany and "if one considers the recent record of German minorities in eastern Europe, it is difficult to wish them back there."[131] She was also convinced, in the case of the Czech expulsions, that Beneš and Ripka had envisioned a slow, orderly 'transfer,' or *Odsun*,* spread over several years, which was frustrated by "a combination of popular exasperation, Communist incitement, and Allied policy."[132] Resettlement, they believed, was the only way to avoid civil war and safeguard the unity and independence of their country. As the opening of East European archives after 1989 revealed, however, the drive for national cleansing was orchestrated from above by Czech authorities, and both Beneš and Ripka were more hardline than she realized, convinced that the removal of all Germans must be accomplished quickly to prevent any future demands for Sudeten autonomy.

Far less controversial were the chapters that examined the Federal Republic's social and economic integration of the expellees and their contribution to the German 'economic miracle' or *Wirtschaftswunder*. The integration of 9.4 million people constituted an enormous challenge in terms of housing, jobs, and food and required the rapid rebuilding of German industries and an expansion of technical training. The resettlement of displaced farmers was even more difficult. But after several hard years of overcrowding and underemployment, most refugees had flourished, aided by Adenauer's Equalization of Burdens Law of 1952.† Those who were public servants were incorporated into the civil service and teaching, while skilled workers found jobs with the extra stimulus provided by the Korean War industrial boom; small businesses multiplied with the help of loans, and cultural integration grew, as evidenced by steadily increasing statistics of intermarriage between 'natives' and expellees. Among the communities Wiskemann visited was Neugablonz, the center of glass bead and button manufacturing. Resettled in Bavaria, the Bohemian glassmakers from Gablonz had created a whole new township ("with streets named after the old ones in Bohemia") based upon glassmaking with exports to the United States.[133] And yet some refugees— possibly as many as 200,000—were still living in camps, obliged to admire the 'economic miracle' "through barrack windows."[134] Gloomy prognostications in 1946 about whether West Germany might be dependent and unable to feed itself because of the huge loss of predominantly agricultural lands to the east had vanished; by 1954 better techniques had significantly raised productivity,

---

* The terminology used is politically significant. Germans used the word *Vertreibung*, or 'expulsion,' while Czech accounts mostly use the more innocuous term *Odsun*, or 'transfer' ('removal'), of population.

† The Equalization of Burdens (*Lastenausgleich*) Law was passed by the West German parliament in May 1952. It was a tax on wealth, the proceeds of which were distributed to those most damaged by the war. By the end of 1971 some 82.8 billion marks had been paid out, 67% of which had gone to refugees and 20% to war wounded.

while industrial exports paid for larger grain imports. In postwar Europe national self-sufficiency was no longer a relevant goal. Finally, Wiskemann examined the economic repercussions of this massive migration on areas the refugees left and the situation of the small ethnic German minority that still resided in Poland and Czechoslovakia. She had not visited these areas but from secondary sources showed how agriculture had suffered from the exodus of farmers. And while the industrial base of the two states was larger, they were deprived of Western markets and complained that Silesia's economic power was being exploited more for the Kremlin's benefit than their own.

Over 16% of West German citizens in the mid-1950s were expellees from the East and they quickly organized themselves into effective political and communal associations. The British and American occupation authorities had outlawed separate refugee organizations pursuing political objectives, but by 1950 the ban had been lifted and all the major political parties supported their calls for revision of the postwar boundary settlement. In 1950 the *Bund der Heimatvertriebene und Entrechteten* [BHE] was formed to advocate for their interests, and by 1955 expellees had formed some twenty *Landsmannschaften* with over 1.3 million members. Wiskemann worried that this large nationalist and anti-communist bloc could become a serious threat to West German democracy. She quoted an article in the *Times* in December 1950: "To a demagogue, refugees are what blood in the water is to a shark and the refugee problem is large enough to create a revolutionary situation."[135]

While attending meetings about the return of the Saar she was alarmed at their Nazi-sounding rhetoric and began following closely the personnel and the internal politics of these organizations. The BHE, whose leadership was dominated by former Nazis, gained seats in several state legislatures, and after his 1953 electoral victory Adenauer gave them two ministerial posts in his governing coalition, one—Theodor Oberländer—as Minister for Expellees.[136] Many mainstream politicians, Wiskemann admitted, found the BHE's irredentist language perilous and unrealistic, but none, outside the Communist party, was willing to accept publicly the Oder–Neisse border. All felt compelled "to behave as if the recovery of the lost territories lies within the range of possibility," while many former expellees who were happy in the West and had no desire for return remained silent, fearing to be "branded as acceptors or approvers of the *status quo.*"[137] She knew that many older expellees were simply homesick or having difficulty adjusting to their new home, but she emphasized political speech ("the right of return") more than the abstract, cultural power of Heimat as a focus of imaginary longing. She also emphasized the role of what we might call the *Ostforschung* industry, the network of exile scholars, publishers, research institutes, and publicists, liberally funded by the German government, that focused on the "lost lands."[138] While Wiskemann deemed some of the research respectable (for example the volumes edited by Theodor Schieder and Hans Rothfels[139]) much, she suggested, had the aim of keeping alive the project of restoring German power in the East so that a reinvigorated German nationalism might in the future "get back something like the frontiers of 1914 either in the name of Germany or of Europe."[140]

Germany's Eastern Neighbours was written with an eye to informing policy-makers. But when Wiskemann submitted her manuscript in August 1955, the international situation was in flux. Stalin's death in 1953 was followed by a power struggle in which Khrushchev emerged as leader, but he had not yet delivered his speech to the Twentieth Congress of the Communist party (February 1956) repudiating Stalinism—a speech that quickly reverberated through Eastern Europe with its rhetoric about "*different* roads to socialism; even a peaceful, *non-revolutionary* path."[141] By 1955, however, there were signs of a possible thaw in foreign policy, as Hugh Seton-Watson had anticipated. There was talk of peaceful coexistence; Soviet troops left Austria, once its neutrality was settled; and a rapprochement was negotiated with Tito's Yugoslavia, which the Soviet leadership seems to have viewed as part of a larger pattern whereby it could consolidate its Eastern European gains behind a buffer of neutral states. What all this might mean for Poland, Czechoslovakia, and the two Germanys was still unclear. Wiskemann organized her conclusions around two questions: Could any frontier adjustments be made, and could some form of international cooperation be devised to ameliorate the longstanding antagonisms of the eastern borderlands?

On the first, she was clear: that Soviet power determined the frontiers and there was no chance of reversing what had been done at Potsdam or the expulsion of Germans. Even minor border adjustments were unlikely, let alone German reunification—indeed "a new Russo-German rapprochement would be the most alarming possibility for the western world."[142] As for the Oder–Neisse border, the dispute between the powers at Potsdam had been over whether the line should be at the eastern or western Neisse river; the physical presence of Soviet troops had enabled Stalin to force adoption of the latter, significantly increasing Polish territory and the number of Germans expelled. In his "iron curtain" speech at Fulton, Missouri, in March 1946, Churchill had condemned Poland's "enormous and wrongful inroads upon Germany...on a scale grievous and undreamed of," while some months later US Secretary of State James Bynes and Labour Foreign Secretary Ernest Bevin had challenged the Oder–Neisse line. But, Wiskemann argued, the die was cast and such declarations merely reconciled Poles to the one great power that guaranteed their new territories.[143]

In answer to the second question, she suggested that a reduction in the antagonism between Germans and Slavs could only be achieved if there was more of a leveling up of living standards in the East. If anything, West Germany's postwar economic success had vastly increased the gulf between them and strengthened German claims to be the natural economic engine for Eastern Europe. If Poles and Slavs were to gain more independence from Moscow and German economic penetration increased, this would require a level of tact that Germans had shown toward their neighbors in the West but might find difficult in the East. "Nothing," she warned, "might do greater harm to German-Slav relationships than for Poles and Czechs to feel that, no sooner they are free of the communists' yoke than they must go into German economic harness."[144] As a first step, now that a decade had passed, West Germany should accept the expulsions as irreversible and recognize the Oder–Neisse line as unalterable, not simply *de facto* but *de jure*. This was essential to reducing the dependence of East European states upon Moscow and might eventually promote ties between an integrated Western Europe and "an East European union which included German representatives."[145] Wiskemann's brand of *Ostpolitik* focused on achieving greater independence for East European states (rather than German reunification), and throughout the 1960s she continued to advocate border acceptance as a way of loosening the grip of Stalinist-style regimes in the East.

British reviewers applauded her achievement in glowing terms. "No British publicist," wrote G.P. Gooch, "possesses a more intensive knowledge of the tangled skein of mid-European politics and we could desire no surer guide…not a sentence can be skipped."[146] The *Spectator* described it as "a book which should be pondered by anyone grooming himself to become, let us say, Under-Secretary of State for Foreign Affairs."[147] W.N. Medlicott, Professor of International Relations at London University, found it an "admirable book" convincing in its claims that the existing border arrangements must be accepted.[148] In the *New Statesman*, Richard Crossman praised Chatham House for sponsoring the book, calling it "succinct, detailed and scrupulously objective" and suggesting: "It should be made compulsory reading for anyone who enters into the controversy about the terms of a final German peace agreement." He also correctly predicted that it would not be popular in the Foreign Office and the US State Department, while in Bonn it would be "regarded as diabolically unfair by everyone." However, he added, "This should not disturb Miss Wiskemann. It is the price she must pay for her almost inhuman detachment."[149] Equally glowing was the verdict of Geoffrey Barraclough, who called it "extraordinarily impressive." A "rising crescendo" of officially sponsored propaganda was demanding a re-drawing of Germany's eastern frontiers, but Wiskemann's historical, strategic, and economic analysis left "nothing of the German case standing." Barraclough hoped, "though it would be purblind to expect, that her words will be heeded in Whitehall and Washington."[150] The book, wrote the *Manchester Guardian*'s Bonn correspondent, Terence Prittie, contained lessons Germans needed to learn; it "will be bitterly resented…and it may do no good there, but the enlightenment which it brings can be useful elsewhere."[151] Much more critical was John Midgley in the *Times Literary Supplement*. A former correspondent in Bonn, he found the book far too anti-German— "deceptively academic but…not in the least detached"—although it drew attention to the way that Bonn's stubborn support for the lost homelands campaign was "a source of fresh tensions and disturbance which will grow as the reunion of Germany draws nearer."[152] Several British reviewers called Wiskemann's book "timely," coinciding with perceived opportunities in the post-Stalin Kremlin; however, by the end of 1956, Moscow's pendulum was already swinging in a different direction as growing unrest and national self-assertion in Poland and Hungary produced a harsh crackdown that dispelled Western illusions about a new Soviet model.

From Prague there was no public response to the book, but Polish writers (and Polish-Americans) were delighted with its vindication of their border claims.[153] However, Wiskemann was completely unprepared for the apoplectic reception her book got in West Germany, where it was reviled as "an apologia of inhumanity" and "a tendentious conglomeration with questionable motives" put out by a "dilettante" and a "pupil of Beneš." The former mayor of Gleiwitz in Upper Silesia allegedly wrote in protest to the Queen of England.[154] Attacks orchestrated by the refugee lobby—including the *Verband der Vertriebenen*, the Herder (Marburg) and Osteuropa (Munich) research institutes, and public officials at the Ministry for Expellees—became increasing nasty and personal, vilifying Wiskemann's motives and integrity. Adenauer's office informed the Ministry for Expellees: "The Chancellor wishes that preparations be made for a coordinated German response to Miss Wiskeman's [sic!] book."[155] A particularly scurrilous brochure was published by Hilmar Toppe, connected with the Munich Osteuropa institute, who dismissed Wiskemann as a mere "dilettante," a Czech defender who had attended Beneš's cocktail parties before the war and whose earlier book *Czechs and Germans* and her lectures in the USA simply aped Czech propaganda. It was well known, argued Toppe, that she was the "mouthpiece" [*Sprachrohr*] of Beneš's lawyer friend and advisor Hubert Ripka, who, it was intimated, had lived with her and had been her lover.[156]

Why did Wiskemann's book produce such a furor in the Federal Republic? In part, the outrage of the *Ostforschung* institutes can be explained by the way she belittled their work as morally unacceptable and academically deficient: "inevitably [they] tend to become centres of irredentist propaganda, pressing German claims rather than weighing data objectively."[157] But the immediate political context was also important. Adenauer was then at the pinnacle of his power; his alignment with the West had paid off handsomely, including the Schuman Plan as a step towards European integration, West German sovereignty, and agreement on German rearmament within NATO. He had also negotiated successfully with Moscow for the release of remaining German prisoners of war. But he faced growing pressure from expellee groups and members of his own coalition government over the lost East. In early October 1956, as the *Times* reported, a huge rally of over 30,000 people gathered in Bonn. Speakers at the event blamed Churchill for bartering away historic German territory and railed against Adenauer's cowardice and inaction. They also vilified Wiskemann and her book as further evidence of a growing readiness to accept the permanence of Germany's losses and division. Adenauer was determined to integrate refugee groups into his Christian Democratic Union with anti-communism as its unifying ideology, while also taming their noisier revanchist elements in preparation for the 1957 elections. He feared that attacks on the expellees' lobby, like Wiskemann's, inflamed that group and also played to Western alarm about the resurgence of neo-Nazi and chauvinist elements.[158]

In the summer and fall of 1956 the Chancellor was also deeply alarmed by the Cold War crises developing over Suez and Hungary. Adenauer's strategy was a strong Western alliance to deter Soviet aggression and, if possible, eventually a rollback of Soviet power in Central Europe. In 1955 the FRG had adopted the so-called 'Hallstein doctrine' by which Bonn would break off diplomatic relations with countries (except for the USSR) that recognized the German Democratic Republic. He feared that Khrushchev's moves towards liberalization would be tempting to Western allies and groups in the FRG that had shown interest in opening dialogue and settling border issues, attracted by Soviet talk about linking German reunification to neutralism. This, in Adenauer's view, would be a downward spiral to Soviet dependency. In an unguarded moment in 1956 the German Foreign Minister, Heinrich von Brentano, had admitted that Bonn's intransigence over the Oder–Neisse line was "somewhat problematic" and might have to be changed to accomplish reunification—remarks he quickly disavowed amid expellee demands for his resignation.[159] Also, as the year continued, Adenauer became increasingly worried that the Western alliance was being undermined by the split between the US and the Franco-British allies over Suez, which might eventually produce an American-Soviet deal involving disengagement in Central Europe. Above all, he feared that a weakening of the Western consensus and a revival of separate national policies might produce a solution to the "German Question" without West German participation—one predicated on freezing the Potsdam borders and two Germanies. Wiskemann's book, published by Chatham House and welcomed by reviewers, stirred these anxieties about a larger drift of British and American politicians towards accepting existing borders and recognition of the GDR as a way of promoting *détente* with Moscow.[160]

Wiskemann was not surprised that German reviewers criticized her book, but she was shocked at the viciousness of the attacks on her scholarly and personal integrity. Seeing her reputation at stake, to say nothing of her livelihood as a journalist, she turned to Chatham House for support. The institute had commissioned the book and Alan Bullock and Hugh Seton-Watson had accepted the manuscript with almost no revisions. She would have liked some public riposte from Chatham House denying the German polemics and libels—a statement that could then be communicated to the British press and would be picked up by Continental papers. Her friend Alan Bullock said he would bring the request before the Board: "We have, as you know," he wrote in a letter to Monty Woodhouse, the Director of

Chatham House, "been persistently ignoring attacks from Germany on the book, but Elizabeth now contends that things have got beyond the possibility of toleration." Toppe's article was "exceedingly offensive, under the guise of scholarship, both against Elizabeth and against Chatham House." And yet, Bullock acknowledged, "so far as Chatham House's reputation is concerned, I am personally most strongly opposed to publishing formal denials or retorts of any kind."[161] Others, notably Charles Lambert Bayne, a former Assistant Secretary at the War Office and an old friend of Wiskemann, urged the board to "take the strongest action possible in her support."[162] But the Research Committee and Woodhouse, who was in general less sympathetic to Wiskemann than his predecessor Toynbee, while agreeing that the imputations against her were "entirely deplorable," decided "as a matter of principle it would be undignified for the Institute to take any public position in reply to such an attack."[163] There is no evidence of Foreign Office involvement in the dispute, although Richard Crossman had predicted that the book would be construed in that quarter as unfair to Bonn.[164] British policy in the mid-1950s was engaged in a delicate dance, trying to move towards détente with the Communist bloc, which required tacit acceptance of the Oder–Neisse line, while doing everything possible to avoid offending West Germany and making soothing noises about the desirability of German unification.[165]

Snubbed by Chatham House's response, Wiskemann turned to her own network of friends to mobilize a response to Toppe and the other attempts to blacken her reputation. To Arnold Künzli, who was working for the Swiss *National-Zeitung*, she wrote:

> You will have seen that since Crossman's article about my book I have become Public Enemy No. 1 in Germany. I am '*Emigrantin*', paid agent, Ripka's mistress etc. etc. – altogether a most peculiar outburst of hysteria even for Germany...I rather hope someone here will write a comment on this singular outburst in Germany – evidently my friends there are too frightened to speak. But most of all I would like something to be said in Switzerland. Do you see any possibility in the *National Zeitung*? I could supply some of the cuttings, but I think it would not be difficult to find the *Schimpfereien* [Ranting or name-calling].[166]

Another person she contacted was Alfred Wiener, founder of the Wiener Library: "I shall be grateful for all the help you can give me –it is disgusting and false – utterly."[167] She added: "My friends regard this as one of the worst bits of neo-Nazism there has been. If you could make a written protest, it would carry weight in Germany and be important."[168] Wiener contacted several German historians, including Helmut Krausnick at the Munich Institut für Zeitgeschichte; he also raised the issue at the German Embassy.[169] Wiskemann also enlisted her friend and Labour party leader Hugh Gaitskell to intercede with the German Embassy.

Finally, the *Manchester Guardian* editor, Alastair Hetherington, published a strong statement in her defense which concluded: "The Nazi leaders, their programme and their policy are treated [in Toppe's pamphlet] as a temporary and regrettable aberration...This is the kind of publication which will inevitably increase the suspicions felt by Germany's neighbours – and by many Germans too – whenever the question of Germany's eastern frontiers is made." Feeling "handsomely rehabilitated," Wiskemann responded: "That leader of yours did exactly what was needed, and the wicked Nazi professor has been made to feel a tiny bit foolish, I gather."[170] Several years later she wrote to Kenneth Younger, the new Chatham House Director and a former Labour politician: "That mad outburst in Germany was very odd, now I can see fairly clearly that the book was all right. But I did feel terribly upset at the time, the worst thing being the feeling that Chatham House was unfriendly about it – perhaps this was just the technique of the then D-G [Director Monty Woodhouse]. Once I got over the whole thing it helped me to know that, if about nothing else, I'm sane about the German question which has been nagging at me since just about the day I was born."[171] *Germany's Eastern Neighbours*, like her earlier study *Czechs and Germans*, influenced Anglo-American scholarship over the following decades, but neither book was translated into German.[172]

*   *   *

After spending the early postwar years as a journalist writing about Italy, Wiskemann found herself increasingly drawn back to Germany and its relationship to the rest of Europe. The 1950s also saw her devote less time to journalism and more to reviewing and academic research. Her journalistic articles focused mostly on Switzerland, Austria, and disputed borderlands like the Saar, Tyrol, and Trieste, places and stories not already covered by full-time correspondents posted to Europe's capitals; this also meant constantly petitioning editors with suggestions for stories. Reviewing for the the *Spectator*, the *Times Literary Supplement*, and other periodicals provided a more regular and predictable income; it also brought her growing recognition in academic circles, especially among the fairly small group of historians working on Germany and the Second World War.

The later success of West Germany can make Wiskemann's anxieties about a resurgence of German nationalism and the nation's failure under Adenauer to confront its past seem overblown and irrational. But in the early 1950s she was far from alone even among British historians, as Astrid Eckert has shown in her analysis of "the struggle for the files"—the German government documents, seized by British and American forces. Wiskemann played a very minor role in this controversy, but one that illuminates both her reputation among professional historians and the prevalence of anti-German prejudice in their ranks.

Already before the war's end several prominent British historians argued that the captured German files should not be left in the hands of Germans, as had happened after 1918.[173] This, they argued, had resulted in *Die Grosse Politik*, a well-known documentary collection, edited by Dr. Friedrich Thimme, which obscured German responsibility for the outbreak of war in 1914, fueled myth-making in the Reich, and provided grist to the mill of revisionist historians.[174] Instead, they urged that the Allies commission their own authoritative *Documents on German Foreign Policy* [DGFP] to set the record straight. The project got underway in 1946 with John Wheeler-Bennett and Raymond Sontag of Berkeley as joint editors-in-chief, supervising a large team of researchers. Progress was slow, and already by 1949 the FRG was insisting on restitution of the files as essential to its sovereignty. As one newspaper put it: "If its archives are taken away, a nation is stripped of its history and is robbed not only of the sources of its history but also of the possibility to write its own history."[175] Negotiations dragged on for years, including periodic quarrels between the British and Americans; even a request for the appointment of a German co-editor got nowhere. But by 1953, eager to improve relations with Bonn, both the British Foreign Office and the US State Department were moving towards returning the documents. This aroused bitter opposition and a threat of resignation from the advisory committee of the DGFP,‡ whose work was still in its early stages.[176]

Predictably, the dispute spilled over into the pages of the *TLS*, thereby publiciz-ing the issue more generally within academia. This occurred in a review by Wiskemann of the fifth volume of the Anglo-American *DGFP* series.[177] The review (anonymous in those days) was unremarkable except for its concluding statement: "Above all, so long as these German archives are in the hands of the Western Allies there need be no fear of manipulations of the texts such as those which have been discovered to have taken place in Germany after the other war. It will be a depressing day for historians if and when the German claim to the return of their Foreign Office documents is recognized."[178] Her declaration triggered a swift response from Oxford's A.J.P. Taylor, who challenged the reviewer to pro-vide details of political falsifications in Thimme's documents, although it soon became clear that his animus was chiefly directed at the team of Allied editors. Given that so far they had only managed to publish five volumes compared to Thimme's "virtually unaided" production of fifty-four in roughly the same time, he suggested: "At this rate it will take them another 50 years to complete their task. It would be better to boast of our achievement when we have achieved it."[179] Over the next two months a heated exchange of letters to the *TLS* debated the errors and distortions of *Die Grosse Politik*. Senior diplomatic historians joined in, Wiskemann defended her claim, Agnes Headlam-Morley, Professor of International Relations at Oxford, saw no reason why Allied scholars should have

---

‡ Consisting of John Wheeler-Bennett, Sir E. Llewellyn Woodward, W.N. Medlicott, Sir Lewis Namier, and Margaret Lambert, who eventually took over as chief editor from Wheeler-Bennett. The Foreign Office librarian, E.J. Passant, was also important in discussions about the files.

exclusive access to the files of the Weimar Republic, and then changed her mind.[180] Evidence from the Holstein and Stresemann papers was also said to prove Thimme's politically motivated distortions.[181] Finally, James Joll took a moderate, Solomonic position, recognizing that Thimme had been under constant pressure from the German Foreign Office to suppress material, while also praising his enormous industry. The *Grosse Politik*, Joll wrote, remained a valuable source, especially since only eleven volumes of British documents had been published for the pre-1914 years and state archives were still only open to 1902.[182] Three more years went by before control of the files was relinquished; most of the diplomatic documents were transferred to West Germany between 1956 and 1958.[183] Frank Roberts, Under-Secretary at the Foreign Office, commented: "the UK historians seem obstinately determined that history shall be the only field in which we refuse absolutely to work with the Germans."[184]

As Astrid Eckert has written, the timing of Wiskemann's *TLS* review was "no accident." What is interesting is that the editorial committee, feeling beleaguered and under growing pressure to surrender the files, chose her to air their objections publicly. She knew the committee members and was a close friend of the current editor-in-chief Margaret Lambert, who probably asked for her help.[185] It also reflected the reputation Wiskemann had gained through her publications and her status as a regular reviewer for the *TLS*, then at the height of its influence. As a freelance historian and journalist her position was somewhat anomalous, on the fringes of both. Her only institutional affiliation was her contract work for Chatham House but that brought her into contact with most of the historians, many with experience in intelligence and the armed services, who in the 1950s were attempting to gain recognition for contemporary history as a legitimate subdiscipline of the historical profession. This drive to move History forward in time, to institutionalize historical study of Fascism, Nazism, and the Second World War, was taking place across Europe and in the United States, and Wiskemann soon found herself invited to participate in international conferences attempting to shape the narrative and key themes for research in these areas. In September 1950 Louis de Jong, Director of the Dutch National Institute for War Documentation, organized a conference in Amsterdam, "World War II and the West." No German historians were invited, while the focus on the West left out the Soviet Union and Eastern Europe. Among the British delegates were A.J. Toynbee and the joint editors of the official British war histories, Cambridge Regis Professor J.R.M. Butler and W.K. Hancock. Wiskemann was invited as a replacement for Sir Lewis Namier. Her presentation examined how recently published political memoirs (by Ribbentrop, Schacht, Ciano, von Papen, Gisevius, and others), if judiciously used, might supplement and provide correctives to official documents which were often pruned, had passages deleted, or were circulated in several versions by the Fascist and Nazi regimes[186] Pleased with her performance, she told A.H. Wadsworth of the *Manchester Guardian*: "I found that I was a less obscure participant than I had expected and my own lecture 'came off', I think—usually I'm a bad speaker, but occasionally not, and this was one of the better occasions."[187]

Other invitations followed, including one in May 1956 (just prior to the furor over *Germany's Eastern Neighbours*) to attend the Institut für Zeitgeschichte's [IfZ] conference on the "Third Reich and Europe" at Tutzing on Starnbergersee.[188] The Institute's founding in 1949 coincided with that of the Federal Republic and it had an implied political mission: to educate Germans about the Nazi past as part of the task of building a democratic state. It also played an important role in the "struggle for the files." The Tutzing conference, in which over sixty scholars from several countries participated, was particularly important for Wiskemann since it opened her eyes to a whole cohort of mostly young historians associated with the *IfZ*, which was emerging as the FRG's chief center for research and documentation about the Third Reich.[189] While deeply critical of the older generation of conservative nationalist German historians, she became a fervent admirer of historians connected with the Institute, like Helmut Krausnick, Thilo Vogelsang, Martin Broszat, Wolfgang Sauer, and especially Karl Dietrich Bracher, whom she was soon referring to as the greatest authority on the Weimar Republic and the rise of Nazism. Her reviews praised their courage and objectivity and helped publicize their work in Britain. She was also instrumental in the publication in English of an influential essay collection by IfZ scholars, *Anatomy of the S.S. State*, written as testimony for the 1963 Frankfurt Auschwitz trials. "This accurate, lucid, dispassionate examination," she wrote in her Introduction, "seems to me far and away the most informative and illuminating statement about Hitlerism that there has been in the last thirty years or so."[190]

By the end of the 1950s, along with her esteem for the new generation of German historians and perhaps influenced by them, she also became noticeably less critical of West Germany. She continued to criticize Adenauer's intransigence over recognizing existing borders and Bonn's support for the *Unteilbares Deutschland* [Indivisible Germany] campaign, but her worries about the stability of German democracy receded. On a visit to Berlin in August 1960 she seemed far happier than before with West German society and politics. She was especially impressed by students and young people under twenty-five who were eager to learn about the Nazi years, "usefully skeptical" towards old political myths and "genuinely international" in their outlook. She even found "enlightened influences at work" in the new German armed forces attached to NATO. Berlin was again a focus of international tension, with Khrushchev threatening access to the city, arguing that the Western presence must end, while the East German leader, Walter Ulbricht, searched for ways to stem the tide of those fleeing to the West—a year later barbed wire and a concrete wall sealed the border altogether. And yet West Berliners and their popular mayor, Willy Brandt, seemed unshaken and had "no illusions about 'democracy' under Ulbricht for they live too close to it."

"The atmosphere," she wrote, "seemed less hectic in Western Germany than it was a few years ago, more quiet and secure," with popular attitudes "conditioned by their miraculous prosperity, expanding welfare benefits and good wages." "By contrast with the Weimar Republic the Federal Republic is generally accepted. This hitherto paternal type of democracy, with adequate freedom of opinion, seems to suit a great many Germans; it is well known that 4 million of them have visited the Bundestag since its inauguration, displaying an interest that seemed real."[191]

Since leaving her wartime job in Bern, Wiskemann had accomplished a great deal. Shortly after completing *Germany's Eastern Neighbours* she published a history of her favorite newspaper, the Swiss *Neue Zürcher Zeitung*, and also accepted the position of director of a major research project on the Italian–Yugoslav territorial dispute over Trieste, funded by the Carnegie Foundation.[192] She had written four books, five if one counts her contributions to the volumes of Toynbee's *Survey of International Affairs*. If anything, she took on too much and risked spreading herself too thin. Working with such Stakhanovite intensity, no wonder she often complained of exhaustion.[193] Not far off her sixtieth birthday, she probably anticipated little change in her professional career, but life often moves in unplanned directions. Despite the controversy it sparked, *Germany's Eastern Neighbours* had increased her visibility as an authority on Central and Eastern Europe and produced new offers of research projects. More surprisingly, in 1958 it also brought about her return to academe with the offer of a Chair at Edinburgh University.

6

The Academic Life and After

"My English friends told me," wrote Franca Magnani, a young Italian who got to know Wiskemann well in the early 1950s, "that Elizabeth had begun her career with two essential prerequisites: unusual intelligence and little money."[1] Always thrifty, she had from the early 1930s struggled to make ends meet as a journalist and researcher. In Rome living costs had been cheap and her income from journalism reasonably predictable. London was far more expensive, payment schedules for freelance articles and reviews had scarcely changed since before the war, and the type of books she wrote earned little. In addition, rationing, shortages of food and basic goods, and higher rates of taxation and inflation during these years of postwar austerity impacted middle-class living standards disproportionately.

Just before Christmas 1947 when Harry Bergholz, now living in the United States, offered to send a parcel of food, she replied: "The tables are turning now for I am far less well off than I was in Switzerland... Now I am certainly not starving, and I know you have to send a lot to your mother. But you would give me a treat which I would love to have if you could just once send me a parcel of food. The most useful and delicious thing I can think of would be ham."[2] A few weeks later she hastened to reassure him: "I said that it would be a treat that I should enjoy, not that the reductions have been <u>so</u> drastic. As a matter of fact, they have so far been slighter than I had allowed for; we are certainly not starving and things are about as well arranged as they could be. I do hope you haven't deprived yourself... but I am <u>very</u> grateful."[3] And when Bergholz brought up her financial help to him during their Swiss years, she dismissed any idea that he owed her anything: "I <u>never</u> lent you money – I wouldn't – I shared some with you... and I haven't the very faintest idea how much."[4] Replying to her Italian friend Guglielmo Alberti, she wrote: "DON'T believe all the propaganda against Socialist England. We are too well off still and not the tiniest bit dictated to or oppressed. My <u>class</u> is being impoverished less suddenly than in Italy or France, but it is an inevitable process and not pleasant."[5]

Although Wiskemann continued to worry about money and making a living, her situation had improved significantly during the war. Her mother came from a wealthy Ipswich mercantile family and two uncles who died in 1942 and 1943 made bequests for their niece, in one case a sum of £10,000.[6] At the time, salaries of the solid middle class ranged from about £700 to £1,200, so her windfall represented a significant financial cushion. Wiskemann probably used some of the

Elizabeth Wiskemann: Scholar, Journalist, Secret Agent. Geoffrey Field, Oxford University Press.
© Geoffrey Field 2023. DOI: 10.1093/oso/9780192870629.003.0007

money while writing *The Rome-Berlin Axis*, but her frugal habits were by this time too ingrained to change and she worried about her future, since she could not expect any job-related pension when it came time to retire.[7] Taxation rates rose substantially in the late 1940s and there was talk of further increases for unearned income and even of a capital levy. Hoping both to preserve her capital by owning something and to throw off additional income that would supplement what she made from writing, she decided in 1951 to give up her rented flat in St. George's Square and invest in a property on Moore Street in Chelsea. More than a room of her own, this was a small house. Now fifty-two years old, she explained to Harry Bergholz: "Prices are very bad and of course worst for people like me. So I put my little inheritance into a pretty little house in Chelsea just near Sloane Square, i.e. perfect position, really very nice and I want paying guests i.e. I am starting up other professions (might go back to univ. teaching). Anyway, if you should hear of anyone who wants a DELIGHTFUL bed-sitting-room with a little washing-room with hot water and breakfast Aug. 20-Sept. 20 send them to me please. I have two Americans sort of sharing the house already (hard currencies are so consoling)."[8] Another letter asked: "If you know anyone nice and also quiet who might prefer my house for anything between 3 nights and 6 weeks and would come as a p.g. [paying guest] will you think of me? I do a nice simple breakfast and occasionally another meal or so. Rooms very nice. U.S. professor 'on vacation' and I might be mutually agreeable and useful."[9] Some of her lodgers became close friends. Among the first was a smart, vivacious young woman, Heather Fenwick Brown, who had just left Cambridge with a classics degree and was enrolled in a management trainee program at Selfridges. She roomed at Moore Street for about a year, before marrying a British diplomat and moving to Washington. She and Wiskemann got on famously, and when she returned to London, Heather Brigstocke (her married name) became a well-known teacher and head mistress of St. Paul's school for girls. Other "p.g.s" included a Swiss foreign correspondent, Erik Mettler, and in late 1955 Noémi Ripka and her young physicist son. Noémi, whom Wiskemann first met in Prague, was teaching French and German literature at the lycée in South Kensington until her husband Hubert returned from teaching in New York.[10]

Renting rooms became important in her efforts to make ends meet; she continued to take in lodgers until 1955 or 1956 and worried when they left and rooms were unfilled. When two bookings fell through early in 1955, she wrote to Arnold Künzli: "I am not altogether sorry to have the house empty until August 1st while I try to finish my book [*Germany's Eastern Neighbours*] and then have a fortnight's holiday. But financially it is bad, and it is imperative that I fill the house in August and September and, if possible, from then to Christmas. If you should hear of anyone nice... Position of house very central but quiet. I supply breakfasts and constant hot water and for short periods in August or September would do suppers too but prefer not... I can't have noisy people nor couples but single man or woman of any age!"[11] To Harry Bergholz she admitted: "Prices go up and up, and every time I think that I need not be so careful, they go up again."[12] When one compares the circumstances of her male peers, both journalists and academics, with secure jobs and predictable incomes, the contrast is striking. To Guglielmo Alberti, she confessed: "I am pretty tired, the eternal struggle of doing my job and all the domestic things is just too much."[13]

* * *

Wiskemann had last taught undergraduates in 1936 and she had no expectation of landing an academic post at age fifty-nine. But in March 1958, shortly after the controversy in West Germany over *Germany's Eastern Neighbours*, she wrote Alastair Hetherington of the *Guardian*: "I've been asked up to Edinburgh to discuss a professorship – can't think I'll get it, but if I did I should try to call on you in Manchester one day."[14] The Edinburgh position for which she successfully interviewed was the Montague Burton Chair of International Relations, a professorship established in 1948 to foster the study of international relations and peace, based on the ideals of the United Nations.

Much had changed since Wiskemann was last employed by a university, but with respect to women's representation among faculty there was little difference. The number of female students taking university degrees grew in the 1950s, but the percentage of women faculty, about 13%, was little altered since the early 1930s.[15] Faculties were still overwhelmingly male clubs, anchored by secure tenure, where teaching was prioritized over research and writing; professors, if they chose, could lead a relatively leisured, free, and unpressured existence. But while some could look back on this period as a 'golden age,' it had no such resonance for women. Research grants were few and prejudice against hiring women remained strong, while those who were hired clustered at the lower junior ranks and salary ranges. Women's colleges at Oxford and Cambridge employed women staff and offered opportunities for senior positions, so did London's Royal Holloway and Bedford Colleges. But in most departmentally organized universities women still mostly found their way blocked. Provincial universities had fewer women faculty than London, and even there LSE was the exception, long a pioneer with respect to its number of women students, degree candidates, and faculty. An analysis of LSE's early years 1895–1932 shows that already 20% of its regular teaching staff were women, although their presence was highly concentrated in the Department of Social Science and Administration. Already in the interwar years Eileen Power and Lilian Knowles became professors of Economic History at LSE, while in the 1950s the senior faculty included Vera Anstey in economics and social anthropologists Lucy Mair and Audry Richards.[16] Had Wiskemann pursued a doctorate there in 1921 instead of Cambridge, perhaps she would have remained within the confines of academia.

Traveling to her Edinburgh interview for the Burton Chair, Wiskemann probably anticipated that her age, long absence from academia, and above all her career as a journalist might harm her chance of success. She always liked to think of herself as a scholar-journalist, although in doing so she risked being depreciated as merely or primarily a journalist. In fact, she worked on a frontier between the two; her scholarly credentials were unmistakable in her writing, while her long association with Chatham House also worked in her favor. The job for which she was being considered was in International Relations [IR], which in Britain, in contrast to the United States, barely existed as a theorized discipline with its own claims for a distinctive mode of thinking about international issues. At the time there were still very few academic programs, teaching positions, or endowed Chairs in IR. The latter included the Wilson Chair of International Politics at Aberystwyth (established in 1919); the Montague Burton Chairs at Oxford and LSE (established in 1930 and 1936); the Stevenson Chair of International History at LSE (1926); and the Cassel Professorship of International Relations, also at LSE (established 1924). Additional programs developed slowly, and existing curricula structures often created obstacles. At Oxford, for example, politics and IR were taught under the rubric of a "Modern Greats" or PPE [Politics, Philosophy, and Economics] degree, which was established in 1920–with IR as an option within the Politics part.[17] Those teaching IR were mostly trained as classicists, political scientists, philosophers, legal scholars, or (increasingly) diplomatic historians. Joining LSE as a lecturer in 1956, Hedley Bull recalled: "I had not done a course of any kind in International Relations, nor made any serious study of it and…I wondered how I was to go about teaching the subject and even whether it existed at all."[18] In Wiskemann's case, she taught diplomatic history years before and much of her journalism had focused on international relations; moreover, her major publications were recognized as significant contributions to the field, and, except for *The Rome-Berlin Axis*, each had an underlying objective to influence policy. This was also true of her current research project, which she had embarked upon shortly before going to Edinburgh: a study of the Italian–Yugoslav territorial dispute over Trieste, funded by the Carnegie Foundation.[19]

As the first woman to occupy a Chair in any discipline at Edinburgh, it would be gratifying to see Wiskemann's appointment as a major breakthrough for gender equality. But the truth is a little more complex, for the Burton endowment's terms made the position more difficult to fill than one might expect. The pay was far from generous and the job was only part-time, requiring an incumbent to reside each spring term for three years in Edinburgh and to give a series of lectures.[20] This made it difficult to attract distinguished scholars with full-time positions elsewhere—their universities were unlikely to agree to their combining a senior faculty position with a three-year partial commitment to Edinburgh. The previous occupant had been C.A. Macartney, a distinguished scholar of Central Europe, who was a fellow of All Souls, Oxford, where he had no formal teaching or administrative responsibilities. Also, Edinburgh did not have a separate department or degree course in IR and so the Burton lectures (not fully integrated into the existing degree offerings) had trouble attracting students.

Already in 1957 there was some discussion about revising the endowment's terms and converting the Chair into an annual series of lectures given by several distinguished outside scholars.[21] W.N. Medlicott, Stevenson Professor of International History at LSE, was consulted about the situation and he made a strong case that Edinburgh should seek additional funding, make the post full-time, and establish a new department.[22] These suggestions did not get very far. The Burton endowment was unwilling to increase its contribution substantially, while—presumably fearing competition—"neither the Faculty of Law nor the Department of History considered that such a step would be in accordance with their educational policy for the next decades."[23] Medlicott then put forward three candidates for the existing post: John Wheeler-Bennett, who had been commissioned to write the official biography of King George VI and probably wouldn't be available; Elizabeth Wiskemann, whom he described as "a pleasant, active middle-aged woman," well-known as a writer but not a university teacher; and finally, Guy Chapman, a French specialist previously at Leeds, "a vigorous and stimulating lecturer, although less of a specialist in international problems...than Miss Wiskemann." On balance he believed that Wiskemann was the person most likely to accept the position since she could live in London part of the year and still travel regularly to the Continent as a journalist.[24]

By the end of Macartney's tenure, the Burton lectures seem to have become rather moribund, with few attendees and little relationship to the rest of the curriculum. Wiskemann worked hard to resuscitate them, developing a following among students and staff in other disciplines, taking pains to publicize lectures, and choosing topics that, in her view, students ought to be discussing irrespective of her own areas of research. Her offerings for spring 1959 seem to have been lost from the files, but in spring 1960 she gave two courses: "Retreat from Empire to Commonwealth and Community" and "International Negotiations in the Modern World." The following year she lectured on "Aspects of the German Question" and, particularly interested in the rapid pace of independence movements in Ghana, Nigeria, and the Congo, she decided to tackle a completely new area: "The United Nations and Africa." The Suez Crisis followed by MacMillan's "wind of change" speech (February 1960), the French failure in Algeria, and the redirection of British overseas policy towards Europe was the larger context for this choice; she was also interested in the parallels between the birth of African and Arab nationalism and the re-emergence of nationalist challenges to the Soviet *imperium* in Hungary and Eastern Europe.[25]

In addition, to raise the public profile of the chair, Wiskemann began a regular series of Thursday evening seminar discussions and invited distinguished outside experts to open these sessions. She petitioned the Burtons for additional money, although it was barely enough to cover travel expenses. Edinburgh is not the easiest place to get to and the discussants, sometimes braving snow (and in the case of

Margaret Lambert a rail strike), clearly came out of respect and affection for her. The 1960 list of these invitees indicates their range and quality as well as Wiskemann's connections in the worlds of journalism, wartime intelligence, Chatham House, and Carnegie:

"Europe in the Thaw," Peter Calvocoressi (Bletchley intelligence; assistant prosecutor at Nuremberg; editor of 5 volumes of the *Survey of International Affairs*; publisher).

"The Central African Federation and related issues," Hester Marsden Smedley (War service in British intelligence; journalist in Europe and Africa).

"Realists and Idealists between the Wars," Margaret Lambert (Historian at St Andrew's, Editor of the captured German Foreign Office Documents).

"European Unions," W. Horsfall Carter (journalist; former head of the West European section of the Foreign Office; Secretariat of the Council of Europe at Strasbourg).

"Patterns of Conflict: Recent Research at the Carnegie Endowment for International Peace," John Goormaghtigh (International lawyer; Director of the European Centre of the Carnegie Endowment).

The following year her invitees were:

"France under De Gaulle," Darsie Gillie (War service in P.W.E. and *Manchester Guardian* correspondent in Paris).

"The International System after the U.N. Assembly," Elisabeth Barker (War service in P.W.E. and BBC Diplomatic Correspondent).

"Africa on the March," Hester Marsden-Smedley (journalist just returned from French-speaking Africa).

"The Arab World," H.E. Tütsch, (Middle East correspondent for the *Neue Zürcher Zeitung*, just back from the Middle East).

"Contemporary Germany," Golo Mann (historian and son of Thomas Mann).[26]

To all appearances, Wiskemann's own lectures and these Thursday evening sessions were a big success. The Marxist historian V.G. Kiernan made efforts to publicize the gatherings and to recruit other faculty, like Lionel Kochan, who had recently been hired to teach European history. Surviving evidence is rather sparse, but Wiskemann clearly enjoyed teaching and the recognition that came with a professorship, although she was sometimes taken aback by the undercurrent of Scottish nationalist sentiment she encountered.

The Edinburgh University administration was well-satisfied with Wiskemann's performance as Chair and disappointed when, in July 1960, she gave notice that she would not stand for re-election to a further three years. The chief reason for her decision was her deteriorating eyesight; especially in the dark winter months of January and February, this made moving around the city hazardous. She first had trouble with her left eye in 1955 but reported to her friend Margaret Cleeve at Chatham House: "I am told I have achieved a marvelous recovery and there is no reason to suppose that I shall not be leading a completely normal life after the end of the month."[27] Further complications led to a cataract operation at the end of 1959, which seems to have been botched. As she explained to Professor A.H. Campbell of the Law faculty: "One of the reasons for my not feeling able to go on in Edinburgh is the condition of my left eye. Three specialists have now told me that it should not have been operated and that I shall just have to make the best of present discomforts perhaps for 10 or 15 years. This is really more difficult away from home at the darkest time of the year. I only knew about the cataract after I had accepted the Edinburgh Chair and then had the operation done last November because a first-rate Harley Street man assured me that he could, as it were, put me right by last January. Now I know that he was taking a big risk without telling me."[28] To her novelist friend Richard Hughes she explained: "Through the tomfoolery of a quite eminent eye-surgeon I've lost the use of my left eye, the detachment of the retina being quite unnecessary. I hope this hasn't happened to you."[29] "I have finished with Edinburgh," she wrote to Guglielmo Alberti, "which has been made difficult by a lot of eye trouble. The first operation was no good and now I have to go nearly blind in the next few years (no one knows how many) before a second one may help."[30]

She probably believed that her teaching career was over, but another opportunity soon arose closer to London at the new University of Sussex. It was part of a major expansion in the early 1960s that created seven new universities to cater to the growing cohort of eighteen- to twenty-one-year-olds applying for degree programs. Previously only a tiny fraction of the population studied at a university; students were overwhelmingly male and middle class (about 3% of working-class adolescents went to university). After 1962, when local councils began paying the tuition and residential fees of those accepted to a university, the number of students rose rapidly, more than doubling in the next decade.

Founded in 1961 at the very beginning of this expansion, Sussex was an exciting place, eager to experiment with innovative curricula that promoted multidisciplinary work and committed to teaching by seminars and tutorials rather than large lectures. Asa Briggs had been recruited as Professor of History and Dean of Social Studies and he hired Martin Wight, then beginning to emerge as one of the leading thinkers in international relations, as the first Dean of its School of European Studies."[31] The academic structure consisted not of departments but of Schools of Studies in which students would study one major discipline within the context of courses in several others. Writing to Isaac Deutscher, who was being considered for a Chair in Russian Studies, Wight wrote: "This means that every undergraduate does at least one piece of written work a week and spends an hour discussing it with a tutor. Lectures are entirely ancillary. We are asking people we appoint to undertake 12 hours a week of tutoring, which is a very heavy load compared with Redbrick." There was also considerable written work to "plough through" outside regular teaching hours.[32] Initially, before most of the new buildings were finished, students in the sciences were a minority and the History faculty played an important role since they taught every student in the Arts. Wight and Wiskemann had worked together on the *Survey of International Affairs* at Chatham House and had also reviewed each other's books in glowing terms. Wight was eager to have her on his staff and hired her as Tutor in Modern European History.[33]

The curriculum Wight designed was a kind of "European Greats" in which students studied European civilization by combining history, philosophy, literature, and politics—reminiscent of the way the civilization of Antiquity was taught at Oxford, but with a strong emphasis on the contemporary. Students, the School's prospectus declared, were "to concern themselves with contemporary as well as inherited culture, with history in the making as well as history that is already made."[34] Little information has surfaced about Wiskemann's time there (the Sussex archives are surprisingly meagre for these earliest years), but the whole idea of cross-disciplinary area studies and tutorials must have been very appealing to her, and in the first years some 60% of the undergraduates were women (compared to 10–15% at Oxbridge). She arrived in the autumn of 1961 with the first fifty-one Sussex students (thirty-seven were women), who were being taught in rented premises in Brighton until the new campus was opened in autumn 1962. She stayed three years, leaving just as the first entrants graduated. By this time the student body had grown to over two thousand and the place was gaining the press soubriquet of "Balliol by the sea." Proximity to London, the BBC, and Fleet Street meant that Sussex gained inordinate media coverage compared to other new universities in these early years; it also attracted an array of talent to the school, many of them non-academics. For example, *New Statesman* journalist Norman Mackenzie was appointed to teach sociology in 1962; like Wiskemann, he had worked for PWE during the war and had close ties to British intelligence agencies. A few years after Wiskemann retired, her publisher friend Peter Calvocoressi also joined the faculty, becoming Reader in International Relations, and Quentin Bell, Bloomsbury chronicler and brother of Julian, was recruited as Professor of Art History.

Teaching at Sussex also brought Wiskemann into more regular contact with Leonard Woolf, who lived nearby at Monks House in Rodmell. She had first met him while working in Birrell and Garnet's bookshop as a young girl and over the years had contributed numerous essays to journals he edited, like the *Contemporary Review* and the *Political Quarterly*. In January 1957 she wrote asking his advice about a summer rental: "I have taken on too much work – much – but one bit is well paid. This means that for the first time in my life I can afford to take a cottage or flat or bungalow next summer for the month of August or anyway for the two middle weeks. Only condition that it should be vaguely between Lewes and the sea so that I can bike to the sea easily." She apologized for asking his help, "but I feel you are the uncrowned king of outer Lewes and must know."[35] The following summer she again rented in the area and visited him and the artist Trekkie Parsons (for twenty-five years after Virginia's suicide, Trekkie spent weekdays with Leonard and weekends with her publisher husband, Ian Parsons). She consulted him about an article she was writing for the *Neue Zürcher Zeitung* on Bloomsbury and invited him to "a picnic sort of meal with a bottle of wine to make up for the absence of comfortable chairs." Wiskemann seems to have enjoyed her Sussex students and attended a wedding reception for two of them a year after she left. At times she probably felt like an anachronism, mystified by the Sixties' generation, writing to Leonard on one occasion: "Two young creatures, *first* years at Sussex, are much excited about 'Bloomsbury'. Would it amuse you to talk to them? They would think it FABULOUS or whatever their word is by now."[36] Leonard sent her the first volume of his autobiography,[37] which she read with "fascinated interest," praising "your candour over non-existence," the rather bleak fatalism with which he described life.[38] His example may have been a stimulus to begin her own memoir a few years later. Shortly after she left Sussex in the summer of 1964, she was reading "Beginning Again," his third volume of autobiography, along with Christopher Hassall's biography of Rupert Brooke: "I have been buried in the period of my childhood, those glowing days."[39]

The campus was a short train journey from Wiskemann's home on Moore Street in Chelsea; she spent two or three days a week at Sussex and the rest of her time doing research and writing. She continued to review almost monthly for the *TLS* and frequently contributed articles and reviews to the *Spectator*, the *Times,* the *Listener,* and *International Affairs*. With her friend Marion Jackson she also worked on an English translation of Wolfgang Leonhard's *The Kremlin since Stalin*. How she knew Leonhard, a defector from East Germany, is unclear, but he spent two years at St. Antony's in the late 1950s and so it was perhaps through these circles that they came in contact.[40] Believing that scholars had a duty to address as wide a public as possible, she also wrote for the popular magazine *History Today* from its inception in 1951 until her death. Founded by Brendan Bracken, chairman of the *Financial Times* parent company, it was edited by Peter Quennell, whom Wiskemann had known since her early twenties, and Alan Hodge.[41] She also became a more frequent broadcaster. Ever since the 1930s Wiskemann had cultivated relationships at the BBC, writing scripts for radio programs and presenting them herself, sometimes in Italian and German for overseas audiences.[42] She was not a natural radio performer and had to work at it with help from friends like fellow Newnham alumna Mary Adams of the Talks Department, Leonard Miall, Elisabeth Barker, and Trevor Blewitt. Others at the

BBC were critical, believing her voice and delivery unsuitable and her accent too "Mayfair." However, she persevered, becoming by the 1960s a more proficient and confident 'media don.'"[43]

Her busy professional life left little time for much else, but friendship was always important to Wiskemann and she kept in contact with a wide circle of people. Some were old English friends she had known for many years, like Violet Bonham Carter, Rebecca West, and 'Boofy' Gore. Some dated from her Cambridge days, like the novelist Richard Hughes and actor Michael Redgrave, who she urged in 1961 to get involved in a public campaign to do something about the unfinished National Theatre: "We all thought it would be so valuable if you could write the Times as soon as possible." Ever the activist, she added: "I think it will be too awful if all Europe is honouring Shakespeare in 1964, but our theatre will scarcely be ready...I am also putting a friend onto worrying the L.C.C. and shall be stirring up the Fine Arts Commission for what it's worth. Perhaps we can get some questions asked in Parliament."[44] Another old friend from her time as a journalist in Berlin was William Robson Scott, now married and teaching at Birkbeck College in London. William had spent the war working for MI5, running informers and gathering information about suspected Communists among German-speaking political exiles. She enjoyed seeing him, but their friendship was fraught and unpredictable, and a final breach seems to have occurred in 1958. To Harry Bergholz she explained: "William has seemed to me almost unbalanced for some time and nearly two months ago he suddenly displayed great hostility to me *a propos* – of all things – my last book [*Germany's Eastern Neighbours*] of which he had until then warmly approved...Often I am to blame but in this case I really was not...Possibly, I had annoyed him over something else, but if so, I don't know what."[45] Until about 1953 Francesco Antinori lived close by in London and worked at the Italian Embassy, although earlier ideas about their eventual marriage had clearly disappeared, and he returned to Rome sometime after.[46] She was also a frequent presence at the Italian Cultural Institute in London, whose Director in the early 1960s was Gabrielli Baldini, the husband of Natalia Ginzburg.[47] Historian and diplomat Stanislaw Kot was another friend; she first met him on a pre-war visit to Warsaw when, like Sikorski, he was under house arrest. In the war he had served the Polish exile government in several posts, including as ambassador to Moscow, and afterwards for two years in Rome, where she often visited him, sometimes bringing Silone and others along. Fearful of returning to Communist Poland, Kot had resigned in 1947 and remained in exile in London until his death.

On trips to the Continent gathering material for her articles, she planned her itineraries to include visits to friends like Guglielmo Alberti, the Oprechts, and Erika Düby in Zurich, and the Szilasis in Freiburg. In Paris she saw Enid McLeod and her partner Ethel Whitehorn. Wiskemann had become acquainted with Enid, a scholar of French literature and biographer of Heloise, in the war years as head of the French Section of the Ministry of Information. Applying for a permanent job in government service in 1945, McLeod alarmed her male interviewers by announcing her preference for the Foreign Office (at that time closed to women). Then, "having thoroughly enjoyed this spectacle of discombobulated bureaucrats, she let them off the hook, revealing that she had received an offer from the British Council [an arms-length cultural agency of the Foreign Office] and 'of course they instantly begged me to take it.'" By 1954 McLeod had become the Council's Director in Paris, the first woman to achieve such a high-ranking overseas post in the organization.[48]

At home on Moore Street, Wiskemann liked having people over; many were academics, journalists, broadcasters, editors, and publishers. But she also enjoyed counseling young researchers and reporters, many of them from abroad. Among the earliest was Franca Magnani (neé Schiavetti), then in her twenties. The daughter of exiled Italian anti-fascists, Franca spent the war years in Zurich, where her parents had founded a school. There the Schiavettis' social circle overlapped with that of Wiskemann, including the Oprechts and the art historian Giuseppe Delogu, who, Franca recalled, always referred to the "mysterious Elisabetta." In 1944 Franca married a Swiss philosophy student, Arnold Künzli, who worked as a journalist first in Rome and then in London. Wiskemann counseled Franca as she embarked on her career in journalism, helping with her articles and opening doors to British life. "When I first got to know Elizabeth," Magnani recalled, "she was a woman of 50, lean, if not to say thin, and spectacled. Her face was wrinkled but youthful and almost mischievous when sometimes a cryptic smile spread over her face. Her grasp of situations was as quick as her movements. Her mind was lively, always ready, and so sharp that she sometimes consciously held herself back...Elizabeth liked to listen. She let others talk and she possessed an un-English characteristic which I have only encountered in her: she asked questions...she was 'liberal' and valued truth and freedom over everything."[49] Among others, Wiskemann introduced Franca to her friend Moura Budberg, whose regular salon at Ennismere Gardens in Kensington included a wide circle of foreign friends, writers, actors, filmmakers, politicians, and Whitehall officials, as well as spies like Guy Burgess and Anthony Blunt. One of the more colorful social figures of the time, whose former lovers included Bruce Lockhart, H.G. Wells, and Maxim Gorky, Budberg had lived in England since 1929; she knew everybody, including numerous people in intelligence, and was well-informed, so much so that MI5 thought her a security risk and, suspecting she was a Soviet agent, kept a large file on her.[50] Franca and Künzli's marriage broke down; they divorced in 1952 and she married Valdo Magnani, a young Italian resistance fighter and Communist who had fought alongside Yugoslav partisans.[51] Wiskemann remained friends with both Künzli and Franca; indeed, her correspondence with Künzli, who took up a post in Bonn, shows how helpful he was to her, sharing information, answering queries, and checking facts for her articles.[52] Later he

Figure 6.1 "Elizabeth Wiskemann's home at 41 Moore Street, London, S.W.3."

switched from journalism to academia, becoming a professor of philosophy at Basel in the 1970s, while Franca, based in Rome, achieved success first as a print journalist interpreting Italy for German readers before, in 1964, becoming the first woman foreign correspondent for West German TV.

*   *   *

When Wiskemann was hired at Edinburgh very few academic programs in International Relations existed; in many universities it was taught within political science departments, while in Oxford, as we have seen, it was a minor option within the hybrid PPE undergraduate degree. The distinction between international history and IR was extremely vague until at least the early 1960s and, arguably, well beyond that. Scholars in both areas focused largely upon statecraft and interpreting the perceptions, beliefs, and actions of leading foreign policy makers. The approach in many cases was straightforwardly historical and cultural, and many of those who taught the subject had no training in the social sciences and little appetite for theory-building. Wiskemann's work, empirical in character, was not untypical of the eclectic, under-theorized IR scholarship of the 1950s.[53] She was happier emphasizing the specificities of each situation, under-scoring, for example, the differences between Nazism and Italian Fascism rather than positing a generic model of fascism, much in vogue in the 1960s. A regular contributor to *International Affairs*, she did not engage with discussions in the journal about IR as a discipline. And while she largely shared the perspective of the so-called 'English school' of IR, underpinned as it was by a skeptical liberalism and focused upon international order, the balance of power, and the ability of prudent policy to mitigate international conflict and anarchy, she was not tempted to intervene in theoretical debate about power, mass politics, or the international system. Indeed, as British IR became more professionalized, drawing closer to American social sciences, she increasingly identified herself as a scholar of modern and contemporary history.[54]

Contemporary history, as indicated in the last chapter, also developed slowly and had little presence as a legitimate subdiscipline within the historical profession, not only in British universities but across most of Europe before the 1960 or even later in many cases. Both World Wars were a catalyst, but it was especially after the Second that pressure intensified for expanding the traditional periodization of history. At the heart of this project was a recognition that it was imperative for historians (along with other humanists and social scientists) to put analytical history to work to understand and explain the extraordinary ruptures and turmoil of the twentieth century: two World Wars, Communist revolutions and fascism, concentration camps and racial genocide, and the collapse of liberalism in so many places.[55] Historians, wrote Eva Reichmann, had "a moral duty" to understand and explain "the collapse of the bastions of reason... of common human decency."[56] There was, in particular, a need to situate Nazism and the war years within that framework, including different nations' experiences of occupation, collaboration, and resistance. In this respect contemporary history reflected the process of reconstructing national identity postwar, establishing dominant narratives and also national mythmaking.

Nowhere was this urgency felt more than in West Germany, where, from the beginning, contemporary history focused upon confronting the nation's recent past, discrediting the historical falsehoods purveyed by the Third Reich, and helping to construct a democratic polity and a new civic morality. The key institution in the FRG was the publicly funded Institut für Zeitgeschichte [IfZ], which originated outside the university system and whose remit was overtly political as well as scholarly: to create a reliable documentary record of the Nazi years so that Germans could both learn from their past and 'overcome' it. When the Institute's house journal, the *Vierteljahrshefte für Zeitgeschichte* [*VjZ*, Contemporary History Quarterly] appeared in 1953, its first issue began with a brief essay by Hans Rothfels, a conservative historian who had spent the Nazi years in exile in the United States. In it he designated 1917 as the starting point for contemporary history, a year that began a new "epoch of universal history" with the Russian Revolution and American entry into the Great War, a "moment of crisis when international, social and ideological conflicts began to be globalized." The task was to situate democracy, fascism, and communism within this revolutionary dynamic. To a degree this reduced the significance of national criteria for German historians tasked with coming to terms with Nazism. But Rothfels also played a central role—including with his own research on the conservative German resistance—in initiating serious West German research into Nazism, combining rigorous professional standards and moral and political engagement. In the next decades the *IfZ* played a huge role, not only in shaping research on Nazism, but more generally in the emergence of contemporary history in Europe.[57]

In Britain, a country less directly affected by the crises and ruptures of the recent past than Continental Europe and where more emphasis was placed upon historical continuity and gradualism, the push for 'contemporary history' came less from the state and official circles, less top-down, and more from individual scholars specializing in Central Europe and international affairs. For many their war service in the forces, government, or intelligence was the decisive factor.[58] They had been suddenly immersed in an exciting new world and understandably wished to write it once the war was over. At Oxford it was a group of Europeanists associated with St. Antony's College who took the lead. William [F.W.] Deakin, James Joll, Alan Bullock, and A.J.P. Taylor formed a Recent History Group in 1950 to stimulate research and persuaded the University press to inaugurate a new series, *The Oxford History of Modern Europe*. Bullock's bestselling Hitler biography grew out of his work under Noel Newsome at the BBC European Service, Joll was in SOE, and Deakin parachuted into the Montenegrin highlands to act as liaison with Tito's partisans. Others who belonged to this war cohort obtained posts in provincial universities, where they shaped research into Germany's recent past; they included former diplomats Robert Cecil and Michael Balfour at Reading and East Anglia, A.J. Ryder at Lampeter, Margaret Lambert at Exeter, William Carr at Sheffield, and Richard Hiscocks, who was hired at Sussex just before Wiskemann retired.[59] There were also refugees from Nazi Germany, although many of the younger ones chose to specialize in British history. Eva Reichmann became Director of Research at the Wiener Library, which had relocated to London in 1938 and became a leading center for the study of Nazism. In 1964 it established the Institute of Contemporary History, and two years later two German-Jewish refugees, Walter Laqueur and George Mosse, founded the first British journal in the field, the *Journal of Contemporary History*.

Within British university departments there remained considerable resistance to contemporary history, and few undergraduate degree courses reached far into the twentieth century. At Oxford, where curricula change moved slowly, the Modern History syllabus went to 1878 in 1946 and had reached 1939 only in 1965.[60] Conservative colleagues sniffed that historians writing about their own lifetimes was really journalism with footnotes, and those rash enough to venture into these waters often made a point of separating their "journalistic" and "scholarly" sides. D.C. Watt recalled that he was often "advised to abandon the study of the twentieth century for safer and more distant pastures" where academic appointments were more plentiful.[61] The 'objective' study of the past, many historians insisted, required large collections of official documents, archives, and the passage of several generations to transform 'current' events into 'History.' Contemporary history seemed a contradiction in terms. Most nations imposed fifty- or seventy-year delays on the opening of government documents. In the 1940s the most recent British ones available were from 1885, and for much of the 1950s it was 1902. As for private papers, the British Museum and many other libraries adopted their own fifty-year rules. Only after a sustained campaign was a thirty-year rule adopted in 1967. For the Third Reich, however, the enormous cache of captured German files already available supplied ample official documentation to satisfy the attributes of professionalism.

Compared to West Germany, discussion in Britain about the status, periodization, and methodology of contemporary history was under-theorized and, in Jane Caplan phrase, "rather pallid."[62] One exception was Geoffrey Barraclough, who insisted that historians were urgently in need of "a new vision"; too much of what was written "did nothing to prepare us for the emergence of the world in which we live, and offers us no clue to its understanding."[63] Contemporary history, he argued boldly, "begins when the problems which are actual in the world today first take visible shape," which for him meant the period 1890–1960, and it required more theorization, distinctive research methods, a global and transnational perspective, and less of a Eurocentric and nation-state focus.[64] His *Introduction to Contemporary History* (1964), which originated as a paper to the Oxford Recent History Group, defined the purpose of contemporary history as explaining the key forces, trends, "actual in the world today." In Britain this seemed excessively 'presentist' to most historians and most declined his invitation to become globalist, preferring to work within national confines. They seemed less intent on defining the field than defending its respectability and Rankean professionalism. They pointed to the diversity of sources already available to historians and reasoned that 'objectivity' was no more a problem with respect to the recent past than it was for earlier centuries—indeed, proximity in time could give historians greater understanding and empathy with the climate of ideas than was possible with remote periods. The "the training and discipline of the historian" was the strongest safeguard against ideological bias, and to leave the terrain to political scientists, non-professionals, or "quasi-historical journalism" would be an abdication of responsibility.[65] The contrast between historians and journalists came up frequently, although journalist practitioners were conspicuous in contemporary history's early years, both as authors and as teachers—aside from Wiskemann, one can point to Soviet experts Edward Crankshaw and Victor Zorza, Walter Laqueur in Middle East and Soviet studies, Guy Wint on China and the Far East, and Alistair Horne's works on the First World War and Algeria.[66]

The fledgling and somewhat fragile status of contemporary history contributed to the academic furor that erupted in 1961 over A.J.P. Taylor's *The Origins of the Second World War*.[67] Compared to Continental historians' battles over collaboration, resistance, deportation, and popular support for Fascism and Nazism, British contemporary historians had little to confront. Certainly, on Britain's involvement in the Second World War there was strong agreement: a critical verdict on Neville Chamberlain's Appeasement policy, positive views of the way that British society and politics rose to the challenge of the war, and an equally strong consensus that it was 'Hitler's War' caused by Nazism's drive for domination of Europe and the conquest of empire in the East. Taylor challenged these established verities, especially what he saw as "the Nuremberg thesis" about the war's origins that he associated with "Namier, Wheeler-Bennett, and Wiskemann in English and the Sorbonne's Maurice Baumont in French."[68] As early as October 1959 Taylor informed Basil Liddell Hart of his plan to write a book about the Second World War's origins, "mainly to make the point that it was not planned by Hitler but that he scrambled into it by mistake."[69] Taylor's strong conviction was that wars were more accidental than deliberate, that men like Bismarck and Hitler had no master plan but improvised and reacted to circumstances as they went along, and that events invariably turned out different than policymakers planned. Postwar circumstances also shaped his views. Active in the Campaign for Nuclear Disarmament, he feared that miscalculation in the nuclear age could trigger unintended war and he was also troubled by arguments that strong opposition to the Soviet Union was essential since the failure to challenge Hitler had resulted in the Second World War.

At the time, Taylor was arguably the most famous historian in Britain. He was prolific, the author of numerous books, a frequent newspaper columnist, and a radio and television celebrity, appearing regularly on nationally popular programs. He was also well-known as a maverick and controversialist. Fellow historians were used to his provocative Shavian tone, his love of paradox and overstatement, but with *The Origins* many believed he had gone way beyond acceptable limits. The brilliance of some early sections of the book was widely acknowledged: his analysis, for example, of European diplomacy in the 1920s. But, as he moved closer to 1939, the book became increasingly unsatisfactory and one-sided. There was nothing in the book about race and *Lebensraum*, nothing about structural changes in Nazi Germany, particularly the regime's revolutionary dynamism after 1936. The significance of Nazi ideology was also dismissed as "dogmas which echo the conversation of any Austrian café or German beer house."[70] For Taylor, foreign policy was determined by *raison d'etat*, not ideology, and politicians' adapted, reacted, and improvised to deal with ever-changing, contingent circumstances. Viewed in this way, Hitler emerges in *The Origins* as a German *Realpolitiker*, little different from Stresemann or Brüning, a politician seeking treaty revision and "in principle and doctrine, no more wicked and unscrupulous than many other contemporary statesmen."[71] He is seen as planning very little but seizing upon opportunities created by the blunders of others. As Tim Mason recognized, the best passages dealt with countries other than Germany whose statesmen were pragmatic, seeking limited goals by conventional means. Taylor argued unconvincingly that Nazi foreign policy was roughly the same. By omitting the centrality of the Third Reich's racial project and the consistency of Hitler's aims for a massive expansion of German territories in the East, he concluded that the outbreak of war resulted from an unintended sequence of events and misjudgments, rather like a road accident; indeed, he couldn't resist baiting historians by remarking at one point: "it seems that Hitler became involved in war through launching on 29 August a diplomatic maneuver which should have been launched on 28 August."[72] He also rejected the conventional view of Chamberlain's diplomacy, portraying him sympathetically as a high-minded activist who sought with "skill and persistence...to follow a moral line," attempting to redress German grievances over the Versailles treaties, but ultimately convincing Hitler of Britain's weakness. But here too his tone was guaranteed to provoke, claiming that the Munich pact, "was a triumph for all that was best and most enlightened in British life; a triumph for those who had preached equal justice between peoples."[73]

Taylor predicted that his book would "annoy the old boys who thought they had settled everything," but he seriously underestimated the storm it created. "Critics descended on the book," as his biographer Adam Sisman noted, "like angry birds."[74] Most prominent was Regius Professor Hugh Trevor-Roper, whose devastating critique in *Encounter* led to a televised debate with Taylor that was covered in the national press. Dozens of historians leapt into the fray.[75] Reviewers accused Taylor of misusing evidence, ignoring documents that hurt his case while mishandling others. Most rejected his portrayal of Hitler. James Joll welcomed the book's insights on 1920s diplomacy in the *Spectator* but added: "It is misleading to write about Hitler as if he were just another ordinary German politician. If Hitler was a rational statesman, then Eichmann was a conscientious civil servant."[76] A curiously oblique review in the *Times Literary Supplement* [by C.M. Woodhouse, Conservative MP but formerly Director of Chatham House] praised Taylor's "methodical and impeccable logic," noting "the perversity which has prevented any university institution in the country from giving a professorial chair to one of England's two or three outstanding historians."[77] But this review, which avoided analysis of Taylor's specific claims, elicited its own irate responses from several scholars, including Hugh Trevor-Roper and A.L. Rowse, who decried the book as "intellectually deplorable," a violation of the historian's duty to the public to "get things right and state them scrupulously, as against this frivolity."[78] Margaret Lambert attacked Taylor's reinterpretation of the November

1937 Hossbach Memorandum as a tactical ploy of domestic politics rather than a blueprint for Hitler's foreign aims. And W.N. Medlicott focused on "Taylor's failure to substantiate his more startling statements" so that readers were left with a "mass of assertion"; he worried that it was "likely to confuse undergraduates and other impressionable readers" who had no direct experience of the 1930s.[79]

As one of the historians identified by Taylor as responsible for the consensus view of Hitler's foreign policy, it was predictable that Wiskemann would wish to reply. Her role in the controversy was minor, but she took it very seriously, not least because she had developed a visceral dislike of Taylor. They had sniped at each other in reviews, and she deplored his persona as a maverick and *enfant terrible*, ready to express a provocative opinion on almost anything. In the *TLS* she regretted that *The Origins* had reinforced the revisionism of right-wing nationalists and Nazi apologists in West Germany—a point echoed by several other critics, including German historians associated with the IfZ, who almost unanimously rejected the book.[80] She had written to the Wiener Library's Director, asking for "German press reactions to A.J.P. Taylor's iniquitous book," adding, "Like Miss Lambert I should like to get some kind of press campaign hooked on to neo-Nazi comments. Shall be very grateful for any help you can provide."[81] Her letter gave several examples of the book's reception by extreme right German newspapers.[82] She also published reviews in *History Today* and the the *Listener*. "Mr. Taylor's admirers," she noted, "no doubt glory in this new display of 'originality of insight and liveliness of style' the criteria of fashion. Otherwise, the book is a virtuoso's display of impish inconsistency in the name of rationality."[83] Taylor had disregarded "the ever-growing mountain of evidence" for Hitler's "long-term programme for the extermination of the races the Führer despised"; "Adolf Eichmann's trial," she added, "tells the story once more. To plan destruction on this scale was to plan war and court disaster. Mr. Taylor, being understandably bored by repetition, discards the evidence."[84] Still not content, she contacted overseas editors and asked Trevor-Roper: "Whether you would like to have another fling at Mr. T. in the N.Z.Z.? [*Neue Zürcher Zeitung*]. If not, Margaret Lambert and I may have another go."[85] But Trevor-Roper declined: "I feel I have had my say and would like to forget about him. I think that what I did say got fairly widely quoted…parts of it were broadcast in German to Germany by the B.B.C."[86]

The Origins was a flawed book and it damaged Taylor's career, although it became a bestseller and was translated into several languages.[87] It had very little impact on historians' depiction of Hitler, the Third Reich, and Nazi foreign policy, but did influence more sympathetic evaluations of Chamberlain and Appeasement. This may have happened anyway as anger about Munich and the so-called 'Guilty Men' subsided and historians turned more to the structural limitations upon British foreign policy imposed by Treasury priorities, imperial overstretch, and military and strategic considerations.[88] Taylor never really changed his views; indeed, never short of conceit, he tended to believe that others had cashed in on his ideas.[89] For Wiskemann the craft of history was a pursuit of truth, or at least as close as one could get to it, through careful evaluation of multiple and diverse sources; she also believed it was the best training for political policymakers. To her, Taylor's technique in argument, his selective use of evidence and stretching the truth to fashion a pithy phrase, was perverse, even dangerous.

Taylor's self-image as a troublemaker and outsider also grated; to her he seemed a consummate insider—denizen of Oxford common rooms, friend of Lord Beaverbrook, fellow of the British Academy, a favorite performer for BBC radio and TV. Their paths had intersected many times: they wrote for the same newspapers and magazines and knew many people in common; both began their careers with research in Vienna; both focused on the Habsburg Monarchy and later developed strong interests in Czechoslovakia, Yugoslavia, and Trieste, although Taylor was on the inside, close to Crozier and Wadsworth at the *Manchester Guardian* and part of the male club of Oxbridge historians, to which no woman really belonged. Having formed a negative view of someone, Wiskemann seldom changed it, and she repeatedly criticized *The Origins*, either explicitly or in scarcely veiled references. After Taylor savaged the book [*The Approach of War, 1938–1939*, 1967] of her young Sussex colleague Christopher Thorne in the *Observer*, she retaliated calling it "a *tour de force*, clear, exciting, accurate," and added, "mercifully for history, however, he is concerned with the truth as demonstrated by the evidence rather than with startling his readers with smart novelties."[90] Dispatching an article to her editor at the *Listener*, we find her attaching a note: "Please be sure to cut and by Mr. A.J.P. Taylor on p. 2 if there is any risk of libel, but I should like it to go in because it's true."[91] And even in 1970, while praising K.D. Bracher's analysis of the Hossbach Memorandum, she couldn't resist summing up: "and Mr. A.J.P. Taylor is left without a leg to stand on."[92]

*   *   *

Sending Christmas greetings to Harry Bergholz in December 1963, Wiskemann explained: "My excuses for not writing are: a) that being fairly blind makes me slow, b) at 64 I do just about as much as at 34 which is really too much…Anyway, I still find life interesting." She had also decided to leave Sussex the following summer: "I shall have done it for three years and I shall stop and try to write three books (if I can still see enough)."[93] In fact, she published four books in the space of six years, as well as numerous book reviews and articles. She wrote quickly but her busy schedule and failing eyesight meant that she was incapable of producing the kind of deeply researched major book that many prominent scholars publish as the capstone of their careers. Instead, all four books were short: it was a case of high productivity on a small scale. Three were syntheses designed for sixth-formers and undergraduate courses and resulted from suggestions by publishers; the fourth was a memoir focusing on her experiences in the 1930s and 1940s.

Growing numbers of high school students were taking 'O' levels and 'A' levels in the 1960s; teacher-training colleges grew rapidly; and the figures for British students in higher education more than doubled.[94] Publishers were quick to see in this dramatic expansion a growing market for new texts, sold in cheap paperback form which, if they were successful, might enjoy a crossover potential to general readers and the much larger American market. This was the case with Wiskemann's *Europe of the Dictators, 1919–1945* (1966), part of Harper-Collins Fontana History of Europe series, edited by J.H. Plumb. It sold over 80,000 copies, many more than her earlier books.[95] She agreed to write *Europe of the Dictators* during her last year at Sussex, but warned Plumb: "I am not free to begin on the book in question until after this academic year, the last one during which I expect to teach two days a week."[96] Working with the exceptionally able editor Richard Ollard, himself a stylish historian, Plumb had signed up a brilliant array of 'stars' for the series.[97] Originally, Martin Wight had agreed to write the 1919–45 volume, but, after reviewing his heavy commitments at Sussex and his work for the British Committee on the Theory of International Relations, he withdrew and recommended Wiskemann, citing, "Her knowledge of the period, both from practical experience and as a historian." Wight added: "She has talked to me about her uncertainty of what her next book will be, and her next book is also likely to be her last."[98] Ollard was delighted with the suggestion: "I remember reading her *Rome-Berlin Axis* with the greatest enjoyment and admiration some ten or twelve years ago"; Plumb too thought it "an admirable idea, indeed far better than Wight himself. I have always read her with great interest, she has a lively mind and we shall be fortunate to get her."[99] Wiskemann estimated that she would need nine months to a year to finish the book and, with her usual discipline, submitted the manuscript on time and at the prescribed length. Plumb (who regarded Geoffrey Elton's *Reformation Europe, 1517–1559* as exemplary) was elated: "Up to Elton's standard and should do very well indeed."[100]

It was an accomplished synthesis, presenting a substantive treatment of the period in a mere 260 pages; "a little masterpiece," G.P. Gooch called it, full of astute observations and sharply drawn vignettes of policymakers she had met and events she had witnessed first-hand. Without mentioning him, it was also in many ways another rejoinder to Taylor's *Origins*; indeed, Wiskemann's Foreword began with a declaration that would have resonated with many participants in the recent debate: "I make no claim to detachment about the history of Europe between 1919 and 1945, but I do not believe that to be involved with it obliges one to be inaccurate or dishonest." The book was also written more from a Continental perspective than most British accounts and devoted closer attention to how events looked from an East European vantage point.[101] Even her very abbreviated chapter on cultural developments was full of acute insights, personal and opinionated. Describing the emotional impact of Spain's Civil War on British and

American intellectuals, she couldn't resist a waspish comment that they seemed "less completely shattered" by Hitler's *Machtergreifung* or the Austrian and Czech crises: "One can, after all, understand that Czechoslovakia was little but a clumsy name, one of many new states far away and land-locked in Central Europe." Spain was quite another thing, a land to which English-speaking travelers had flocked in the 1930s; when the Civil War began "only Central European specialists were aware that Austria and Czechoslovakia were in grave danger."[102]

These were sentiments she had expressed at the time. Similarly, her views about political events and policymakers had changed little. She still believed that the League of Nations could have done much to modify and improve the Versailles peace settlement had the major powers been willing to commit to it. For all his tactical flexibility, she argued, Hitler never varied his territorial and racial goals, which were evident in *Mein Kampf* and documents like the November 1937 Hossbach Memorandum (largely dismissed as a domestic tactic by Taylor). Nor had her criticism of Neville Chamberlain ("stubborn, vain, naif, and ignorant") and Appeasement softened. Although many historians were becoming more sympathetic to Appeasement by the late 1960s, Wiskemann thought they went too far in replacing "guilty men" by "helpless men."[103]

The book got a very favorable reception from reviewers. In the *Sunday Times* Cyril Connolly wrote a glowing review—"a book of which one would not miss a word," especially her brilliant analysis of the complex affairs of Eastern Europe; he wished she had included more on public opinion and a chapter on interwar journalists who were alert to the dangers of the dictators while "so many statesmen slept or politicians appeased or generals played for safety."[104] Academic reviewers were equally laudatory. George Mosse declared that it "holds the reader spellbound...I cannot think of a better introduction...and one which deals not only with the big powers but the smaller nations as well."[105] Christopher Thorne, then working on his own study of international affairs leading up to 1939, wrote that "the author's familiarity with the language, literature and politics of so much of the region frequently reveals little-known facets of the period, enriching the book's character sketches...giving weight to its judgments." Above all, she "succeeds in recapturing the particular hope, turmoil and fear of the inter-war years."[106] And American historian Robert Pois called it "a work of compelling power, tinctured with strong emotion," well-researched and factual "yet not detached" and "much more than the mixture of studied objectivity and platitudes one often associates with histories of this era."[107] Wiskemann had reminded readers that it was "the great age of the critical journalist" which prompted Malcolm Muggeridge to reflect how much had changed since the 1930s: "As the Cold War set its grip on the Continent, activities like hers [Wiskemann's] became largely impossible. Requests for visas and interviews in the Soviet satellite countries remained unanswered, public relations men barred the way to the mighty in their seats; the handout replaced the confidential chat. Even Tabouis* appearing briefly on the postwar scene was unable to make much headway, and Mr. Gunther's wanderings seemed pallid by comparison with his pre-war junketings."[108]

Perhaps most pleasing of all was a glowing review in the *TLS*, anonymous as was its custom, but written by Zara Steiner, then working on British diplomacy before the First World War. "Eye-witnesses," she wrote, "are not always the best of historians, but even before the war Miss Wiskemann demonstrated that she could shape direct observation into scholarship." Steiner especially praised the sections on Eastern Europe: "These could only have been written by someone in full-command of the tangled interwar histories of the individual states." The review ended with the hope "that Miss Wiskemann will be called on to do a new diplomatic history of the period which would give her the scope necessary for such an undertaking." Such a project was impossible for Wiskemann at this point; it was left for Steiner herself to fulfill the task years later in two magisterial volumes (the only female author in the Oxford History of Modern Europe series).[109]

After *Europe of the Dictators* Wiskemann published a memoir which focused exclusively on two decades of her life, 1928–48, when she was a foreign correspondent in Central Europe and a secret agent in Switzerland. As she saw it, the great cause of her life had been anti-Nazism, and this became the main thrust of her account, essentially inserting her personal story or rather her public life into the historical period about which she had written so much. The book is full of tantalizingly brief pen portraits of prominent figures she met—diplomats, politicians, artists, and academics—and her first-hand knowledge is apparent on every page. But *The Europe I Saw* (1968)—poignant for someone going blind—is aptly titled, for it relates the Europe she *saw* rather than reflecting upon how she was changed or formed by her experiences. Self-revelation was not Wiskemann's style and, aside from her consuming hatred of Nazism, she is largely silent about her own thoughts and emotions, and many aspects of her life are simply omitted. Always reticent and very private, she remained "dauntingly discreet" in the words of Michael Ratcliffe, a colleague at the *Times* and later theatre critic at the *Observer*.[110] Ratcliffe called it "her Cambridge manner," but her model may have been Iris Origo, equally reserved, whose two memoirs Wiskemann reviewed and greatly admired. She even remained silent about many aspects of her service for PWE, perhaps feeling bound by the secrecy rules. The rancor between PWE and SOE that bedeviled wartime intelligence continued to fester postwar. The work of PWE had largely been forgotten (and David Garnett's official history had been suppressed), while SOE's exploits were celebrated in books and successful films, several of them highlighting female agents.[111] Perhaps she wished to counterpose

---

* Geneviève Tabouis (1892–1985) was the most famous female foreign correspondent in France in the 1920s and 1930s. Like Wiskemann, she repeatedly warned readers about the danger posed by Hitler and German rearmament and advocated intervention to support Czechoslovakia.

a different narrative. Reviewers praised the book, several of them expressing their high regard for her career as a journalist and her knowledge of European affairs, but those who knew her best were disappointed; it seemed rather bland when compared to her pungent comments in conversation.[112]

In her last two books Wiskemann turned her attention again to Italy. The first, *Fascism in Italy* (1969), was written for St. Martin's series on "The Making of the 20th Century." Contributors included many of the best-known historians working on the period since the First World War and the books were designed to provide undergraduate and lay readers with brief, insightful overviews.[113] Wiskemann's volume—really an extended essay of about 120 pages—was a model of clarity and compression. Intended as an introduction to the topic, the book requires no detailed analysis. It examined the origins, domestic policies, and institutional evolution of the Fascist regime and its foreign policy, while the final chapters focused on its impact on Nazism and extreme right regimes in Austria, Hungary, Romania, France, Spain, and Portugal. In every case she found Mussolini's impact slight and largely superficial and emphasized the ideological, structural, and cultural differences that distinguished new ultra-right movements in these countries from Italy, belying Fascist claims that theirs was a "conquering creed." This was especially true of Nazism, whose racism, use of terror, relationship to industry and religion, and non-corporate structure were quite different, to say nothing of the two dictators' personalities and the degree to which the Italian and German populations succumbed to their ideologies. Compared to Nazism, she wrote, Italian Fascism was a regime of compromise—with respect to the Crown and the Catholic Church, its less efficient structure of control, and its treatment of opposition. This allowed anti-fascists like Cesare Pavese and Carlo Levi to survive *confino* in the South and men like Benedetto Croce and Luigi Einaudi to remain unpenalized while making little secret of their liberal sympathies. In consequence, in 1943 far more anti-fascist Italians than anti-Nazi Germans survived to take over the state. As for those tempted to view Fascism as a catalyst of modernization in Italy, Mussolini's regime, she concluded, brought "no gains and several grave disadvantages": economic development was retarded, education declined, the illiteracy and misery of the *Mezzogiorno* was unchanged, and the power of the Catholic Church increased. The only purpose it served, she reflected, was in totally discrediting the Monarchy and bringing about a republic—but even here, she added, the real debt was to Mazzini.[114]

In these final sections Wiskemann was responding to a growing number of comparative fascism studies in the 1960s and to historians' preoccupation with developing a checklist or basic minimum of indispensable characteristics that linked different far right movements. The broad use of 'fascism' and 'anti-fascism' by Marxists and the left in the 1930s and 1940s was, she believed, justified politically at the time (in, for example, the Action party's efforts to construct a broad progressive coalition), but, for serious historians, generic theories of fascism could also lead to confusion and misunderstanding, blurring important distinctions. The editors of the *Journal of Contemporary History* declared in their first issue that fascism was a key neglected topic for historians and political theorists, and it quickly became a central theme in the emerging field of contemporary history and a catalyst for transnational European studies.[115] That this comparative approach opened many new areas of research is undeniable, and Wiskemann recognized this in her book reviews, but she also saw potential dangers—downplaying, for example, national differences and in detaching the problem of fascism from the question of why liberal democracy was in crisis and so vulnerable to the assault of the right both in the West and in the peasant societies of Eastern Europe in the interwar years.[116] For Wiskemann, like many older historians, this required both close attention to the role of traditional elites who supported the new far right politics and careful attention to the specific characteristics of longer national trajectories: under-development and the flaws of the Risorgimento in Italy, for example, and in Germany the abortive liberal revolution of 1848 and the destructive impact of Bismarck.

Deceptively simple and straightforward, *Fascism in Italy* was a clear, intelligent analysis by a writer who had read all the major sources in both Italian and English and had her own firm convictions. In Britain it gained positive reviews—the journalist and politician Vernon Bartlett, for example, recommended it as "an excellent little book"[117]—and it proved a valued aide for beginning students, but reviewers for MacMillan, the US distributors, raised difficulties. Charles Delzell, whose book on the Italian resistance to Mussolini Wiskemann admired, argued that it offered nothing new by way of interpretations, while John Weiss of New York's Lehmann College (who had written on "The Fascist Tradition" in Europe) wanted something more structured and thematic. Both were doubtful it would suit the more problem-oriented undergraduate courses in the United States.[118]

Wiskemann's last book, *Italy since 1945* (published posthumously in 1971), was another brief text and not her best, but given her increasingly blindness, merely finishing it was a victory. It examined the complicated birth of the Italian Republic and the fissiparous political parties and coalitions that emerged in the quarter century after the war. Italy appears as a kaleidoscope of party alliances, continually recycled political figures, legislative efforts, and crises, as recounted by a particularly astute observer with an unusual capacity for ordered detail. In this short study there is no complex analysis of the underlying social and political themes. The major themes of the period are all there—the 'economic miracle' in the northern industrial cities and the massive exodus from rural areas and the South; the complex relationship of the state and the Catholic Church; and the pervasiveness of political corruption—but they receive brief insightful sketches rather than systematic analysis. In 1970 Wiskemann recognized that a crisis was overtaking Italy. She pointed to widespread student and labor unrest, the threat of violence especially from neo-fascists, and political blocs too divided and riven with rivalries to cope; indeed, politics had become an excuse for not governing. But she offered no conjecture as to where the impending crisis might lead. Part of the problem, perhaps, is that the book appeared too early: the '*anni di piombi*' [the years of lead] reached their violent climax a decade after with the Red Brigades and the kidnapping and killing of Christian Democratic leader Aldo Moro, while northern separatism and systemic 'Tangentopoli' corruption climaxed still later. At times the book has the feel of an intelligent conversation, of words spoken to a tape recorder or an amanuensis. It does, however, demonstrate Wiskemann's immersion in Italian affairs, including film, literature, theatre, and music, to the very end of her life.

*   *   *

After retiring from Sussex, Wiskemann kept to an exhausting schedule. Aside from writing four books, there were articles, media appearances, and numerous reviews (nineteen for the *TLS* alone in 1967, seventeen in 1968, and sixteen in 1969), some of them extended essays like her analysis of Swiss literature in the 1950s and her critique of Albert Speer's memoirs.[119] She continued to broadcast for the BBC, participating in two lecture series for Radio 3 (successor to the Third Programme) on "The Thirties in Britain" and "The Threat of Fascism" and serving as general editor of another series, "Between the Wars".[120] Thanks to Grace Wyndham Goldie, she also began making appearances on BBC TV, discussing, for example, the history of Switzerland and her experiences as a foreign correspondent.[121] There were also gratifying marks of academic recognition. High praise for *Europe of the Dictators* turned readers back to her earlier books, three of which were re-issued in new editions. C.L. Mowat asked her to write the section on "Germany, Italy and Eastern Europe 1898–1945" for a volume of the *New Cambridge Modern History*,[122] and she was delighted by the award of an honorary D.Litt from Oxford in 1965, especially when the public orator described her as "a Cassandra who lived to record the war she had foretold."[123]

Wiskemann had good friends in Oxford and made trips there to see fellow historians Robert Blake, Hugh Trevor-Roper, James Joll, Bill Deakin, and Lucy Sutherland, one of the most influential women at the university, who was the head of Lady Margaret Hall. In 1966 Wiskemann gave a course of lectures there on interwar Europe.[124] She also traveled up to Cambridge regularly, seeing old friends at Newnham, including Kay Baxter, a former actress who taught theology but was also Secretary of the Women's Appointments Board working to enhance the status of women at the university.[125] Historians and graduate researchers, some from Central Europe and the United States, sought her advice, and she enjoyed meeting with and mentoring young historians and foreign correspondents. Often these meetings were over lunch; she enjoyed good food and cooking and liked organizing lunch parties at her Moore Street home.[126] "You met interesting people and you took along a bottle of wine," recalled one journalist. "She never lived well off her books and articles notwithstanding their stature."[127]

When Sally Marks, later a leading authority on interwar diplomacy, arrived in London in early 1966 to work for a Ph.D. at LSE, she sought out Wiskemann in hopes of studying with her but was told she was now fully retired.[128] A graduate of Wellesley then in her mid-thirties, Marks had worked for the US Defense Department before turning to an academic career and teaching at a small college. She admired *Czechs and Germans* and was thinking of writing about the Munich crisis. Wiskemann invited her to lunch and steered her towards the 1920s and working with LSE's George Grün. More lunch invitations followed, and they met frequently over the next two years; indeed, Marks recalled: "For a while she rather tried to take me over, and I had to establish my independence." Wiskemann advised Marks on her dissertation and introduced her to her former colleague Christopher Thorne and to the journalist Hester Marsden Smedley, who provided "fabulous" contacts in Belgium and Luxembourg, where Marks did her archival research.[129] Wiskemann and Marks enjoyed each other's company and yet, the younger woman recalled, though very friendly, their relationship was always a little formal: "She was very reserved about anything personal. I never learned anything about her family or youth. She was slightly prissy and a bit prickly... She would tell me about other historians, but she was not gossipy and very rarely catty.... Elizabeth was a stickler for the proprieties and had her Standards... I always felt I had to be on my best behavior, even when it was just the two of us and even after two years."[130]

Throughout her life, it seems, there was only a very small circle of friends with whom Wiskemann fully opened up. She could draw upon a vast network of colleagues and acquaintances but was in some ways quite solitary. Her closest friend in these years was Heather Brigstocke (*neé* Renwick Brown), who had been one of the first "paying guests" at Moore Street. Heather and her diplomat husband and three children had returned from Washington in 1963; she took a job teaching classics at Francis Holland School at Sloane Square, close to Wiskemann's home, and then became a dynamic reforming head mistress there in 1965. Both women loved the theatre and art, and Wiskemann became godmother to Heather's second son, Julian. They also traveled together to the Greek islands, where Heather was impressed by Wiskemann's intrepid cycling despite her poor vision.[131]

It was a busy and full life, with trips to museums, the ballet, concerts, and the theatre, but the deterioration of Wiskemann's eyesight gave her much anxiety. In 1961 Hugh Trevor-Roper had put her in contact with his brother Patrick, a distinguished eye surgeon (and one of only three gay men who appeared openly as witnesses before the 1955 Wolfenden Committee).[132] She liked and trusted him, but there was little he could do to improve her bad eye and she worried that if anything went wrong with the other one, she would be completely blind. Meeting J.H. Plumb for the first time at Prunier's restaurant in London to discuss what became *Europe of the Dictators*, she warned: "Please don't be surprised if

I behave rather like a bat – I was recently blinded in one eye by an operation which should not have been performed and see badly with the other one (work at present not affected)."[133] She tried not to let her sight prevent her from attending gatherings with friends, and she remained a lively, interesting guest whom people were anxious to meet.[134] But she was less mobile than before. In January 1966, invited to a dinner in Brighton by former students, where Leonard Woolf would be present, she wrote: "I'd like to come but am a bit immobilized in the winter because I can't see much in the dark."[135] Ever stoic, to an enquiry from her novel-ist friend Richard Hughes, she wrote: "I can see enough to crawl along, right eye only."[136] When, after her death, Sir Michael Redgrave starred in John Mortimer's play "Voyage Around My Father" (about the playwright's father, who went blind in mid-life), he was asked how he captured so well the details of blindness and recalled watching his friend Elizabeth in her home "especially the delicate motion of her hands feeling the surfaces and objects."[137]

Somehow she continued to travel, though less than before: to Switzerland, Italy, and she even returned to Prague briefly in January 1969, five months after Soviet invasion forces had destroyed the democratic aspirations of the "Prague Spring."[138] Along with numerous British experts on Soviet and East European affairs, she signed a letter to the *Times* in October 1968 condemning Brezhnev's use of force and urging all Britons who were invited to the Soviet Embassy's cele-bration of the October Revolution not to attend (three of the thirty-one who signed the letter were women).[139] She was deeply shocked by the Soviet invasion and horrified that Gomulka, hero of the Polish October of 1956, had chosen to help crush the Czech reformers.[140] But traveling around Prague she was relieved to find that a kind of normality had returned to the city and believed that Soviet occupation had strengthened the unity of Czechs and Slovaks, intellectuals, stu-dents, and workers in opposition. This was overly optimistic: 'normalization' soon brought the harsh re-imposition of a police state and hopes for reform perished for a generation.

To Harry Bergholz, always an important confidant, she wrote: "As I'm sure I have said before, I'm very bad at growing old and can't face the prospect of death with much satisfaction. But it is the problem of my sight which plagues me most. I am to go to an eye-surgeon tomorrow [Patrick Trevor-Roper] and I'm sure he will want to operate, and I'm terrified of that after my bad experience." She added: "I'm also at sixes and sevens because I think I must sell this house and look for a flat which would be easier to live in."[141] The house was packed with books, and just the thought of downsizing and moving must have been alarming. Her older sister Eugenia was still alive, but there is no evidence that they were still in con-tact or that she could expect help from family.

She continued writing reviews and somehow finished her last book, *Italy since 1945*. "So far," she confided to Bergholz, "I go on much the same, reviewing a good many books. My sight is bad, everything looking fearfully smudgy, but with a very good reading lamp etc, I manage somehow, though winter is awful to get through. I lose my nerve if I look ahead, so I just try not to." "The world," she added, "gets nastier and nastier by my standards."[142] She did not elaborate, but one can guess at least some of her meaning. It was indeed a grim period: atrocities in Vietnam and the bombing of Cambodia, Enoch Powell and 'Paki-bashing' at home, violence in Northern Ireland, Baader-Meinhof in Germany and, of course, the crushing of the Prague Spring and the reassertion of Soviet power in Eastern Europe. She also felt increasingly at odds with what she took to be the cultural atmosphere of the time: "the unbridled hostility of intellectuals on the left and the right," the attacks on liberalism, and "the Fascist and Nazi phrases in current use among those who think themselves Maoists."[143] Her own politics, which were a combination of liberal and socialist during the war, had by the Sixties become more centrist. Christian Democratic rule in West Germany and Italy, which she once deplored, seemed now at least to offer practical managed democracy, sustained by unprecedented economic progress. Asked by Leonard Woolf about her politics in 1965, she replied: "I suppose my political standpoint just about the same as that of Maynard [Keynes] and Beveridge"; she had returned to their brand of social liberalism.[144] Wiskemann was very much a product of the 1920s and loved the artistic experimentation, the sense of hope and possibility that she remembered as the *leitmotif* of the decade before the harsh realities of the 1930s dominated. "The strangest characteristic of the European consciousness in the twenties, even in the early twenties," she recalled, "was a romantic optimism, a starry-eyed belief that paradise was round the corner."[145] This feeling, especially among the young, was gone, replaced by a negative, debunking spirit.

Sally Marks had returned to London for further research in 1970–71 and was living in north London; she "saw a good deal of Elizabeth at first at her house, then more often at an Italian restaurant near Piccadilly Circus that she fancied." Wiskemann put her in touch with a literary agent who got her a contract for her first book: *The Illusion of Peace* (1976). "I knew," Marks recalled, "that she was worried about her eyes and another operation necessary in the coming summer. Perhaps I should have known that if she mentioned it at all, she was *extremely* worried, but I didn't."[146] She was very good at hiding her anxieties. There is fragmentary evidence of Wiskemann's depressed mood in the months before her death. She had finished and sent off her last book to the publisher and completed several promised book reviews (they appeared in the months after her death). She was tired from the effort and possibly plagued by insomnia, a recurrent problem. When her good eye began to deteriorate with a cataract, she grew increasingly fearful that another operation might fail, leaving her completely blind. Her Swiss friend Erika Düby urged her to have it done there, to no avail. Perhaps she offered a hint as to her own views when years before she wrote to Leonard Woolf, just about to turn eighty: "Please live as long as you can with satisfaction: I shall hope to see you many summers yet."[147] As she looked ahead, Wiskemann saw no satisfaction, no palatable future; she had always been independent, made her own choices, and valued her autonomy. That she should choose when her life would end was very much in character. If she lost her sight completely, remaining in her house would almost certainly be impossible; her likely fate would be a nursing home where, unable to work, travel, and go out, her life would lose its meaning and purpose. In this sense her suicide was rational, thought out, and pre-emptive.

In late April 1971 Wiskemann made a brief trip to Israel to give a lecture and seemed cheerful enough in her correspondence with C.H. Rolph, whom she was helping with his biography of Kingsley Martin.[148] She had dinner with Heather Brigstocke on June 25; a week later Heather sent a postcard from Edinburgh and got a reply "which said she was feeling low and asked me to get in touch with her." Returning to London, Heather phoned but got no answer. On July 5 Wiskemann was found dead in her house. She had taken a lethal dose of barbiturate capsules washed down with alcohol. Such a massive overdose could only have been taken deliberately. Her head was on a cushion in front of a gas fire; she had taken, the coroner noted, "steps to gas herself if the drug-taking had no effects."[149] She had made a will, even leaving her books to Lucy Sutherland's college (Lady Margaret Hall, Oxford), her Piranesi drawing to the Fitzwilliam Museum at Cambridge, and her property to Heather Brigstocke.[150] Typically, she attended to last details, leaving clear instructions for the charlady, who she knew would find her.

*   *   *

At her death Wiskemann was well-known as a journalist and historian; reviewers praised her "as one of the best informed and in judgment, most balanced observers of the international scene."[151] She enjoyed life, the company of her friends, travel, art, and literature, but was also ambitious, driven, and extremely hard-working. Her professional career always came first and, as a woman, a freelance journalist, and a scholar on the fringes of academia for the most part, she felt a strong need to prove herself, to show she could match the full-time professionals in both fields. In her entry for the *Dictionary of National Biography*, James Joll described her as "a small, vivacious woman of great charm and independence, always outspoken in defense of her strongly held opinions, sensitive and quick to reply to criticism, and justly proud of her record." This was accurate; she could be difficult, prickly, and quick to react to perceived slights or condescension, especially from male colleagues, whether it was uncooperative government officials at the British legations in Prague or Bern, the West German campaign against *Germany's Eastern Neighbours*, or academic skirmishes with A.J.P. Taylor. For most of her life, she lived by her pen, always a formidable challenge. All this took its toll, emotional and psychological, and she often complained of insomnia and nervous exhaustion. But she was also determined, cool-headed, and psychically tough: it took courage to pursue stories amid the growing violence of Nazi Berlin;

daring to travel across Vichy France in 1941 without papers; and a different kind of courage to end her own life.

Looking back, it is clear how deeply formative two sets of experiences were in Wiskenann's life. First, the Bloomsbury circles of her youth and at Cambridge. She celebrated Bloomsbury for its rejection of Victorian constraints and sexual morality, its liberal politics, its receptivity to Freud, modern art, and literature, and the value it placed on friendship and personal relations. Forster, Keynes, the Woolfs, and her old friend Francis Birrell had a lasting impact on her social values and intellectual outlook, her sense of self. The second defining influence on her life was her long and intense engagement with Nazism, beginning in 1930 and lasting some fifteen years and more. While silent about many things, her memoir makes clear that confrontation with Nazism turned her into a political activist. Wiskemann grasped immediately its significance and the threat it posed not only to Weimar democracy and the rule of law but to peace in Europe. Expelled from the Reich by the Gestapo, she became a Cassandra and a wandering scholar, earning very little, but touring Eastern Europe, including places where there were few Western journalists, doing all she could to publicize Nazi political and economic subversion of the states created by the Treaty of Versailles.

Becoming a journalist was not something Wiskemann had planned on doing; she first traveled to Berlin as an escape, a change of scene from Cambridge after the downgrading of her doctoral thesis and the Empson scandal. Cambridge connections—especially Kingsley Martin and Leonard Woolf at the *New Statesman*—got her foot in the door, but drive and sheer talent did the rest. Dividing her time between stints of adjunct teaching at Newnham and pursuing news stories in Germany, she quickly emerged as a regular member of the foreign correspondents' 'fraternity' in Berlin. By 1935 she was regularly publishing articles in the leading left-liberal magazines as well as the *Scotsman*, *Manchester Guardian*, and *News Chronicle*, and newspapers throughout Britain carried news of her arrest and expulsion the following year.[152] Her articles in the mid-1930s were outstanding; complex, analytical, full of local eyewitness detail, and unafraid to forecast likely outcomes. Friends described her as a great watcher and listener. Living in Rome immediately after the war, Wiskemann again had the luxury of following a major story—the birth of the Italian Republic—but once she returned to London, while her articles on the Saar especially were excellent, in general her journalism was more fragmentary. There were fewer opportunities for a freelance reporter: she had to choose stories that full-time correspondents were not addressing, while the Cold War made impossible the access to politicians and freewheeling travel she had enjoyed earlier. To make ends meet she turned more and more to book reviewing, "a full-time job with a half-time salary," as Cyril Connolly once called it.[153]

Wiskemann's work as a historian is more difficult to evaluate. She was a pioneer in the new field of contemporary history and, as such, her books were inevitably superseded in later decades. She wrote quickly, always on tight deadlines, and three of her books were syntheses written for students. Writing the kind of book that takes a decade and more of research was not something she could ever contemplate. But reviews of her books attest to their significance and quality. *The Rome-Berlin Axis* was the first major study in English of the Hitler–Mussolini relationship, while *Germany's Eastern Neighbours* remained for many years the only serious study in English of the expulsion of ethnic Germans from Eastern Europe. The most common criticism of *Europe of the Dictators, 1919–1945*, her concise survey for the Fontana paperback series, was that it should have been longer. Even so, it had an impact; referring to the book in 2007, one historian wrote: "Elizabeth Wiskemann will be familiar to every British history student who completed their schooling by the early 1990s."[154] Above all, there is *Czechs and Germans*, still widely cited over eighty years after its publication.[155] That she was able to research the book in under a year and write it in four months is astonishing. As a doctoral candidate at Cambridge her chosen topic had been a conventional one in diplomatic history about Louis Napoleon and the Vatican. But her experience as a journalist not only shifted her interests to contemporary affairs, it encouraged a multi-dimensional approach to politics, embracing economics, cultural life, political geography, and social structure. To understand the contested borderlands of Europe, the Sudetenland, Saar, Trieste, and Tyrol, she had to combine a journalist's eye for social detail and geography with a historian's longer view of, for example, the clash of Slav and German cultures. Today Europe's eastern borderlands are once again high on the agenda of contemporary historians and IR specialists. Lucian Ashworth, for example, has recently criticized the way that Eastern Europe has figured in traditional IR theorizing, arguing that that the "wide gulf between the study of global order and foreign policy...can only be successfully bridged by using the kind of detailed knowledge constructed by Wiskemann" in *Czechs and Germans*. Her empirical approach, he suggests, which begins with a ground-eye view, paying close attention to history, ethnic and class analysis, and political geography, offers a useful corrective to abstract models of global order and better foreign policy prescriptions.[156]

As indicated throughout this biography, Wiskemann's career, while unique and defined by her choices and circumstances, should also be viewed as paradigmatic of a larger group of women, mostly from upper-middle-class families, who graduated from university in the 1920s and 1930s and attempted to carve out careers for themselves in international politics. They belonged to the first large cohort of female graduates looking to build their careers without reliance on inherited or married wealth. They grew up in the wake of the First World War; many, inspired by the spirit of liberal internationalism, were ardent supporters of the League of Nations Union [LNU], but, as the international order broke down in the 1930s, they became active in anti-fascist and anti-Appeasement campaigns. With few opportunities available within the universities, many turned to journalism and broadcasting to pursue their interests or worked for pressure groups like the LNU or the agencies of the League of Nations. Some have made an appearance in earlier chapters since their lives intersected with Wiskemann's either in Prague or PWE or Chatham House, whose importance in launching their careers, providing research projects, contacts, and publishing opportunities, can hardly be overstated. When war came, they were recruited into the expanded wartime state, especially in propaganda and intelligence, and for many—as was true of Wiskemann—these years were critical in shaping their future direction and in forging networks of ties in the postwar era. Along with Wiskemann, a brief list of this cohort would include Doreen Warriner, Elizabeth Monroe, Anne Lambton, Dorothy Pickles, Margaret Lambert, Elizabeth Barker, Phyllis Auty, and Violet Connolly. By the 1970s their contributions to studies of Eastern Europe, the Middle East, Soviet affairs, peasant economies, and other areas were widely recognized.[157]

Wiskemann career trajectory fits into this pattern. Not only were two of her books sponsored by Chatham House, but work on its *International Survey* and other projects was crucial for her finances. After a serious setback in her aspirations for an academic career, she reinvented herself as a journalist in Berlin. Like the others mentioned above, the Second World War had a crucial impact on Wiskemann's career. Her experience was different from that of Monroe at MOI, Barker at PWE, or Grant Duff at the BBC, since she was posted abroad and was for the most part a one-person operation, gathering intelligence on Axis Europe. Sent to Switzerland originally on a short-term basis, her commitment stretched to the entire war as the country became increasingly important as an intelligence hub. Again, the speed with which she managed, virtually unaided, to establish a network of informants and to respond to multiple agencies requiring both straight intelligence and content for propaganda is remarkable. Her personal dynamism and information-gathering skills made her a highly effective covert agent. She trod a precarious line, having to protect her sources, avoid alienating the Swiss authorities, and guard against German counterespionage agents. These were years of intense living, but also of strain and overwork, and Harry Bergholz was her confidant in difficult periods when her "nerve-controls," as she put it, were working badly. Some of her problems came from within her own legation, where she faced resistance and non-cooperation from diplomatic colleagues and members of rival covert units. She was undoubtedly the victim of male chauvinism and dislike for a tough-minded woman, but her difficulties also resulted from larger internecine struggles that hampered British intelligence organizations during the war. One of her solutions was to forge a close alliance with Allen Dulles, sharing information to their mutual benefit. Her postwar journalism and books on Italy and Central Europe were greatly influenced by wartime experience, especially in the case of Italy, by her personal contact with numerous Italian exiles who occupied important positions in Italian politics and society in later decades.

By most measures Wiskemann enjoyed a good deal of success, and her work received the recognition she craved. But her career also illustrates the challenges that women of her era faced in professional life, especially if they lacked private means. Along the way, she was helped by both male and female networks. However, in none of the realms in which she operated—journalism, government service, and academia—did she enjoy the same opportunities as men, and she encountered barriers, slights, sometimes outright obstruction because of her sex. She was not an outspoken feminist like Warriner and, from surviving evidence at least, was not active in feminist organizations. But the circles she moved in could all be labeled feminist: from Newnham with its connections to the suffrage campaigns, to friends like James and Alix Strachey, Kay Baxter, and Rebecca West. She was proud of being among the first women to get full diplomatic status and equally delighted at being the first woman elected to a Chair in any discipline at Edinburgh. But she mostly resisted strong identification by sex and disliked being called a *woman* journalist, preferring the "universal neuter," a space open to talent and blind to gender limitations. Her feminism was defined as independence and equality of opportunity—or, as Virginia Woolf put it, as humanism applied to women—and this included sexual freedom, divorce reform, and easy access to birth control. "She was for me," wrote Franca Magnani, "the prototype of an emancipated Englishwoman, even though she didn't use the word emancipation."[158]

On July 6, news of Wiskemann's death was reported in the press and tributes began to appear. RW in the *Times* recalled her help when he was starting out as a young correspondent in Bonn and praised both her "superb intellectual standards and her deep sense of loyalty to the cultural values underlying Europe's political history."[159] An editor at *History Today* recalled how "her precise and high-pitched voice on the telephone somehow conveyed the strength and acuteness of her personality." "Few people," he wrote, "have combined so admirably a deep knowledge of recent and contemporary European history with the gift of lucid expression."[160] More personal was Christopher Sykes, whom she had helped with his biography of Adam von Trott. They had clearly formed a close bond; everyone, he wrote, concerned with Europe must feel a sense of "irreparable loss" at the news, and those "who knew and loved her must be conscious of a gap in their own lives."[161] From the war years, which played so large a role in her life, came an anonymous tribute, but probably from Arthur 'Boofy' Gore, Lord Arran, who first met her at the British Legation in Bern and found her courage inspirational in the desperate summer of 1940. The tribute celebrated "a very special person," an outstanding scholar, and a patriot who risked her life for her country. She was also, the letter continued, "a gay and witty person whose company was pure joy. But over her life there hung the darkest shadow of all, the shadow of blindness. I don't think that any of us realized...just what it meant to the scholar and historian that slowly and inexorably her eyes dimmed, her vision faded...I cannot think of Elizabeth as dead. Despite her poor eyes, she shone too brightly for anything so trivial as death to extinguish so blazing a light."[162]

Notes

1. *Times*, July 9, 1971, p. 14.
2. Leonard Woolf to EW, March 20, 1968, Leonard Woolf papers.
3. EW, *The Europe I Saw* (London, 1968), p. 61.
4. On at least two occasions, in 1958 and 2008, the *New Statesman* reprinted her article "The Nazi Haven," which originally ran in the February 11 issue, 1933, immediately after Hitler was appointed Chancellor.
5. Timothy Garton Ash, *History of the Present* (London, 1999), p. xviii.
6. M. Gellhorn, "Obituary of a Democracy," *Colliers Weekly*, Dec. 10, 1938. Gellhorn turned this article into a novel with the same title in 1940, describing life in Prague after the surrender of the Sudetenland at Munich.
7. Julie V. Gottlieb, *'Guilty Women,' Foreign Policy, and Appeasement in Inter-War Britain* (London, 2015).
8. Mark Cornwall, "Elizabeth Wiskemann and the Sudeten Question: A Woman at the 'Essential Hinge' of Europe," *Central Europe*, 1, 1 (May 2003), p. 75.
9. J. Hagen, "Redrawing the Imagined Map of Europe: The Rise and Fall of the 'Center,'" *Political Geography*, 22 (2003), pp. 489–517.
10. The three aristocrats of the cohort considered here were: Shiela Grant Duff (1913–2004), granddaughter of Liberal politician Lord Avebury; Ann Lambton (1912–2008), granddaughter of the earl of Durham, whose family had great wealth in land and coal mines; and Margaret Lambert (1906–95), daughter of Liberal peer Viscount Lambert, a close friend of Winston Churchill.
11. Julie V. Gottlieb, *'Guilty Women'*. Helen McCarthy, *The British People and the League of Nations. Democracy, Citizenship and Internationalism, c. 1918–45* (Manchester, 2011). Deborah van Seeters, "Women's Foreign Policy Advocacy in 1930s Britain," Ph.D. diss., University of Toronto, 1999.
12. S. Oldfield, Doers of the World: British Women Humanitarians 1900–1950 (London, 2006); S.L. Roberts, "Place, Life Histories and the Politics of Relief: Episodes in the Life of Francesca Wilson, Humanitarian, Educator, Activist," Ph.D. diss., University of Birmingham, 2010. Wilson published a memoir and accounts of relief work in inter-war and postwar Europe.
13. Warriner destroyed most of her personal papers, but her nephew has been able to piece together many details of her life: Henry Warriner, *Doreen Warriner's War* (Kibworth, Leicestershire, 2019). Also, William Chadwick, *The Rescue of the Prague Refugees, 1938–39* (Leicester, 2010). D. Warriner, "Winter in Prague," *Slavonic and East European Review*, 62, 2 (April 1984), pp. 209–240.
14. Women played a central role in the BBC's Foreign Department in the 1930s: Kate Murphy, "Isa Benzie, Janet Quigley and the BBC's Foreign Department, 1930–1938," *Feminist Media Histories*, 5, 3 (2019), pp. 114–139.

15. Just about all the British women pioneers in the field of international relations appear in Chatham House publications as authors of essays or reviews. For example: Shiela Grant Duff, Elisabeth Barker, Margaret Lambert, Ann Lambton, Lucy Mair, Susan Strange, Cora Bell, Phyllis Auty, Barbara Ward, Dorothy Pickles, and many others.

16. Eleanore Breuning, "Margaret Lambert: Obituary," the *Independent*, Feb. 1, 1995. John Gurney, "Ann Katharine Swynford Lambton, 1912–2008," *Biographical Memoirs of Fellows of the British Academy*, 12 (2013), pp. 235–273.

17. Henry Warriner, *Doreen Warriner's War*. A Durham University research project funded by the Leverhulme Trust is examining PWE's role in British cultural life and those who worked for the agency, including women. James Smith *et al.*, "The Political Warfare Executive, covert propaganda, and British culture." Other women recruited by PWE included novelist Muriel Spark, poet Kathleen Raine, film critic Dilys Powell, Freya Stark, BBC woman's hour producer Joanna Scott-Moncrieff, and calligrapher Elizabeth Friedlander who produced printed propaganda and forged documents.

18. E. Barker, *Truce in the Balkans* (1948); *Macedonia and its Place in Balkan Power Politics* (1950); *Britain in a Divided Europe* (1971); *The Cold War* (1972); *Austria 1918–1972* (1973); *British Policy in South East Europe in the Second World War* (1976); *Churchill and Eden at War* (1978); *The British Between the Super Powers 1945–1950* (1983).

19. Warriner's books included: *Food and Farming in Postwar Europe* (1943), *Land and Poverty in the Middle East* (1948); *Revolution in Eastern Europe* (1950); and *Land Reform in Principle and Practice* (1969).

20. Barker and Shiela Grant Duff never became academics; Monroe entered academia in her fifties; Warriner was a lecturer at the School of Slavonic and East European Studies, London University, until 1960 when she was promoted to Reader. Her appointment as Professor came in 1965, one year before her retirement.

21. The *Kindertransport* required a different kind of organization because of the need to organize foster families to take the children in the UK. Wiskemann admired Warriner who after the war recommended her as possible author of a study being contemplated by Chatham House on the economies of Eastern Europe. "Economies of Eastern Europe," April 28, 1948, 4/Warr (Warriner file), Chatham House Archives. Also, Laura E. Brade and Rose Holmes, "Troublesome Sainthood: Nicholas Winton and the Contested History of Child Rescue in Prague, 1938–1940," *History & Memory*, 29, 1 (spring/summer 2017), p. 12.

22. In 2016 the British Political Science Association established an annual prize in Wiskemann's honor, awarded to the best dissertation on issues of inequality and social justice.

23. Apart from reviews of her books and articles, there are, I believe, only two studies about her: Mark Cornwall, "Elizabeth Wiskemann and the Sudeten Question" and Peter Kamber, *Geheime Agentin* (Berlin, 2010). Kamber's massive and insightful documentary novel deals with Switzerland during the war and Wiskemann is one of several central figures. Quite reasonably for a work of fiction, the novel also invents meetings, interactions, etc. for which no documentary evidence exists.

24. Some of Wiskemann's friends and acquaintances did not leave an archive or the documents that survive do not include correspondence from Wiskemann—for example,

Dory von der Mühll (sister of Carl Burckhardt), a close friend, and F.W. Deakin (first Warden of St. Antony's College, Oxford), whose interests in Yugoslavia and Italy she shared.

25. Recent examples include: Sarah Watling, *The Olivier Sisters. A Biography* (Oxford, 2019); Sarah Lonsdale, *Rebel Women between the* Wars (Manchester, 2020); Francesca Wade, *Square Hunting: Five Women in London between the Wars* (New York, 2020), which includes a chapter on Virginia Woolf.

26. Mark Cornwall, "Elizabeth Wiskemann and the Sudeten Question," p. 57. In interwar fiction, women journalists were often represented unsympathetically as intruders with masculine traits (a threat to a male profession) and as deviant, lesbian types. Sarah Lonsdale, "'We Agreed That Women Were a Nuisance in the Office, Anyway': The Portrayal of Women Journalists in early twentieth century British fiction," *Journalism Studies*, 14, 4 (2013), pp. 461–475.

27. EW to Martin Wight, Feb. 14, 1966, Martin Wight papers, 233/36.

Chapter 1

1. Emily Myra Burton (1863–1918) studied at the Ipswich School of Science and Art and almost certainly strongly encouraged Elizabeth's artistic interests.

2. Sir Bunnell Henry Burton (1858–1943) was mayor of the city; Sir William Parker Burton (1864–1942) was a friend and business partner of Sir Thomas Lipton and made a fortune in the sugar, biscuit, and tea trade. He was also renowned as a yachtsman who came close to winning the Americas Cup captaining Lipton's boat in 1920.

3. Eugenia Myra Wiskemann (1890–1979) was active in the suffrage campaign. In 1915 she joined the United Suffragists, founded by George Lansbury and Elizabeth Pethwick-Lawrence, which admitted men and, unlike the Women's Social and Political Union, argued that the campaign for the vote must be continued during wartime. She married a civil engineer, Cecil Holmes Waghorn, in 1917; they separated around 1924/5 and later divorced. George O. Wiskemann (1892–1963) was in business in London, traveled frequently, and died on a ship in New Zealand. He may have worked for British intelligence during the Second World War; Nigel West mentions a George O. Wiskemann who ran a Scandinavian sub-section of SOE. N. West, *Secret War. The Story of S.O.E. Britain's Wartime Sabotage Organisation* (London, 1992), pp. 26, 79, Appendix, p. 256.

4. *Notting Hill High School Magazine* (online): March 1910; March 1911; March 1912; March 1913; March 1914; March 1915; March 1916; 1920; 1921;1925; 1933; 1937; 1941; 1949; 1951; 1955; 1956; 1958; 1960; 1971. J. Kamm interviewed EW for her history *Indicative Past. A Hundred Years of the Girls' Public Day School Trust* (London, 1971), p. 58.

5. EW, *The Europe I Saw*, p. 8.

6. HC Debate on Enemy Aliens, Nov. 12, 1917.

7. *The London Gazette* 1888, filing against H. Wiskemann in the High Court of Bankruptcy, Nov. 1888. Possibly his wife's family helped him get over this first crisis. On his bankruptcy: *The London Gazette*, May 23, 1922. EW's mother left over £3,000

at her death, most of which went to her husband. Also, EW to Julian Trevelyan, Aug. 30, 1930, Julian Otto Trevelyan papers.

8. EW, *The Europe I Saw*, p. 7.

9. Rita McWilliams Tullberg, *Women at Cambridge* (Cambridge, 1998).

10. Kathleen Raine, *The Land Unknown* (London, 1975), pp. 23–4. Raine was a student at Girton 1926–29. On Newnham, see: E.M. Butler, *Paper Boats* (London, 1959).

11. J. Lehmann, *In My Own Time* (Boston, 1955), p. 88.

12. Sir Charles Tennyson (1879–1977) was a grandson of the poet Alfred Lord Tennyson; his wife, Ivy Gladys (1880–1958), was the daughter of a government Inspector of Factories. After working for Emily Hobhouse, she became Secretary of the Free Trade Union in 1903. Hallam Tennyson, *Studies in Tennyson* (London, 1981). The papers of Charles Tennyson and Ivy Gladys are in the Tennyson Research Centre, Lincoln.

13. EW, *The Europe I Saw*, p. 29. Neither Birrell nor Garnett (nor Ralph Wright, who later became a partner) was cut out for business. Birrell saw the shop more as a gathering place for intellectuals than a commercial enterprise. Frances Partridge (*née* Marshall, educated at Bedales and Newnham) also enjoyed working in the bookstore for several years: "It was as if a lot of doors had suddenly opened out of a stuffy room which I had been sitting in for far too long." F. Partridge, *Love in Bloomsbury. Memoirs* (Boston, 1981), pp. 75–6. EW seems to have fallen out with Partridge in later years, describing her somewhat tartly as "*eine dekorativer Verkäuferin*" in the Birrell/Garnett bookstore. EW, "Was war Bloomsbury," *Neue Zürcher Zeitung* Literatur und Kunst, Oct. 12, 1958, p. 5.

14. St. Felix School, Southwold, in Suffolk. She taught there 1921–22. EW to Colonel Kerr, May 11, 1945, NA: FO 898/257.

15. J. Holland Rose letter March 9, 1925; W.F. Reddaway "Draft Report on Wiskemann's Dissertation" and Reddaway to Pernel Strachey, June 23, 1925; Pernel Strachey to EW, July 18, 1925. Newnham College Archives. EW indicated that, if the fellowship committee required further references, they could contact Miss Cooke (Director of Historical Studies at Newnham) and Eileen Power of LSE. How well she knew Power is unclear. A possible link between them was Karin Costelloe, a close Girton friend of Power, who later married Adrian Stephen (Virginia Woolf's younger brother, who was a friend of EW).

16. D. Fair, *Harold Temperley. A Scholar and a Romantic in the Public Realm* (Newark, 1992), p. 172 and p. 321, fn. Slow to respond to demands for graduate degrees, Cambridge introduced a Ph.D. program in 1920 and an M.Litt. in 1921.

17. Pat Thane, "The Careers of Female Graduates of Cambridge University, 1920s–1970s," in D. Mich, J. Brown, and M. Van Leeuwen (eds.), *Origins of the Modern Career* (Aldershot, 2004).

18. EW, *The Europe I Saw*, p. 9; Mark Cornwall, "Elizabeth Wiskemann and the Sudeten Question: A Woman at the 'Essential Hinge' of Europe," *Central Europe*, 1 (2003). p. 57.

19. EW, *The Europe I Saw*, pp. 94–6. Also, R. Hughes to EW, Oct. 20, 1966, Richard Hughes papers. Hughes (1900–76) also addressed the Heretics Society in 1926–27. His best-known novels were *High Wind in Jamaica* (1929) and the first part of an unfinished trilogy, *The Fox in the Attic* (1961), about Hitler and the early Nazi movement, for which he used some of EW's work.

20. On this circle of friends and their magazines: Sir Michael Redgrave papers, Victoria and Albert Museum, Theatre and Performance Art Archives (Olympia) 31/3/5/4/1–4; 31/3/5/10/1–10; 31/3/5/31/1–18. Also, Peter Stansky and William Abrahams, *Julian Bell: From Bloomsbury to the Spanish Civil War* (Stanford, 2012). *Experiment* also included illustrations of artworks by Cartier-Bresson, Georges Braque, and Max Ernst. K.L. Donaldson, "*Experiment*: A Manifesto of Young England, 1928–1931," Ph.D. diss., University of York, Sept. 2014. Jason Harding, "*Experiment* in Cambridge," *The Cambridge Quarterly*, 27, 4 (1998), pp. 287–309.

21. Margaret Gardiner (1904–2005), *A Scatter of Memories* (London, 1988), p. 75. Educated at Bedales and Newnham, Gardiner was wealthy and aided her artist friends, including Barbara Hepworth, Ben Nicolson, and W.H. Auden. Other Heretics members included: mathematician Frank Ramsey, I.A. Richards, Maurice Dobb, J.B.S. Haldane, Dora Russell, and economist Joan Maurice (later Robinson).

22. Kathleen Raine, *The Land Unknown*, p. 44.

23. John Haffenden, *William Empson, vol. 1: Among the Mandarins* (Oxford, 2009), p. 241. Entry in the diary of Ivor and Dorothea Richards "To Empson and met Elizabeth Wiskermann" [sic!].

24. John Haffenden, *William Empson, vol. 1: Among the Mandarins*, pp. 240–1. "The attraction for Empson of such a vital, intelligent older woman was obvious...He was drawn to strength of will, uncomplicated vigour, self-sufficiency, and not to passiveness or pliancy. Delicate femininity was not so fetching to him" (p. 241). Haffenden's source was two Newnham alumnae: literary scholar E.E. Phare (better known as Elsie Duncan-Jones) and novelist and biographer Elizabeth Jenkins.

25. EW, "Was war Bloomsbury" *Neue Zürcher Zeitung* Literatur und Kunst, Oct. 12, 1958, p. 5.

26. A.O. Bell and A. McNeillie (eds.), *The Diary of Virginia Woolf*, vol. 3, entry 27 Oct. 1928, p. 201 (New York, 1980); H. Lee, *Virginia Woolf* (Vintage, p. 556;. Some of Wiskemann's letters to Julian Trevelyan in 1930 echo Woolf's comments about the freedom that came with £500 a year.

27. J. Haffenden (ed.), *Selected Letters of William Empson* (Oxford, 2006), pp. 8–9 (Empson to I.A. Richards, n.d., summer 1929). Another example from 1924 of college morality codes: mathematician Frank Ramsey's intense anxiety that he might lose his fellowship at King's if his premarital relationship with Lettice Baker (later his wife) were discovered. Cheryl Misak, *Frank Ramsey: A Sheer Excess of Powers* (Oxford, 2020).

28. John Haffenden, *William Empson, vol. 1: Among the Mandarins*, pp. 240–59; J. Haffenden (ed.), *Selected Letters of William Empson*, p. 9–10. J.B.S. Haldane to J.M. Keynes: "I tried to make him fight the matter, but he would not as he feared that the name of the woman in the case would come up." *Ibid.*, p. 13, fn 2 and p. 9. Haffenden believes that EW's relationship with Empson continued after he relocated to London and that he may have accompanied her to Berlin in 1930. I have found no evidence of this.

29. J. Haffenden (ed.), *Selected Letters of William Empson*, p. 10.

30. D. Franke, *Modernist Heresies. British Literary History 1883–1824* (Columbus, 2008), pp. 98–100.

31. Julian Trevelyan, *Indigo Days* (London, 1957; repr. Scolar 1996), p. 11. Other speakers who came in early 1930 were Naomi Mitchison and Adrian Stephen. N. Mitchison to 'Betty' [EW], n.d. but late 1929 or early 1930; A. Stephen to 'Betty', Jan. 21, 1930, I/53, I/52 Julian Trevelyan papers.

32. Julian Trevelyan, *Indigo Days*, pp. 21–46.

33. EW to Julian Trevelyan, Dec. 16, 1929; Jan. 1, 1930, Julian Trevelyan papers.

34. EW to Julian Bell, Christmas Day 1935, Julian Bell papers.

35. EW to Julian Trevelyan, Dec. 16, 1929; Jan. 1, 1930, Julian Trevelyan papers.

36. EW to Guglielmo Alberti, April 22, 1930, Alberti papers.

37. EW to Julian Trevelyan, March 17, 1930, Julian Trevelyan papers.

38. EW to Julian Trevelyan, April 5, 1930; she added: "Promise never to say you're frightened of me again." Julian Trevelyan papers.

39. EW to Julian Trevelyan, July 16, 1930; also, June 28, 1930, Julian Trevelyan papers.

40. Julian Trevelyan, *Indigo Days*, p. 32.

41. EW to Julian Trevelyan, July 16, 1930. Also, about a year later, "I have also just heard that my ridiculous father has pawned all my mother's furniture and silver so that I shan't even get a *saltspoon*. Some of the silver was beautiful and anyway I'm quite a weak fool over my mother." EW to Julian Trevelyan, Aug. 30, 1931, Julian Trevelyan papers. Her father returned to Germany and died there in December 1932.

42. EW to Julian Trevelyan, April 5 [no year given, but likely 1931], Julian Trevelyan papers.

43. She translated documents for the economist Ernest Rowe-Dutton, then financial attaché to the British Embassy, whom she described as her mentor when she first arrived in Berlin.

44. EW to Julian Trevelyan, Aug. 12, 1930 (later letters put her in Italy in December 1930). Julian Trevelyan papers.

45. Colin Storer, *Britain and the Weimar Republic: The History of a Cultural Relationship* (London, 2010). Norman Page, *Auden and Isherwood: The Berlin Years* (New York, 1998). She writes: "I never stayed in Munich for long so that I never really came to terms with its strange jumble of leftist writers and artists, clerical politicians and rabid Pan-Germans who crystallized into Nazis." EW, *The Europe I Saw*, p. 18.

46. Haffenden interview with Julian Trevelyan, John Haffenden, *William Empson, vol. 1: Among the Mandarins*, pp. 242, 612, fn 56. At the time, however, the scandal caused her a good deal of grief, some from Empson's male friends.

47. EW to Julian Trevelyan, Dec. 23, 1930, Julian Trevelyan papers.

48. EW to Julian Trevelyan, Dec. 23, 1930, Julian Trevelyan papers.

49. EW to Julian Trevelyan, Jan. 17, 1931, Julian Trevelyan papers. "Opium" refers to Cocteau's *Opium: Journal d'une désintoxication* (1930), a journal of his drug addiction and cure. Julian had given a copy to EW.

50. EW to Julian Trevelyan, Nov. 29, 1930, Julian Trevelyan papers; EW, *The Europe I Saw*, p. 24.

51. EW to Julian Trevelyan, Feb. 18, 1931, Julian Trevelyan papers.

52. EW to Julian Trevelyan, April 4, 1931 [postcard], Julian Trevelyan papers.

53. The marriage of Cambridge economist Maurice Dobb and his wife Phyllis had broken down; she was in Berlin with Trevor Blewitt whom she later married; together, they translated numerous German literary texts into English. EW to Julian Trevelyan, July 1, 1930, Julian Trevelyan papers.

54. EW, *The Europe I Saw*, p. 14.

55. EW to Julian Bell, Aug. 18, 1931, Julian Bell papers.

56. EW to Julian Trevelyan, Oct. 10, 1931, Julian Trevelyan papers; EW, *The Europe I Saw*, p. 25: "The interplay of teaching about the past and playing with the fire of the present was extraordinarily stimulating." She was uncertain about the direction of her writing and toyed with several ideas, including a "history of Germany for the fairly young." She contacted T.S. Eliot, who thought it merited discussion and suggested they meet. But Faber's board decided there was probably little prospect of success for such a book on Germany. She then wrote that she had been "reading a good deal about Catherine the Great lately which makes me contemplate a quite different piece of writing viz. about her currency and credit notions as compared with her and our contemporaries." Eliot again responded: "If you think that some of the material could be cast in the form of an article for the *Criterion* I should be interested in that, and would be in a better position to speak about the book." Nothing came of either project. T.S. Eliot to E. Wiskemann, Oct. 2, 1931; Nov. 19, 1931; Dec. 2, 1931 in V. Eliot and J. Haffenden (eds.), The Letters of T.S. Eliot, vol. 5, 1930–1931 (New Haven, 2015), pp. 676, 748, 761.

57. EW, *The Europe I Saw*, p. 17.

58. Review of Peter Gay, *Weimar Culture: The Outsider as Insider*, *Spectator*, May 22, 1969, p. 18.

59. EW, "A City Divided," *Times Literary Supplement*, July 24, 1959, p. 431.

60. EW to Julian Trevelyan, Aug. 18, 1930, Julian Trevelyan papers.

61. EW to Julian Trevelyan, Dec. 23, 1930, Julian Trevelyan papers.

62. EW to Julian Trevelyan, March 14, 1931, Julian Trevelyan papers.

63. EW to Julian Trevelyan, Oct. 31, 1931, Julian Trevelyan papers.

64. EW to Julian Trevelyan, Jan. 2, 1932, Julian Trevelyan papers.

65. EW to Julian Trevelyan, May 30, 1932, Julian Trevelyan papers.

66. EW to Julian Trevelyan, July 1 and July 16, 1931, Julian Trevelyan papers.

67. Of her evenings with Breitscheid and his wife, she wrote: "But it was saddening each time because he could see no solution; he was too obedient to the rules of his party and he was temperamentally unable to devise any ingenuity to help defeat the hostile forces whose strength gathered the moment prosperity faltered." EW, *The Europe I Saw*, p. 16.

68. EW, *The Europe I Saw*, pp. 22–3; Voigt to W.P. Crozier, July 14, 1932, *Manchester Guardian* archives: "Several times I have taken people who were incredulous to his [Hitler's] and other Nazis' meetings and in every case they have been astounded, especially at what I have referred to as the lynching spirit. A meeting addressed by Hitler, Goebbels or the other leaders is simply a mob that lynches in imagination. Ebbutt (a first-rate man, by the way) went to such a meeting for the first time a few weeks ago and told me that it made him physically sick."

69. EW, "Frederick Augustus Voigt," in E.T. Williams and H.M.Palmer (eds.), *Dictionary of National Biography*, Supplement 7: 1951–60 (Oxford, 1971), p. 1015.

70. Aside from Kingsley Martin, many of Wiskemann's friends and acquaintances were connected to the magazine, including Leonard Woolf, David Garnett, Francis Birrell, and Peter Quennel. On the weekly press: Benny Morris, *The Roots of Appeasement. The British Weekly Press and Nazi Germany* (London, 1991).

71. EW to Julian Trevelyan, June or July (unclear) 17, 1932, Julian Trevelyan papers. Kingsley Martin, like many of EW's friends, was an undergraduate at Magdalene College; his wife and sister were also at Newnham with her. EW to C.H. Rolph, Feb. 23, 1971. C.H. Rolph papers.

72. EW to J. Trevelyan, July 16, 1930, Julian Trevelyan papers. She interviewed Brüning several times after his resignation in 1932.

73. EW, "Brown Army and Iron Front," *New Statesman and Nation*, April 16, 1932, p. 473. Three months later she praised Brüning's courage in coping with mounting unemployment: shortening hours, organizing relief, creating *Arbeitsdienst*, etc. EW, "Whither Germany?" *The Nineteenth Century*, July 1932, p. 32.

74. EW, "Brown Army and Iron Front," p. 473.

75. EW, "Brown Army and Iron Front," p. 473.

76. EW, "Whither Germany?" p. 28.

77. EW, *The Europe I Saw*, p. 25.

78. EW to 'Willow,' spring 1932 (no date); 'Willow' to EW, April 23, 1932 ['Willow' was probably Mary Adams (1898–84), who had been at Newnham and joined the BBC in 1930]. Wiskemann did, however, secure some work sub-editing for Bartlett's foreign affairs program. EW to J.R. Ackerley (Talks Department), Oct. 24, 1934; EW to 'Willow' Feb. 26, 1935, March 12, 1935, and June 16, 1935. RCONT1 Radio Talks, Wiskemann 1932–61, BBC Written Archives.

79. Voigt to W.P. Crozier, Sept. 23, 1932. Also, EW to Julian Trevelyan, Sept. 15, 1932, Julian Trevelyan papers: "The Berlin correspondent of the *Manchester Guardian* offered me to be MG in Rome the other day which stirred my very guts – but I do not think the job is in his giving at all. He is, I believe, writing to the editor." Crozier had already hired someone, although some months later Alexander Werth again recommended EW: "She is, I think, a very capable journalist...and says that she would gladly go up to Manchester if there were any chance of getting the Rome job." A. Werth to W.P. Crozier, Feb. 6, 1933, Manchester Guardian Archive.

80. On Ebbutt: Frank McDonagh, "*The Times*, Norman Ebbutt and the Nazis 1927–37," *Journal of Contemporary History*, 27 (1992), pp. 407–24.

81. EW, *The Europe I Saw*, pp. 20–1.

82. Dennis Sefton Delmer (later an important figure in PWE and wartime intelligence) worked for the *Daily Express*. Some fellow journalists suspected him of being on the Nazi payroll or at least compromised by his closeness to elite Nazis.

83. E.J. Passant (1890–1959) was a fellow of Sidney Sussex College. He became head of the German section of the Foreign Office Research Department and then Foreign Office Director of Research and Librarian.

84. Ebbutt's flat was another gathering place, see the description in Martha Dodd, *Through Embassy Eyes* (New York, 1939), pp. 101–5.

85. Lilian Mowrer, *Journalist's Wife* (New York, 1937), p. 286.

86. John Gunther, "Dateline Vienna," *Harper's Magazine*, July 1935.

87. EW, *The Europe I Saw*, pp. 13, 17, 19, 21.

88. EW, *The Europe I Saw*, p. 19. Voigt's views became more conservative and Christian later. For Voigt's bed: David Ayerst, *Guardian. Biography of a Newspaper* (London, 1971), p. 501.

89. EW, *The Europe I Saw*, p. 31. Also, [Unsigned] "Reaction in Germany," *New Statesman and Nation*, July 30, 1932; [Unsigned] "Bayonets or Faction in Germany?" *New Statesman and Nation*, Sept. 17, 1932.

90. Planck and Marcks were influenced by Hans Zehrer and the group around the right-wing journal *Die Tat*. EW was clearly reading the journal. Also: EW, "Prospects for Germany," *Contemporary Review* 143 (Jan–June 1933) pp. 155–163.

91. EW, Review of Alan Bullock, *Hitler, A Study in Tyranny*, *History Today*, December 1952. On the Potempa affair: Paul Kluke, "Der Potempa Fall," Vierteljahreshefte für Zeitgeschichte, 5 (1957), pp. 279–97; David Siemens, *Stormtroopers. A New History of Hitler's Brownshirts* (New Haven, 2017).

92. For Alfred Rosenberg's defense of the SA in the *Völkischer Beobachter*, see: I. Kershaw, *Hitler: 1889–1936 Hubris* (New York, 1999), p. 383; for the solicitor: EW, *The Europe I Saw*, pp. 28–9.

93. EW to Julian Trevelyan, Sept. 15, 1932, Julian Trevelyan papers.

94. EW, *The Europe I Saw*, pp. 29–30. She wrote: "although he was notorious as a 'misogynist,' he was exquisitely good to me. I have never known anyone more civilised."

95. EW, "The Defeat of Hugenberg," *The Nineteenth Century and After*, 113 (Jan. 1933), pp. 36–46.

96. EW, "Schleicher: The Up-To-Date General," *New Statesman and Nation*, Dec. 17, 1932, pp. 789–790.

97. EW, "Schleicher: The Up-To-Date General." Her views were influenced by Erwin Planck, State Secretary in the Reichschancellory under Papen and Schleicher.

98. EW, *The Europe I Saw*, p. 30.

99. EW, "Schleicher: The Up-To-Date General," p. 789.

100. EW, "Whither Germany?" p. 33.

101. EW, "Prospects for Germany," *Contemporary Review* 143 (Jan.–June 1933), p. 157.

102. F.A. Voigt to W.P. Crozier, Dec. 4, 1932, Manchester Guardian Archive.

103. EW, "Prospects for Germany," *Contemporary Review* 143 (Jan.–June 1933), p. 163.

104. EW "The Nazi Heaven," *New Statesman and Nation*, Feb. 11, 1933, p. 153. "There has been," she wrote, "a skillfully organized Nazi stampede of the nation, by a dexterous combination of honeyed words from Hitler with the seduction of pageantry against a background of terrorism."

105. EW, *The Europe I Saw*, pp. 35–6.

106. F.A. Voigt to W.P. Crozier, March 15, 1933, Manchester Guardian Archive.

107. EW, *The Europe I Saw*, p. 34. This may have been Sefton Delmer or perhaps Rothay Reynolds, Berlin bureau chief for Lord Rothermere's *Daily Mail*.

108. EW, *The Europe I Saw*, p. 34.

109. EW, *The Europe I Saw*, pp. 34–5.

110. Heuss became the first President of the German Federal Republic in 1949; he and his wife remained friends of Wiskemann. On Stolper: Toni Stolper, *Ein Leben in Brennpunkten unserer Zeit: Gustav Stolper 1888–1947* (Tübingen, 1967). EW also remained friendly with Toni Stolper into the postwar years.

111. EW, *The Europe I Saw*, pp. 36–7.

112. EW, *The Europe I Saw*, p. 37.

113. EW,"Germany's Magna Carta," *New Statesman and Nation*, April 1, 1933, p. 404. And again April 22, "Hitler's Way": "War propaganda among the youth organizations, is particularly rampant." "Hitler has promised ten years of peace. But even should we have them, who dares to think what will follow after" (p. 497).

114. EW, *The Europe I Saw*, pp. 37–8. Geoffrey Mander, *We Were Not All Wrong* (London, 1941). She knew Sir Herbert Samuel's son Philip from Trinity, Cambridge, and also the two daughters of Lib-Lab politician Colonel Josiah Wedgwood who went to Newnham. Unfortunately, EW commented, Sir Herbert was too cautious and the Colonel too old to respond very much.

115. F.A. Voigt to W.P. Crozier, July 12, 1933; May 9, 1933; March 28, 1933; July 12, 1933; also, Voigt to Crozier, Dec. 15, 1933, Manchester Guardian Archive.

116. On her return to London, she accompanied Carl Ossietzky's fourteen-year-old daughter, Rosalinde. Her father was in a concentration camp where he would die. Wiskemann did not like the girl and rather harshly described her as "a typical product of the Berlin of the intellectuals, helping herself to everyone's cigarettes." EW, *The Europe I Saw*, p. 39. Previously editor of *Die Weltbühne*, Ossietzky was awarded a Nobel Prize in 1935.

117. [Unsigned] *New Statesman and Nation*: "Adolf Hitler Will Give You –?" May 6, 1933; EW,"Truce in Germany?" July 22, 1933 and "Nazi Laurels," Nov. 18, 1933. Also, for EW's sense of the economic and political tensions in Germany before and after the Röhm putsch: EW, "The Second Spring," *New Statesman and Nation*, April 28, 1934, pp. 630–631 and "The Riddle of Germany: Hitler or Reichswehr?" *Nineteenth Century and After* 116 (Aug. 1934), pp. 162–173.

118. EW, "On the Cultural Front: The Nazi Drive to Instill their Doctrine of Blood and Soil," *New York Times*, May 27, 1934; EW, "Woman's Changing Role in Nazi Germany," *New York Times*, Sept. 2, 1934. On the Nazi Christian movement (*Glaubensbewegung Deutsche Christen*) which sought to integrate Nazi racial doctrines and Protestantism: EW, "Germany's Second Reformation," *Contemporary Review* 145 (Jan.–June 1934).

119. Some, like Dorothy Thompson and John Gunther, attended at various times both groups. On the Café Louvre circle and foreign correspondents in Vienna from 1931 until the crisis of February 1934, see John Gunther's *roman à clef: The Lost City* (New York, 1964, although it was actually written in 1937).

120. She met Musil again in Geneva during the Second World War; he died there in exile in April 1942.

121. EW, *The Europe I Saw*, pp. 65–6.

122. EW, "Chancellor Tom Thumb," *New Statesman and Nation*, June 17, 1933.

123. EW, "Thin Ice in Austria," *New Statesman and Nation*, Dec. 30, 1933.

124. EW, "Austria and the Vatican: A Check for National Socialism?" *Nineteenth Century*, vol. 114, Jan. 1934, pp. 176–187. She also met and was impressed by the leftist Catholic Vice Mayor of Vienna, Ernst Karl Winter, who worked unsuccessfully to bring Social Democrats and Catholics into a common front to defend Austria against Nazism.

125. EW, "Catholic Austria and the Hapsburgs," *Nineteenth Century and After*, vol. 115, Jan. 1934, pp. 643–654. On Catholics in Bavaria: EW, "Persecution," *New Statesman and Nation* June 2, 1934, pp. 837–838.

126. EW, *The Europe I Saw*, p. 68. Also, similar description: EW, "The Austrian Tragedy," *New Statesman and Nation*, March 31, 1934, pp. 477–478.

127. G.E.R. Gedye, "Austria – Whose Revolt?" *New Statesman and Nation*, Feb. 24, 1934. EW "The Austrian Tragedy."

128. On Gaitskell: Philip Williams, *Hugh Gaitskell* (London, 1979), pp. 53–9; Others who were living in Vienna at the time and were associated with Gaitskell's activities were: Kim Philby and John Lehmann.

129. N. Mitchison, *Naomi Mitchison's Vienna Diary* (London, 1934). Mitchison arrived on February 26 and returned to London on March 22. The Chicago heiress Muriel Gardiner, who was living in Vienna and training as a psychoanalyst, was also active in the political underground and in touch with Gaitskell, Mitchison, Gedye, etc., see: M. Gardiner, *Code Name "Mary": Memoirs of an American Woman in the Austrian Underground* (New Haven, 1983). Muriel Gardiner's story seems to have inspired a character in Lillian Hellman's memoir *Pentimento* (1973) and subsequently the Oscar-winning film, *Julia* (1977). Hellman denied the character was based on Gardiner but never identified an alternative, nor did she explain the insertion of herself into the story. Also, Dorothy Thompson's account of the assault on Red Vienna: "A Wreath for Toni," *Harper's Magazine*, July 1934, pp. 136–47.

130. Elwyn Jones (1909–89) appears in Mitchison's diary as Glyndwr and Gaitskell as Sam. Postwar, Jones was a Labour MP, a prosecutor at Nuremberg, and Lord Chancellor (1974–79).

131. Voigt seems to be V, whose pessimism greatly disturbed Naomi Mitchison when he described both the Brown terror of Nazi Germany and the Polish atrocities against Ukrainians. Pointing to the recent bloodshed of February 6 on the streets of Paris, he mused that "the world was going fascist," and, unlike Mitchison, he placed little hope in the Soviet Union. She writes: "It was as though he had taken the lid off hell, like the fifteenth century German painters did." *Naomi Mitchison's Vienna Diary*, pp. 209–10.

132. EW, "Mittel-Europa," *New Statesman and Nation*, May 12, 1934, p. 701.

133. EW, "Repercussions in Austria," *New Statesman and Nation*, July 14, 1934, pp. 40–41.

134. EW, "Catholic Austria and the Hapsburgs," *Nineteenth Century and After*, vol. 115, Jan. 1934, pp. 652–654.

135. EW "Austria since July," *New Statesman and Nation*, Sept. 15, 1934, p. 317.

136. Via an introduction from Wheeler-Bennett, she was also able to interview Franz von Papen, now Hitler's special envoy to Austria.

137. EW "Austria since July," *New Statesman and Nation*, p. 317.

138. "Austria since July," p. 318.

139. EW, *The Europe I Saw*, pp. 69–72. Also, EW, "Will Austria Become German?" *Fortnightly*, 140, July 1936, pp. 567–574.

140. EW, "The Problem of the Saar," *New Statesman and Nation*, Jan. 13, 1934, pp. 33–34.

141. EW, "The Problem of the Saar"; also EW, "A Running Sore," *New Statesman and Nation*, Dec. 1, 1934, p. 800.

142. EW, *The Europe I Saw*, pp. 44–5. Sir Geoffrey George Knox (1884–1958). Knox was soon transferred to become British Ambassador at Budapest. Wiskemann gossiped to Julian Bell: "Also I have been seeing my old friend Knox who is now H.M. Minister at Budapest. I may tell him my dirtiest stories, so that is good." EW to Julian Bell, Christmas Day 1935, Julian Bell papers. Another person she met in the Saar was the actor James Robertson Justice, then a volunteer policeman for the League who would get drunk and disorderly and then urge her to intervene with Knox on his behalf.

As a professor at Edinburgh over two decades later she met him again when Justice was Rector of the university. EW, *The Europe I Saw*, p. 46.

143. EW, *The Europe I Saw*, p. 46.

144. [Unsigned], "The Struggle in the Saar," *New Statesman and Nation*, June 23, 1934, pp. 937–938. Also, EW, "In the Saar This Summer," *Contemporary Review* 146 (July–Dec. 1934), pp. 316–324.

145. EW, "Before the Plebiscite in the Saar," *Nineteenth Century and After* 116, Dec. 1934, p. 630.

146. [Unsigned], "The Struggle in the Saar," p. 938.

147. EW, "Before the Plebiscite in the Saar," p. 638.

148. EW, "In the Saar This Summer," p. 317.

149. [Unsigned], "The Struggle in the Saar," p. 938.

150. The Social Democratic and Communist workers were divided, but Hitler was perceived to have moved to the right with the Night of the Long Knives in which he turned against the SA.

151. EW, "The Struggle for the Saar," *New Statesman and Nation*, Oct. 6, 1934, p. 426.

152. EW, *The Europe I Saw*, pp. 44–7. Some, of course, like Voigt, Vernon Bartlett, Alexander Werth, and Kingsley Martin, were seasoned observers.

153. EW, "The Riddle of the Saar," *New Statesman and Nation*, Dec. 13, 1934, pp. 893–4.

154. EW, "A Saar Close-Up," *Contemporary Review* 147 (Jan.–June 1935), pp. 296–304 (quote from p. 304).

155. EW, "A Saar Close-Up," p. 301.

156. Shiela Grant Duff, *The Parting of Ways: A Personal Account of the Thirties* (London, 1982). Shiela's mother, Ursula Grant Duff (1885–1959), was educated at home by governesses but pushed for her daughter to attend St. Paul's school and Oxford. Ursula was active in the Abortion Law Reform Association, the birth control movement, the Eugenics Society, and the National Council of Women.

157. This is especially evident in Shiela's correspondence with her friend Diana Hubback (daughter of Eva Hubback, feminist and social reformer). Both were intensely focused on doing something of social significance; neither wanted to marry and settle down after Oxford, but rather to engage actively in politics, international affairs, or social reformism. Shiela's hope in 1934 was "to contribute something to prevent war and bring about better peace conditions in Europe, especially in Germany and Austria" (*The Parting of Ways*, p. 63). Also, Grant Duff Sokolov papers, Oxford, Box 40.

158. Shiela Grant Duff to Christopher Sykes, May 23, 1967, Box 25/5 Grant Duff Sokolov papers. Historian Agnes Headlam-Morley (1902–1986) was a fellow of St. Hugh's College, Oxford; she was appointed Montague Burton Professor of International Relations at Oxford in 1948.

159. Shiela Grant Duff, *The Parting of Ways*, chapter 8.

160. E.A. Mowrer to Shiela Grant Duff, Aug. 22, 1935, Box 2/1 Grant Duff Sokolov papers.

161. Shiela Grant Duff, *The Parting of Ways*, p. 94.

162. EW, *The Europe I Saw*, pp. 93–4.

163. EW, *The Europe I Saw*, p. 100.

164. EW to Julian Bell, Dec. 23, 1935, Julian Bell papers.

165. On British women travelers in the Balkans: J.B. Allcock and A. Young, *Black Lambs and Grey Falcons: Women Travelling in the Balkans* (Oxford/New York, 2000).

166. EW, "Yugoslavia since Marseilles," *The Political Quarterly*, 6, 3 (July 1935), pp. 369–378; EW, "Yugo-Slavia and the *Anschluss*," *Contemporary Review* 148 (July–Dec. 1935), pp. 46–54; EW, "The Elections in Yugo-Slavia," *Time and Tide*, May 4, 1935, pp. 645–646. At the year's end she published two articles on the consequences of the Ethiopian War for Austria and Yugoslavia: "Austria and the Abyssinian War," *News Chronicle*, Nov. 20, 1935, p. 14; "Yugoslavia," *News Chronicle*, Dec. 4, 1935, p. 8.

167. M.J. Bonn, *Wandering Scholar* (London, 1949); Patricia Clavin, "'A Wandering Scholar' in Britain and the USA: The Life and Work of Moritz Bonn," in Anthony Grenville (ed.), *Refugees from the Third Reich in Britain* (Amsterdam, 2003). EW was friendly with the Bonns in London until they left for the US in 1939 and seems to have remained in contact until the early 1960s.

168. David Ayerst, *Guardian. Biography of a Newspaper* (London, 1971), pp. 513–16.

169. W.P. Crozier to F.A. Voigt, June 23, 1935, Manchester Guardian Archive B/V51A 213/400. Also, Crozier to Voigt, Jan 12, 1936: "In any case what is important for you to remember is this: that you are the channel through which practically all the damning exposures of what goes on in Germany get into the paper, and it must long ago have occurred to these people – what, by the way, is true – that if they could get rid of you they would stop off the supply of damning stuff to the M.G. I hope, therefore, that you will distrust everybody and everything, and take great care not to be alone in lonely places."

170. Dorothy Thompson, "Good-bye to Germany," *Harpers Magazine*, Nov.–Dec. 1934.

171. J. Wheeler-Bennett, *Knaves, Fools and Heroes. Europe Between the Wars* (London, 1974), pp. 073–5, 91–2.

172. Frank McDonagh, "*The Times*, Norman Ebbutt and the Nazis 1927–37," *Journal of Contemporary History*, 27 (1992); EW, *The Europe I Saw*, pp. 242–4.

173. EW, "A Land Fit for Heroes," *New Statesman and Nation*, July 13, 1935, pp. 53–54, reprinted in EW, *The Europe I Saw* (Appendix), pp. 242–5. Also, on the army's position: EW, "The Will of the Führer has the Force of Law," *New Statesman and Nation*, June 21, 1934, pp. 83–84.

174. EW, "A Land Fit for Heroes," p. 53.

175. EW, "A Land Fit for Heroes," p. 53.

176. [Unsigned], "The Expansion of Germany," *New Statesman and Nation*, Dec. 7, 1935, pp. 839–40.

177. EW, *The Europe I Saw*, p. 48.

178. Including *Contemporary Review, Nineteenth Century and After, Scotsman, Spectator, Time and Tide, Manchester Guardian*.

179. Mark Cornwall, "Elizabeth Wiskemann and the Sudeten Question," pp. 74–5.

180. EW to 'Willow,' Feb. 26, 1935. She planned to visit Vienna, Zagreb, and Belgrade to report on developments in Yugoslavia (including the May elections) after the October 1934 assassination of French Foreign Minister Barthou and King Alexander of Yugoslavia in Marseille.

181. Christopher Isherwood, *Mr. Norris Changes Trains* (London, 1935), p. 35.

182. Christopher Isherwood, *Mr. Norris Changes Trains*, p. 180.

183. Christopher Isherwood, *Mr. Norris Changes Trains*, p. 186.

184. Depiction of Helen Pratt as a lower-middle-class graduate of London University was perhaps part disguise (EW was a Londoner) and possibly a dig from landed

gentry-born Isherwood. Isherwood was at Cambridge 1923–25, where he was close to Bloomsbury circles (e.g. John Lehmann and Humphrey Spender and his wife). He lived in Berlin 1929–33; there he enjoyed journalists' company and mixed with the foreign press corps. He knew Norman Ebbutt and, we are told, frequented the Taverne. He was also introduced by F.A. Voigt to William Robson Scott, a close friend of EW from her Berlin days until the late 1950s. Robson Scott, who was teaching English at the Friedrich-Wilhelm (later Humboldt) University, was portrayed as Peter Wilkinson in *Goodbye to Berlin*. Isherwood also dedicated *Lions and Shadows* (1938) to him. EW and Isherwood earned money teaching English and may well have shared students; both were also acquainted with Erika and Klaus Mann and Wilfrid Israel (depicted as Bernard Landauer). Fearful that the German police might seize them, Isherwood destroyed the diaries he kept from his Berlin years.

Chapter 2

1. J. Lehmann, *The Whispering Gallery* (London, 1955), p. 225.
2. EW [Unsigned] "The Expansion of Germany," *New Statesman and Nation*, Dec. 7, 1935. Also, EW, "The Rhineland. The Election and the Coup: Nazi Unpopularity," *The Scotsman*, March 28, 1936. EW, "Hitler's 'Rhineland Election,'" *New Statesman and Nation*, April 4, 1936, pp. 518–519: "In many families to-day politics are never mentioned, because such bitter cleavages exist, and the closest relations are afraid of one another. During the winter discontent and boredom have, of course, been increasing. The Catholic Rhineland was especially critical; in spite of Nazi attacks against Catholicism the churches were everywhere fuller than when Brüning ruled. People complained that they were taxed to death on behalf of rearmament and got nothing from it. There was certainly plenty of work at Essen or, for example, at the Opel Motor works between Frankfurt and Mainz, but Frankfurt itself, with the destruction of so many Jewish concerns, had been placed upon a special distressed-area list, while the Saarlanders (except for the metal workers) were bitterly disillusioned."
3. EW, "Between France and Germany," *Contemporary Review*, 149 (Jan.–June), 1936, p. 678.
4. She got to Switzerland slightly later (March 30), immediately after witnessing and reporting on Hitler's plebiscite to affirm his remilitarization of the Rhineland. As was often the case, she had important contacts in these areas: historian and journalist Hermann Wendel showed her around his native Metz; in Luxembourg her guides were the Vienots (especially Pierre Vienot), and through their family connection she got to tour the huge ARBED steel works; she also met the Luxembourg Prime Minister, Joseph Bech. She also had good friends in Cologne.
5. EW, "Between France and Germany," pp. 681, 685; EW, "The German Coup in France's Recovered Provinces," *Scotsman*, March 26, 1936, p. 13. Also, EW, "In the Rhineland," *New Statesman and Nation*, March 28, 1936 and "In the Rhineland Today," *Scotsman* March 30, 1936. She found greater complacency in Luxembourg.
6. EW, "Switzerland To-Day," *New Statesman and Nation*, April 18, 1936. The leader of the Nazis in Switzerland, Wilhelm Gustloff, had been assassinated a month earlier in February 1936 by a Croatian Jewish student.

7. EW, *The Europe I Saw*, p. 130.

8. EW, "Between France and Germany," p. 686; Also, much later: EW, "Two Views: Ancient and Exquisite Cities," *Times*, Feb. 15, 1964; EW, "Basle: City Rich in Colours," *Times*, Sept. 3, 1966.

9. EW, "Hitler's 'Rhineland Election,'" *New Statesman and Nation*, April 4, 1936, p. 519.

10. EW, *The Europe I Saw*, p. 52.

11. EW, "Hitler's 'Rhineland Election,'" p. 518. She found more criticism of the Nazi regime in Cologne among Catholic clergy and workers: "In Cologne one has a strong impression that the clergy is thoroughly active, and that the Nazi attacks upon the wealth of the Catholic Church have, up to the present, failed to paralyze its organization." EW, "The Rhineland, the Election and the Coup," *Scotsman*, March 28, 1936, p. 17.

12. EW, "Hitler's 'Rhineland Election,'" p. 519.

13. On the Nazification of education: EW, "The Education of the Young," *New Statesman and Nation*, May 30, 1936. EW, "Education and International Relations," *Contemporary Review*, 152 (July–Sept.) 1937. Around this time, she called in to the *Times* office in Printing House Square and editor A.L. Kennedy recorded in his diary (May 15, 1936): "Miss Whiskemann [sic!] called at the office this morning, an intelligent and nice woman of the *Manchester Guardian* type of mind. She studies German education and fully realizes the appalling outlook of superiority and defiance to which the youth of Germany is being brought up."

14. EW, "Danzig's Nazi Regime: Relations with Poland," *Scotsman*, July 25, 1935. Also, EW, "Poland and Germany Today," *Fortnightly*, 138 (July 1935), pp. 304–313.

15. EW, *The Europe I Saw*, pp. 49–50.

16. He later wrote two very influential analyses of Nazism: *Die Revolution des Nihilismus. Kulisse und Wirklichkeit im Dritten Reich* (Zurich, 1938; English translation 1939) and *Gespräche mit Hitler* (Zurich, 1940; English translation 1940); also *Die konservative Revolution: Versuch und Bruch mit Hitler* (New York, 1941; English translation same year).

17. EW, *The Europe I Saw*, pp. 49–50. Returning to London, she informed Rex Leeper at the Foreign Office of her conversations with Rauschning and delivered messages for him and Vansittart.

18. EW, "The Conflict in Memel," *Contemporary Review*, 148 (July–Dec.) 1935, pp. 531–538; also, EW, "The Struggle for Memel: A Broken Statute," *Scotsman*, Aug. 2, 1935 and "Memel – Land of Spies," *News Chronicle*, Aug. 16, 1935. In Memel she was subjected to a barrage of propaganda from both Lithuanians and Germans and came away appalled by both sides. There was little room for a moderate middle between the extremes. The Lithuanians feared that at any moment they could become Hitler's Abyssinians, while the Germans there had no idea that the oppressive aspects of Lithuanian rule were everyday reality in the German Reich. EW, "What of Memel?" *Time and Tide*, Aug. 3, 1935.

19. Through the efforts of Wiskemann, Voigt, and other journalists, these representatives met with Lord Cecil of the League of Nations Union and Labour party people. Their timing was inauspicious: King George V had died, Parliament was on its Christmas break, and the Ethiopian crisis was preoccupying the government. Also, Polish leader Beck's aim was to accommodate the new Germany. M. Andrzejewski, *Opposition und*

Widerstand in Danzig 1933 bis 1939 (Bonn, 1994), p. 114; D. Gazeby, *The Last General Secretary. Sean Lester and the League of Nations* (Dublin, 1999), p. 131. When the *Manchester Guardian*'s Geneva correspondent, Robert Dell, visited England in August 1936, he wrote: "I find opinion here worse than I thought. The ignorance of people that ought to be well-informed about the real situation on the Continent is alarming and the apparent indifference to what may happen even more so." He added that Hitler "is likely to be master of Europe in about six months without firing a shot." R. Dell to W.P. Crozier, Manchester Guardian Archives.

20. In June 1936 Berlin sent the naval cruiser *Leipzig* to Danzig and its commander was ordered not to call on Lester, a deliberate insult; local Nazis were also intent on boycotting the High Commissioner. Marit Fosse and John Fox, *Sean Lester: The Guardian of a Small Flickering Light* (Lanham, MD 2016).

21. EW, "Danzig Situation. Fight for the Freedom of the City: Mr. Sean Lester's Task," *Scotsman*, July 14, 1936.

22. EW, "The Free City of Danzig," *New Statesman and Nation*, July 18, 1936. EW, "Poland and Germany Today," *Fortnightly*, 148 (July 1935), pp. 304–313. EW, "City in Fetters – and They Call It Free!" *Daily Herald*, July 16, 1936.

23. EW, *The Europe I Saw*, p. 54. In fact, she had been under surveillance for six months: Wiskemann's police file included a Feb. 17, 1936, letter from the Bavaria Political Police to numerous police and official agencies in the Reich to the effect that two of her July 1935 articles had "reviled" National Socialism "in unexampled fashion." It added that if she returned to the Reich, "it is to be reported at once without preventing her entry into Germany." Wiskemann, *The Europe I Saw*, pp. 240–1 (Appendix 1). Also, EW's review of I.A. Morrow, *The Peace Settlement in the German-Polish Borderlands* (Oxford, 1936) in *New Statesman and Nation*, Aug. 15, 1936, pp. 227–228.

24. EW, *The Europe I Saw*, pp. 42, 54–5. Peter Day, *The Bedbug: Klop Ustinov: Britain's Most Ingenious Spy* (London, 2014). Ustinov continued working at the embassy until 1935 and, together with his diplomat friend Wolfgang von Putlitz, supplied MI5 with important information. During the war and after, Ustinov continued to work for the British secret service.

25. EW, *The Europe I Saw*, p. 55.

26. Ebbutt reached the First Secretary, Ivone Kirkpatrick, and the Military Attaché. For Kirkpatrick, see his memoir, *The Inner Circle* (London, 1959).

27. EW, *The Europe I Saw*, pp. 54–9.

28. "Englishwoman's Berlin Arrest: Questions about a Review Article," *Observer*, July 12, 1936, p. 20; "Englishwoman Arrested in Berlin," *Times*, July 13, 1936; "London Teacher's Arrest. Berlin Interrogation," *Manchester Guardian*, July 13 and 14, 1936; "London Girl Arrested in Berlin by Secret Police," *Evening Standard*, July 11, 1936, p. 1; "Woman Grilled by Nazis is Going Back," *Daily Herald*, July 15, 1936. The *Sunday Times* gave an accurate description of her arrest, release, and expulsion from Germany, ending with the patronizing comment: "Miss Wiskemann was then able to return to the polishing of her nails, an operation which the untimely intrusion of politics had interrupted." "Secret Police Arrest London Girl," *Sunday Times*, July 12, 1936. A week later, the newspaper (owned by the Camrose, Kemsley brothers and edited by W.W. Hadley) corrected its earlier description of her as "a socialist writer and

economist," noting that she was a student of international relations without party affiliation. "Arrested in Berlin," *Sunday Times*, July 19, 1936.

29. Parl. Deb. Commons, July 20, 1936, questions put by Mr Vyvyan Adams (Conservative MP) to Mr Anthony Eden. Adams also suggested to Winston Churchill that he see Wiskemann: "She has a great deal of information about the position of Danzig, and I thought you would be interested if she passed it on to you first-hand. I hope you will be able to see her." In the end, because of pressing political and literary work, Churchill was unable to talk to her. Adams to Churchill, July 15, 1936; Wiskemann to Churchill, July 16 and 23, 1936; Churchill (private sec.) to Wiskemann, July 24, 1936. W.S. Churchill papers, CHAR 2/275, Churchill College, Cambridge University.

30. EW to Julian Bell, Dec. 14, 1936, Julian Bell papers.

31. EW, *The Europe I Saw*, p. 60.

32. 'Rex' Leeper also played a role in Wiskemann's wartime career as head of the Political Intelligence section of the Foreign Office. He was a close confidant of Sir Robert Vansittart, Permanent Under-Secretary at the Foreign Office 1930–38 and a fierce opponent of Appeasement.

33. EW, "Poland's Camp of National Unity," *Fortnightly*, 142 (July 1937), pp. 41–51; EW, "Poland and the Colonels," *New Statesman and Nation*, April 24, 1937; EW, "Poland after Pilsudski," *Scotsman*, April 14, 1937; EW, "The Abortive March on Budapest," *New Statesman and Nation*, March 27, 1937; EW, "The Nazis and Rumania," *New Statesman and Nation*, June 20, 1936; EW, "Rumania without Titulescu," *New Statesman and Nation*, Nov. 7, 1936; EW, "From Masaryk to Beneš," *Contemporary Review* 149 (Jan.–June 1936), pp. 154–161; EW, "The Little Entente," *Contemporary Review* 150 (July–Dec.), 1936, pp. 675–685; "German Minorities and the Little Entente," *New Statesman and Nation*, Jan. 11, 1936. EW, "Germany, Hungary, Rumania," *Hungarian Quarterly* 3,1 (Jan. 1937), pp. 71–78.

34. EW, "Will Austria Become German?" *Fortnightly*, 140 (July 1936), pp. 567–574. EW, "Germany and Austria," *New Statesman and Nation*, Oct. 3, 1936; EW, "Dr. Schuschnigg and His Neighbours," *New Statesman and Nation*, June 5, 1937. EW, "Austrian Independence: Schuschnigg's Firm Stand," *Scotsman*, June 1, 1937.

35. EW, "Czechoslovakia Prepares," *New Statesman and Nation*, Oct. 31, 1936, p. 659.

36. EW, *The Europe I Saw*, p. 94.

37. EW, "From Masaryk to Beneš," *Contemporary Review* 149 (Jan.–June), 1936, p. 154.

38. EW, *The Europe I Saw*, pp. 74–5; EW, *The Rome-Berlin Axis* (Oxford, 1949), p. 116. In 1934 when American journalist Hubert Knickerbocker asked European political leaders if they thought another war might break out, only two—Thomas Masaryk and Admiral Horthy of Hungary—replied there would be no war. H.R. Knickerbocker, *Will War Come to Europe?* (London, 1934).

39. EW, *The Europe I Saw*, p. 76. Her journalist friend Darsie Gillie sent her to the Ripkas.

40. Keith G. Robbins, "Konrad Henlein, the Sudeten Question and British Foreign Policy," *The Historical Journal*, 12, 4 (1969), pp. 674–697. The Henlein movement was receiving Nazi subsidies from 1934. How much control that gave Berlin is questionable, but certainly it grew dramatically from 1937. The French military attaché in Prague, General Faucher, whom Wiskemann knew and admired, reported to Paris by 1935 that Henlein was receiving Nazi funds. The Foreign Office was also aware by 1937 that Henlein's denials were lies.

41. Addison informed the Foreign Office that "order, method, punctuality, honesty in dealing with one's fellow human beings are as alien to the Slav character as water to a cat." I. Lukes and E. Goldstein, *The Munich Crisis of 1938: Prelude to War* (New York, 1999), p. 259.

42. Aside from Wiskemann: Elizabeth Monroe, Doreen Warriner, Elisabeth Barker, Margery Perham, Agnes Headlam-Morley, and Margaret Cleeve.

43. The other two were: Ian Morrow, *The Peace Settlement in the German-Polish Borderlands* (1936) and C.A. Macartney, *Hungary and her Successors* (1937).

44. EW, *The Europe I Saw*, p. 51.

45. A. Crozier, "Chatham House and Appeasement," in Andrea Bosco and Cornelia Navari (eds.), *Chatham House and British Foreign Policy 1919–1945* (London, 1994), pp. 205–259.

46. EW, *Czechs and Germans: A Study of the Struggle in the Historic Provinces of Boehmia and Moravia*, preface to the second edition, p. vii. (London, 1966). EW, *The Europe I Saw*, p. 82.

47. Jocelyn to A.J. Toynbee, Feb. 10, 1937, Chatham House (RIIA) Archives 16/23 (Elizabeth Wiskemann, "Czechs and Germans").

48. H. Josephine Pybus to A.J. Toynbee, Feb 11, 1937, Chatham House (RIIA) Archives 16/23.

49. EW to A.J. Toynbee, Feb. 9, 1937, Chatham House (RIIA) Archives 16/23.

50. D. Cameron Watt, "Women in International History," *Review of International Studies*, 22 (1996), p. 436.

51. A.J. Toynbee to EW, Feb. 19, 1937; EW to A.J. Toynbee, Feb. 22, 1937, Chatham House (RIIA) Archives 16/23.

52. Shiela Grant Duff, *The Parting of Ways*, p. 116.

53. Shiela Grant Duff to Diana Hubback, Aug. 29, 1936, Box 40/1 Shiela Grant Duff papers. For letters, etc. introducing her: Box 1/folders 1–2.

54. Shiela Grant Duff papers Box 6 (Ripka correspondence); Box 2/3 (letters concerning her work in Prague and Germany 1934–46). Shiela Grant Duff to Diana Hubback, Nov. 22, 1936, Box 40/1.

55. Shiela Grant Duff to Diana Hubback, Aug. 29, 1936, Box 40/1.

56. Shiela Grant Duff to Diana Hubback, Sept. 24, 1936, Box 40/1.

57. Shiela Grant Duff to Diana Hubback, Nov. 22, 1936, Box 40/1.

58. Shiela Grant Duff to E.A. Mowrer, Feb. 5, 1937, Box 2/1.

59. Shiela Grant Duff, *The Parting of Ways*, pp. 148–50.

60. Shiela Grant Duff to E.A. Mowrer, n. d., probably end of February 1937, Box 2/1.

61. EW to Shiela Grant Duff, March 24, 1937, Box 2/4.

62. E.A. Mowrer to Shiela Grant Duff, April 5, 1937, Box 2/1.

63. Shiela Grant Duff to J.L. Garvin, May 24, 1937, Box 2/5.

64. Shiela Grant Duff papers: Box 2/2 (press cuttings on the Saar 1935, etc.); Box 2/4; Box 3/4–5 (Churchill correspondence).

65. EW, *Czechs and Germans*, preface to the second edition, p. viii.

66. EW, *The Europe I Saw*, p. 83. Otakar Odlozilik (1899–1973), Czech historian and archivist; he was an expert on Protestantism in Bohemia and Moravia and wrote about the Hussite movement. After the Second World War, he moved to the United States and taught at Columbia and the University of Pennsylvania.

67. EW, *The Europe I Saw*, p. 84. Addison was removed from Prague in 1936 because of his evident hostility toward Czechs and Beneš; he was posted to Chile but chose to retire from the diplomatic service instead. Prior to service in Prague, he had spent seven years in Berlin and two in the Baltic states, tours of duty that reinforced his sympathy for Germans and racial disdain for Slavs. His deputy, Robert Hadow, remained in Prague until October 1937, when he returned to London. In August 1937 Hadow had written to Sir Anthony Eden that Wiskemann had "taken somewhat violent exception to any suggestions I made" (quoted by Mark Cornwall, "Elizabeth Wiskemann and the Sudeten Question," p. 63). Addison's successor was Sir Basil Newton, whom EW had known as head of Chancery in Berlin; she said he told her he didn't read books and asked for a four-page guide to Czech-German relations.

68. Before researching her book, EW had written several articles on Czechoslovakia: "Masaryk's Resignation," *New Statesman and Nation*, Dec. 21, 1935; "From Masaryk to Benes," *Contemporary Review* 149 (Jan.–June), 1936; "German Minorities and the Little Entente," *New Statesman and Nation*, Jan. 11, 1936; "Czechoslovakia Prepares," *New Statesman and Nation*, Oct. 31, 1936; "Czech and German," *New Statesman and Nation*, April 17, 1937.

69. Mark Cornwall, "Elizabeth Wiskemann and the Sudeten Question: A Woman at the 'Essential Hinge' of Europe," *Central Europe*, 1,1 (May 2003), p. 59. [Cornwall fn: V. Král (ed), *Die deutschen in der Tschechoslowakei 1933-1947* (Prague, 1964), document 47, p. 100, Rutha to Sudetendeutsche Partei leadership, June 1936].

70. EW, *Czechs and Germans*, preface to the second edition, p. x.

71. Cornwall, "Elizabeth Wiskemann and the Sudeten Question," p. 62.

72. EW, *The Europe I Saw*, p. 88.

73. EW, *Czechs and Germans*, preface to the second edition, p. ix.

74. Cornwall, "Elizabeth Wiskemann and the Sudeten Question," p. 61. EW was not Jewish.

75. EW, *The Europe I Saw*, p. 90.

76. Cornwall, "Elizabeth Wiskemann and the Sudeten Question," p. 61.

77. On the Küdlich affair: Cornwall, "Elizabeth Wiskemann and the Sudeten Question," pp. 62–5. Without naming Küdlich, Wiskemann's *Czechs and Germans* (pp. 231–4, 261–2) used him as a source for Czech mismanagement of communal relations in the area and deliberately rough police methods in Ostrava. Küdlich was well known in the area for having acted as defense lawyer for schoolteacher Richard Patscheider. Patscheider moved to Troppau from the Tyrol and became involved in pro-Nazi and anti-Czech activities in Silesia. He was convicted of treason in 1935 but then escaped from prison and gained political asylum in Nazi Germany, where he worked for the Sudeten Homeland Association in Bavaria.

78. Cornwall, "Elizabeth Wiskemann and the Sudeten Question," p. 64.

79. Cornwall, "Elizabeth Wiskemann and the Sudeten Question," p. 65, and fns 47, 48.

80. Cornwall, "Elizabeth Wiskemann and the Sudeten Question," p. 65.

81. EW, *Czechs and Germans*, preface to the second edition, p. x.

82. The meeting is named after the military adjutant, Colonel Hossbach, who took notes and authored a memorandum. See J. Noakes and G. Pridham (eds), *Nazism 1919-1945. 3: Foreign Policy, War and Racial Extermination* (Exeter, 1988), pp. 679–91.

83. G.E.R. Gedye papers, Imperial War Museum (documents 22,580) contain an unpublished account of his escape.
84. EW, *Czechs and Germans*, p. 283.
85. Mark Cornwall, "A Fluctuating Barometer. British Diplomatic Views of the Czech-German Relationship in Czechoslovakia 1918–1938," in Eva Schmidt-Hartmann and Stanley B. Winters (eds.), *Grossbritannien, die USA und die böhmischen Länder 1848–1938* (Munich, 1991), pp. 313–333.
86. EW, *The Europe I Saw*, p. 85.
87. Cornwall, "Elizabeth Wiskemann and the Sudeten Question," p. 66. The head of the Southern Department of the Foreign Office also commented that Wiskemann was "a dangerous busybody journalist."
88. On Hadow: Lindsay M. Eades, *Portrait of An Appeaser: Robert Hadow, First Secretary in the British Foreign Office, 1931–1939* (Westport CT and London, 1996).
89. Hadow to Toynbee, Dec. 30, 1937, RIIA [Chatham House] archive 16/23, includes Hadow's notes on chapter one. The final published version was altered, but still referred to the Germans as 'colonists.' EW's source was Professor Wilhelm Wostry, head of the Verein fur Geschichte der Deutschen in Böhmen.
90. F. Ashton-Gwatkin to A.J. Toynbee, Jan. 6, 1938, RIIA [Chatham House] archive 16/23. Ashton-Gwatkin was soon to accompany Lord Runciman on his mission to Czechoslovakia.
91. A.J. Toynbee to Hadow, March 11, 1938, RIIA [Chatham House] archive 16/23.
92. A. Crozier, "Chatham House and Appeasement," in Andrea Bosco and Cornelia Navari (eds.), *Chatham House and British Foreign Policy 1919–1945* (London, 1994). Toynbee's articles in the *Economist*, July 10 and 24, 1937.
93. Hadow to A.J. Toynbee, May 16, 1938, RIIA [Chatham House] archive 16/23. The Hadow Affair should be placed in the larger context of governmental efforts under Chamberlain to control the media and the flow of news reporting. This involved flattery and access, telephone calls to press owners and editors, and censorship of the BBC aimed at excluding anti-Appeasement views and dampening criticism of the Nazi regime.
94. A.J. Toynbee to Hadow, May 19, 1938, RIIA [Chatham House] archive 16/23.
95. A.J. Toynbee to I. Macadam, May 17, 1938, RIIA [Chatham House] archive 16/23.
96. A.J. Toynbee to I. Macadam, May 17, 1938, RIIA [Chatham House] archive 16/23.
97. When D.C. Watt, in a book about postwar British attitudes towards Germany, seemed to lump Wiskemann together with Toynbee, she responded angrily in a review in the *Listener*, Feb. 11, 1965, p. 237.
98. Paul Vysny, *The Runciman Mission to Czechoslovakia, 1938: Prelude to Munich* (New York, 2003). J.K. Roberts and Sir L. Mallet acquired the book for the FO library and alerted Runciman to it.
99. A member of the Runciman Commission, whom EW had known for some years, Robert Stopford, did consult her "without much conviction." Later, she wrote, he was so remorseful about what happened to Czechoslovakia that he worked closely with Doreen Warriner to bring Czech refugees to Britain, despite the Home Office's lack of enthusiasm. EW, "Munich and After," *New Statesman and Nation*, Nov. 1, 1968, p. 587.
100. The influential Foreign Office official Frank Roberts also wrote that "it gave a very good and unbiassed picture of the Czech problem." M. Cornwall, "Elizabeth

Wiskemann and the Sudeten Question," p. 55 [Cornwall source: fn 4: FO 371/21761, C 5651/4770/18, Minute by Roberts, June 7, 1938]. After the appearance of her book EW continued to report on the crisis: EW, "Germany and the Czechs: How Prague met the recent crisis," *Scotsman* June 3, 1938, p. 13; "Czechoslovakia and Her Future," *Fortnightly* 144 (July 1938), pp. 57–65.

101. *Manchester Guardian*, July 8, 1938 (review by F.A. Voigt). *Sunday Times*, Aug. 21, 1938 (review by David Stephens).

102. George Glasgow, "Germans and Czechs: An Old Problem," *Observer*, June 19, 1938.

103. *Times*, June 4, 1938; *Nation* Aug. 13, 1938, p. 159; *Spectator* (R.W. Seton-Watson), July 1, 1938, p. 25.

104. *Daily Telegraph*, July 5, 1938 (by J.C. Johnstone, author of *Germany: Hammer or Anvil?* London, 1939). There were also many academic reviews, e.g. *American Sociological Review*, 4, 3 (June 1939), pp. 421–2 (by Oscar Jaszi); *The Slavonic and East European Review*, 17, 49 (July 1938), pp. 239–40.

105. E.H. Carr to A.J. Toynbee, Nov. 19, 1938, RIIA 4/Carr, Chatham House Archives.

106. The level of EW's activity for the Czech Association is unclear. Indicative perhaps of her prominence is the curious part-fiction, part-diary *Peterley Harvest*, published under a pseudonym in 1960. Its author was probably Richard Pennington, who was librarian at the National Liberal Club and in May 1938 became secretary of the Czech Association. The 'diarist' describes several meetings with EW to discuss the Association, its aims, and differences of opinion within it. Peterley Harvest. The Private Diary of David Peterley (London: Penguin Classics, 1985, preface by Michael Holroyd), pp. 215, 225, 227–8, 229, 233, 238, 242.

107. C.H. Rolph, *Kingsley. The Life, Letters and Diaries of Kingsley Martin* (London, 1973), pp. 237–46.

108. *New Statesman and Nation*, Aug. 27, 1938, p. 301.

109. Robert Skidelsky, *John Maynard Keynes: Fighting for Britain 1937–1946* (London, 2000), pp. 35–7.

110. Others who lodged protests were Aylmer Vallance, Raymond Mortimer, Leonard Woolf, Profs J.D. Bernal and Lancelot Hogben, and Professor Vocadlo from Prague.

111. For his biography, Rolph interviewed Wiskemann several times. C.H. Rolph papers SX Ms55/1/1/115. After Rebecca West was particularly damning in her assessment of Kingsley (R. West to Rolph, n. d., 1971), Rolph replied: "Your response delighted me. I've been getting panegyrics from everyone. Well, except perhaps Malcolm Muggeridge and poor Elizabeth Wiskemann [a reference to her suicide], both of whom seem to have seen the side of him that presented itself to you. He wasn't as bad, I think, as Beaverbrook – now that was an evil man." (Rolph to Rebecca West, Nov. 7, 1971). Michael Ratcliffe (literary editor of the *Times* and theatre critic of the *Observer*) recalled that she "used to speak of Kingsley Martin's editorial compromise over Czechoslovakia in 1938 when her own observed evidence was set aside, as if it only happened a few weeks previously, and she was ready to argue it out again with him at any time…" M. Ratcliffe, "The Editor and His Conscience," *Times*, April 12, 1973.

112. EW, *The Europe I Saw*, p. 91; EW, "1938: Was the Left as Ignorant as Chamberlain?" *Times* (London), April 6, 1968, p. 21.

113. Shiela Grant Duff, *Europe and the Czechs* (London, 1938); also, Diplomaticus (pseud. Konni Zilliacus), *The Czechs and Their Minorities* (London, 1938). Eunice Frost for

Penguin Books to Shiela Grant Duff, Dec. 1, 1938, Box 4/folder 3, Shiela Grant
Duff papers.

114. Shiela Grant Duff to Victor Gordon Lennox, Aug. 7, 1936; Shiela Grant Duff to David
Scott Fox, April 2, 1938. Shiela Grant Duff papers, Box 2/4. This contained the
undated letter to Hadow. Grant Duff was close friends with David Scott Fox, a young
diplomat in Prague, despite their strong differences over British foreign policy. It is
not clear that this letter to Hadow was sent; she may have sent it to Scott Fox on April 2
for his opinion. She was particularly enraged at Hadow's claim that he was "defending" men like her father who had died in the previous war against her. To Lennox,
who wrote for the *Daily Telegraph*, she complained: "It is very difficult to become a
journalist and I am not becoming it at all well. I write very little and when I do the
Observer does not print it... The legation is not at all what you pictured it as being
and is intensely suspicious of me. Hadow would help me perhaps if I asked definite
things, but nothing is volunteered. He thinks I am prejudiced and am earnest and
sighs that you, at any rate, were never earnest" (Aug. 7, 1936).

115. Morley College for Working Men and Women, autumn 1937 series on the
Contemporary World. A later series in spring 1939 included Freda Utley, Cecil
Sprigge, Elizabeth Monroe, Madeleine Kent, and Sir Bernard Pares. Eva Hubback, the
mother of Grant Duff's close friend Diana, went to Newnham, taught there and
became Principal of Morley College in 1927.

116. The summer school's focus was contemporary dictatorships and their challenge to
liberal democracy and justice. Participants included F.A. Voigt, Francis Muir, Moritz
Bonn, Lord Samuel, Geoffrey Crowther, Sir Archibald Sinclair, Roy Harrod, and Sir
Walter Layton. *Manchester Guardian*, July 28 (p. 5) and Aug. 2, 1938 (p. 12).

117. She also lectured at women's colleges, including Bryn Mawr and Radcliffe. *Bryn
Mawr Alumni Bulletin 1939*.

118. EW, *The Europe I Saw*, p. 92.

119. *Scarsdale Inquirer*, 42, November 18, 1938.

120. EW to Hamilton Fish Armstrong, Dec. 20, 1938, Hamilton Fish Armstrong papers.

121. EW to Hamilton Fish Armstrong, Dec. 20, 1938. Clarence Streit (1896–1986) was a
journalist and an Atlanticist, who founded the Federal Union. After covering the
League of Nations in Geneva, he became a strong advocate of a union of democracies, modeled on American federalism. His 1938 book *Union Now* was a huge
best-seller.

122. M. Newman, "British Socialists and the Question of European Unity, 1939–45" and
R.A. Wilford, "The Federal Union Campaign" in *European Studies Review*, 10, 1
(1980) pp. 75–100 and pp. 101–114. P. Wilson, "The New European Debate in
Wartime Britain," in P. Murray and P. Rich (eds.), *Visions of European Unity* (Boulder,
CO, 1996), pp. 39–62. R.M. Douglas, *The Labour Party, Nationalism and
Internationalism 1939–1951* (London, 2004). Supporters of the Federal Union cam-
paign in Britain included G.D.H. Cole, C.E.M. Joad, Barbara Wootton, William
Beveridge, Julian Huxley, Leonard Woolf, and Kingsley Martin.

123. EW to Margaret Cleeve (of Chatham House), Oct. 9, 1938. She was approached about
at least four books "with quite good advances." She did not know whether she was
free to consider these offers. "On the other hand I can't afford to reject them all unless

I know that I'm otherwise employed." RIIA [Chatham House] archive 16/23. EW, *The Europe I Saw*, p. 92.

124. EW–Alan Harris (Duckworth editor) correspondence June 1938–Feb. 1939, MS 959/109; 959/119; 959/1/137, Gerald Duckworth & Co. Archive. Harris responded: "Very well, OH BUSINESS WOMAN, I give it up – needless to say with the very greatest regret." A. Harris to EW, Feb. 1, 1939, Duckworth & Co. Archive.

125. EW, *Undeclared War* (New York, 1939). Also, her two excellent articles for *Foreign Affairs* evaluating the social and economic consequences of Munich and Prague: EW, "Czechs and Germans after Munich," *Foreign Affairs*, 17, 2 (Jan. 1939), pp. 291–304; EW, "The *Drang nach Osten* Continues," *Foreign Affairs*, 17, 4 (July 1939), pp. 764–773.

126. EW, *Undeclared War*. Aside from *Foreign Affairs*, she also completed several articles for other periodicals and papers: *Nation*; *Fortnightly Review*; *Spectator*; *Scotsman*; *New Statesman and Nation*. On Nazi efforts to destabilize Poland and Romania by advancing the cause of Ukrainian nationalism: EW, "Greateer Ukrainia," *Nation* 145, 9 (Feb. 25, 1939), pp. 224–227.

127. R. Vambery, "An Epilogue to Peace," *Nation*, 150, 8 (Feb. 24, 1940), p. 284.

128. EW, "The Fathers of German National Socialism," *The Nineteenth Century and After*, 125 (Jan. 1939), pp. 446–456.

129. EW, *Undeclared War*, p. 262 and Introduction to the second edition (1967), p. ix. She contrasted the quality of *Menschenwürde* or human dignity, as embodied in the Swiss poet Gottfried Keller and the historian Jacob Burckhardt, to the dehumanizing process of National Socialism.

130. The title was soon changed, once the real war began, to *Prologue to War*.

131. This was also the verdict many years later of her friend and Sussex colleague Christopher Thorne, "Versailles to Potsdam," *Spectator* April 22, 1966, p. 504.

132. *Observer*, Jan. 7, 1940, p. 3 (Keith Feiling); *New Statesman and Nation*, Nov. 18, 1939, p. 718 (Coventry); *Manchester Guardian*, Dec. 27, 1939, p. 3 (Voigt); *Spectator*, Nov. 9, 1939, p. 22 (Wickham Steed). Sir Lewis Namier and Sir Ronald Storrs, both friends, also expressed great admiration for the book, as did Rustem Vambery, the exiled Hungarian professor of criminal law. R. Vambery, "An Epilogue to Peace," *Nation*, Feb. 24, 1940, pp. 283–4: "her book reveals the most stupendous knowledge of the turmoil in all those countries east and west of the axis upon which Nazi imperialism is anxious to bestow its benefits." Academic reviews included: *Journal of Modern History*, 13, 1 (March 1941), by Bernadotte Schmitt; *Annals of the American Academy of Political and Social Science*, 210 (July 1940), by Hans Kohn; *Politique étrangere*, 5, 1 (Feb. 1940), by J.P. Buisson; *The Slavonic Year Book*, vol. 19, 53–4 (1939–40), by W.J. Rose; *International Affairs*, vol. 18, 6 (Nov.–Dec. 1939), by R.W. Seton-Watson; Waldemar Gurian, "Some Problems of War," *The Review of Politics*, 2, 2 (April 1940). Also, R.E. Lengyel, "How Nazism Works," *New York Times*, March 3, 1940, p. 93.

133. Julie V. Gottlieb, '*Guilty Women, Foreign Policy and Appeasement in Inter-War Britain* (London, 2015); also, "'Broken Friendships and Vanished Loyalties': Gender, Collective (In)Security and Anti-Fascism in Britain in the 1930s," *Politics, Religion & Ideology*, 13, 2 (June 2012), pp. 197–219; "Varieties of Feminist Responses to Fascism in Interwar Britain," in N. Copley and A. Olechnowicz (eds.), *Varieties of Anti-Fascism. Britain in the Inter-War Period* (New York, 2010), pp. 101–118. Carol Miller,

"'Geneva – The Key to Equality': Inter-war Feminists and the League of Nations," *Women's History Review* 3, 2 (1994), pp. 219–245. Deborah Van Seters, "Women's Foreign Policy Advocacy in 1930s Britain," Ph.D. diss, University of Toronto, 1999. Helen McCarthy, *The British People and the League of Nations. Democracy, Citizenship and Internationalism c. 1918–45* (Manchester, 2011), especially chapter 7.

134. "Books and Exhibitions of the Year," *Times*, Jan. 2, 1939, p. 42.

135. Catherine Clay, *Time and Tide. The Feminist and Cultural Politics of a Modern Magazine* (Edinburgh, 2018).

136. Vera Brittain papers, cited by R. Overy, *The Morbid Age: Britain between the Wars* (London, 2009), p. 247.

137. Storm Jameson's path from pacifism to a belief that war was inevitable and necessary can be traced in her correspondence; she finally broke with pacifism after Munich.

138. EW to J.G. Crowther, Nov. 6, 1934, J.G. Crowther papers.

139. EW to 'Willow' [Mary Adams], June 16, 1935. RCONT1 Radio Talks, Elizabeth Wiskemann. BBC Archives. J.R. Ackerley was editor of the BBC's magazine, the *Listener*.

140. EW to Julian Bell, Christmas Day 1935, Julian Bell papers.

141. EW to Julian Bell, Dec. 14, 1936, Julian Bell papers. Graham Bell was from South Africa and unrelated to Julian. Julia Strachey was Lytton's flamboyant niece; she was a novelist and had worked as a model for the fashion designer Poiret.

142. Christopher Andrew, *Her Majesty's Secret Service. The Making of the British Intelligence Community* (New York, 1986), p. 415.

143. F.A. Voigt's book *Unto Caesar* (London, 1938) examined the similarities between Bolshevism and Nazism, which he viewed as revolutionary, totalitarian regimes and secular religions.

144. EW to L. Miall, Aug. 25, 1939 (answering Miall's note of Aug. 22), RCONT1 Talks Dept. Elizabeth Wiskemann file 1, BBC Written Archives.

Chapter 3

1. Initially she contemplated another American tour to publicize the book. EW to Robert Bendiner, managing editor of the *Nation*, July 19, 1939, The Nation Archive, Houghton Library, Harvard University.

2. Some scholars criticized Toynbee's decision to in effect turn Chatham House into a quasi-governmental research organization. Doreen Warriner, for example, decided to resign her membership, informing Margaret Cleeve: "At the time of Munich some correspondence I had with Sir John Hope Simpson led me to feel some misgiving about the danger that Chatham House might be too much under the influence of circles too closely in sympathy with the policy of appeasement, and now I feel that the present function of Chatham House, however useful, does destroy its independence and does indicate a departure from principles which I understood it was founded to promote." D. Warriner to M. Cleeve, June 30, 1940. 4/WARR, Chatham House Archives.

3. R.H. Keyserlingk, "Arnold Toynbee's Foreign Research and Press Service, 1939–43 and its Post-war Plans for South-east Europe," *Journal of Contemporary History* 21

(1986), pp. 539–558. Christopher Brewin, "Arnold Toynbee, Chatham House, and Research in a Global Context," in D. Long and P. Wilson (eds.), *Thinkers of the Twenty Years' Crisis: Inter-War Idealism* Reassessed (Oxford, 1995), pp. 277–301. The Foreign Office chose Toynbee's team in preference to a rival bid from London University under E.H. Carr. Academics associated with it included: G.N. Clark, C.K. Webster, Sir Alfred Zimmern, C.A. Macartney, and B.H. Sumner. Also, C. Thorne, "Chatham House, Whitehall and Far Eastern Issues, 1941–1945," *International Affairs*, 54 (1978), pp. 1–29.

4. MI5, for example, had a total staff of thirty-six officers.

5. Anthony Read and David Fisher, *Colonel Z. The Life and Times of a Master of Spies* (London, 1985).

6. Christopher Andrew, *Her Majesty's Secret Service. The Making of the British Intelligence Community* (New York, 1985); Keith Jeffery, *MI6. The History of the Secret Intelligence Service 1909–1949* (London, 2010); on Dansey and much else: Anthony Read and David Fisher, *Colonel Z.* ; Wesley Wark, *The Ultimate Enemy: British Intelligence and Nazi Germany* 1933–1939 (Ithaca, NY, 1985).

7. EH was the Department of Propaganda in Enemy Countries. It was soon merged with two other departments (Section D, created by MI6, and MI/R, created by the War Office) and absorbed into the Special Operations Executive (SOE.). F.A. Voigt also worked for EH early in the war. For an account of the squabbling between rival bureaucratic organizations to gain control of secret intelligence and propaganda in the early war period, see: Michael Stenton, *Radio London and Resistance in Occupied London. British Political Warfare 1939–43* (Oxford, 2000). The struggle between MOI and the FO for control of propaganda was intense from the beginning. E.H. Carr was placed in charge of the FO's Foreign Policy Directorate, but he soon quit in frustration after being overruled in several of these disputes. Robert Cole, *Britain and the War of Words in Neutral Europe, 1939–1945. The Art of the Possible* (London, 1990).

8. EW, *The Europe I Saw*, pp. 139–40.

9. EW to Eidgenössisches Politisches Departement, Jan. 16, 1940. Schweizerisches Bundesarchiv, E 2001 (D), 3, Bd 14 (A.15.47.11).

10. She continued her journalism, doing some work for the *Neue Zürcher Zeitung*, *Weltwoche*, and also *Listener*, *Spectator*, and *Foreign Affairs* (EW to Bergholz, April 24, May 28, 1940).

11. EW to Crozier, Nov. 28, 1939, Manchester Guardian Archive, C1/W9/11.

12. Crozier to EW, Nov. 30, 1939, Manchester Guardian Archive C1/W9/13. She replied on Dec. 3, 1939: "As for caution and scepticism I tend to carry them to the point of dullness, but I will try to avoid that too! I wish the British public hadn't been fed on talk about Germany cracking up tomorrow – they're in for disappointment for some time to come, I fear."

13. Anthony Read and David Fisher, *Colonel Z.*, p. 174; Sarah Lonsdale, *The Journalist in British Fiction and Film. Guarding the Guardians from 1900 to the Present* (London, 2016), chapter 4.

14. L. Miall to EW, Feb. 2, 1940, BBC Archives Caversham.

15. EW to L. Miall, Feb. 28, 1940, BBC Archives Caversham.

16. She was back in Zurich in April. While she was in London, Hitler occupied Denmark and Norway.

17. EW, *The Europe I Saw*, p. 151.

18. Alfred A. Häsler, *Das Boot ist voll. Die Schweiz und die Flüchtlinge 1933–45* (Zurich, 1962). Independent Commission of Experts, Switzerland – the Second World War, *Switzerland and Refugees in the Nazi Era* (Bern, 1999). Over the course of the war some 300,000 refugees entered the country; 104,000 were foreign troops and the rest civilians.

19. Neville Wylie, *Britain, Switzerland and the Second World War* (Oxford, 2003); Wylie, "'Keeping the Swiss Sweet': Intelligence as a Factor in British Policy towards Switzerland during the Second World War," *Intelligence and National Security* 11, 3, (July 1996), pp. 442–467.

20. EW, *The Europe I Saw*, p. 131.

21. Peter Stahlberger, *Der Zürcher Verleger Emil Oprecht und die deutsche politische Emigration 1933–1945* (Zurich, 1970).

22. Enormously effective and successful, *Die Pfeffermühle* gave over one thousand performances in Zurich; Erika Mann wrote most of the scripts and also performed. The cabaret's satires of Hitler and Nazism led to German pressure on the Swiss authorities and it was closed down in 1937.

23. EW, *The Europe I Saw*, p. 152.

24. Hitler's invasion of Western Europe sharply diminished the flow of intelligence; also, later, when the USSR entered the war, the decision to terminate direct intelligence work against the Soviet Union (so as not to jeopardize the Anglo-Soviet alliance) further reduced the information deriving from covert operations. As a result, open-source intelligence became much more important; indeed, it has been estimated that 60% of economic intelligence obtained about Germany and occupied Europe came from newspapers and similar sources. Regional centers sent the information to Britain where Toynbee's Foreign Research and Press Service (later the Foreign Office Research Department) and other agencies analyzed it. Elisabeth Pares, daughter of the Slavic historian Bernard Pares, became the head of the Baltic states section of Toynbee's FRPS and chief analyst of the intel coming from Stockholm on north-east Europe. Ben Wheatley, *British Intelligence and Hitler's Empire in the Soviet Union, 1941–1945* (London, 2017).

25. NA: FO 371/24537. Robert Cole, *Britain and the War of Words in Neutral Europe, 1939–1945*, p. 23. To be fair, Daniels had a great deal of work, answering the needs of London with correspondence and reports and at the same time interpreting British policy and actions for the Swiss press. In addition, since British papers were in short supply and there was no BBC Swiss Service, the legation began putting out a news bulletin. Initially, roughly eighty copies a week were circulated, but soon demand grew (including among the Swiss population) and it began appearing twice a week with a print-run of about 2,000 and by Jan. 1942, with increased Treasury funds, had reached 60,000 copies. Daniels did not seem dynamic or youthful enough to run it and was replaced. In addition to Cole, *Britain and the War of Words in Neutral Europe, 1939–1945*, Sir David Kelly, *The Ruling Few or the Human Background to Diplomacy* (London, 1952), pp. 174–5; M.R.D. Foot, *Resistance. European Resistance to Nazism 1940–1945* (New York, 1977), p. 216.

26. EW to Rex Leeper, Sept. 4, 1941, NA: FO 898/256. EW admitted that in Paris she and Daniels's subordinates, David Scott, Thomas Cadett, and Thomas Barman, had laughed a lot at his expense. EW, *The Europe I Saw*, p. 141.

27. Marie Noëlle Kelly, *Dawn to Dusk* (London, 1960), with a preface by Rebecca West. EW, *The Europe I Saw*, p. 141.
28. Elizabeth Montagu, *Honourable Rebel* (Beaulieu, Hampshire, 2003).
29. EW, *The Europe I Saw*, p. 141. On the opposition to women within the Foreign Office, see Helen McCarthy, "Petticoat Diplomacy: The Admission of Women to the British Foreign Service, 1919-1946," *Twentieth Century British History*, 20, 3 (Sept. 2009), pp. 285-321.
30. Anne Sebba, *Battling for News. The Rise of the Woman Reporter* (London, 1995), p. 147.
31. EW, "Sword of Freedom," *Fortnightly* 150, July 1941, pp. 129-134.
32. EW was fond of describing a walk in Bern with her friend 'Boofy' Gore. Speaking perfect German in his loud Etonian voice, Gore soon drew around them a hostile Bernese crowd who made abusive remarks about *Sauschwaben* until EW managed to explain in her halting Swiss dialect that they were British. EW, *The Europe I Saw*, pp. 143-4.
33. EW, "Switzerland in Wartime," *TLS*, Dec. 29, 1961, p. 923.
34. EW, "The Sword of Freedom," *Fortnightly* 150, July 1941, pp. 129-30. She was silent about Swiss failure to extend political rights to women, something she took up post-war. EW, review of "Switzerland in Wartime," *TLS*, Dec. 29, 1961, p. 923.
35. EW, "The Swiss Confederation and the War," *Fortnightly* 147, Jan. 1940, p. 388. Also, EW, "Swiss Listening-Post," *Spectator*, Feb. 2, 1940, p. 136; EW, "Switzerland Waits," *Spectator*, May 16, 1940, pp. 9-10; EW, "The Sword of Freedom."
36. Crozier used some of what she had sent him as a letter to the paper, inadvertently including her initials, E.W., and placing her name in the general index. She responded that this "is a very serious matter and either you or I have been most dangerously careless to have allowed this to happen – it may lead to my expulsion from Switzerland at any moment and to other complications." Crozier apologized, adding that those dealing with her contributions have "now been warned about the importance of anonymity." EW to Crozier, March 30, 1940; Crozier to EW, April 1, 1940, Manchester Guardian Archive, C1/W9/15 and C1/W9/17.
37. EW, "Wenn der Krieg richtig anfängt," *Neue Zürcher Zeitung*, May 2, 1940, p. 3. Also, Werner Vogt, *Winston Churchill: Mahnung, Hoffnung, und Vision 1938-1946. Das Churchill-Bild in der Berichterstattung und Kommentierung der Neuen Zürcher Zeitung* (Zurich, 1996), pp. 126, 188.
38. His letters to EW have not survived. Bergholz (1908-94) needed to fix up a job in the US before he could hope to get a visa. The Swiss declared his French visa invalid and, with internment of aliens underway in Britain, he also learned that he would not be granted re-entry to Britain. EW mentions him indirectly but not by name in her memoir.
39. Mary jean Woodruff, "Unusual Experiences: Bergholz Works Against Nazi Regime," *Michigan Daily*, 64, 156, May 23, 1954.
40. EW to Bergholz, card Jan. 11, 1940; Feb. 19, 1940.
41. EW to Bergholz, March 7, 1940.
42. No date, possibly late April but more likely early May, 1940.
43. EW to Bergholz, May 16, 1940.
44. EW to Bergholz, March 12, May 20-5, 1940.
45. EW to Bergholz, May 20-5, 1940.
46. EW, "Sword of Freedom," *Fortnightly* 150, July 1941, p. 130.

47. EW to Bergholz, May 20–25, 1940. Refers to the January 1889 suicide pact of the star-crossed lovers Habsburg Crown Prince Rudolf and his mistress, Baroness Mary Vetsera.

48. EW to Bergholz, May 20–5, 1940.

49. EW to Bergholz, n.d (a Thursday evening), possibly May 30, 1940.

50. EW to Bergholz, June 1–5, 1940.

51. EW to Bergholz, June 1–5, 1940.

52. EW to Bergholz, June 5–8, 1940.

53. There are signs that she had suffered an appendicitis attack while staying with French-Swiss friends near Morat in early May, but it passed. Later another flare-up was probably masked by her pregnancy until it ruptured or became severely inflamed.

54. EW to Bergholz, June 13, 1940. She also writes: "Anyway I fancy I and a good many of my English friends hate an affaire to be admitted because it amuses us to keep people guessing…I fancy that sort of attitude is anything but sympathique to you, but it was sure to emerge from me at some point."

55. EW, *The Europe I Saw*, p. 145.

56. EW to Bergholz, June 26, 1940.

57. EW to Emmie Oprecht, June 27, 1940, Oprecht Nachlasse.

58. EW to Bergholz, July 6, 1940.

59. EW to Bergholz, July 18, 1950.

60. EW to Bergholz, no date, but early August 1940 (Monday).

61. EW to Bergholz, August 12, 1940.

62. EW to Bergholz, Sept. 2, 1940.

63. EW to Bergholz, Sept. 9, 1940.

64. EW, *The Europe I Saw*, pp. 146–7; EW to Emmie Oprecht, June 27 and August 7, 1940, Oprecht Nachlasse. She mentions to Carl Burckhardt, who had invited her to a dinner party, that she needed to be in Bern that day; she had "said goodbye to René and it was better to let him go, however sadly." EW to Carl Burckhardt, Oct. 16, 1940, Burckhardt Nachlass.

65. EW, *The Europe I Saw*, pp. 146–7. Immediately after the war, Vaidie played a major role in the investigation of Nazi (Jewish) gold smuggled into Switzerland. On Vaidie's role in the financial negotiations between Switzerland and France (including the liquidation of German assets in Switzerland): J.M. Schaufelbuehl, *La France et la Suisse ou la force du petit* (Paris, 2009).

66. EW, "Danzig before the Storm," *TLS*, June 10, 1960, p. 371.

67. Douglas Gageby, *The Last General Secretary. Sean Lester and the League of Nations* (Dublin, 1999). See also: Sean Lester diary (accessible online), United Nations Archives, Geneva. EW, "Low Treason" (review of a book about Avenol), *Spectator*, Sept. 2, 1970, p. 589: "Avenol seemed increasingly to lose his head. More and more he was found to advocate the surrender of the League to become Hitler's instrument in the refashioning of the European order. The defeat of France seemed to blind him completely."

68. EW to Sean Lester, Dec. 16, 1940, Sean Lester Diaries, p. 661, United Nations Archives, Geneva.

69. Charles Paravicini to C.J. Burckhardt, March 19, 1936, Burckhardt Nachlass.

70. Burckhardt was vain and she flattered him: "I so much enjoyed our lunch the other day and all the indiscretions…it cheered me up marvelously and altogether I have decided that I must visit Geneva oftener in order to preserve my own wavering morale and in order to clutch at the last fragments of civilization." EW to C.J. Burckhardt, Oct. 16, 1940, Burckhardt Nachlass.

71. Burckhardt had tried to act as a channel of communications with British Ambassador Kelly until Churchill shut down these peace feelers. Later in 1941 he opened talks with Ulrich von Hassell, former diplomat active in resistance circles, and Ernst von Weizsäcker. Burckhardt had originally met Weizsäcker when he was German Consul in Basel. The British Ministry of Economic Warfare was angered by Red Cross efforts to send supplies to Greece and Belgium, which they viewed as breaking the British blockade, while the British also wanted more done for their POWs. Burckhardt lamented the collapse of the Habsburg Monarchy and had little sympathy for Czechs, Poles, and Slavs generally. EW, "Danzig before the Storm," *TLS*, June 10, 1960. Baron Ernst von Weizsäcker was State Secretary in the German Foreign Office 1938-43 and then German Ambassador to the Vatican 1943-45. Convicted for war crimes at Nuremberg, he was released in 1950 after a public campaign in his defense.The view prevailing in postwar West Germany that the Foreign Office was a centre of anti-Nazi resistance was substantially revised as a result of a study commissioned by Foreign Minister Joschka Fischer in 2005. See: E. Conze, N. Frei, P. Hayes, M. Zimmermann, *Das Amt und die Vergangenheit: deutsche Diplomaten im Dritten Reich und der Bundesrepublik* (Munich, 2010) and the review by R.J. Evans, "Nazis and Diplomats" in Evans, *The Third Reich in History and Memory* (Oxford and New York, 2015), pp. 262–93.

72. EW to C.J. Burckhardt, Nov. 24, 1940. Erich Podach (1894–1967) and his wife Jenny. Erich was a literary scholar and expert on Nietzsche.

73. EW to C.J. Burckhardt, Dec. 6, 1940; telegram from Burckhardt to EW, Dec. 9, 1940. Michael Fleming (1913–40) was the brother of explorer Peter Fleming and writer Ian Fleming, the creator of James Bond.

74. "The Battle of Whitehall," Robert Bruce Lockhart noted tartly in 1940, "is far more important to civil servants than the Battle of Britain." *The Diaries of Sir Robert Bruce Lockhart* vol. 2, 1939–45 (London, 1981), p. 85.

75. Neville Wylie, *Britain, Switzerland and the Second World War*, p. 272. Far more successful than Cartwright was the Air Attaché at Bern, 'Freddie' West (1896–1988). P.R. Reid, *Winged Diplomat. The Life Story of Air Commodore 'Freddie' West* (London, 1962).

76. E.g. EW to Bergholz, May 28, 1940.

77. The German Abwehr claimed to have a thousand agents in the country, and a Gestapo branch office (Bureau F) was attached to the Reich's Bern embassy.

78. EW to 'Rex' Leeper, Aug. 19, 1941, NA: FO 898/256.

79. EW to Harry Bergholz, Sept. 2, 1940. 'Boofy' Gore was transferred to Lisbon in February or March 1941.

80. EW to Emmie Oprecht, Oct. 9, 1940, Oprecht Nachlasse.

81. Swiss neutrality prevented the use of air routes to get to London. In her memoir she explained simply: "The state of Europe had changed so remarkably since I had left

London in April 1940 that I felt in great need of consultations at home. I was, moreover, dissatisfied with my position and so I asked to go home in any case." EW, *The Europe I Saw*, p. 153.

82. EW, *The Europe I Saw*, p. 153. When she reached London, "Rex" Leeper (head of PWE) told her the war would be won by the end of 1942. She declared that he was being optimistic and he thought she was being defeatist.

83. EW to Walter Adams, May 7, 1941, NA: FO898/256.

84. M. Muggeridge, *The Infernal Grove* (London, 1973).

85. She felt a little guilty about Scott. They were good friends and enjoyed each other's company, but she frequently criticized his gullibility and readiness to believe whatever stories were being spread around. The night before she left Lisbon they dined together. She retired early but Scott knocked on her door with news that Rudolf Hess had landed in Scotland. She thought the story ridiculous and sent him away. They never met again, and he died at an early age. EW, *The Europe I Saw*, pp. 155–6.

86. EW to Bergholz, May 10, 1941.

87. EW to Emmie Oprecht, May 12, 1941.

88. Neill Lochery, *Lisbon: War in the Shadows of the City of Light, 1939–1945* (London, 2012); E.M. Remarque, *The Night in Lisbon* (New York, 1962); A. Koestler, *Arrival and Departure* (London, 1943).

89. She later wrote to Leeper (Sept. 4, 1941, NA: FO 898/256): "I suppose you realize that SOMEONE was quite deliberately fabricating Colonel D's hostility to me and he is very angry with them; if I had not unearthed this piece of malice it might have been used against me indefinitely and I must confess that I find it very extraordinary that quite unscrupulous people are allowed into highly confidential places." It is unclear to whom she refers, in Bern possibly Henry Cartwright or John McCaffery, SOE's head of operations in Switzerland.

90. W. Adams to Brigadier Dallas Brooks, May 6, 1941.NA: FO 898/256.

91. Philip Ziegler, *London at War* (New York, 1995), pp. 160–1.

92. EW to Bergholz, May 29, 1941.

93. She first met Sikorski in Warsaw in 1937; he was under house arrest, and she had to walk past a guard of gendarmes. He promised not to forget that EW had visited him and kept his promise. She thought he was perhaps the most attractive public figure she had ever encountered. In Fife he made her an honorary Colonel of the Second Polish Brigade and presented her with a badge and ribbon. EW, *The Europe I Saw*, pp. 125–8. She also found time to put in an appearance at a PEN congress in Sept. 1941: "Being in government service I'm not free to make statements in public but I suppose one can join in the congress in other ways." EW to Storm Jameson, Aug. 25, 1941. PEN Archive.

94. Philip Williams, *Hugh Gaitskell* (London, 1979), p. 96ff.

95. Pauline Elkes, "The Political Warfare Executive. A Re-Evaluation Based on the Work of the German Section," Ph.D. diss., Sheffield University, 1996. In February 1942 Dalton was moved from the Ministry of Economic Warfare to the Board of Trade. He vented his frustrations in his diary. On February 6, 1942, for example, he wrote: "I think that we just don't deserve to win the war. We are all fighting each other instead of the enemy, and with such great zest." *The Second World War Diary of Hugh Dalton, 1940–1945* (London, 1986).

96. Sir David Kelly to H.L. d'A Hopkinson (Counsellor at the Foreign Office), April 16, 1941, NA: FO 898/256.

97. EW to 'Rex' Leeper, Aug. 19, 1941, NA: FO 898/256.

98. EW to Leeper, Aug. 19, 1941, NA: FO 898/256.

99. EW to Leeper, Aug. 19, 1941, NA: FO 898/256.

100. 'Rex' Leeper to Sir Charles Hambro, Sept. 2, 1941, NA: FO 898/256. She wrote to Emmie Oprecht: "It is marvelous to find my friends here again. I have various possibilities for work and must decide. It is not out of the question that I'll be back in Switzerland again soon." EW to Emmie Oprecht, June 4, 1941. If the Swiss job fell through, she intimated that she might work at the Czech Legation in London. EW to 'Rex' Leeper, July 24, 1941, NA: FO 898/256.

101. Helen McCarthy, *Women of the World. The Rise of the Female Diplomat* (London, 2014); "Petticoat Diplomacy." Also, FCO Historians, *Women and the Foreign Office: A History* (London, 2018).

102. Stephen Heald, an old friend from Chatham House, was now working at MOI.

103. She may have been slightly wrong; Helen McCarthy says that Freya Stark and Nancy Lambton, attached to the legations in Baghdad and Tehran, also got diplomatic status. H. McCarthy, *Women of the World*, pp. 183–4. McCarthy argues that their professional competence helped destroy much of the Foreign Office case against women.

104. EW to 'Rex' Leeper, Sept. 4, 1941, NA: FO 898/256.

105. EW, *The Europe I Saw*, p. 157.

106. R.G. Leddy was at that time working for the FBI and was sent by Hoover to investigate security breaches at US embassies in Europe. Later he became a senior CIA operative with a great deal of experience in Cuba, Guatamala, Venezuela, etc.

107. Soon after her return she visited Sean Lester but their encounter was more combative than usual—EW having raised the topic of Eire's neutrality. Lester recorded in his diary: "I get tired of Elizabeth…Gave her an outburst on Ireland: in the good old style. She's not at all anti-Irish but was quoting some folk in London. I said no Englishman should open his mouth about Ireland…Dec [De Valera] and Co. may be wrong – but no coercion! She's very intelligent, however, and her books are sound." Sean Lester Diaries, Oct. 20, 1941, p. 846. She was soon lunching with him again. Sean Lester Diaries, Dec. 20, 1941, p. 928, United Nations Archives, Geneva.

108. EW to Colonel Nigel Sutton, Oct 21, 1941, NA: FO 898/256. Colonel Sutton was PWE Regional Director for France in 1941 and in January 1943 became Director of Political Warfare for Occupied Territories.

109. EW, *The Europe I Saw*, p. 149. This was possibly someone from Buro Hä.

110. EW, *The Europe I Saw*, p. 165. Whitehall officials also insisted that she keep and submit a regular tally of her train expenses and justify taking taxis rather than buses; she eventually explained that she was switching from 3rd class train travel to 2nd, which was less crowded and less exhausting.

111. Elizabeth Montagu, *Honourable Rebel*, chapters 1–6, quotation on p. 97.

112. Elizabeth Montagu, *Honourable Rebel*, pp. 213–337 describe her experiences during the war years and pp. 292–297 her escape from France into Switzerland. Scott-Montagu probably took over some of EW's duties reading the foreign press while she was in England. After EW's return in October 1941, Scott-Montagu's duties expanded.

A film, based on the memoir, appeared in November 2015: "The Honourable Rebel," directed by Mike Fraser, with Diana Rigg and Dorothea Myer-Bennett.

113. Elizabeth Scott-Montagu also knew Shiela Grant Duff and Moura Budberg.

114. Elizabeth Montagu, *Honourable Rebel*, p. 314. Scott-Montagu was bi-sexual and had a long relationship with the classical pianist, Renata Borgatti, who at this time was running a music school in Switzerland.

115. Elizabeth Montagu, *Honourable Rebel*, p. 314: "Elizabeth was not generally popular with the Legation staff who afforded her little cooperation. However, her work was paramount to her and woe betide anyone who impinged on this." An Anonymous letter to the *Times* after EW's death, probably from 'Boofy' Gore, recalled how they always laughed "at the absurdities and ignorances of our colleagues." *Times*, July 9, 1971, p. 14.

116. *Honourable Rebel*, p. 313.

117. *Honorable Rebel*, pp. 314–315. While EW was in England from May to September 1941, she probably underwent espionage training at Woburn.

118. *Honourable Rebel*, pp. 316–18.

119. The National Archives include a good deal of information about 1941–42 and 1944–45; the information is thinner for 1943 (much of it dispersed in different agencies), but luckily the OSS Archives in Washington contain a good deal about that year.

120. The report on French workers' morale probably came via Vaidie; it was written in late September 1941: "L'opinion ouvrière et de syndicalisme en France," NA: FO 898/256, 1941–42.

121. M. Balfour (?) to EW, Oct. 4, 1942, NA: FO 898/257. EW was also asked to comment on the effectiveness of British radio propaganda. EW, "Memorandum on BBC Broadcasts," March 30, 1942, NA: FO 898/256. She also criticized British propaganda aimed at Hungary as confused, muddled: NA: FO 898/150.

122. There were four Swiss medical missions to the eastern front. The first to Smolensk (Oct. 1941–Jan. 1942) originated with a right-wing nationalist and pro-German, Dr Bircher. It was not endorsed by the Swiss Federal Council. The Swiss military took an interest in later missions. Later missions took place: a) Jan.–April, 1942 (to the General Government area of Poland); b) June–Sept. 1942 (Latvia and Estonia); this is the mission referred to by London; c) Dec. 1942–March 1943 (Ukraine). The teams of doctors and nurses usually numbered about seventy to eighty people. They were instructed not to give aid to Soviet POWs and to reman silent about what they saw. Members of the missions often kept diaries, which record that later missions found their German hosts less arrogant, less confident of victory, more pessimistic. Dr Rudolf Bucher, a member of the first mission, spoke out (in public lectures and press interviews) after his return about the murder and inhuman treatment of Jews and partisans that he had witnessed in Warsaw and Smolensk. The German Ambassador protested and the Swiss army tried to muzzle him, to little avail. Diaries from later missions do not mention Jews—possibly because of tighter censorship or because their movements were more restricted.

123. Telegram FO to Bern, Oct 25, 1942; EW to M. Balfour, Oct. 28, 1942, NA: FO 898/256.

124. EW to Michael Balfour, Oct. 5, 1942, NA: FO 898/257.

125. EW telegrams, March 3, 1943; Feb. 5, 1943, NA: FO 898/257.

126. "La situation en France." Wiskemann sent this long document to Allen Dulles June 19, 1943. NAWA RG 226 Entry 210, Box 362 (OSS documents).

127. Report on "Foreign Workers in Germany," May 13, 1942, NA: FO 898/257.

128. EW to Dulles, April 15, 1943 (on the growing power of Goebbels and Bormann); EW telegram, Dec. 19, 1942, to the effect that Himmler and Ribbentrop were said to be ailing and had disappeared into nursing homes for some weeks. NAWA RG 226 (OSS documents).

129. EW telegram, Dec. 19, 1942: "Hitler's condition has been alternating between outbursts of rage and long dazed periods of frightened silence. He had recently been supplied with a certain Fraulein Braun with whom his behavior is pathologically depraved." [In fact, Eva Braun had appeared on the public scene a good deal earlier.] NA: FO 898/257.

130. EW, *The Europe I Saw*, p. 161. Also, Wiskemann to Dulles, Feb. 26, 1944 (with information on the French Maquis and Darnand, etc.).

131. EW, *The Europe I Saw*, p. 162. After hearing that her parents had been killed in a concentration camp in 1944, Emmy committed suicide.

132. Pierre Dubois also played an important role in smuggling Elizabeth Scott-Montagu into Switzerland. See: Elizabeth Montagu, *Honourable Rebel*, pp. 292-297.

133. David Garnett, *The Secret History of P.W.E.* (London, 2002), p. 142.

134. Visser 't Hooft informed her about the increased persecution of Berlin Jews in March 1943 and asked her to pass a letter to Dulles urging him to intercede over the US's indiscriminate bombing of Dutch targets like the Philips factory at Eindhoven by Flying Fortresses, which caused large civilian casualties. EW to Dulles, March 25, 1943, NAWA RG 226 (OSS documents).

135. W.A. Visser 't Hooft, *Memoirs* (London, 1973), quote, p. 142. For a detailed study of the Swiss Road: Megan Koreman, *The Escape Line: How the Ordinary Heroes of Dutch-Paris Resisted the Nazi Occupation of Western Europe* (Oxford, 2018). Only one group of documents sent by EW via the Swiss Road has survived: NIOD 455, J. van Borssum-Buisman, Swiss Road, inv. No. 2.11 MI and FO documents sent by Elizabeth Wiskemann, (1943-44), Nederlands Institut voor Oorlogsdocumentatie, Amsterdam.

136. EW met Barth in the autumn of 1941 and visited him many times. EW, *The Europe I Saw*, p. 162; Eberhard Busch (ed.), *Die Akte Karl Barth: Zensur und Uberwachung im Namen der Schweizer Neutralitat 1938-1945* (Zurich, 2008), pp. 257, 505-6. Barth worked with both the Oprechts and Visser 't Hooft. EW also put Dulles in contact with Barth: EW to Dulles, Jan. 22, 1943, NAWA RG 226 (OSS documents).

137. She looked for anyone who could provide knowledge of conditions inside Germany. When the Oprechts' German maid, Maria, who had previously worked in Thomas Mann's household (where EW first met her ten years before), returned to Munich for a month, she was debriefed by EW on her return. Maria also regularly passed along letters from her parents. EW to Allen Dulles, Sept. 25, 1943; Oct. 12, 1943, NAWA RG 226 (OSS documents).

138. The industrial population of German-speaking Switzerland was overwhelmingly Social Democratic. For EW, the split between Capital and Labour was "the most serious cleavage in Swiss life, a potential hole in Switzerland's armour." EW, "Sword of Freedom," p. 132.

139. Neville Wylie, *Britain, Switzerland and the Second World War*, p. 58, NA: FO 898/256. Also on Bringolf, etc.: Pierre Th. Braunschweig, *Secret Channel to Berlin* (Philadelphia, 2004).

140. Albert Müller was given the code name Q5. EW wrote that he "gives me pretty well all his confidential information from his correspondents in Germany and from other people, stuff which for various reasons (neutrality etc) he cannot publish." EW to Lt.-Colonel Kerr, Jan. 23, 1945. The *Neue Zürcher Zeitung* staff also included Eric Kessler, a close friend of EW, who had worked for the NZZ in London and was then for a time press attaché at the Swiss Embassy there. In 1944 he returned to the NZZ as an editor. Kessler was recruited to MI5 by Guy Burgess and was considered as a possible intermediary for establishing a clandestine radio station for broadcasting propaganda into Germany. Through Burgess, Kessler was also supplying information to the KGB. After the Burgess–Maclean affair, EW wrote: "All along he had been unswerving in his faith in the Allied cause, and we had always treated each other as if we were colleagues." *The Europe I Saw*, pp. 192, 198.

141. EW wrote a brief history of the NZZ: *A Great Swiss Newspaper: The Story of the Neue Zürcher Zeitung* (London, 1959).

142. Her introduction to him came from 'Sigi' (Sir Sigismund) Waley, brother of the orientalist Arthur Waley, and a high official at the Board of Trade.

143. EW, *The Europe I Saw*, p. 153. EW to 'Rex' Leeper, Sept. 4, 1941, NA: FO 898/256. The identity of the Basle banker who gave her the information is unknown (possibly Isidor Koppelmann?). Wiskemann was clearly mistaken in believing she heard about the "Final Solution" at the end of 1941. She probably heard of the mass shootings by Einsatzkommando units in the east, for example at Babi Yar in the Ukraine and Odessa in September and October 1941.

144. Carl Goerdeler was the director of the overseas sales department for Bosch GmbH, which gave him cover to travel and establish an anti-Nazi network. Joachim Scholtyseck, *Robert Bosch und der liberale Widerstand gegen Hitler, 1933 bis 1945* (Munich, 1999).

145. EW, *The Europe I Saw*, p. 161.

146. W. Laqueur, "The Terrible Secret: Some Afterthoughts," in C.Y. Freeze, S.F. Fried, and E.R. Sheppard (eds.), *The Individual in History: Essays in Honor of Jehuda Reinharz* (Waltham, Mass 2015), pp. 403–418. References to Hoffmann LaRoche director: EW to Allen Dulles, June 26, 1943; EW to Allen Dulles, March 21, 1943, NAWA REG 226 (OSS Documents). Hellmich (1880–1949) seems not to have publicly acknowledged his aid to the Allies in the postwar years. EW names him to Colonel G.K. Kerr, April 4, 1945, NA: FO 898/257. Eduard Schulte (1891–1966) was managing director of Germany's largest zinc producer; he made many trips from Germany to Switzerland and cooperated with Allied intelligence services,; he fled to Zurich in December 1943.

147. I found no evidence connecting EW to the two major communist spy networks in Switzerland that passed German military intelligence to the Soviet Union: the so-called Lucy spy ring run by the German refugee Rudolf Roessler and the 'Rote Drei' network run by the Hungarian Sandor Rado which was part of the Red Orchestra. However, among Rado's suppliers of information was the socialist lawyer and journalist Otto Punter in Bern, who, it seems, also provided information to EW. Punter (codename Pakbo) had a connection to the exiled Munich police chief,

Baron Michael von Godin, and to the press attaché in the Vichy French Embassy in Bern, Louis Suss (codename Salter). Schulze-Gaevernitz and Dulles were also in contact with the last two. Punter's books and interviews are riddled with errors, so that it is difficult to be certain about his role.

148. Through Vaidie she also got intelligence from Maurice Couve de Murville, who was head of Vichy's external finances; he broke with Vichy, went to Algiers, and joined the Free French in 1943.

149. EW to Allen Dulles, Sept. 25, 1943, NAWA RG 226 (OSS documents). Before spending a dozen years at the Swiss Embassy in London, Charles de Jenner (1886–1970) had also served in Vienna and Belgrade. He was appointed Swiss Ambassador to China in 1948.

150. EW: "Report on Croatia," April 24, 1942, NA: FO 898/257; also, EW to Michael Balfour, Oct. 24, 1942 (she also included the wavelengths of partisan broadcasts for London to use them) NA: FO 898/256. Nedić was a former Minister of War in Yugoslavia. The Germans turned to him to preside over a Government of National Salvation to defeat the partisans. While EW was highly critical of Mihailović, she did pass on to London the opposing view from Mihailović brought to her by a Czech visitor who ran a travel agency in Yugoslavia. EW to Allen Dulles, June 3, 1942, NAWA RG 226 (OSS documents).

151. EW, *The Europe I Saw*, p. 159. She first met Kramer in October 1941, shortly after she returned from London.

152. Franz Kramer (1900–50) was summoned to Berlin in early 1944 after being accused of "defeatism"; he refused to go and had to break with the German Legation (NA: FO 898/257). A one-page typed summary of Kramer's career (undated but probably 1944) can be found in NAWA RG 226 (OSS documents).

153. D. Garnett, *The Secret History of PWE: The Political Warfare Executive 1939–1945* (London, 2002). Tim Brooks, *British Propaganda to France 1940–1944. Machinery, Method, and Message* (Edinburgh, 2007). Joannis D. Stefanidis, *Substitute for Power: British Propaganda to the Balkans 1939–1944* (Ashgate, 2012). Michael Balfour, *Propaganda in War 1939–1945. Organisations, Policies and Publics in Britain and Germany* (London, 1979), p. 96.

154. Quoted by Neville Wylie, "'Keeping the Swiss Sweet': Intelligence as a Factor in British Policy towards Switzerland during the Second World War," *Intelligence and National Security*, 11, 3 (July 1996), p. 460.

155. Maxwell to M. Balfour, Sept 14, 1942; also H. Paniquian to P. Scarlett, Oct. 22, 1942, NA: FO 898/256.

156. E.M. Barker "Berne Special Pilot, nr. 244," Jan. 31, 1943, NA: FO 898/257. Elizabeth Barker began at P.W.E working under Ralph Murray on the Balkans and south-east Europe; by 1943 she was Director of the south-east Europe section.

157. D. Garnett, *The Secret History of PWE*, p. 97. Also, Noel Newsome, *Giant at Bush House. The Autobiography of Noel Newsome, volume 1: 1906–1945* (Steyning: The Real Press, 2019). Newsome married Sheila Grant Duff during the war.

158. Michael Balfour said that Crossman's weakness was that "he could never resist the lure of a novel idea irrespective of whether it fitted in with his general outlook or not." He also said, "Tom Delmer's virtuoso performance in developing black broadcasting was both inimitable and too successful to be interfered with." Prof. Michael Balfour obituary by Leonard Miall, *Independent*, Sept. 28, 1995, p. 23.

159. See, for example, M. Balfour to P. Scarlett, Aug. 13, 1942; M. Balfour to Lord Cage, Sept. 12, 1942, NA: FO 898/257. Also, Robert Cole, *Britain and the War of Words in Neutral Europe 1939–1945*, p. 122.

160. See chapter 4, pp. 146–7 for Delmer. On one internal memo (March 11, 1944) listing a range of topics on which information was needed, an official wrote asking whether EW could be sent a list of priority questions about Italy without indicating "how far such material is to have precedence over German, French and Balkans," NA: FO 898/257.

161. EW to Colonel Kerr, Sept. 21, 1944, NA: FO 898/257.

162. *The Diaries of Sir Robert Bruce Lockhart, 1939–45*, vol. 2, p. 187 (Aug.13, 1942).

Chapter 4

1. Peter Grose, *Gentleman Spy, A Life of Allen Dulles* (New York, 1994); James Srodes, *Allen Dulles. Master of Spies* (Washington, 1999).

2. Stephen Kinzer, *The Brothers: John Foster Dulles, Allen Dulles and Their Secret World War* (New York, 2014). Allen Dulles and Hamilton Fish Armstrong collaborated on two interventionist books: *Can We Be Neutral?* (1936); *Can America Stay Neutral?* (1939).

3. Christof Mauch, *The Shadow War Against Hitler. The Covert Operations of America's Wartime Secret Intelligence Service* (New York, 2003), p. 109.

4. EW to Allen Dulles, Dec. 11, 1942, NAWA RG 226 (OSS documents) Entry No. 210. Box 362.

5. Michael Balfour to Peter Scarlett (Foreign Office), Aug. 13, 1942, NA: FO 898/257.

6. EW to Sir Bruce Lockhart, Aug. 4, 1942, NA: FO 898/256. She approached both Lockhart and Frank Roberts (FO) about the situation: EW to W. Adams, July 21, 1942 ("everything is done to show resentment at my presence here"). By June 1943 the legation had no fewer than six press attachés so that—as Norton recognized—their 'cover' was not much of a fig leaf.

7. EW to Sir Bruce Lockhart, Aug. 4, 1942, NA: FO 898/256.

8. M. Balfour to Peter Scarlett (Lockhart's personal assistant), Aug. 18, 1942, NA: FO 898/257.

9. J. Arrow (Director of Overseas Division, MOI) to Frank Roberts (FO), Sept. 24, 1942, NA: FO 898/257.

10. M. Balfour to Peter Scarlett, Aug. 13, 1942; Terence Harman (Regional Director for the Low Countries) to M. Balfour, July 11, 1942, NA: FO 898/257.

11. M. Balfour to Peter Scarlett, Aug. 13, 1942.

12. EW to Michael Balfour, Oct. 5, 1942; also, EW to Walter Adams, July 21, 1942 (copies to Balfour and Harman). Saxe had previously worked for the League of Nations and as Swiss correspondent for *Agence Belge*. Harman was still pushing for Saxe several months later: Terry Harman to Brigadier Sachs, April 3, 1943, NA: FO 898/257.

13. EW to Allen Dulles, Dec. 11, 1942, NAWA RG 226 (OSS documents).

14. EW to Bergholz, Dec. 18, 1942: "Though we are very fond of each other you are psychologically very bad for me when my life is being difficult. But yet I've been looking forward to your coming." EW to Bergholz, Dec. 21 and 23, 1942: she says she feels guilty about not inviting him [to Zurich] but she cannot bear his pessimism; says she is sorry: "But honestly it is a bit your fault that you don't know how to help a friend in this kind of difficulty – most of one's other friends do." Also: "No, it wasn't that you get on my nerves as you think. But somehow that if I've lost my courage you make it more difficult for me to recapture it and I MUST of course. I'm difficult to understand, Je · m'excuse."

15. EW to Dulles, Dec. 30, 1942, NAWA RG 226 (OSS documents).

16. EW to Dulles, Feb. 11, 1943, NAWA RG 226 (OSS documents).

17. EW to Allen Dulles, Dec. 11, 1942; EW to Allen Dulles, Feb. 20, 1943, NAWA RG 226 (OSS documents).

18. Douglas Waller, *Disciples: The World War II Missions of the CIA Directors Who Fought for Wild Bill Donovan* (New York, 2015), p. 136.

19. Srodes, *Allen Dulles. Master of Spies*, pp. 257–8. SIS was not happy about Dulles's efforts to establish independent links to the French Maquis; they also felt he was more likely than they to take unwarranted risks.

20. Srodes, *Allen Dulles. Master of Spies*, p. 233.

21. EW to Dulles, early Dec. (Dec. 11?), 1943, NAWA RG 226 (OSS documents).

22. EW to Dulles, Jan. 14, 1944, NAWA RG 226 (OSS documents).

23. EW to Dulles, Dec. 13, 1942. On the rivalry of the O.S.S. and S.O.E.: Britain maintained primacy over policy and operations in Yugoslavia, having had a longer history there, and the Americans were unhappy about the British shift towards Tito and away from Mihailović. In France the two services cooperated effectively. Neither service had expected a strong Italian resistance movement to develop, and when it did they operated separately and in competition. In Switzerland McCaffery eschewed any information-sharing with Dulles or division of responsibilities for Italy (much to Dulles's frustration), but by late 1944, O.S.S. was dominant, sending more men, equipment, and supplies. Tommaso Piffer, "Office of Strategic Service versus Special Operations Executive: Competition for the Italian Resistance, 1943–1945," *Journal of Cold War Studies*, 17, 4 (Fall 2015), pp. 41–58.

24. Kramer comes up several times in their correspondence, e.g. Sept. 24, 1943; Oct. 1, 1943; Oct. 29, 1943; Oct. 26, 1944, NAWA RG 226 (OSS documents).

25. Telegram 5688, Dec. 6, 1942, N.H. Petersen, *From Hitler's Doorstep. The Wartime Intelligence Reports of Allen Dulles, 1942–1945* (University Park, PA, 1996), pp. 23–5.

26. EW to Dulles, May 20, 1943, NAWA RG 226 (OSS documents).

27. EW to Allen Dulles, July 18, 1943, NAWA RG 226 (OSS documents).

28. EW to Allen Dulles, Jan.14, 1944, NAWA RG 226 (OSS documents).

29. EW to Allen Dulles, early March (n.d.) 1943, NAWA RG 226 (OSS documents). EW, *The Europe I Saw*, p. 163.

30. Dulles did pass to SIS important information from Kolbe about V1 and V2 missile sites (Peenemünde), the effects of Allied raids, etc. He shared with EW copies of French resistance clandestine papers and leaflets and much else.

31. EW to Dulles, n.d., probably end of March, beginning of April 1943, NAWA RG 226 (OSS documents). In June she passed along to Dulles a report from Mihailović discussing the situation, opposing a Croatian state, and describing outrages by Tito's pro-Soviet partisans, Wiskemann to Dulles, June 3, 1943. Mihailović was compromised with Nedić, the Serb quisling whom the Germans had established in Belgrade. Nedić supplied Mihailović with arms if he would fight the partisans.

32. EW to Dulles, Dec. 13, 18, and 22, 1942, NAWA RG 226 (OSS documents); EW, *The Europe I Saw*, p. 171.

33. E.M. Barker, memo on Special Pilot no. 244, Jan 31, 1943, NA: FO 898/257.

34. F.W. Deakin, *The Embattled Mountain* (London, 1971). OSS also focused its energies on arming Tito's partisans. There was a bureaucratic battle between PWE, the Foreign Office, and SOE over support for Mihailović, with the FO fighting rearguard action on Mihailović's behalf. E. Barker, "Some Factors in British Decision-making over Yugoslavia," in P. Auty and R. Clogg (eds.), *British Policy Towards Wartime Resistance in Yugoslavia and Greece* (London, 1975), pp. 22–58.

35. EW, *The Europe I Saw*, p. 175. She was somewhat awed by these people on her first visits, writing to Julian Trevelyan: "How ravishing Nicky is. And how can even a Florentine lady withstand Morra?" EW to Julian Trevelyan, Dec. 23, 1930, Julian Trevelyan papers. Morra translated Virginia Woolf into Italian.

36. EW, *The Europe I Saw*, p. 176.

37. Italian anti-fascists made efforts to secure from Britain and the US assurances about the future of Italy and its governmental structure. Some of these approaches in 1942–43 flowed through Geneva and Bern, but the contacts seem to have been through channels other than Wiskemann, for example J. McCaffery of SOE, who was in touch with Adriano Olivetti, R. Matteoli, and others. Both Churchill and Eden were resistant to making any promises. Richard Lamb, *The Ghosts of Peace 1935–1945* (London, 1987), chapters 7, 8.

38. James D. Wilkinson, *The Intellectual Resistance in Europe* (Cambridge, MA, 1981), p. 247. Silone was expelled from the Italian Communist party [PCI] in 1931.

39. *Fontamara* (1936); *Pane e Vino* (1937); *Il seme sotto la neve* (1942).

40. EW, *The Europe I Saw*, p. 177. Sean Lester at the League was also in touch with Silone; when Wiskemann consulted Lester about the prospects for resistance in Italy, he referred to "The seed beneath the snow" (title of the third volume of the Abruzzi trilogy) in his response. Sean Lester to EW, July 22, 1943, Sean Lester papers, Section B IV, League of Nations Secretary-General 1940–47, #50, Archives of University College, Dublin.

41. G. Mayer to Allen Dulles, Jan. 9, 1943, NAWA RG 226 Entry 125, Box 8 (OSS documents). Peter Kamber has published many OSS-Silone files online. Silone supplied information about anti-fascist partisan groups, about Italian Socialists, and about Communist organizations; he also evaluated Allied propaganda targeted at Italy and gave opinions about Italian political figures. Like several of EW's contacts, he was increasingly concerned about Communist strength in the resistance and the dangers it presented for postwar Italy.

42. EW to Dulles, July 18, 1943, NAWA RG 226 (OSS documents).

43. EW to Dulles, July 28, 1943, NAWA RG 226 (OSS documents).

44. EW to Dulles, Aug. 18, 1943, NAWA RG 226 (OSS documents).

45. EW to Dulles, Oct. 13, 1943, NAWA RG 226 (OSS documents).

46. EW, "The Last Phase of the War in Europe: A Personal Impression from Switzerland," *The World Today*, 1, 3 (September 1945), p. 127.

47. EW, "The Last Phase of the War in Europe," p. 127.

48. She saw a good deal of Guglielmo Alberti; he introduced her to various people, including Denise Mayer, wife of René Mayer, later Prime Minister of France in 1953. Luigi Einaudi (1874–1961), Professor of Economics at Turin and a distinguished journalist, was at the center of an anti-fascist group of intellectuals that included Manlio Brosio, Niccolo Carrandini, Gramsci, Togliatti, Silone, Saragat, and Piero Gobetti. Postwar, Einaudi held many offices, including Governor of the Bank of Italy and, in 1948, President of the Italian Republic.

49. EW, *The Europe I Saw*, p. 225. Others in the circle were George Cattaui, Ettore Passerin d'Entrèves, Gianfranco Contini, and Adriano Olivetti.

50. EW, "The Last Phase of the War in Europe," pp. 127–8.

51. EW, *The Europe I Saw*, pp. 182–3.

52. F.A. Voigt to W.P. Crozier, Nov. 2, 1937, Guardian News and Media Archive, online.

53. EW to Dulles, Oct. 13 and 16, 1943, NAWA RG 226 (OSS documents).

54. NA: Prime Minister's Files PREM 3/243/5, folios. 209, 221. Also, M. Gilbert, *Road to Victory. Winston S. Churchill* vol. 7 (London, 1986), pp. 1088–89.

55. Martin Clark, *Modern Italy 1871–1982* (London, 1984), pp. 305–6. On February 22, 1944, Churchill made a much-publicized speech in the Commons in which he praised Badoglio and criticized the Committee of National Liberation. R. Lamb, *War in Italy, 1943–1945* (New York, 1993), p. 206. Immediately after the armistice, Marie-José, Princess of Piedmont, had arrived in Switzerland with her children, including the six-year-old Prince of Naples, next in line to the throne after Umberto.

56. EW, *The Europe I Saw*, p. 182.

57. EW, *The Europe I Saw*, pp. 177–8; I have not been able to identify him. He supplied what London referred to as the Q1 intelligence. NA: FO 898/257, EW to Colonel Kerr, Dec. 4, 1944.

58. "Report on Materials Forwarded from Berne," I.A. Richmond for the head of PWE's Italian section, Oct. 15, 1944, NA: FO 898/257.

59. Even getting agents into Switzerland was proving very difficult, because of the vigilance of the Swiss authorities, who in late 1943 were again deeply worried that the Germans might attempt a full invasion. SOE did nothing to stop the mass of goods flowing across the country into Italy. Also, when McCaffery became ill in late 1943, his SOE replacement had to be parachuted into a resistance circuit in France and then smuggled across the Swiss frontier; after that he was held in a Swiss internment camp before being released to assume his legation duties. Neville Wylie, *Britain, Switzerland, and the Second World War* (Oxford, 2003), pp. 275–7.

60. Tommaso Gallarati Scotti, *Memorie riservati di un ambasciatore. Il dairio di Tommaso Gallarati Scotti 1943–1951* (Milan, 2015), pp. 15–16, 35, 113–14, 130, 140.

61. Martin Clark, *Modern Italy 1871–1982*, p. 306.

62. Charles F. Delzell, *Mussolini's Enemies. The Italian Anti-Fascist Resistance* (Princeton, 1961), p. 430.

63. A little earlier, republics had been declared at Carnia in the north-east (Venetia) and Montefiorino in the central Apennines, aided by British and American liaison officers. These were also defeated.

64. EW, *Italy* (Oxford, 1947), p. 116.

65. EW, *The Europe I Saw*, p. 185. EW to Bruce Lockhart, Sept. 30, 1944, NA: FO 898/257.

66. EW, "The Last Phase of the War in Europe," pp. 128–9. Six days later heavily armed SS troops arrived and drove out these liberators and sacked Cannobio.

67. EW, Italy, p. 117; EW, *The Europe I Saw*, p. 185; EW, "The Breaking of the Axis," *International Affairs*, 22, 2 (1946), p. 239. Wiskemann referred several times to the case of Corinda Menguzzato (she mistakenly called her Clorinda Menguzzo).

68. EW, "The Italian Resistance," in A.J. Toynbee and V.M. Toynbee (eds.), *Hitler's Europe*, vol. 1 (Oxford, 1954), pp. 331–338, quote on p. 337. In a 1947 review, Wiskemann regretted the lack of understanding in Britain about the resistance struggle, almost "as if there had been some deliberate suppression of facts." The subject, she wrote, called for a new Trevelyan. EW, "Resurgent Italy," *Times Literary Supplement*, Jan. 25, 1947, p. 47.

69. EW, "The Italian Resistance," p. 331.

70. I.A. Richmond, "Report on Material Forwarded from Berne, October 15, 1944," NA: FO 898/257.

71. I.A. Richmond to Dr. Klibansky, Sept. 26, 1944, NA: FO 898/257.

72. EW, "Eastern Europe and Western Diplomats," *Fortnightly*, 158 (July 1945), pp. 304–310.

73. EW, *The Europe I Saw*, pp. 191–2.

74. EW to Lt.-Colonel Kerr, Oct. 19, 1944, NA: FO 898/257.

75. EW to Allen Dulles, April 3, 1943, NAWA RG 226 (OSS documents).

76. Neville Wylie, *Britain, Switzerland and the Second World War*, p. 298.

77. *The Diaries of Sir Robert Bruce Lockhart*, vol 2, p. 187. [Aug 13, 1942].

78. EW to Allen Dulles, Jan. 28, 1943, NAWA RG 226 (OSS documents).

79. Lucas Delattre, *A Spy at the Heart of the Third Reich: The Extraordinary Story of Fritz Kolbe* (New York, 2007). Delattre says that it was Kolbe's very good friend Ernst Kocherthler who went to see Cartwright as an intermediary and got thrown out. Most books, however, present the story as I have shown it.

80. Fritz Kolbe's (1900–71) information included details of the V1 and V2 programs; Japanese naval plans; exposure of 'Cicero,' a German spy working as a valet to the British Ambassador in Turkey; information about resistance groups and the Nazi hierarchy in Berlin; German assumptions about Allied landings in Western Europe; Nazi peace feelers, etc. Lucas Delattre, *A Spy at the Heart of the Third Reich*. It was Gerald Mayer who brought him to Dulles. SIS and Bletchley's response to Kolbe was complex. They were able to read a good deal of German signal traffic and knew about a secret German transmitter in Dublin. SIS feared that if Kolbe were captured carrying copies of telegrams to the OSS, the Nazis might learn the extent to which their cables had been intercepted and read and this could jeopardize the Ultra project. Bletchley had already read some of the telegrams Kolbe provided and they didn't want the German espionage unit in Dublin closed down. Dulles knew nothing of Ultra. Nigel West, "Fritz Kolbe and Allen Dulles: Masterspies?" *International Journal of Intelligence and Counterintelligence*, 19, 4 (2008), pp. 756–761.

81. EW, *The Europe I Saw*, p. 168.

82. Horst R. Sassin, *Liberale im Widerstand: Die Robinsohn-Strassmann Gruppe, 1934–1942. Hamburger Beiträge zur Sozial- und Zeitgeschichte, Band 340* (Hamburg, 1993), pp. 224–5, 486, fn 148.

83. EW, *The Europe I Saw*, p. 43.

84. EW, *The Europe I Saw*, p. 167.

85. Wirth knew remarkable things, EW acknowledged, but he drank too much to be reliable. *The Europe I Saw*, p. 169. Wirth was in contact with Sir Robert Vansittart's intelligence service, the French secret service, and the OSS, but he was careless and ultimately of little help to his resistance friends.

86. EW, *The Europe I Saw*, p. 167.

87. Knut Hansen, *Albrecht Graf von Bernstorff. Diplomat und Bankier zwischen Kaiserreich und Nationalsozialismus* (Frankfurt, 1996).

88. EW to Dulles, April 15 and n.d. (April) 1943, NAWA RG 226 (OSS documents). On Dohnanyi: Elisabeth Sifton and Fritz Stern, *No Ordinary Men. Dietrich Bonhoeffer and Hans von Dohnanyi: Resisters Against Hitler in Church and State* (New York, 2013).

89. EW, *The Europe I Saw*, pp. 167–8.

90. Gero Schulze-Gaevernitz (1901–70) had worked for Morgan Livermore in New York. He was the brother-in-law of the German industrialist Edmund Stinnes. He had extensive contacts in banking and diplomacy and was able to travel frequently between Switzerland and Germany.

91. EW, *The Europe I Saw*, p. 168. London knew something of Gisevius and Canaris from other sources, including the remarkable agent Halina Szymańska: see Keith Jeffery, *The Secret History of MI6, 1909–1949* (New York, 2010), pp. 380–82, 511–12.

92. Peter Hoffmann, *The History of the German Resistance, 1933–1945* (Cambridge, MA, 1977), p. 235.

93. Mary Bancroft, *Autobiography of a Spy* (New York, 1983; James Srodes, *Allen Dulles. Master of Spies*, p. 273. Elizabeth Scott-Montagu, *Honourable Rebel*, p. 334. Scott-Montagu probably joined Bancroft in the late spring or early summer of 1943—a particularly busy time for EW when she was under a lot of pressure.

94. Although their paths must have crossed many times, Wiskemann and Bancroft omitted each other from their memoirs, and Wiskemann also made no mention of Scott-Montagu.

95. Much has been written about Adam von Trott. Among his close friends were David Astor and Shiela Grant Duff. Klemens von Klemperer, *German Resistance Against Hitler: The Search for Allies Abroad 1938–45* (Oxford, 1992), pp. 122–129, 264–281; *A Noble Combat—The Letters of Shiela Grant Duff and Adam von Trott zu Solz 1932–1939* (Oxford, 1988). S. Grant Duff, *The Parting of the Ways—A Personal Account of the Thirties* (London, 1982); Christopher Sykes, *Troubled Loyalty* (London, 1968).

96. Clarita von Trott zu Solz, *Adam von Trott zu Solz: Eine Lebenbeschreibung* (Berlin, 2016), p. 276.

97. EW, *The Europe I Saw*, pp. 168–9.

98. Klemens von Klemperer, *German Resistance against Hitler*, p. 304, endnote 88 [source: "Aufzeichnungen von Harry Bergholz, 15.1. 1950," Adam von Trott Archive, Innsbruck].

99. It is unclear whether Trott passed along to Wiskemann a copy of this Memorandum. Correspondence between Visser 't Hooft and Bishop Bell on allied area bombing, contacts with the German opposition, and the need to give the Germans assurances about the future of their nation could not be exchanged via regular post for fear that they would be read by the Nazi secret service; encoded letters were exchanged via the British Embassy in Bern. From surviving documents, it seems that Wiskemann played a role in this.

100. Quoted in P. Hoffmann, "The Question of Western Allied Cooperation with the German Anti-Nazi Conspiracy, 1938–1944," *Historical Journal*, 34, 2 (1991), pp. 437–464, quote from p. 462. Also, Richard Lamb, *The Ghosts of Peace 1935–1945* (Wilton, Salisbury, 1987), p. 257.

101. EW, *The Europe I Saw*, p. 188.

102. EW "Germany Report Nr. 5," Nov. 2, 1944, conveyed information EW had gathered about the fate of von Moltke.

103. EW, *The Europe I Saw*, p. 188.

104. The day before tha coup EW had sent Dulles a report, based most likely on information from the former Democratic Party Reichstag deputy Ernst Lemmer, who had for some years been a reporter for the *Neue Zürcher Zeitung* and traveled frequently from Berlin to Switzerland. Lemmer arrived from Berlin on July 13 and reported to her on Catholic and labor opposition groups that were now active. EW to Dulles July 19, 1944, NAWA RG 226 (SS documents). Lemmer was also in contact with the Rote Kapelle resistance group; he survived the war and was a prominent figure postwar in the Christian Democratic Union. Another undated letter from EW to Dulles (probably written at the end of July or early August) contained early information about the aftermath of the plot: "German official left Berlin early July 22nd. Told old friend here Canaris probably involved in conspiracy against Hitler. Apart from Stauffenberg, source only knew so far that Generals Beck and Fromm and an intelligence officer had been executed. There had been many arrests."

105. EW, *The Europe I Saw*, p. 189.

106. Peter Hoffmann, "The Question of Western Allied Cooperation with the German Anti-Nazi Conspiracy," p. 463 [source: FO 371/39062]. Wheeler-Bennett had been transferred to PWE as an advisor on Europe in 1944; previously his war service was in the US as Assistant Director of the British Press Service in New York 1940–41 and then Special Assistant to the Director-General of British Information Services in Washington 1942–44. On the refusal in Whitehall to take seriously the German opposition around Canaris, see also: P.R.J. Winter, "British Intelligence and the July Bomb Plot of 1944: A Reappraisal," *War in History*, 13, 4 (2006) pp. 468–494.

107. Silvia Daniel, "'Troubled Loyalty'? Britisch-deutsche Debatten um Adam von Trott zu Solz, 1933–1969," *Vierteljahrshefte für Zeitgeschichte*, 52, 3 (July 2004), pp. 409–440. In Germany an increasingly positive focus on the German conservative civilian and military opposition (e.g. in works by Gerhard Ritter and Hans Rothfels) was fueled by anti-communism. Christopher Sykes papers, Box 32, Folders 7, 9.

108. J. Lewis, *David Astor* (New York, 2016), p. 259; C. Sykes to EW, May 8, 1968; EW to C. Sykes, Feb 3, 1966, Christopher Sykes papers. Grant Duff wrote David Astor an uncharacteristically furious letter saying that "the real disaster of Adam's life was that he put his trust in you and Cliveden and Chamberlain in 1939." Lewis, p. 260.

109. Christopher Sykes, "Heroes and Suspects: The German Resistance in Perspective," Encounter (Dec. 1968), pp. 39–47; David Astor, "Why the Revolt Against Hitler was Ignored," Encounter (June 1969), pp. 3–13; Christopher Sykes, "The Revolt against Hitler: A Reply to David Astor," Encounter (July 1969), pp. 90–94; Peter Calvocoressi, "On the Difficulties of Being an Anti-Nazi," plus letters from Sir John Wheeler-Bennett and Hugh Trevor-Roper Encounter (Aug. 1969), pp. 93–95; Harold Kurtz, J.H. van Roijen, C.C. Aronsfeld, W.A. Visser 'tHooft, Harold C. Deutsch, "David Astor and the German Opposition," Encounter (Sept. 1969), pp. 89–96; David Astor, "The German Opposition to Hitler: A Reply to Critics," Encounter (Oct. 1969), p. 97. Wiskemann appeared in the debate (but not by name) when Astor referred to her "unconvincing remark" about Trott's anti-Slav views; Sykes replied: "Mr. Astor faintly but effectively misquotes the lady…I should add that this lady-like personage is a formidable authority on modern Europe of which she is a most distinguished historian." Sykes, "The Revolt against Hitler," p. 94.

110. Wheeler-Bennett's work should also been seen in the context of the rehabilitation of nationalism and the Wehrmacht in Adenauer's Germany and British critiques of early postwar West Germany (see chapter 5, pp. 24–6).

111. P.R.J Winter, "British Intelligence and the July Bomb Plot of 1944: A Reappraisal," War in History, 13, 4 (November 2006), pp. 468–494; also "A Higher Form of Intelligence: Hugh Trevor-Roper and Wartime British Secret Service," Intelligence and National Security, 22, 6 (2007), pp. 847–880.

112. EW, The Europe I Saw, p. 200: "The Russians were more and more suspicious that the British and Americans were intending to make peace with the Germans behind their backs. Naturally the Germans did everything possible to nurture Russian suspicions, and messages poured into us in Switzerland from Nazis of all kinds, indirectly or even directly asserting that all they wished to do was to come over to our side in order to fight with us against the Russians. I remember being visited by a colleague of the Croat dictator, Pavelić…who explained that his heart had always been on our side. More striking perhaps was a message brought to me which purported to come from Heydrich's successor, the Austrian, Ernst Kaltenbrunner who magnanimously offered to give the Allies his support if I would let them know. I did not. The awkward thing was that quite early in 1945 Allen Dulles had encouraged the peace feelers of the SS Chief in Italy, Karl Wolff."

113. Kerstin von Lingen, Allen Dulles, the O.S.S. and Nazi War Criminals: The Dynamics of Selective Prosecution (Cambridge, 2013); also "Conspiracy of Silence: How the 'Old Boys' of American Intelligence Shielded SS General Karl Wolff from Prosecution," Holocaust and Genocide Studies, 22, 1 (Spring 2008), pp. 74–109. After the Eichmann trial German prosecutors found evidence that Wolff had helped speed up deportations of Jews to Treblinka. A Munich court finally found him guilty of complicity in genocide in 1964; further interventions on his behalf secured his release from prison in 1969 on medical grounds. For EW's view of Dollmann and his role in war crimes, see: The Rome-Berlin Axis, pp. 325–6.

114. Allen Dulles, The Secret Surrender (New York, 1966).

115. EW, "The Last Phase of the War in Europe," The World Today, 1, 3 (September 1945), p. 130.

116. EW, The Europe I Saw, p. 200.

117. EW, *The Europe I Saw*, p. 203.

118. EW, "Swiss Positions," *Times Literary Supplement*, March 31, 1966, p. 259: Oscar Düby "devoted himself to helping Jewish refugees get into Switzerland in spite of the thinly veiled hostility to them of the head of the Federal Police Force, Dr. Rothmund." Düby, a lawyer, worked for the Federal Police department dealing with aliens and was head of the section for emigrant and refugee care.

119. EW, *The Europe I Saw*, pp. 166–7. Drs. Otto and Anne Wertheimer ran the Galerie les Tourettes (Paris and Basle) in the postwar years.

120. David Kelly to Rex Leeper, Dec. 10, 1940, NA: FO 371/26508.

121. EW, *The Europe I Saw*, p. 153.

122. NA: HS 8/216, SO2 Executive Committee, Progress report for the week ending 3.4. 1941 (April 3, 1941). SO2 (previously D section) was until Aug. 1941 the active operations section of Dalton's SOE.

123. David Kelly to FO, March 31, 1941, NA: FO 371/26513 (Thorsten Noack, *NS-Euthanasie und international Öffentlichkeit*, [Frankfurt, 2017], p. 220).

124. EW to 'Rex' Leeper. Sept 4, 1941. She had correctly identified two killing centers, Grafeneck in south-west Germany and Sonnenstein in Saxony. On Shirer, see: Thorsten Noack, "William S. Shirer and International Awareness of the Nazi 'Euthanasia' Program," *Holocaust and Genocide Studies*, 30, 4 (Winter 2016), pp. 433–459. Noack says that Wiskemann believed Shirer had received his information from the British secret service, but by September 1941 there were several possible sources. Noack, *NS-Euthanasie und international Öffentlichkeit*, p. 114.

125. EW, "Report on Rumania," April 27, 1942, NA: FO 898/257. EW got this information from Dr. Carlo Fleischmann (1892–1965), the co-owner of a successful grain-trading business and an importer of raw materials, who had gone to Romania with a Swiss commercial group [*Einkaufskommission*].

126. NA: FO 371/34382 (63) March 12, 1943. Michael Fleming thinks that, because the figure was too low, "Wiskemann's data would have been useful to counter any demands to publicize the Jewish death toll at Auschwitz as reported by Rowecki and Jankowski." M. Fleming, *Auschwitz and the Allies* (Cambridge, 2015), p. 353, fn 22.

127. EW to Allen Dulles, March 25, 1943, NAWA RG 226 (OSS documents).

128. Neal H. Petersen (ed.), *From Hitler's Doorstep: The Wartime Intelligence Reports of Allen Dulles, 1942–1945* (Pennsylvania, 1996).

129. Richard Breitman, "Intelligence and the Holocaust," and Shlomo Aronson, "OSS X-2 and Rescue Efforts During the Holocaust," in David Bankier and G.L. Weinberg (eds.), *Secret Intelligence and the Holocaust* (New York and Jerusalem, 2006), pp. 17–48, 65–104.

130. M. Hastings, *The Secret War. Spies, Ciphers, and Guerrillas 1939–1945* (New York, 2016), p. 308.

131. EW, *The Europe I Saw*, pp. 160–1. Exactly what he had told her and what she meant is unclear.

132. Christopher R. Browning, "A Final Decision for the 'Final Solution'? The Riegner Telegram Reconsidered," *Holocaust and Genocide Studies*, 10, 1 (Spring 1996), pp. 3–10.

133. Hungarian diplomat Géza Soos, a leader in the resistance movement in Budapest, made two trips to Switzerland in 1943, one early in the year and the other in March or April. He met with Adolf Freudenberg and Visser t'Hooft and made contact with

EW and Dulles. Around this time in early 1943, EW sent Dulles a report on the situation in Hungary. EW to Allen Dulles, March 2, 1943, NAWA RG 226 (OSS documents).

134. M. Gilbert, *Auschwitz and the Allies* (London, 1981), pp. 232–4.Gerhart M. Riegner, *Never Despair* (Chicago, 2006), pp. 85–7. The combined report had been prepared and sent from Bratislava by Slovak Jewish leaders, led by Oskar Krasnansky. Also, Zoltán Tibori Szabó, "The Auschwitz Reports: Whot Got Them, and When?" in R.L. Braham and W. van den Heuvel, *The Auschwitz Reports and the Holocaust in Hungary* (New York, 2011), pp. 85–120.

135. Gerhart Riegner, interviewed for the Holocaust Museum by R. Breitman April 28 and May 11, 1992, RG – 50.030*0819 (U.S. Holocaust Memorial Museum), p. 433 and diskette 6, especially 01:40 – 01:45). Mark Roseman, *A Past in Hiding: Memory and Survival in Nazi Germany* (New York, 2000), pp. 372–3.

136. Martin Gilbert, *Auschwitz and the Allies*, p. 233.

137. Martin Gilbert, *Auschwitz and the Allies*, p. 233.

138. Ysrael Gutman and Michael Berenbaum, *Anatomy of the Auschwitz Death Camp* (Bloomington, IN, 1998), p. 566, fn 28. Dulles sent it on to Roswell D. McClelland of the War Refugee Board in Bern. War Refugee Board, Box 63. General Correspondence of R. McClelland. F. Misc. Documents and Reports re: Extermination Camps for Jews in Poland.

139. Norton Telegram, No. 2949, Urgent, War Cabinet Distribution, copy in Premier papers 4/51/10. M. Gilbert, "Could Britain have done more to stop the horrors of Auschwitz?" *Times*, Jan. 27, 2005. Michael Fleming, *Auschwitz, the Allies and Censorship of the Holocaust* (Cambridge, 2014), p. 232. Also, p. 369, fn 35 says that no evidence has been located that earlier Polish intelligence about Auschwitz that passed through Bern on its way to Britain was shared with EW. Possibly, this may have been due to the fact that the Poles worked closely with SOE, which often had strained relations with other British agencies. In London, Chaim Weizmann and Moshe Shartok (Secretary of the Jewish Agency) asked Eden to broadcast warnings to Hungarian railroad workers and to bomb the railway lines between Budapest and Auschwitz.

140. M. Gilbert, "Could Britain have done more to stop the horrors of Auschwitz?"

141. M. Fleming, *Auschwitz, the Allies and Censorship of the Holocaust*, p. 233; Tvsi Erez, "Hungary – Six days in July 1944," *Holocaust and Genocide Studies*, 3, 1 (1988), pp. 37–53; M. Mazower, *Hitler's Empire* (New York, 2008), pp. 404–5. Laszlo Borhi has introduced another complexity. He argues that the West was eager to negotiate with Hungary and Romania, believing that their exit from the war would force Hitler to divert major forces from north-west Europe to the area. Borhi argues that Dulles focused on this in late 1943 and early 1944 and seemed little concerned that it might signal disaster for Hungarian Jewry, the last major Jewish community surviving. Borhi's thesis is controversial; the Hungarians had their own reasons for seeking to escape Nazi control and a Soviet occupation (for a time they also believed that a British and American invasion would occur in the Balkans). Laszlo Borhi, *Dealing with Dictators: The United States, Hungary, and East Central Europe, 1942–1989* (Bloomington, IN, 2016), chapter 1. Also, his "Secret Peace Overtures, the Holocaust and Allied Strategy vis-à-vis Germany," Journal of Cold War Studies, 14, 2 (Spring 2012), pp. 29–67.

142. This is also the view of Frank Baron in his detailed analysis of the multiple threads within and outside Hungary that influenced Horthy: Stopping the Trains to Auschwitz: Budapest 1944 (Lawrence, KS 2020), pp. 13–27, 31–38. While busy arranging a brief return to London in October 1944, EW was continuing to provide information on the situation in Hungary and specifically the actions of the Protestant Churches. EW to Kerr, Oct. 25, 1944, handwritten P.S. on October 26, NA: FO 898/257. Dr. Andrea Kirchner (Fritz Bauer Institute, Goethe University, Frankfurt am Main) is working on a study of Richard Lichtheim which may uncover additional information on EW's role.

143. B. Rogers, "British Intelligence and the Holocaust: Auschwitz and the Allies Re-examined," Journal of Holocaust Education, 8, 1 (summer 1999), pp. 89–106; M. Fleming, "Allied Knowledge of Auschwitz: A (Further) Challenge to the 'Elusiveness' Narrative," Holocaust and Genocide Studies, 28, 1 (spring 2014), pp. 31–57. M. Fleming, Auschwitz, the Allies and Censorship of the Holocaust. Also, Walter Laqueur, The Terrible Secret (Boston, 1980). Fleming also points to a PWE-issued aide-mémoire for staff that mentioned the killing at Auschwitz, NA: FO 371/39014 (441) "Special Annex on the Persecution of the Jews," March 24, 1944.

144. M. Fleming, "The Reassertion of the elusiveness narrative: Auschwitz and Holocaust Knowledge," Holocaust Studies (online, April 2020).

145. J.P. Fox, "The Jewish Factor in British War Crimes Policy in 1942," English Historical Review, 92, 362 (Jan. 1977), pp. 82–106. Bernard Wasserstein, Britain and the Jews of Europe, 1939–1945 (Oxford, 1979).

146. M. Fleming, "British Narratives of the Holocaust in Hungary," Twentieth Century British History, 27, 4 (2016), pp. 555–577. Fleming focuses on the role of C.A. Macartney (1895–1978) in framing the coverage of Hungary in the Weekly Intelligence Summary [WIS] and BBC broadcasts to Hungary. Macartney was a student of R.W. Seton-Watson, although they fell out over their respective advocacy of Czechoslovakia and Hungary in the 1920s. Macartney's deep sympathies led him to downplay criticism of Hungary in the WIS coverage. Later he preceded EW as Montague Burton Professor of International Affairs at Edinburgh. Miklos Lojkó, "C.A. Macartney and Central Europe," European Review of History, 6, 1 (1999), pp. 37–57.

147. FO Telegram to EW in Bern, April 15, 1943, NA: FO 898/257.

148. C.J. Child to Lt.-Colonel Kerr, Aug. 12, 1944, NA: FO 898/257.

149. EW cypher from Bern to FO, Aug. 24, 1944, NA: FO 988/257. On Kühne & Nagel: Johannes K. Beermann-Schön, "Taking Advantage: German Freight Forwarders and Property Theft," in C. Kreutzmüller and J.R. Zatlin (eds.), Dispossession: Plundering German Jewry, 1933–1945 (Ann Arbor, MI, 2020), pp. 127–147.

150. EW, The Europe I Saw, p. 203.

151. EW to Kerr, June 9, 1945, NA: FO 898/257. Presumably for use by those preparing for the Nuremberg tribunal.

152. In fact, the Vichy regime continued to use the tricolor flag. She may have seen the original tricolor in place of the Petain tricolor, which had a fransisc or double-headed axe on the white stripe. She may also have seen a tricolor flag with the cross of Lorraine on the white stripe (often flown by the Free French).

153. EW to Lt.-Colonel Kerr, Nov. 2, 1944, NA: FO 898/257. Dulles traveled to London and Washington with Donovan in September and October.

154. EW to Lt.-Colonel Kerr, Oct. 25, 1944, NA: FO 898/257.

155. EW to Lt.-Colonel Kerr, Oct. 14, 1944, NA: FO 898/257.

156. Lt.-Colonel Kerr, memo: "Reinforcement for Miss Wiskemann," Oct. 27, 1944, NA: FO 898/257.

157. Brigadier Eric Sachs memo. Oct. 30, 1944, NA: FO 898/257. A.R. Walmsley (head of the German section) believed that there was a need for several people to gather intelligence for Germany and Austria alone. On one memo about Italy was scrawled a question: Could she be sent a list of priorities for Italy without indicating "how far such material is to have priority over German, French, and Balkans?"

158. Lt.-Colonel Kerr to EW, Nov. 2, 1944, NA: FO 898/257.

159. C.J. Child to Lt.-Colonel Kerr, Aug. 12, 1944, NA: FO 898/257.

160. Lt.-Colonel Kerr to C.J. Child and A.R. Warmsley, Sept. 18, 1944, NA: FO 898/257.

161. Sefton Delmer to Lt.-Colonel Kerr, Dec. 11, 1944, NA: FO 898/257.

162. Lt.-Colonel Kerr to Brigadier Sachs, (DPW1) Top secret, Dec. 16, 1944, NA: FO 898/257.

163. Delmer to DW1, Oct. 31, 1944. Also, Director-General (via J. Wheeler-Bennett), Oct. 30, 1944, NA: FO 898/257.

164. C.J. Child to Lt.-Colonel Kerr, Oct. 21, 1944, NA: FO 898/257.

165. EW to Lt.-Colonel Kerr, Sept. 21, 1944, NA: FO 898/257.

166. Clifford Norton telegrams, June 16, 1944; Sept. 6, 1944, NA: FO 898/257. He asked the FO to take this up with PWE.

167. B.P. Burgess (MOI to W. Stewart Roberts (PID), Aug. 7, 1944; MOI to W. Stewart Roberts, Director of Finance, Sept. 25, 1944, NA: FO 898/257.

168. EW to Lt.-Colonel Kerr, Nov. 4, 1944, NA: FO 898/257.

169. "Cousin Jane": Janet May Brough Pollitt (1899–1986). In *The Europe I Saw* EW refers to her three times without giving any specific information (often the case with those like Harry Bergholz to whom she was close). Jane's mother, like EW's, belonged to a family prominent in Ipswich, and the two women were painters and attended the Ipswich art school. Their daughters were born in the same year and the girls became close friends from an early age. EW indicates that she first went to Naples in 1925 with Jane, who was teaching at an international school there; later in 1934 the two went on a cruise to Greece. Jane seems to have helped EW with her research and writing and in the 1946–47 electoral registers she is listed as sharing EW's flat in St. George's Square.

170. Physicist P.M.S. Blackett and his wife, Constanza, were old friends. Blackett had gone to Magdalene College, Cambridge, in 1919 and his wife was at Newnham, overlapping with EW. It was during the V2 attacks. Showing Elizabeth her bedroom, Constanza commented: "If a V2 comes it will blow you out of the window and then back again, but you'll be dead by then, so you won't mind." *The Europe I Saw*, p. 198. Blackett had also been a member of the Heretics Club at Cambridge.

171. Memo by Lt.-Colonel Kerr, April 4, 1945, NA: FO 898/257.

172. EW to Colonel Kerr, Feb. 10, 1945; Jan 23, 1945, NA: FO 898/257.

173. EW to Kerr, June 4, 1945, FO 898/257. Franco Marinotti (1891–1966) came to the British at the end of 1944 as an intermediary of the SS with overtures that Western Allies should agree to a cease-fire while allowing the continuation of the war against the Red Army. The British rejected the approach out of hand; Dulles probed more

deeply, hoping to find a formula that would satisfy the spirit of unconditional surrender. J.H. Waller, *The Unseen War in Europe. Espionage and Conspiracy in the Second World War* (New York, 1996), p. 367.

174. EW, *The Europe I Saw*, p. 199.

175. She also seems to be referring to Kramer in her criticisms of *Freies Deutschland*: "the leftist grouping of German emigrés calling itself *Freies Deutschland* became increasingly vociferous. A painful situation arose because it felt called upon to denounce the cowardice and treachery of compatriots who had only come out into the open against Hitler since Urach's arrival, one or two of them actual victims of Urach's purge. Inevitably the people attacked included certain persons who had been working for the Allies as long as they could do so without being discovered, and discretion made it almost impossible for them to defend themselves, although a number of *Freies Deutschland* people had contributed much less to the downfall of the Nazis." EW, "The Last Phase of the War in Europe," *The World Today*, 1, 3 (September 1945), p. 134.

176. EW to Colonel Kerr, Feb. 10, 1945, NA: FO 898/257; I have not been able to identify Q1's name.

177. EW to Colonel Kerr, Dec. 4, 1944, NA: FO 898/257.

178. EW to Kerr, Feb. 14, 1945, NA: FO 898/257. At this point Q1 was being detained at Chiasso on the Ticino border between Switzerland and Italy.

179. Patricia Meehan, *The Unnecessary War: Whitehall and the German Resistance to Hitler* (London, 1992), p. 328.

180. Kerr to EW, Aug. 29, 1944. She was asked for details of age, background, views of Great Britain and the US, estimate of professional ability, assistance to Jews or other activities, etc. Among those she recommended as a candidate for reconstruction planning or international relief was Swiss lawyer Oscar Düby, who had worked to facilitate the entry of Jews into Switzerland.

181. EW to General Secretary of PWE, Sept. 21, 1944; Lt.-Colonel Kerr sent EW's questions to the Director of Plans, Oct. 5, 1944, NA: FO 898/257.

182. Trevor Blewitt to EW, March 23, 1945, BBC Archives Caversham.

183. EW to Kerr, April 14, 1945, NA: FO 898/257. PID was established in 1939 under 'Rex' Leeper as the Political Intelligence Department of the Foreign Office. The name continued in use, but after 1943 it was a cover for the Political Warfare Executive [PWE].

184. EW to Kerr, May 11, 1945, NA: FO 898/257. A.R. Walmsley was eager to employ EW but in early May 1945 was not sure she could at that moment be fitted into the German or Austrian section.

185. EW to Lt.-Colonel Kerr, May 21, 1945, NA: FO 898/257.

186. Major Grazebrook to John Wheeler-Bennett, May 29, 1945, NA: FO 898/257. Klibansky himself transferred to the denazification program in Germany before resuming his academic career in 1946, gaining a Chair of Philosophy at McGill University.

187. Michael Balfour, one of those to whom she reported in Whitehall during the war, became Director of Information Services in the British zone in 1946. M. Balfour, *Propaganda in War, 1939–1945* (London, 1979).

188. Michael Balfour, "Intelligence Arrangements in Switzerland: The competence of Miss Wiskemann," April 1, 1943, NA: FO 898/257.

189. EW to Guglielmo Alberti, n.d., December 1943, Alberti papers; EW to Allen Dulles, Dec. 24, 1943; EW to Allen Dulles, Dec. 26, 1943, NAWA RG 226 (OSS documents).

190. EW to Bergholz, Aug. 5, 1943; also, EW to Bergholz, Dec. 23, 1942.

191. Harry Bergholz, "Memoiren Schweiz" (unpublished hand-written manuscript), p. 192ff. Deutsches Exilarchiv, 1933–45 (Frankfurt am Main).

192. EW to Bergholz, March 9, 1943. In a letter to Sean Lester, March 21, 1943, she seems to be eager to downplay any 'suspicions' about her relationship to Gautier: "I want to say, please don't misunderstand my interest in Gautier's return, which was due to the fact that he took various messages for me and then on Nov. 8 became the only means by which the answers can reach me…I just felt I wanted to explain because I gather that some people have been discovering marvelous interpretations…as they always do." Sean Lester papers [P203/50], University College, Dublin Archives.

193. EW to Harry Bergholz, June 2, 1943.

194. EW to Bergholz, June 19, 1943. There was another crisis in October 1943 when she thought she might be pregnant again by Bergholz: EW to Bergholz, Oct. 13, 1943: "Too peculiar - my period ought to have come 1 week plus 1 day ago and there is no sign of it. I've suddenly got panic-stricken…but yet I cannot see how it could possibly be anything terrible, do you?…I want to come to supper with you next Tuesday or Wed. please, but I can't wait so long – please write to me quickly to reassure me or prepare me for the worst. Otherwise, I may be going to have the change of life very young…It seems to me absurd to be scared and yet I am. Much love, E."

195. EW to Bergholz, Aug. 5, 1943.

196. EW to Bergholz, April 20, 1944; EW to Bergholz, April 21, 1944.

197. EW to Bergholz, May 22, 1944; also, May 4 and May 15–17, 1944.

198. EW to Guglielmo Alberti, April 6, 1945, Alberti papers.

199. EW to Guglielmo Alberti, April 27, 1945, Alberti papers. Why EW wanted Francesco to see Mottironi is unclear; perhaps it relates to the attacks on him in Rome or possibly it was about a job. Mottironi was the delegate of the Italian Red Cross in Geneva dealing with the repatriation of Italian prisoners of war.

200. EW to Dr. Klibansky, May 11, 1945, NA: FO 898/257. It is difficult to find out much about the Marchese Francesco Antinori. He was born in Perugia into an ancient aristocratic family, son of Giacomo Antinori and Maria Bourbon del Monte Santa Maria. He had a degree in jurisprudence. Assigned to the press section of the Foreign Service, he was press attaché to the Italian Embassy in Berlin 1929–40; then the Madrid Embassy, 1940–43. He then served at the Italian Legation in Bern 1943–44 and again 1947–51. From 1945–47 he was at the Press Office of Ministry of Foreign Affairs in Rome (De Gasperi and Nenni were Foreign Ministers).

201. EW to Bergholz, n.d.1945.

202. EW to Bergholz, n.d. late 1944 or early 1945.

203. EW to Bergholz, June 5, 1945.

204. Anne Sebba, *Battling for News. The Rise of the Woman Reporter* (London, 1995), p. 239. From 1951 Antinori was at the Italian Embassy in London, from 1953 as press counsellor. *Archivio biographico Italiano. Nuova serie* (1997, microfiche). In the late 1960s he lived in Italy, spending Christmases with the Magnani family (whom he had met through Wiskemann). Information from Prof. Marco Magnani.

205. EW to Guglielmo Alberti, April 13, 1947, Alberti papers.

206. EW, *The Europe I Saw*, pp. 203–4. Kogon's intended transfer from Buchenwald to Auschwitz had been postponed three times and he was scheduled to be shot shortly before the camp's liberation by the Allies.

207. BBC Oral history: Elisabeth Barker, interviewed by Leonard Miall (May 9, 1983), Imperial War Museum, Sound Archive cassette 10606.

208. For example, E.M. Barker, "Berne Special Pilot, No. 244," Jan. 31, 1943, NA: FO 898/257.

209. Obituary by her younger brother Nicholas Barker, *Times*, March 28, 1986; she was awarded an OBE in May 1967. Also N. Barker to G. Field, April 19, 2017.

210. Shiela Grant Duff to Clementine Churchill, Nov. 1940, Box 3/5 Shiela Grant Duff Sokolov papers.

211. Ondřej Koutek, "The Overseas Resistance on the Airwaves of the BBC: Czechoslovak Broadcasts from London, 1939–45," *Behind the Iron Curtain*, 3, 1 (2014), pp. 9–22.

212. *TLS*, Jan. 4, 1947.

213. EW, "Eastern Europe and Western Diplomats, p. 309.

214. EW, "Eastern Europe and Western Diplomats," pp. 309–10.

215. EW, *The Europe I Saw*, p. 204.

216. EW, *The Europe I Saw*, p. 212.

Chapter 5

1. EW (from Rome) to Harry Bergholz, Dec. 8, 1945.

2. EW to Guglielmo Alberti, Oct. 15, 1945, Alberti papers.

3. EW, *The Europe I Saw*, p. 214.

4. EW to Guglielmo Alberti, Jan. 27, 1946.

5. EW to Guglielmo Alberti, Jan. 27, 1946. Alberti was very helpful, introducing her to writer Arturo Luria, poet Eugenio Montale, the editor Alberto Coracci, as well as re-connecting her with people she had previously met, like Umberto Morra.

6. EW, *The Europe I Saw*, pp. 214–15.

7. EW, "Roman Christmas," *Spectator*, Jan. 4, 1946, p. 7.

8. [EW], *Economist*: "Armistice Italy," Nov. 10, 1945, pp. 669–670; "Crisis in Italy," Nov. 24, 1945, pp. 752–753. Correspondents writing for the *Economist* were not identified by name. How much editing/re-writing was done by senior editors is unknown but probably very little in EW's case since she always submitted well-written copy at the prescribed length. Her contributions were usually described as "From a correspondent in Rome" or "From a correspondent in Italy." Here I have used parentheses [EW].

9. EW, "The Poles in Italy," *Spectator*, Feb. 1, 1946, p. 110. Also, "Italians and Anders' Army," *Observer*, Jan. 13, 1946, p. 1. For her view of General Anders, see also EW, "General Anders' Story," *Spectator*, Aug. 5, 1949, p. 184.

10. There were some twenty-five daily newspapers in Italy and innumerable weeklies and magazines, and a readership thirsting for news. On Italian periodicals in this period, see the special issue of *Journal of Modern Italian Studies*, 1 (2016), and the special issue of *Modern Italy*, 2 (Jan. 2016).

11. David Ward, *Antifascisms: Cultural Politics in Italy 1943–1946* (London, 1996).

12. EW, *Italy* (Oxford, 1947), p. 138.

13. EW, *The Europe I Saw*, p. 229. Craveri, one of the founders of *Giustizia è Libertà*, had worked with Allen Dulles and OSS in the war. On this, see: V. Gozzer, "OSS and ORI: The Raimondo Craveri and Max Corvo Partnership," *Journal of Modern Italian Studies*, 4, 1 (1999), pp. 32–36. Both Elena and Raimondo were supporters of the Action party.

14. The first Polish ambassador in postwar Rome was her old friend Professor Stanislaw Kot (1885–1975). A historian, he had been close to General Sikorski and was one of the leaders of the exile Polish government in London during the war. EW knew him from her pre-war travels in Poland, and in Rome she often dined with him, sometimes taking Silone and other friends along. In 1947, with the Communist consolidation of power in Poland, Kot resigned and spent the rest of his life in London.

15. EW, "South Italian Problem," *Spectator*, Aug. 15, 1946, p. 163. On this circle see: Caroline Moorhead, *A Bold and Dangerous Family* (New York, 2017).

16. EW, *The Europe I Saw*, p. 231.

17. Jomarie Alano, *A Life of Resistance: Ada Prospero Marchesini Gobetti, 1902–1968* (Rochester, 2016). Also, Caroline Moorhead, *A House in the Mountains: The Women Who Liberated Italy from Fascism* (New York, 2020).

18. Undated fragment of a letter from EW to Bernard Berenson (probably 1949), Bernard and Mary Berenson papers, Harvard University Center for Italian Renaissance Studies, Villa I Tatti, Florence.

19. EW, *The Europe I Saw*, p. 228.

20. EW to Guglielmo Alberti, May 18, 1946.

21. EW, "Socialism and Communism in Italy" *Foreign Affairs*, 24, 3 (April 1946), p. 492.

22. EW, "Six Parties Will Join Italy's Cabinet," *Observer*, Dec. 2, 1945, p. 5. [EW], "Crisis in Italy," *Economist*, Nov. 24, 1945, pp. 752–3; [EW], "The Italian Scene," *Economist*, Dec. 1, 1945, p. 787.

23. [EW], "After the Crisis," *Economist*, Jan. 19, 1946, pp. 98–99.

24. EW, "Italy's Governments," *Spectator*, Dec. 9, 1945, p. 535.

25. EW, *The Europe I Saw*, p. 217.

26. [EW], "The Italian Parties," *Economist*, Feb. 23, 1946, p. 298.

27. EW, *The Europe I Saw*, p. 218.

28. EW, *The Europe I Saw*, p. 217.

29. EW, "Socialism and Communism in Italy," pp. 484–493. This is an especially astute analysis of the relationship between the Communists and Socialists which attests to EW's intimate knowledge of the two parties and her contacts with leading figures. Also, EW, "Unstable Italy," *Spectator*, Nov. 28, 1947, p. 674.

30. EW, "Socialism and Communism in Italy," p. 489.

31. Liberals gained forty-one and the *Qualunquisti* thirty seats. Wiskemann also noted that in these municipal elections voters (including women) turned out in large numbers (she suggested 80–85%) "which belies the charges of political apathy sometimes made against the Italians." *Economist*, April 20, 1946, p. 641.

32. EW, "The Birth of a Republic," *Fortnightly*, 160, 6 (July 1946), p. 21.

33. [EW], "Italy's Choice," *Economist*, June 1, 1946, p. 886.

34. EW, "The Birth of a Republic," p. 22.

35. [EW], "The House of Savoy," *Economist*, May 11, 1946, p. 748.

36. EW to Guglielmo Alberti, July 3, 1946.

37. [EW], "After the Referendum," *Economist*, June 22, 1946, pp. 1005–1006. Also, EW, "The Papal Victory, 1848–1948," *History Today*, 1, 11 (November 1951), pp. 62–69. Years later Percy Allum made the same point, "The South and National Politics 1945–50," in S.J. Woolf (ed.), The Rebirth of Italy, 1943–1950 (London, 1972), p. 108. EW also criticized the Catholic Church for impeding the building of schools and its

lack of commitment to teachers and education: EW, "The Re-education of Italy," *Spectator*, June 5, 1947, pp. 648–649; EW, "Fascism and Education," *Spectator*, Dec. 27, 1946, pp. 710–712.

38. EW, "Socialism and Communism in Italy," p. 485.

39. EW, *The Europe I Saw*, pp. 222–3. EW had been a strong advocate of easily obtained birth control since her Cambridge days. On this occasion she remembered that her young friend Franca Magnani had just beforehand "been groaning to me over the obstacles to any knowledge of birth control in Italy."

40. Paolo Baffi, "The Bank of Italy and Foreign Economists 1944–1953: A Personal Memoir," *Rivista di Storia Economica*, 2, 2 (1985), p. 5. Baffi (Governor of the Bank of Italy in the 1970s) remembered that EW and Barbara Ward (who was at the time on the editorial staff of the *Economist*) spent time in those postwar years at the Bank of Italy's research department.

41. [EW], "Problems of Italian Reconstruction": 1. "Political Deadlock in Italy," *Economist*, Nov. 30, 1946, p. 872–873; 2. "New Deal for Italian Agriculture," *Economist*, Dec. 21, 1946, pp. 1001–1002; 3. "Italian Economy in the Balance," *Economist*, Feb. 1, 1947, pp. 199–200; "Crisis in Foreign Trade," *Economist*, Feb. 8, 1947, pp. 246–248. As she pointed out, much of the Italian economy was already nationalized (via the IRI, or Institute for Industrial Reconstruction, established during the Depression). Unlike in postwar Britain, political debate was not over nationalization but over what to do with the nationalized undertakings.

42. Ivor Thomas, *The Problem of Italy: An Economic Survey* (London, 1946); reviewed by Wiskemann in the *Spectator* April 26, 1946, pp. 434–5.

43. [EW], "New Deal for Italian Agriculture," *Economist*, Dec. 21, 1946.

44. "In Italy, where the remnants of feudal agriculture and of bastard industrial corporativism lie like chains around the nation's neck, any constructive reform must offend one or other of the Conservative vested interests, and the Christian Democrats rely on them too greatly for their voting strength to risk decisive action." "Political Deadlock in Italy," *Economist* Nov. 30, 1946.

45. For Wiskemann's hopes that Councils of Management in factories might transform Italian industrial relations: EW, "Italians at Work," *Tribune*, June 6, 1947, pp. 8–9.

46. EW, "Unstable Italy," pp. 674–675.

47. Chatham House Archives, RIIA/8/1405. EW, "The Situation in Italy," May 22, 1947, discussion meeting.

48. The mood in her pro-Action circles was captured by Carlo Levi's novel *L'orologio* (Turin, 1950). "Something went out of Roman life after the election," wrote literary translator William Weaver, "a kind of resignation set in as if almost everyone I knew had belonged to a single, widespread defeated party." W. Weaver (ed.), *Open City. Seven Writers in Postwar Rome* (Vermont, 1999), p. 26.

49. EW, *The Europe I Saw*, p. 225. In the summer of 1951 EW returned to cover the local elections that completed the rout as communists and socialists lost power in many northern cities, with the exception of the 'Red Zone' of Emilia Romagna and Tuscany. EW, "Italy's 'Red' Zone," *The Twentieth Century*, 150 (July 1951), pp. 297–306; EW, "The Italian Political Scene: Significance of the Local Elections," *The World Today*, July 1951, pp. 283–292; EW, "Die Linke in Italien: Die entmachteten Starken und die geprellten Zauderer," *Frankfurter Hefte*, 6, Hefte 7 (July 1951), pp. 502–507.

50. EW, "South Italian Problem," *Spectator*, Aug. 15, 1946, pp. 163–164.

51. Leone and Natalia Ginzburg lived 1941–43 in a village in the Abruzzo (viz: Natalia Ginzburg, *Tutti I Nostri Ieri*, Turin, 1952). In 1949, Cesare Pavese's novella *Il Carcere* described his twelve-month confinement in 1935 in the Calabrian coastal village of Brancaleone.

52. EW, "Crisis in Calabria," *Spectator*, Nov. 25, 1949, p. 734.

53. EW, *The Europe I Saw*, p. 232.

54. J.A. Davis, "Christopher Seton-Watson, the Second World War and Italian Liberalism," *Modern Italy*, 16, 4 (Nov. 2011), pp. 411–425 (Howard quoted on p. 413).

55. C. Seton-Watson, *Dunkirk–Alamein–Bologna: Letters and Diaries of an Artilleryman 1939–1945* (London, 1994), p. 254. An obituary for Seton-Watson recalled how "he was shocked by what he perceived as a complete lack of a sense of noblesse oblige on the part of the upper-class Italians he encountered in Rome." *Guardian*, Dec. 3, 2007. His papers have been deposited in the Bodleian Library, University of Oxford, but have not been catalogued and are not yet accessible to scholars. Given that he kept a detailed diary of his travels during the war years, he probably left an account of this expedition with Wiskemann too.

56. C. Seton-Watson, *Dunkirk–Alamein–Bologna*, p. 254.

57. Among the fruits of his research is the magisterial *Italy from Liberalism to Fascism* (London, 1967).

58. EW, *The Europe I Saw*, pp. 232–3.

59. EW, "South Italian Agriculture" [review of *Riforma agrarian e azione meridionalista*], *TLS*, July 8, 1949, p. 439. Also letter from EW to Alan Pryce Jones, editor of the *TLS*, May 31, 1949. Alan Pryce-Jones papers [GEN Mss 513, box 25, Nr. 1310].

60. EW, "Crisis in Calabria," *Spectator*, Nov. 25, 1949. E.W. "Poverty and Population in the South," *Foreign Affairs*, 28, 1 (Oct. 1949), pp. 84–91. EW, "The Land Problem of Southern Italy," *The World Today*, 5, 6 (June 1949), pp. 251–257.

61. EW, "Poverty and Population in the South," p. 87.

62. EW, *The Europe I Saw*, p. 234.

63. EW, *Italy*, pp. 92, 97, 101.

64. EW, *Italy*, p. 102. Closely related in substance to *Italy* are her early articles: "The Breaking of the Axis," *International Affairs*, 22, 2 (March 1946), pp. 227–239 and (published a few years later) "The Italian Resistance," her contribution to A.J. Toynbee and V.M. Toynbee, *Hitler's Europe*, vol. 1. (Oxford, 1954), pp. 327–337.

65. *Italy*, p. 145. Reviews of the book were favorable: Muriel Grindrod, *International Affairs*, 24, 1 (Jan. 1948), p. 131; Janet Trevelyan (wife of G.M. Trevelyan and a leading member of the British-Italian League and the British Institute in Florence), wrote a glowing review ending with the hope that EW would "soon be able to devote her great talents to a study of Italy's recovery." *Spectator*, Sept. 12, 1947, p. 342.

66. The Foreign Office Research Department gave her access to the originals of documents quoted at Nuremberg and to the unpublished letters exchanged between Mussolini and Hitler. Its Director of Research and Librarian was E.J. Passant, a former Cambridge don, whom she knew from Berlin in the early 1930s.

67. Her diplomatic sources included: Vittorio Cerruti (Berlin Ambassador in 1933); Raffaele Guaraglia (Ambassador to France, the Vatican, and Turkey and then Badoglio's Foreign Minister); Count Massimo Magistrati (long-term Counsellor in

Berlin and married to Ciano's sister); Michele Lanza (First Secretary of the Berlin Embassy 1939–43), and, of course, Antinori, who worked closely with Ambassador Attolico in Berlin until they were both transferred in 1940. She also interviewed former Austrian Chancellor Kurt von Schuschnigg and the former Polish and French Ambassadors in Berlin, Josef Lipski and André Francois-Poncet.

68. EW, "Memoirs as a Source of Recent History," *TLS*, Nov. 10, 1950, p. 716.

69. Her friend Cecil Sprigge took over as Rome correspondent: D. McLachlan to C.J. Sprigge, Sept. 10, 1947, Sprigge papers 1703/202.

70. EW, *The Rome-Berlin Axis* (Oxford, 1949), p. 339.

71. Her journalism in the 1930s, focusing on Italian policy towards Austria and the 'Little Entente,' viewed Mussolini as a shrewd operator on the international stage, very different from the "sawdust Caesar" of some early books: George Seldes, *Sawdust Caesar: The Untold History of Mussolini "the Unholy Alliance," and Fascism* (London, 1936). For later British accounts that emphasize Mussolini's lack of a clear set of goals: D. Mack Smith, *Mussolini's Roman Empire* (London, 1976); A.J.P. Taylor, "The Great Pretender," (review of Mack Smith) in *New York Review of Books*, Aug. 5, 1976; Ivone Kirkpatrick, *Mussolini: A Study in Power* (London, 1964); R. Absalom, *Italy since 1800: A Nation in the Balance* (London, 1995), pp. 143–6.

72. Alan Cassels, *Mussolini's Early Diplomacy* (Princeton, 1970); Esmonde M. Robertson, *Mussolini as Empire-Builder: Europe and Africa, 1932–1936* (London, 1977); MacGregor Knox, *Mussolini Unleashed, 1939–1941: Politics and Strategy in Fascist Italy's Last War* (Cambridge, 1982); MacGregor Knox, "The Fascist Regime, its Foreign Policy and its Wars: An 'Anti-Fascist' Orthodoxy?" *Contemporary European History*, 4, 3 (1995), pp. 347–365; R.J.B Bosworth, *The Italian Dictatorship* (Oxford, 1998), chapter 4.

73. G.P. Gooch, *Contemporary Review* 176 (July–Dec. 1949), p. 313.

74. Martin Wight review in *International Affairs 25*, 3 (July 1949), p. 370.

75. H. Trevor-Roper, "The Unholy Alliance," *Observer*, May 1, 1949, p. 7.

76. *Spectator*, April 15, 1949, p. 518 by Alan Bullock. Also, James Joll in *History*, 37, 130 (June 1952), pp. 172–3; W.N. Medlicott, *English Historical Review*, 64, 253 (Oct. 1949), p. 567 also praised the book's high standard of scholarship as confirmation of the legitimacy of contemporary history. Other reviews in academic journals included: *Revue historique*, 212, 1 (1954), pp. 139–41 (J.B. Duroselle); *The American Political Science Review*, 43, 5, (Oct. 1949), pp. 1048–1049 (B. McCown Mattison); *American Historical Review*, 55, 1 (Oct. 1949), pp. 139–140 (Raymond Sontag); *Journal of Modern History*, 23, 1 (June 1951), pp. 177–178 (Eric Kollman).

77. EW, *The Rome-Berlin Axis*, p. 346.

78. EW, *The Rome-Berlin Axis*, p. 344. The linkage of Hitler and Nietzsche was very common in the 1940s: M. Whyte, "The Uses and Abuses of Nietzsche in the Third Reich: Alfred Baeumler's 'Heroic Realism,'" *Journal of Contemporary History*, 43, 2 (April 2008), pp. 171–194. Also, Steven E. Aschheim, *The Nietzsche Legacy in Germany 1890–1990* (Berkeley, CA, 1994).

79. "Two Dictatorships," *TLS*, April 16, 1949, p. 243.

80. James Joll review, *History*, 37, 130 (June 1952), pp. 172–3. Rene Albrecht-Carrié, *Political Science Quarterly*, 65, 2, (June 1950), pp. 305–307 saw the comments on Nietzsche references as a device "which makes for literary quality but which historically, may be open to some question." EW removed the Nietzsche references in a later edition.

81. Taylor wrote two reviews: "The Axis," *Manchester Guardian*, May 3, 1949, p. 4 and "The Supermen: Hitler and Mussolini," originally in the *New Statesman* and reproduced in his book *From Napoleon to Stalin* (London, 1950), pp. 161–166. EW was mostly happy with her reviews, describing them to her friend Richard Hughes as "kind, except for Carr in the TLS [she was mistaken here] and, of course, the pathological Mr. A.J.P. Taylor." EW to Richard Hughes, Dec. 29, 1949, Richard Hughes papers. To Bernard Berenson, she complained that while ready to accept some of Taylor's criticism, "most of his article consists of stuff taken from me but put out as the original thought of A.J.P. Taylor and that angers me." EW to Berenson, n.d., but late 1949 or 1950, I Tatti Archives, Florence.

82. EW, *The Rome-Berlin Axis*, pp. 245, 270, 282. Donald Sassoon, "Italy After Fascism. The Predicament of Dominant Narratives," in R. Bessel and D. Schumann (eds.), *Life and Death. Approaches to a Social and Cultural History of Europe during the 1940s and 1950s* (Cambridge, 2003), pp. 259–290; Rosario Forlenza, "Sacrificial Memory and Political Legitimacy in Postwar Italy: Reliving and Remembering World War II," *History and Memory*, 24, 2 (Fall/Winter 2012), pp. 73–116.

83. EW to A.P. Wadsworth, Nov. 1, 1950, Manchester Guardian Archives.

84. EW's contributions received special praise. In an otherwise critical review of one volume in the series, D.C. Watt wrote: "An exception to the rule is provided by the brilliant essay on the Balkans by Elizabeth Wiskemann," *The Slavonic and East European Review*, 37, 89 (June 1959), p. 558. Publication of these volumes was often delayed. The volumes were: *Survey of International Affairs: The Eve of War* (1953); *Survey of International Affairs: Hitler's Europe 1939–1946* (1954); *Survey of International Affairs: The Realignment of Europe* (1956); and *Survey of International Affairs: The Initial Triumph of the Axis* (1958); all were edited by A.J. Toynbee and Veronica M. Toynbee.

85. EW to A.P. Wadsworth, June 12; Wadsworth to EW, June 14, EW to Wadsworth, June 16, 1953, Manchester Guardian Archives.

86. EW, "Balkan People," *Spectator*, Dec. 17, 1948, p. 26.

87. EW, *The Europe I Saw*, p. 191.

88. Hugh Seton-Watson, *The East European Revolution* (London, 1950). The three stages were genuine coalition, bogus coalition, and then the 'monolithic' regime.

89. Doreen Warriner, *Revolution in Eastern Europe* (London, 1950).

90. EW, "Hungary," in Reginald R. Betts (ed.), *Central and South-Eastern Europe, 1945–1948* (Oxford, 1950), pp. 95–129. During the war R.R. Betts (1903–61) worked closely with Shiela Grant Duff in the BBC Czech broadcasting section. He eventually became Jan Masaryk Professor of Central European History at the School of Slavonic and East European Studies, London University. Shiela Grant Duff papers, Box 7/1 and Box 8/1.

91. EW, *The Europe I Saw*, p. 106.

92. EW, *The Europe I Saw*, p. 110. After her return she addressed a meeting at Chatham House on the situation in Hungary: RIIA 8/1586, Oct. 25, 1948, Chatham House papers.

93. EW, *The Europe I Saw*, pp. 208–9.

94. EW, "Rough Justice in Hungary," *Spectator*, Oct. 14, 1948, pp. 489–490.

95. Reginald R. Betts (ed.), *Central and South-Eastern Europe, 1945–1948*, p. 95, author's note.

96. EW's own name, along with that of Allen Dulles, surfaced in the November 1952 Czechoslovak show trial of Rudolf Slánsky and other former leaders. This was in the cross-examination of Jaromir Kopecky, with whom she had worked in Switzerland.

97. Sean Forner, *German Intellectuals and the Challenge of Democratic Renewal. Culture and Politics after 1945* (Cambridge, 2014).

98. EW, "German History, 1937–1952," in J. Bithell (ed.), *Germany. A Companion to German Studies* (London, 1955), p. 204; EW, review of Trevor-Roper, *Hitler's Table Talk*, and G. Reitlinger, *The Final Solution, TLS*, May 1, 1953, p. 279; "Bismarck and His Opponents," *TLS*, July 5, 1957, pp. 405–6.

99. EW to Harry Bergholz, July 18, 1950.

100. EW to William Clark, June 22, 1950, William Clark papers. Also, A.H. Wadsworth to EW, July 21, 1950 and July 25, 1950, Manchester Guardian Archives.

101. W. Dirks, "Der restaurative Charakter der Epoche," *Frankfurter Hefte*, 9 (1950), pp. 942–946.

102. EW, "German History, 1937–1952," p. 204.

103. EW, "The Second German Aftermath," *Spectator*, July 20, 1950, pp. 75–76. In literature she pointed to the vogue for Ernst Jünger and the Catholic novelist Stefan Andres; she seems not to have known at this time about Gruppe 47 or Heinrich Böll.

104. EW, "Trends in Germany," *Spectator*, June 29, 1950, pp. 878–879.

105. EW, "New Ideas Versus Old in Western Germany," *The World Today*, 6, 8 (Aug. 1950), p. 334. The *Brüderschaft* was founded in 1949 in Hamburg by former SS officers of the *Grossdeutschland* Division who had been POWs in England. It had about 2,500 members, many of them former army officers, spread across West Germany and had ties to right-wing groups and parties and to neo-Fascist and neo-Nazi organizations abroad. Opposed to both the Atlantic alliance and the Soviet Union, it aimed to overthrow the Federal Republic and its constitution and favored dictatorship by an officer elite. Among its leaders was SS Colonel Alfred Franke-Gricksch (SS Death's Head Division and then Heydrich's *Reichssicherheitshauptamt*—Reich Security Main Office) and Karl Kaufmann (Gauleiter of Hamburg 1929–45). It rapidly became the object of Allied surveillance and disintegrated in 1951 from factional splits. R. Breitman and Norman J.W. Goda, *Hitler's Shadow: Nazi War Criminals, U.S. Intelligence, and the Cold War* (Washington, 2011), pp. 53–9.

106. EW–Arnold Künzli correspondence, 1950–54; Künzli was based in Bonn. Also, EW, "A Short History of the German Student Corporations," *History Today*, 4, 12 (Dec. 1954), pp. 835–843.

107. EW, "New Ideas Versus Old in Western Germany"; EW, "Italians at Work," *Tribune*, June 6, 1947.

108. On French control of the Saar: Bronson Long, *No Easy Occupation. French Control of the German Saar, 1944–1957* (Rochester, N.Y., 2015).

109. EW, "The Saar as an International Problem," *The World Today*, July 1952, pp. 299–307; "The Future of the Saar," *The World Today*, May 1953, pp. 193–201; "Important Concessions to the Saar. Political and Economic Relations with France," *Manchester Guardian*, June 26, 1953, p. 6. Wiskemann also sketched the history of the Saar for a new popular history magazine: EW, "The Saar," *History Today*, 3, 8 (Aug. 1953), pp. 553–560.

110. EW, "Bone of Contention," *New Statesman and Nation*, May 10, 1952, p. 544.

111. EW, "Another Saar Plebiscite," *Spectator*, Oct. 21, 1955, pp. 4–5. EW "The Saar Moves Towards Germany," *Foreign Affairs*, 34, 2 (Jan. 1956), pp. 287–296; EW, "The Return of the Saar to Germany," *The World Today*, Jan. 1957, pp. 27–36.

112. Daniel L. Cowling, "Britain and the Occupation of Germany, 1945–49," Ph.D. diss., Cambridge University, 2018, especially chapter 5. Also, Cowling, "Anglo-German Relations after 1945," *Journal of Contemporary History*, 54, 1 (March 2017), pp. 82–111.

113. Drew Middleton, *The Renazification of Germany* (New York, 1949). D. Middleton, "Neo-Nazism: A Cloud Like a Man's Hand," *New York Times*, July 1, 1951. Sefton Delmer, "Is a New Hitler Rising?" *Daily Express*, July 6, 1951. There were exceptions, like Terence Prittie, the *Manchester Guardian*'s Bonn correspondent, who dismissed as exaggerated claims about a Nazi resurgence. On this general theme: Gavriel D. Rosenfeld, *The Fourth Reich. The Specter of Nazism from World War II to the Present* (Cambridge, 2019). H.R. Trevor-Roper, "The Danger of a Neo-Nazism," *New York Times*, July 27, 1947. Also, the feature article in *Picture Post*, June 16, 1951.

114. *Daily Express*, quoted by Karen Bayer, *"How dead is Hitler?" Der britische Starreporter Sefton Delmer und die Deutschen* (Mainz, 2008), p. 184.

115. Norbert Frei, *Adenauer's Germany and the Nazi Past* (New York, 2002). Jeffrey Herf, *Divided Memory. The Nazi Past in the Two Germanys* (Cambridge, 1997).

116. Hugh Seton-Watson to Margaret Cleeve, July 22, 1953, RIIA 17/73, Chatham House Archives.

117. Hugh Seton-Watson to Margaret Cleeve, July 22, 1953.

118. Including Donald McLachlan, who had once been Norman Ebbutt's assistant in Berlin and became foreign editor of the *Economist* in 1947. He commented on the preliminary outline that EW submitted. M. Cleeve "Notes," Aug. 10, 1953; McLachlan comments, Dec. 7, 1953, RIIA 17/73, Chatham House Archives.

119. RIIA 17/73, "Germany's Eastern Neighbours," Chatham House Archives. "Note by Seton-Watson on Germany's Eastern Frontiers," July 24, 1953, RIIA 17/73. Doreen Warriner encouraged the Committee to choose Wiskemann for the task. Several years earlier she had suggested that EW work for Chatham House on a pamphlet on "The Economies of Eastern Europe," RIIA 4/WARR, April 28, 1948. EW knew Hugh and the whole Seton-Watson family well. For her reviews of Hugh's work: EW, "Eastern Europe Today," *TLS*, Nov. 3, 1950, p. 687; EW, "Eastern Europe and Western Diplomats," *Fortnightly*, 158 (July 1945), pp. 304–310.

120. RIIA 17/73, Chatham House Archives.

121. Especially helpful were the excellent library and press clipping files at Chatham House.

122. R.M. Douglas, *Orderly and Humane. The Expulsion of the Germans after the Second World* War (New Haven, 2012), pp. 73–4. Matthew Frank, *Expelling the Germans. British Opinion and Post-1945 Population Transfer in Context* (Oxford, 2007), p. 47ff.

123. R.M. Douglas, *Orderly and Humane*, p. 76.

124. In addition to Douglas and Frank, Vit Smetana, *Exile in London: The Experience of Czechoslovakia and Other Occupied Nations, 1939–1945* (Prague, 2018); Martin D. Brown, "Forcible Population Transfers – A Flawed Legacy or an Unavoidable Necessity in Protracted Conflicts? The Case of the Sudeten Germans," *The RUSI journal*, 148, 4 (2003), pp. 81–87, which has an excellent bibliography.

125. R.M. Douglas, *Orderly and Humane*, pp. 288–9, 293, 238; Matthew Frank, *Expelling the Germans*, pp. 183–8.

126. R.M. Douglas, *Orderly and Humane*, pp. 290–2. Shiela Grant Duff papers, Bodleian Library, Box 5/2–3 and Box 8.

127. Matthew *Frank, Expelling the Germans*, pp. 188–92.

128. EW, "Eastern Europe and Western Diplomats," *Fortnightly*, 158 (July/Aug. 1945), p. 310. EW, [review of R.W. Seton-Watson, *Twenty-Five Years of Czechoslovakia*] *International Affairs*, 22, 1 (Jan. 1946), p. 140.

129. EW, *Germany's Eastern Neighbours*, p. 133. She also waded into the minefield of rival statistics for the numbers of deaths caused by the expulsions, questioning the figures given in many German sources as inflated. The expulsions from the Polish areas, she argued, resulted in "well under 1 million deaths" while those from the Sudetenland she put at roughly 100,000, not the 300,000 or more in many German sources. EW, *Germany's Eastern Neighbours*, pp. 121–2, 130. The issue remains highly controversial, but a 1995 joint German and Czech Commission concluded that up to 30,000 Sudeten Germans were killed.

130. T. Prittie, "Harsh Frontier," *Manchester Guardian*, June 15, 1956, p. 6.

131. EW, *Germany's Eastern Neighbours*, pp. 61, 112, 294.

132. EW, *Germany's Eastern Neighbours*, p. 69.

133. EW, *Germany's Eastern Neighbours*, pp. 159–60.

134. EW, *Germany's Eastern Neighbours*, p. 165. She is quoting the words of Wenzel Jaksch, leader of the Sudeten Social Democrats.

135. EW, *Germany's Eastern Neighbours*, p. 191.

136. BHE gained 27 seats in the 1953 Bundestag election. Waldermar Kraft, the leader of the BHE, was a former SS member. Theodor Oberländer, who had once worked in Alfred Rosenberg's *Ostministerium*, resigned his post as Minister for Expellees in 1960 when it was alleged that he had participated in the murder of Jews in the Ukraine in 1941.

137. EW, *Germany's Eastern Neighbours*, pp. 202, 205.

138. EW, *Germany's Eastern Neighbours*, pp. 179–209. See also her correspondence with Anrold Künzli, Künzli Nachlass, Bern. EW reviewed critically these *Ostforschung* studies: for example, those of K. Turnwald: EW reviews in the *TLS*, "Minority Report," Feb. 11, 1955, p. 87 and "German Minority," Aug. 12, 1955, p. 463. The first of these was a selection of personal accounts produced by the Association for the Protection of Sudeten German Interests, and her old friend Voigt (whose politics had moved sharply to the right) wrote a Foreword for it.

139. EW, *Germany's Eastern Neighbours*, p. 190. On Schieder and Rothfels: R.G. Moeller, *War Stories: In Search of a Usable Past in the Federal Republic of Germany* (Berkeley and Los Angeles, 2003), chapter 3.

140. EW, *Germany's Eastern Neighbours*, pp. 202–9 (quote on p. 209); also p. 195.

141. William Taubman, *Khrushchev, the Man and his Era* (New York, 2003), p. 271.

142. EW, *Germany's Eastern Neighbours*, p. 292. At the Teheran and Yalta Conferences it had been agreed by Churchill, Roosevelt, and Stalin that the Soviet Union would retain eastern Poland (up to the so-called Curzon line, the 1920 armistice line between Poland and the Soviet Union). Poland would be compensated by the gain of former German lands to the west, east of the Oder-Neisse rivers. This meant that East Prussia, all of Silesia, Pomerania, and East Brandenburg ceased to be German. Germany lost roughly 25% of its former territory compared to its 1937 borders.

143. EW, *Germany's Eastern Neighbours*, chapters 9, 12, 15.

144. EW, *Germany's Eastern Neighbours*, p. 295.

145. EW, *Germany's Eastern Neighbours*, pp. 294–5.

146. G.P. Gooch, "Central Europe," *Contemporary Review* 190 (July–Dec. 1956), Literary Supplement, July 1, p. 48.

147. "Slav versus German," *Spectator*, Aug. 31, 1956, p. 276.

148. W.N. Medlicott review in the *English Historical Review*, 73, 286 (Jan. 1958) pp. 186–7. Also, J. Geiner review in *International Journal*, 13, 2 (1958), p. 159; S. Sharp review in *American Political Science Review*, 51, 2 (1957), pp. 527–528; Piotr S. Wandycz review in *The Historian*, 20, 3 (1958), p. 362–363; A.D. review in *The Geographical Journal*, 122, 4 (Dec. 1956) pp. 497–8; Paul E. Zinner review in *Political Science Quarterly*, 72, 2 (June 1957), pp. 301–3; Charles Morley review in *American Historical Review*, 62, 2 (Jan. 1957), pp. 391–2.

149. Richard Crossman, "The Oder-Neisse Line," *New Statesman and Nation*, Aug. 4, 1956, p. 125.

150. G. Barraclough in *International Affairs*, 32, 4 (Oct. 1956), pp. 495, 496.

151. T. Prittie, "Harsh Frontier," *Manchester Guardian*, June 5, 1956, p. 6. Also, the letter exchange: "Beyond the Oder-Neisse: A Bismarckian Solution," *Manchester Guardian*, Feb. 12, 1958, p. 6.

152. "Expulsions from Eastern Europe," *TLS*, Sept. 21, 1956, p. 555.

153. M. Cornwall, "Elizabeth Wiskemann and the Sudeten Question: A Woman at the 'Essential Hinge' of Europe," *Central Europe* 1, 1 (May 2003), p. 73, fn 92 cites a positive, unpublished appraisal in the Czech archives which, however, questioned the number of Sudeten German deaths mentioned by EW and her verdict that agriculture in the region had deteriorated. A.J. Kaminski, "Zachodnio-Niemieckie glossy o pracy Elizabeth Wiskemann," *Przeglad Zachodni*, 12, 5/6 (1956), pp. 28–41. Bernard Ziffer (an international lawyer who worked for Radio Free Europe), "Elizabeth Wiskemannn's Book and Nationalist German Propaganda," *The Polish Review*, 1, 4 (Autumn 1956), pp. 107–114; Alexander Korczynski's review in *The Polish Review*, 2, 1 (Winter 1957), pp. 77–83 was positive but disputed EW's comments about Polish repression of Ukrainians.

154. The Minister for Refugees, Theodor Oberländer, gave a press interview announcing that an extensive refutation of the book would soon appear by German scholars. *Die Brücke*, Sept. 15, 1956; R. Crossman, "Miss Wiskemann Raises a Storm," *Times*, Aug. 8, 1956; "Germany's Eastern Frontier: Angry Book Critics," *Manchester Guardian*, Aug. 10, 1956; *Frankfurter Allgemeine Zeitung*, Aug. 18, 1956 (this review by Rudolf Urban of the Herder Institut at Marburg was a spiteful personal attack); *Ost-West Kurier*, Sept 22, 1956; *Schlesische Rundschau*, Sept. 15, 1956. Fritz T. Epstein, review in *The Journal of Modern History*, 29, 2 (June 1957), pp. 162–3. H. Kraus, "Verteidigung des Unrechts," *Das Ostpreussenblatt*, Aug 25, 1956, p. 1. M. Gärtner, "Eine englische Studie über die Oder-Neisse Linie," *Zeitschrift für Politik*, new series, 3, 3 (Dec. 1956), pp. 270–278. Also, *Historische Zeitschrift*, 185, 3 (1958), pp. 638–40. E. Birke's review in *Zeitschrift für Ostforschung*, 5 (1956), pp. 570–6.

155. Politisches Archiv, B 12/257, Staatssekretär des Bundeskanzleramts to the Bundesvertriebenenministerium, Aug. 23, 1956. The Foreign office contacted all diplomatic and consular offices about the book, Politisches Archiv, B 12/263, Oct. 11, 1957; also, B 12/260, Bundesarchiv Koblenz. Corinna R. Unger, "'Objektiv aber nicht neutral': Zur Entwicklung der Ostforschung nach 1945," *Osteuropa*, 55, 12

(Dec. 2005), pp. 121–2. An essay collection on the issue that was officially supported was Göttinger Arbeitskreis (eds.), *Deutschlands Ostproblem: Eine Untersuchung der Beziehungen des deutschen Volkes zu seinen Nachbarn* (Würzburg, 1957).

156. The most offensive pamphlet was Hilmar Toppe, "Elizabeth Wiskemann und Deutschlands Nachbar Polen," *Wirtschaft und Wissenschaft. Sonderdruck des Stifterverband für die deutsche Wissenschaft* (Munich and Essen, 1957). She had first been introduced to the Ripkas in the 1930s by Darsie Gillie. Later Mrs Noemi Ripka lodged for a while at Moore Street. In *The Europe I Saw* Wiskemann wrote (p. 204) about Toppe's "tissue of falsehoods" and added rather nastily: "certain things that I knew could have been said with some truth about a quite different person were laid at my door." She seems to have been referring to Shiela Grant Duff. A review in *Die Zeit* had been critical of Wiskemann's book, but the paper found Toppe's personal attack on her integrity completely unacceptable: "Toppe hat es sich zu leicht gemacht," *Die Zeit*, May 15, 1958.

157. EW, "Historians on Thin Ice: German Scholars Examine Nazi Records," *Times*, June 4, 1956, p. 11.

158. "Four Cabinet Resignations," *Times*, Oct. 8, 1956; M. Frank, *Expelling the Germans*, p. 1.

159. On Brentano, H. Gerald Hughes, "Unfinished Business from Potsdam: Britain, West Germany, and the Oder-Neisse Line, 1945–1962," *International History Review*, 27, 2 (June 2005), p. 268. Swiss journalist Fritz René Allemann also argued that border recognition would loosen Polish and Czech ties to Moscow: *Bonn ist nicht Weimar* (Cologne and Berlin, 1956).

160. Jost Dülffer, "'No More Potsdam!' Konrad Adenauer and the Basis of his International Orientation," *German Politics and Society*, 25, 2 (Summer 2007), pp. 19–42.

161. Alan Bullock to Monty Woodhouse, Jan. 8, 1958, RIIA 17/73, Chatham House Archives.

162. C.L. Bayne to C.M. ('Monty') Woodhouse, Jan 12, 1958, RIIA 17/73.

163. Extract from the minutes and agenda of the RIIA Research Committee meeting Jan 14, 1958, RIIA 17/73. C.M. Woodhouse to EW, Jan 15, 1958; EW to Woodhouse, Oct. 1, 1958, RIIA 4/WISK.

164. R. Crossman, "The Oder-Neisse Line," *New Statesman and Nation*, Aug. 4, 1956, p. 125.

165. H. Gerald Hughes, "Unfinished Business from Potsdam." Also, Daniel Gossel, *Briten, Deutsche und Europa. Die Deutsche Frage in der britischen Aussenpolitik 1945–1962* (Stuttgart 1999). In 1962 British officials secretly guaranteed the inviolability of Poland's western borders. MacMillan had hopes of making a breakthrough on East–West relations, but he was distrusted by Bonn. The American Embassy in Bonn followed the dispute over Wiskemann's book closely, and Elim O'Shaughnessy, the *chargé d'affaires*, wrote a report on the German response, Debra J. Allen, *The Oder-Neisse Line: The United States, Poland and Germany in the Cold War* (Westport, CT, 2003), p. 171 and footnotes.

166. EW to Arnold Künzli, Aug. 27, 1956, Künzli Nachlass, Bern.

167. EW to Alfred Wiener, Jan. 6, 1958, Elizabeth Wiskemann Correspondence File, Wiener Library Archives.

168. EW to Alfred Wiener, Jan. 27, 1958, Wiener Library Archives. In another letter she referred to the British slowness to take the Nazis seriously in the 1930s and the danger of such views in contemporary Germany: "And this is the point. The last book of

mine has only one *These* i.e. that this man Hitler caused all this ghastly suffering first to the Poles and Czechs and then to the Germans. That only our friends can face." EW to Alfred Wiener, Feb. 7, 1958, Wiener Library Archives.

169. Frank Sikora, *Als Deutscher unterwegs. Gelebte Zeitgeschichte* (Munich, 2006). In the 1950s Sikora worked for the German Ambassador in London, Herwarth von Bittenfeld. He recalls deep British suspicions about German *Ostpolitik* and he became involved in the furor over Wiskemann's book (p. 140, etc). The embassy was troubled by the leader in the *Manchester Guardian* which attacked German expellees and the institutes in West Germany focusing on *Ostpolitik*. Herwarth claimed that he had advised Wiskemann against writing for Chatham House about Germany's eastern borders as too controversial; she had ignored his counsel and he felt snubbed.

170. Ci/W9 Manchester Guardian Archive: Wiskemann to Hetherington, Feb. 5, 1958; Hetherington to Wiskemann, Feb. 7, 1958; Wiskemann to Hetherington, Feb. 9, 1958; Wiskemann to Hetherington, March 25, 1958. "Scholarship or Slander?" *Manchester Guardian*, Feb. 8, 1958. Toppe remained unrepentant and withdrew none of his claims: Hilmar Toppe to Wiskemann, Feb. 18, 1958, RIIA 17/73.

171. RIIA 4/Wisk, EW to Kenneth Younger, Oct. 21, 1966. She used pretty much the same phrase in her memoir, *The Europe I Saw*, p. 205.

172. E. Hahn, "Die 'Sudetendeutsche Frage' und die Historiker in den U.S.A.," *Bohemia* 39, 2 (1998), pp. 435–437. Eva Hahn praised *Czechs and Germans* and *Germany's Eastern Neighbours*. See: "Sudeten Dialogues. Martin D. Brown and Dr Eva Hahn," *Central European Review* 3, 16 (May 7, 2001), online at ce-review.org. Reviewing Wiskemann's memoir, *The Europe I Saw* (which was translated into German), Martin K. Bachstein praised her work and saw her recognition of the borders in the east as an early anticipation of Willi Brandt's *Ostpolitik*, acceptance of the post-1945 realities being the only way to overcome Europe's ideological division. Bachstein, a Sudeten émigré to the US, wrote books about Wenzel Jaksch and Sudeten Social Democracy and worked for many years for Radio Free Europe. "Eine unerbittliche Journalistin: Elizabeth Wiskemann," *Bohemia*, 13 (Jan. 1972), pp. 458–460.

173. The key figures were Sir Lewis Namier and Sir E.L. Woodward.

174. Astrid M. Eckert, *The Struggle for the Files. The Western Allies and the Return of German Archives after the Second World War* (Cambridge, 2012). Also, D.C. Watt, "British Historians, the War Guilt Issue, and Post-War Germanophobia: A Documentary Note," *Historical Journal*, 36, 1 (1993), pp. 179–185. At a March 1950 editorial meeting John Wheeler-Bennett noted, "If the unreliability of the *Grosse Politik* could be proved, it would be an irrefutable argument for not admitting German historians to the project," Astrid M. Eckert, *The Struggle for the Files*, pp. 316–17.

175. *Rheinzeitung* (Koblenz), April 26, 1956, quoted by Astrid M. Eckert, *The Struggle for the Files*, p. 296. At no point did Bonn argue that it needed the records to prosecute Nazi war criminals (p. 376).

176. Concern about neo-Nazism was especially high in 1953 after British occupation authorities arrested Werner Naumann and several other Nazi loyalists, accusing them of conspiring to overthrow the West German government. Widely publicized in Britain, the case was turned over to the Bonn authorities, who found insufficient evidence, dropped the charges, and released the men. EW reviewed Naumann's memoir, calling him "an unabashed fascist" and adding "like Senator McCarthy he finds

Moscow's hidden hand at work in every American and British ministry." *International Affairs*, 30, 1 (Jan. 1954), p. 98.

177. Some months before, she had also written a signed article discussing the different national documentary series being prepared: EW, "Documents and the Historian," *TLS*, Oct. 3, 1952, p. 652.

178. EW, "Hitler and the Smaller Powers," *TLS*, July 31, 1953, p. 490. Astrid Eckert was unaware that the review was written by Wiskemann. She wrote: "the apparent insider-knowledge it displays suggests that the anonymous reviewer either was associated with or had strong ties to the Foreign Office Library or the *Documents on German Foreign Policy* project" (*The Struggle for the Files*, p. 323). In a later review of another volume of the German Foreign Policy documents, Wiskemann wrote: "The more that one reflects upon the German Foreign Office Documents the more satisfied one becomes that they should have been published by non-German historians, for it would have required phenomenal courage for Germans so completely to expose a former German regime." "Pretexts for War," *TLS*, March 1, 1957, p. 123.

179. A.J.P. Taylor letter, *TLS*, Aug. 7, 1953, p. 507.

180. E.L. Woodward, J.R. Butler letters, *TLS*, Aug. 21, 1953, p. 535 and Sept. 25, 1953, p. 613. "Your Reviewer" (EW), *TLS*, Aug. 21, 1953, p. 535. There was, of course, a personal side to these letters. Woodward had been a strong supporter of Taylor's career, but since 1947 they had become bitter enemies. Taylor suspected Woodward of blocking his candidacy for an Oxford Chair in 1952. A.J.P. Taylor letter, *TLS*, Sept. 4, 1953, p. 565. Agnes Headlam-Morley letters, *TLS*, Aug. 14, 1953, p. 521 and Sept. 18, 1953, p. 597.

181. Isabella Massey, editor and translator into English of Luigi Albertini's three-volume *Origins of the War of 1914*, *TLS*, Sept. 11, 1953, p. 581 and Oct. 16, 1953, p. 661.

182. James Joll letter, *TLS*, Sept. 25, 1953, p. 613.

183. Restitution of the military records was slower and more piecemeal, continuing well into the 1960s.

184. D.C. Watt, "British Historians, the War Guilt Issue, and Post-War Germanophobia," p. 180. As Eckert noted, early access to this huge cache of documents boosted the careers of a group of historians, including Wiskemann, who used them for *The Rome-Berlin Axis*.

185. In a letter recommending EW for radio broadcasts, Lambert wrote: "She does know Germany well and has the right ideas (at least they agree with mine)." Margaret Lambert to Mrs Horton (Talks Department BBC), Dec. 22, 1950. BBC Archives, Caversham, Elizabeth Wiskemann file.

186. EW [Unsigned], "Historians of World War II," *Manchester Guardian*, Sept. 25, 1950, p. 8.

187. EW to A.H. Wadsworth, Sept. 10, 1950, Manchester Guardian Archives. On Chester Wilmot's suggestion, she approached the BBC Talks Department about broadcasting her talk, but nothing seems to have come of this. The conference was covered by the BBC, and Toynbee's address on contemporary history seems to have been broadcast.

188. For the Tutzing conference: letters between Paul Kluke and EW, Nov. 22, 1955–March 23, 1956, ID 102/43; also, ID 102/47 (which includes extract of letter from EW concerning the criticism by Hilmar Toppe of her book *Germany's Eastern Neighbours*). Hausarchiv [Paul Kluke] *IfZ*. EW participated in the 1959 European Forum Alpbach,

an interdisciplinary forum designed to promote closer European integration among scholars and students. She also attended the 11th International Congress of Historical Sciences held in Stockholm in August 1960 and wrote an article about it for the *Manchester Guardian*.

189. EW, "Historians on Thin Ice.," *Times* June 4, 1956, p. 11. Also, her review of the subsequent conference book in *International Affairs*, July 1958. She praised several of the papers, including that of philosopher Theodor Litt (1880–1962), a critic of Nazism who had been forcibly retired from Leipzig University in 1937. His lecture, she wrote, formulated the underlying theme of the conference and the problem of the age: "How is democracy to be reconciled with technical advance and its totalitarian affinities."

190. H. Krausnick, H. Buchheim, M. Broszat, and H.A. Jacobsen, *Anatomy of the S.S. State* (London, 1968), Introduction, p. ix. [EW], "How Was It Possible?" *TLS*, March 17, 1961; [EW], "Hitler's Rise to Power," *TLS*, July 26, 1963. She was also greatly impressed by Fritz Fischer's study of Germany's aims in the First World War, *Griff nach der Weltmacht* (Düsseldorf, 1961). On *IfZ* historians and the Auschwitz trial (1963–65): Mathew Turner, *Historians and the Frankfurt Auschwitz Trial: Their Role as Expert Witnesses* (London, 2018); also, M. Turner, T. Joel, and D. Lowe, "Between Scholarship and Politics. The First Decade of the Institut für Zeitgeschichte," *European Studies Quarterly*, 49, 2 (April 2019), pp. 250–271.

191. EW, "Berlin Between East and West," *The World Today*, 16, 11 (Nov. 1960), pp. 463–472 quotes p. 467.

192. EW, *A Great Newspaper: The Story of the Neue Zürcher Zeitung* (London, 1959). John Goormaghtigh, Director of the European Center of the Carnegie Endowment, hired EW to direct the Trieste project. Primarily because of her failing eyesight, she later handed the project's direction over to her French historian friend J.B. Duroselle.

193. She complained: "The trouble is that I simply do not do half the things I need to and get into a panic and that makes things worse – the usual *cercle vicieux*. A year's holiday would be the thing, but no one knows how one could arrange that." EW to Harry Bergholz, July 18, 1950. And again: "I'm just as busy as ever – sometimes I think I must organize my life very badly, but I think the chief and perhaps insoluble problem is to combine the feminine domesticities with an otherwise professionally full life." EW to Harry Bergholz, Oct. 10, 1948. The publications she wrote for in these years included: *Economist, Manchester Guardian, Observer, Spectator, Neue Zürcher Zeitung, Il Ponte, Foreign Affairs, Fortnightly, The World Today, International Affairs, Tribune, Frankfurter Hefte. Times*, and *Sunday Times*.

Chapter 6

1. Franca Magnani, *Eine italienische Familie* (Munich, 1993), p. 282.
2. EW to Harry Bergholz, Dec. 7, 1947.
3. EW to Harry Bergholz, Jan. 16, 1948; also, March 1, 1948; Dec. 18, 1952. In 1947 Jane Pollitt shared the flat at St. George's Square. At Wiskemann's request, Bergholz also sent a parcel to a Sudeten-German family in an internment camp in Passau: "I particularly wanted to help them as soon as possible. I have managed to give some clothes for them to someone who was going to Germany, so now I feel I've done my bit." EW to H. Bergholz, Nov. 11, 1948.

4. EW to Harry Bergholz, Nov. 11, 1948.

5. EW to Guglielmo Alberti, Sept. 8, 1947.

6. Last Will and Testament of Sir William Parker Burton (died Nov. 1942; probate Feb. 3, 1943), who left EW £10,000 and similar sums to her brother and sister, and Last Will and Testament of Sir Bunnell Henry Burton (died May 1943; probate Sept. 22, 1943), who left EW £250. My thanks to George and Charles Burton for sending me these documents from the District Probate Registry at Ipswich.

7. EW to Harry Bergholz, Dec. 18, 1952: "food prices have gone up so alarmingly."

8. EW to Harry Bergholz, May 11 (1952).

9. EW to Harry Bergholz [card], Feb. 9, 1952.

10. EW to Harry Bergholz, Nov. 17, 1955. Hubert Ripka (1895–1958) was a close associate of Beneš; he served in the Czech government until the coup of 1948 and also wrote about the coup, etc. Hubert Ripka to Shiela Grant Duff, May 29, 1955, Shiela Grant Duff papers, Box 6/3, Bodleian Library. Erik Mettler was a journalist for the *Neue Zürcher Zeitung*. Another guest was Erika Rathgeber, wife of the physicist Henri Rathgeber. An architect and a planner, she later became President of the Women's International League for Peace and Freedom. EW to A. Künzli, April 27, 1952, Künzli Nachlass; EW to A. Wiener, Feb. 7, 1958, Wiener Library Wiskemann correspondence.

11. EW to Arnold Künzli, Jan.18, 1955, Künzli Nachlass.

12. EW to Harry Bergholz, Nov. 17, 1955.

13. EW to Guglielmo Alberti, Feb. 20, 1955.

14. EW to A. Hetherington, March 25, 1958, Manchester Guardian Archives.

15. Carol Dyhouse, *No Distinction of Sex? Women in British Universities 1870–1939* (London, 1995).

16. See the excellent online information put out by LSE Archivist Sue Donnelly and others: "Women at LSE 1895–1932: Facts and Figures"; "The Hidden Women of LSE." Several came from Girton, finding LSE a lot more congenial. Maxime Berg has suggested that several of the economic historians might have become economists but for Professor Alfred Marshall's infamous attitude towards women in the profession.

17. C. Hood, D. King, and G. Peele (eds.), *Forging a Discipline. A Critical Assessment of Oxford's Development of the Study of Politics and International Relations in Comparative Perspective* (Oxford, 2014), especially the chapter by Martin Ceadel, "The Academic Normalization of International Relations at Oxford 1920–2012: Structures Transcended" (pp. 184–201). The IR option within PPE remained a minor component of the degree; not until 1960, for example, did the Cold War enter the undergraduate syllabus. It also had few dedicated teachers; the colleges simply relied on historians and others to lend a hand. Instead, at Oxford scholarship on IR, contemporary history, and area studies was concentrated in two postgraduate specialist colleges, Nuffield and St. Antony's. For a transnational analysis of IR's development as an academic discipline, see: Jan Stöckmann, *The Architects of International Relations: Building a Discipline and Designing a World, 1914–1940* (Cambridge, 2022).

18. Hedley Bull, "Martin Wight and the Theory of International Relations," *British Journal of International Studies*, 2 (1976), p. 101.

19. John Goormaghtigh, Director of the European Center of the Carnegie Endowment, hired Wiskemann to direct the project. Primarily because of her failing eyesight, Wiskemann turned its direction over to her French historian friend J.B. Duroselle.

It was eventually published as *Le conflit de Trieste, 1943–1954* (Brussels, 1966). In the preface, Duroselle made generous reference to Wiskemann's contribution. Not long after her appointment as Professor at Edinburgh, Wiskemann also published a book about the *Neue Zürcher Zeitung*, which she considered one of the best papers in Europe; she had many friends among its editors and correspondents: *A Great Swiss Newspaper: The Story of the Neue Zürcher Zeitung* (London, 1959).

20. The two other Burton Professorships at Oxford and LSE were full-time and came with a much higher salary.

21. International Relations Chair, Wiskemann files, shelf Mark: EUA-A-83, Edinburgh University Archives.

22. W.N. Medlicott to J. Macpherson, Jan. 16, 1958, Edinburgh University Archives.

23. Minutes of Special Committee concerning the Chair of International Relations, Feb. 18, 1958.

24. W.N. Medlicott to J. Macpherson, Jan. 14, 1958. Medlicott was well-acquainted with Wiskemann's journalism and her books, which he had reviewed favorably.

25. EW, "Communism and Nationalism," *Sunday Times*, June 18, 1961. EW, review of H. Stuart Hughes, "Contemporary Europe," in *International Affairs*, 38, 2 (April 1962), p. 254.

26. EW to Miss Giles, Jan. 13, 1960 and Oct. 23, 1960.EW to Golo Mann, Jan. 13, 1961; Mann to EW Jan. 26, 1961, Golo Mann Nachlass, Bern.

27. EW to Margaret Cleeve, March 21, 1955, 4/Wisk, Chatham House Archives.

28. EW to Prof. A.H. Campbell, July 28, 1960; also, July 1, 1960, Edinburgh University Archives. The problem with her eye is a little unclear: I would guess that she first had a retina tear or detachment and that later a cataract developed in the same eye and the operation was a failure. Before the operation she was quite confidant, explaining to her writer friend Joseph Breitbach, who had just sent her a book: "I just have to have a small eye operation and will not be allowed to read for three weeks." EW to J. Breitbach, Nov. 9, 1959, Breitbach Nachlass, Marbach.

29. EW to 'Diccon' (Richard Hughes), Dec. 10, 1961, Richard Hughes papers.

30. EW to Guglielmo Alberti, Dec. 1960 [postcard], Alberti papers.

31. See, for example, Robert Jackson, "Martin Wight's Thought on Diplomacy," *Diplomacy and Statecraft*, 13, 4 (Dec. 2002), pp. 1–28. The Martin Wight papers at L.S.E. contain information about the early years of Sussex and Wight's plans for the curriculum, e.g. boxes 49,56, 2014 and the correspondence files 233/49-56.

32. M. Wight to I. Deutscher, Dec. 10, 1962, in David Caute, *Isaac and Isaiah: The Covert Punishment of a Cold War Heretic* (New Haven, 2013), p. 276. Caute examines in detail the role of Sir Isaiah Berlin in blocking Deutscher's appointment, although Asa Briggs, Wight, and others were enthusiastically in favor.

33. At Sussex the salary for senior lecturers was from £1,650 to £2,250. Given her experience and standing, EW was probably at the upper end of the scale. By this time, she was more secure financially and no longer rented out rooms in her house.

34. Matthew Cragoe, "Asa Briggs and the University of Sussex, 1961–1976," in Miles Taylor (ed.), *The Age of Asa: Lord Briggs, Public Life and History in Britain since 1945* (Basingstoke, 2015), p. 232. Also, David Daiches, *The Idea of a New University: An Experiment in* Sussex (London, 1964); Michael Beloff, *The Plateglass Universities* (London, 1968). Sybil Oldfield, starting her first job as a history lecturer, found this

"New Map of Learning" (Asa Briggs's mantra) exhilarating: "subjects were not separated each from each but *connected*. Literature with History and Philosophy and Sociology and Psychology. No students would leave us with the delusion that they had 'done' English or French or History...Bliss was it in that dawn" Sybil Oldfield, "Sybil Oldfield at Seventy-Two: Humanistic Feminism—or Thinking Back through our Grandmothers," *Women's History Review*, 19, 5 (Nov. 2010), p. 749.

35. EW to Leonard Woolf, Jan. 22, 1957, Leonard Woolf papers, The Keep, Sussex.

36. EW to Leonard Woolf, Nov. 21, 1964, Leonard Woolf papers. Victoria Glendinning in her biography, *Leonard Woolf* (London and New York, 2006), p. 424, says the students were Clare Cherrington and her friends Julia Flint and Kay (Catherine) Jones. They invited LW to become honorary chair of the Sussex University Fabian Group. EW also introduced him to fellow historians Christopher Thorne and Richard Hiscocks. Woolf received an Honorary Doctorate of Letters from Sussex in 1964.

37. L. Woolf, *Sowing: An Autobiography of the Years, 1880–1904* (London, 1960).

38. EW to Leonard Woolf, Nov. 22, 1960, Leonard Woolf papers.

39. EW to Leonard Woolf, Aug. 16, 1964, Leonard Woolf papers.

40. Wolfgang Leonhard, *The Kremlin since Stalin* (Oxford, 1962), translated by Elizabeth Wiskemann and Marion Jackson. She may have met Leonhard through F.W. Deakin, James Joll, or David Footman—all at St. Antony's.

41. Over the years she contributed a number of reviews and six essays to *History Today*, the last being EW, "Masaryk and Czechoslovakia," *History Today*, 18, 12 (Dec. 1968), pp. 845–851.

42. Requisition, June 11, 1949, for a broadcast in Italian aired on June 10. Requisition for a talk about the Saar in German ("German Features"), Aug. 22, 1956. RCONT1 Radio Talks, E. Wiskemann 1932–61, BBC Written Archives Caversham.

43. Note in the files by unidentified author, probably addressed to John Coatman of the News Department, April 21, 1939, RCONT1 Radio Talks, E. Wiskemann 1932–61, BBC Written Archives Caversham. Ronald Lewin (Organiser, Third Programme Talks) to EW, Sept. 28, 1950: "The reactions to your last broadcast...suggested that your performance at the microphone had not entirely done justice to the interest of the script, and we feel that we should have the reassurance of a preliminary recording of a portion of the lecture." Also, Trevor Blewitt to A.C. (H), Aug. 30, 1945. RCONT1 Radio Talks, E. Wiskemann 1932–61, BBC Written Archives. Two powerful critics of her voice and delivery were Third Programme's Lord Archie Gordon and the formidable producer Anna Kallin. EW to Ronald Lewin, April 17, 1953, about a proposed talk on the Saar: "I should add that I know that my B.B.C. dossier will inform you that my voice is unsuitable for broadcasting. This may have been so when I was on the verge of a bad nervous breakdown a few years ago. But I listened critically to a record of myself broadcasting in German to Switzerland the other day and was surprised to hear how well I came across, better in fact than my masculine partner. I am fairly sure that I do not come across worse in my own language." Apparently, BBC officials agreed about her improvement: Elisabeth Rowley, Talks organizer, to Miss Rowntree, July 29, 1953. Jean Rowntree, granddaughter of the Quaker philanthropist, Joseph Rowntree, was a producer for the Third Programme. After working to help Jews and socialists escape from Prague in 1938, she joined the BBC in 1940.

44. EW to Michael Redgrave, Sept 14, 1961. Michael Redgrave papers.

45. EW to Harry Bergholz, March 6, 1958. An attempt at reconciliation some years later proved disastrous: EW to Harry Bergholz, Oct. 29, 1966.

46. Prof. Marco Magnani says that he remembers Marchese Francesco Antinori attending the family Christmases in Rome when he was young. The Brigstocke family also became close friends with the Magnanis.

47. Vittorio Gabrieli, "Minima Personalia: England, My England," *Belfagor*, 63, 3 (March 2008), p. 194. The first Director in the early postwar years had been EW's friend Umberto Morra. Natalia Ginzburg was in London 1960–62; EW wrote an obituary for her husband, Director Baldini, for the *Times*, June 25, 1969, p. 12.

48. EW to Guglielmo Alberti, Feb. 20, 1955, Alberti papers. Enid McLeod, *Living Twice* (London, 1982). McLeod (1896–1985) became a close friend of Alberti, Umberto Morra, and Alexander d'Entréves of the Potigny group in the years before the war. She attended St. Hugh's Oxford, wrote several books and translations, worked for the League of Nations in Geneva 1926–29, and for MOI (French section under Raymond Mortimer) during the war. She had also previously worked for Chatham House on the *African Survey*. Postwar she ran the British Council in Paris. Also, H. McCarthy, *Women of the World: The Rise of the Female Diplomat* (London, 2014), p. 258.

49. Franca Magnani, *Eine italienische Familie* (Munich, 1993), pp. 281–3.

50. Deborah McDonald and Jeremy Dronfield, A *Very Dangerous Woman: The Lives, Loves and Lies of Russia's Most Seductive Spy* (London, 2015).

51. Valdo Magnani (1912–82) at first seemed destined for a chequered career in the Italian Communist party but he became increasingly critical of Stalinism and Nenni's socialist party. In 1951 he formed an alternative socialist party with Aldo Cucci. He continued to be active in politics, especially in the cooperative movement.

52. The Wiskemann–Künzli letters date from June 1950 to August 1956. Arnold Künzli Nachlass, Schweizerisches Literaturarchiv.

53. A British Committee was established in 1959, aided by the Rockefeller Foundation, to theorize IR. Brunello Vigezzi, *The British Committee on the Theory of International Politics (1954–1985)* (Milan, 2005). The Committee was chaired by Cambridge historian Herbert Butterfield, among its most active members was Martin Wight.

54. When asked for information in preparation for awarding Wiskemann an honorary doctorate, Lucy Sutherland (Principal of Lady Margaret Hall) explained that EW identified herself as "a writer on modern and contemporary history." Lucy Sutherland to A. Bryan Brown, March 1, 1965, Sutherland papers, Oxford.

55. Already in the 1930s there were criticisms that so many academic historians made little or no contribution to public debate about the contemporary political crisis and the struggle between fascism and democracy. John Kenyon, *The History Men* (second ed. London, 1993), p. 288.

56. E. Reichmann, "The Study of Contemporary History as a Political and Moral Duty," in Max Beloff (ed.), *On the Track of Tyranny* (London, 1960), p. 191. Reichmann (1897–1998) fled from Berlin to London in 1939. Her best-known work is a study of anti-Semitism, *Hostages of Civilization* (London, 1950).

57. Jane Caplan, "Contemporary History: Reflections from Britain and Germany," *History Workshop Journal*, 63 (Spring 2007), pp. 230–238. By the 1990s German historians had become bitterly divided over Rothfel's legacy as they debated how postwar conservative nationalist historians had grappled with the Nazi era. See: N. Berg, "Hidden

Memory and Unspoken History: Hans Rothfels and the Postwar Restoration of Contemporary German History," *The Leo Baeck Institute Year Book*, 49, 1 (Jan. 2004), pp. 195–220; J. Eckel, "Hans Rothfels—An Intellectual Biography in the Age of Extremes," *Journal of Contemporary History*, 42, 3 (July 2007), pp. 421–446.

58. In 1950 the two best-known historians who had written about the origins of the Second World War and Nazism were Sir Lewis Namier and Hugh Trevor-Roper, specialists on Britain in the eighteenth and seventeenth centuries. In 1948 Namier was seriously considered for the Burton Chair in International Relations at Oxford. C. Hood, D. King, and G. Peele (eds.), *Forging a Discipline*, p. 193.

59. One can point to many other examples: M.R.D. Foot, Michael Howard, Christopher and Hugh Seton-Watson, to name only four.

60. 1939 was still the end date in the 1980s. Remarkably, in 1930, while the Oxford undergraduate curriculum ended in the 1870s, G.N. Clark, editor of the *Oxford History of England*, commissioned a volume covering the years 1870–1914. Authored by the liberal progressive Robert Ensor, who had spent most of his career as a journalist and leader writer, it was published in 1936 and by the 1980s had sold over 100,000 copies.

61. D.C. Watt, "Contemporary History: Problems and Perspectives," *Journal of the Society of Archivists*, vol. 3, Oct. 1969, pp. 511–525, quote from p. 512. Alan Bullock recalled being taken aside by J.C. Masterman and told: "You know, if you really want a career as a historian, you must stop this." i.e. his focus on the recent past. A. Bullock to Ian McIntyre, *Independent*, June 20, 1991.

62. Jane Caplan, "Contemporary History: Reflections from Britain and Germany," p. 235.

63. G. Barraclough, "The Larger View of History," *TLS*, June 6, 1956, p. 14.

64. K.C. Dewar, "Geoffrey Barraclough: From Historicism to Historical Science," *The Historian*, 56, 3 (March 1994), pp. 449–464. G. Barraclough, "History, Morals and Politics," *International Affairs*, 34, 1 (Jan. 1958), pp. 1–15; *History in a Changing World* (Oxford, 1955); *An Introduction to Contemporary History* (London, 1964).

65. Alan Bullock, "Is it Possible to Write Contemporary History?" in M. Beloff, *On the Track of Tyranny* (London, 1960), pp. 67–77. Also, Alan Bullock, "Is History Becoming a Social Science? The Case of Contemporary History," *The History Teacher*, 11, 4 (Aug. 1978), pp. 549–561.

66. Guy Wint's books included *Spotlight on Asia* (1955); *The British in Asia* (1947); *Dragon and Sickle* (1958) on the Communist revolution in China, and *Total War* (1972) for Penguin with Peter Calvocoressi. He had close connections to St. Antony's College, as did Zorza and Crankshaw. In the 1960s St. Antony's scholarly reputation was burdened by reports that it was a training school for spies; this was because of the role of Deakin, David Footman, and others who had worked in intelligence during the war. Footman had run the Central European desk at MI6 until 1953 and then returned to teaching; Guy Wint was said to have been a key journalist contact of the postwar Information Research Department. P. Lashmar and J. Oliver, *Britain's Secret Propaganda War: The Foreign Office and the Cold War 1948–1977* (London, 1998).

67. Debate about the nature of history and historians' methodology seemed to be on the increase with E.H. Carr's 1961 Trevelyan Lectures at Cambridge, published as *What is History?* Carr attacked the "cult of facts" and settled scores with Isaiah Berlin and Karl Popper, who had accused him of determinism and of presenting history through the

eyes of the 'winners'. See also: Ved Mehta's highly entertaining *The Fly and the Fly-Bottle: Encounters with British Intellectuals* (Boston, 1962).

68. A.J.P. Taylor, *The Origins of the Second World War* (London, 1961), pp. 9, 12–13, 69 (here Hugh Trevor-Roper is added). Already in his Ford Lectures of 1956 Taylor had named Wiskemann along with Namier, Wheeler-Bennett, and Toynbee as the authorities from which "our present attitude" towards the origins of the Second World War For was derived. A.J.P. Taylor, *The Trouble Makers: Dissent over Foreign Policy, 1792–1939* (London, 1957), pp. 16–17.

69. Quoted in Adam Sisman *A.J.P. Taylor: A Biography* (London, 1995), p. 288.

70. A.J.P. Taylor, *The Origins of the Second World War*, p. 69.

71. A.J.P. Taylor, *The Origins of the Second World War*, p. 71.

72. A.J.P. Taylor, *The Origins of the Second World War*, p. 278.

73. A.J.P. Taylor, *The Origins of the Second World War*, p. 189. Taylor said later that he meant this ironically.

74. Adam Sisman, *A.J.P. Taylor: A Biography*, p. 294.

75. Critics came from across the political spectrum: for G.F. Hudson the book was "An Apologia for Adolf Hitler," *Commentary*, Feb. 1, 1962, pp. 178–184, while labour historian Alan Fox complained that Taylor's leveling down was "perverse and irresponsible." Fox, "Was Hitler Guilty?" *Socialist Commentary*, June 1961, pp. 5–7. Isaac Deutscher even saw a connection between Taylor's treatment of Hitler and contemporary favor for West German rearmament under NATO. Deutscher letter, *TLS*, June 2, 1961.

76. James Joll, "The Ride to the Abyss," *Spectator*, April 21, 1961, p. 561.

77. [Anon., in fact C.M. Woodhouse], "Why Did We Fight?" *TLS*, April 21, 1961, p. 244. 'Monty' Woodhouse was Director of Chatham House and had fought with the partisans in Greece.

78. A.L. Rowse and H.R. Trevor-Roper, "Letters to the Editor," *TLS*, May 21, 1961, p. 325. David Thomson, "Letters to the Editor," *TLS*, May 5, 1961, p. 277, Isaac Deutscher, M. Lambert, and W.N. Medlicott, Elizabeth Wiskemann, "Letters to the Editor," *TLS*, June 2, 1961, p. 341. Trevor-Roper was concerned about university students who had little grasp of the mood of the 1930s.

79. "Letters to the Editor," *TLS*, June 2, 1961 (Isaac Deutscher, M. Lambert, and W.N. Medlicott).

80. Including Trevor-Roper, Gordon Craig, and Golo Mann. Gordon Craig, "Provocative, Perverse View of Pre-1939," *New York Herald Tribune*, Jan. 7, 1962. Golo Mann, "Hitlers britischer Advokat: A.J.P. Taylors Revision des Geschichte," *Der Monat*, 11, 96 (Sept. 1961), pp. 79–86.

81. EW to C.C. Aronsfeld, May 24, 1961; C.C. Aronsfeld to EW, May 25, 1961, Wiener Library Archives, London. Wiskemann Correspondence File.

82. "Sir, – On April 22 the *Reichsruf*, the organ of the neo-Nazi *Reichspartei* in the Federal Republic, jubilantly welcomed Mr. Taylor's misreading of the Hossbach Memorandum and attacked German historians who had read it with greater care. The *Deutsche Soldatenzeitung* of April 28 was happy to note that Mr. Taylor had made nonsense of the Nuremberg trials. The May number of *Nation-Europa* (published in Coburg by Artur Ehrhardt, formerly a Major in the S.S., on behalf of the chief neo-Nazi international organization) was gratified to observe that Mr. Taylor had explained away the responsibility of Nazi Germany for the Second World War. Sir Oswald Mosley's *Action*

has expressed similar appreciation of Mr. Taylor." EW, "Letters to the Editor," June 2, 1961, p. 341.

83. *Listener*, April 20, 1961, p. 707.

84. EW, "Hitler's Reputation," *History Today*, (June 1961), p. 429.

85. EW to Hugh Trevor-Roper, July 5, 1961, Lord Dacre of Glanton papers, Christ Church College, Oxford.

86. H.R. Trevor-Roper to EW, July 20, 1961, Lord Dacre of Glanton papers.

87. W.R. Louis (ed.), *The Origins of the Second World War: A.J.P.Taylor and His Critics* (New York, 1972); E.M. Robertson (ed.), *The Origins of the Second World War: Historical Interpretations* (London, 1971); G. Martel (ed.), *The Origins of the Second World War Reconsidered: The A.J.P. Taylor Debate After Twenty-Five Years* (Boston, 1986); G. Martel (ed.), *The Origins of the Second World War Reconsidered: A.J.P. Taylor and the Historians* (London, 1999).

88. S. Aster, "Appeasement: Before and After Revisionism," *Diplomacy and Statecraft*, 19, 3 (2008), pp. 443–480. A.J.P. Taylor to Kingsley Martin (n.d. but in the early 1960s): "Chamberlain ought to have regretted what he did. But he didn't. He was an obstinate and narrow-minded man who, when things went wrong, always put the blame on others – Baldwin, Hitler, anyone but himself. In my book on the origins of the Second World War, I slipped towards the same mistake as Bright, and gave the impression of excusing Hitler. I didn't mean to. All I wanted to say was that he planned much less and improvised much more than people made out at the time." "Letters to the Editor – written by his contributor, A.J.P. Taylor, to Kingsley Martin of the 'New Statesman' at various times from 1951 to 1964," *London Review of Books*, May 10, 1990, p. 12.

89. A.J.P.Taylor, *A Personal History* (London, 1983), p. 235: "Every historian cashes in on my views perhaps without knowing that he is doing so."

90. EW, "The End of Peace," *Sunday Times*, April 23, 1967. Thorne, who became a leading historian of international affairs, was teaching at Charterhouse School when he first met EW. She advocated strongly for him to be hired at Sussex: EW to Martin Wight Jan 18, 1966; Nov. 29, 1967; Dec. 14, 1967. Martin Wight papers, 233/36, folder 21.

91. EW to Anthony Thwaite, No. 47 (n. d., probably 1965), Anthony Thwaite papers. Also, Sally Marks to Geoffrey Field, Jan. 10, 2016.

92. EW, "The German Brand of Dictatorship," *Government and Opposition*, 5, 2 (April 1970), p. 252.

93. EW to Harry Bergholz, Dec. 21, 1963.

94. In 1960/61 there were 107,000 full-time university students in Britain; by 1967 there were well over 200,000 (plus 18,000 part-time students). Brian Harrison, *Seeking a Role* (Oxford, 2009), pp. 357–370. Other sources give the number of students in full-time education as roughly 450,000 by 1971.

95. Ms. Dawn Sinclair (Harper-Collins) email to G. Field, June 8, 2017.

96. EW to J.H. Plumb, Oct. 19, 1963. J.H. Plumb papers.

97. They included: George Holmes, J.R. Hale, Geoffrey Elton, J.H. Elliott, David Ogg, Olwen Hufton, George Rudé, Jacques Droz, and J.A.S. Grenville. Ollard and Plumb also seem to have discussed who would do the period 1878–1919; the names of George Kennan and Eugen Weber were mentioned. It was eventually assigned to

Norman Stone, but not published until 1983. By the time Wiskemann came on board, Elton's contribution on Reformation Europe was finished and they regarded it as the model.

98. Martin Wight to Richard Ollard, Sept. 24, 1963. J.H. Plumb papers.

99. R. Ollard to J.H. Plumb, Sept. 25, 1963; J.H. Plumb to R. Ollard, Oct. 4, 1963. J.H. Plumb papers.

100. J.H. Plumb to R. Ollard, Nov. 4, 1965. J.H. Plumb papers.

101. Zara Steiner, "Axis Turns Again," in *TLS*, June 2, 1966, p. 487.

102. EW, *Europe of the Dictators 1919–1945* (London 1966), pp. 249–50.

103. S. Aster, "Appeasement: Before and After Revisionism."

104. Cyril Connolly, "Lest We Forget This Too," *Sunday Times*, April 10, 1966.

105. George Mosse, publisher's blurb for the Harper & Row edition. Mosse to Hugh van Dusen, March 16 and Hugh van Dusen's reply March 21, 1966. George Mosse papers, Madison Wisconsin microfilm reel 80, nrs 345–349. Also, review by René Albrecht-Carrié in *The Political Science Quarterly*, 83, 4 (Dec. 1968), pp. 617–619. For a negative review and one that seems more focused on her earlier study about the postwar expulsion of the Sudeten Germans, see: James H. Wolfe, *World Affairs*, 129, 4 (Jan.–March 1967), pp. 265–7.

106. C. Thorne, "Versailles to Potsdam," *Spectator*, April 22, 1966, p. 505.

107. Review by Robert A. Pois in *The Historian*, 30, 1, November 1967, p. 100.

108. Malcolm Muggeridge, "Europe That Never Was," *Observer*, Feb. 4, 1968.

109. "Axis Turns Again" [Zara Steiner], *TLS*, June 2, 1966, p. 487. Zara Steiner, *The Lights That Failed: European International History, 1919–1933* (Oxford, 2007); The Triumph of the Dark: European International History, 1933–1939 (Oxford, 2013).

110. M. Ratcliffe, "Memoirs of a Great Watcher," *Times*, Feb. 17, 1968, p. 21. Ratcliffe was a student of J.H. Plumb at Cambridge.

111. In 1946 Wiskemann's old friend David ('Bunny') Garnett had been hired to produce an official history of PWE. He had completed it by 1947 but was all too frank about the inter-agency power struggles. As a result, it was conveniently buried for over half a century. Even when published in 2002, many passages were deleted as "potentially embarrassing and/or libelous." David Garnett, *The Secret History of P.W.E.: The Political Warfare Executive* (London, 2002). On media coverage of SOE, see: Juliette Pattinson, *Behind Enemy Lines: Gender, Passing and the Special Operations Executive in the Second World War* (Manchester, 2007).

112. Review by I.F.D. Morrow in *International Affairs*, 44, 3 (July 1968), pp. 503–4; J.W. Brügel in *Sozialdemokratische Zeitschrift für Politik, Wissenschaft und Kultur*, 47 (1968), pp. 233–234; F.P. Habel in *Bohemia*, 13 (Jan. 1972), pp. 458–61. Christopher Seton-Watson, "Travelling Scholar – Journalist," *TLS*, March 7, 1968, p. 226; C.L. Mowat, "One Woman's Worlds," *Listener*, April 4, 1968, p. 447: "Miss Wiskemann wears her gifts lightly: her courage, her quick intelligence, her unselfish care for others." Paul Stauffer, "Die Schweiz in Britischer Sicht, 1935–1945," *Schweizer Monatshefte*, 47 (Oct. 1968), pp. 707–710.

113. The series was edited by Geoffrey Warner, a historian of France, and later by Christopher Thorne, Wiskemann's young colleague at Sussex.

114. EW, Fascism in Italy (London, 1969), pp. 120–1.

115. See also the insightful analysis of Mark Mazower, "Fascism and Democracy Today: What Use is the Study of History in the Current Crisis?" *European Law Journal*, 22, 3 (May 2016), pp. 375–385.

116. She praised, for example, Ernst Nolte's *Der Faschismus in seiner Epoche* (1963) because it related *Action Française*, Fascism, and Nazism to the crisis of liberalism, and H.R. Kedward's *Fascism in Western Europe 1900–1945* (1970) because it was careful to distinguish the differences between these movements as well as their common attractions. [EW], "Not All as Bad as Hitler," *TLS*, July 11, 1968.

117. Vernon Bartlett, "The Feeble Tyrant," *TLS*, Aug. 21, 1969.

118. File on EW, "Italian Fascism in Europe," Box 587, St. Martin's Press Archive, Brown University. MacMillan raised doubts about distributing the book and eventually lowered the number they had agreed to take. Wiskemann made it clear that she would not consider a re-write. One American review praised it as "a masterpiece of condensation" "in clear and forceful prose" and recommended it as the best introduction to the subject: William Ebenstein, *The Annals of the American Academy of Political and Social Science*, 389 (May 1970) pp. 152–4.

119. EW, "Contemporary Writing in Switzerland," *TLS*, July 4, 1958, pp. 381–382; EW, "Hitler and His Architect," *TLS*, Oct. 16, 1969, pp. 1173–1174. The digitized online version of the *TLS*, which includes authors, lists EW and Ernest Borneman (writer, filmmaker, musicologist, etc.) as co-authors of a detailed critique of German theatre in the 1960s: "German Theater in the 1960s," *Times Literary Supplement*, April 3, 1969, pp. 337–340 (see the response "Was ankommt, wird verurteilt," *Der Spiegel*, 18, 1969). I have not been able to discover if this is an error or if EW knew Borneman. As a youth Borneman had known Brecht, he was in Berlin in the early 1930s, and his wife Eva Geisel worked at one time as a theatre critic for the *New Statesman* where she could have met EW. Detlef Siegfried, *Modern Lusts: Ernest Borneman: Jazz Critic, Filmmaker, Sexologist* (London, 2020).

120. "The Thirties in Britain" and "The Threat of fascism" were compiled by Constantine FitzGibbon. Other participants included: Lord Boothby, A.K. Chesterton, Sir Colin Coote, Walter Laqueur, and Philip Toynbee. For "Between the Wars," EW recruited E.H. Carr, Jean-Baptiste Duroselle, Elie Kedourie, A.J. Nicholls, and Philip Noel-Baker. Her own talk for the series was "Italy and the Successor States," broadcast on Nov. 29, 1967. EW also participated with her old friend Lord Arran ('Boofy' Gore) and the Dutch Prime Minister, Joseph Luns, as they reminisced about Arran's wartime experiences in the Foreign Service. Home Service, Jan. 6, 1967, "The Decline and Fall of Arthur Gore," Genome Radio Times, 1923–2009.

121. BBC TV: "News Map," June 1, 1948 (on Switzerland); "Foreign Correspondent," Nov. 11, 1949, produced by Grace Wyndham Goldie.

122. The New Cambridge Modern History XII: The Shifting Balance of World Forces 1898–1945, edited by C.L. Mowat (Cambridge, 1968), chapter 16 (pp. 473–511). She also contributed to a history of Italy edited by the photographer and art critic Milton Gendel.EW, "Modern Italy: 1870 to the present," in M. Gendel (ed), *An Illustrated History of Italy* (London, 1966). All the contributors were distinguished in the field, including Denis Mack Smith, Michael Grant and Peter Burke. Wiskemann's section was co-authored with the journalist Peter Nichols, Rome correspondent for the London *Times*.

123. "Elizabeth Wiskemann (1899–1971)," *Dictionary of National Biography, 1971–1980* (Oxford, 1986), p. 918, edited by Lord Blake and C.S. Nicholls, entry by James Joll. *Guardian*, March 20, 1965, p. 3. Also, EW to Leonard Woolf, May 22, 1965, Leonard Woolf papers.

124. My thanks for this information to Mr Frank Sinanan, then a PPE student, who attended the lectures in Hilary term 1966.

125. Phyllis Hetzel, "Obituary: Kay Baxter," *Independent*, Feb. 15, 1994.

126. To the poet and *Listener* editor, Anthony Thwaite, she wrote that she preferred having about five people, adding "*Pro tem* I have enough domestic help, almost too much, so I'm entertaining while it lasts..." EW to Anthony Thwaite, Jan 26, 1964, Thwaite papers.

127. R.W., "Elizabeth Wiskemann: Guidance to Young," *Times*, July 15, 1971, p. 18.

128. EW knew everybody in History/International Affairs at LSE, and Sally Marks thought she might have done a little teaching for them after Sussex. I have not been able to confirm this, but she did on occasion act as an external examiner for L.S.E, Edinburgh, and Sussex.

129. EW and Hester Marsden Smedley first met in Switzerland, where EW was assistant press attaché; both served in wartime intelligence. From the Belgian–Luxembourg border Hester sent back some of the earliest reports of the German invasion in May 1940. While retreating from France she also encountered Kim Philby and recommended that MI6 recruit him. Marks's dissertation was published as *Innocent Abroad: Belgium at the Paris Peace Conference* (Chapel Hill, NC, 1981) and she had previously published *The Illusion of Peace: International Relations in Europe, 1918–1933* (New York, 1976).

130. Sally Marks to Geoffrey Field, Jan. 10, 2016. Marks wrote: "Elizabeth sent me in 1971 to a young man who was starting a literary agency with a friend. They did not succeed in placing my insufficiently revised diss. (just as well) but did get me the contract for *The Illusion of Peace* [Her first book]...A lucky break." Also, Christoph Kimmich to Geoffrey Field, Nov. 27, 2017. Kimmich was writing a dissertation about Danzig. Wiskemann met with him, gave him names of people who might be helpful, invited him to lunch, and later came to the viva for his D.Phil. She also recommended his finished Oxford thesis for publication by Chatham House. K.O. Younger to EW, Oct. 15, 1964; Alan Bullock to K. Younger, Oct. 2, 1964; K. Younger to Alan Bullock, Sept. 29, 1964, RIIA 4/WISK, Chatham House.

131. In 1974 Heather Brigstocke became High Mistress of St. Pauls' Girls' School, the leading private girls' school in London, and served there until 1989. In 1990 she was created a life peer; she served on many boards and committees and in 2000 was awarded a CBE for her service to the English-speaking Union. In March 1974 her husband, diplomat Geoffrey Brigstocke, died in the crash of Turkish Airlines flight 981 on its way from Istanbul to Paris. She remarried a fellow peer, law lord Hugh Baron Griffiths, in 2000. Lady Brigstocke died tragically in 2004 just south of Athens, killed by a speeding driver as she crossed the road after a meeting of the children's charity Home Start International, of which she was the founding chairperson. Obituary by Katharine Whitehorn, "Baroness Brigstocke of Kensington," *Guardian*, May 3, 2004. Visiting Paris in March 1965 and hoping to see her friend Joseph Breitbach, EW wrote: "The beautiful young Frau Brigstocke, my adopted daughter, is coming too." EW to J. Breitbach, March 30, 1965, Breitbach Nachlass. My thanks to David and Julian Brigstocke for sharing their recollections with me.

132. EW to Hugh Trevor-Roper, July 5, 1961; Hugh Trevor-Roper to EW, July 30, 1961. Lord Dacre of Glanton papers, Christ Church College, Oxford. She also seems to have consulted the distinguished Swiss ophthalmologist Prof. Hans Goldmann. In the 1990s Hugh Trevor-Roper himself suffered from glaucoma and a cataract and, like Wiskemann, feared risking an operation, which he was told might leave him blind.

133. EW to J.H. Plumb, Jan. 2, 1964 [postcard], J.H. Plumb papers, Cambridge University Library.

134. When Lucy Sutherland invited EW to a dinner party during an Oxford vacation and was concerned whether dons would still be around, she was shocked by the eager responses to her invitation. Letters to Dame Lucy Sutherland, Oct. 1969–Jan. 1970, Lucy Sutherland papers, Bodleian Library, Oxford. Guests included Robert Blake and Raymond Carr and their wives, Herbert Nicholas of New College, P.G.M. Dickson, and Richard Cobb, the latter rearranging flight plans to Brussels to attend.

135. EW to Leonard Woolf, Jan. 16, 1966, Leonard Woolf papers.

136. EW to Richard Hughes, March 17, 1968, Richard Hughes papers.

137. Alan Strachey, *Secret Dreams: The Biography of Michael Redgrave* (London, 2004), p. 408.

138. EW, "Thomas Masaryk's Legacy," *Spectator*, Oct. 24, 1968, pp. 573–574; "The Freedom to Joke," *Spectator*, Jan. 16, 1969, p. 70; "Prague Spring 1968," *Spectator*, Feb. 6, 1969, p. 178. Also, the biographical tribute: EW, "Masaryk and Czechoslovakia," *History Today*, 18, 12 (Dec. 1968). Her shock at the invasion is mentioned in a letter to the *Times*, July 6, 1971. These events seem to have precipitated the suicide of her former colleague in Berlin, Alexander Werth, in March 1969, although I have found no mention of his death by Wiskemann.

139. Letter to the *Times*, Oct. 28, 1968, p. 9; the other two female signatories were Agnes Headlam-Morley and Violet Connolly, author of several books on the Soviet economy.

140. EW, "Vicious Circle," *Spectator*, July 11, 1969, p. 47. Frank Giles, editor of the *Sunday Times*, wrote to her, "it was very useful for me to be able to pick your brains and thereby supervise and, where necessary, to amend the material which our man in Prague sent through for that weekend." ST/ED/FG/1/03, News International Record Office, London.

141. EW to Harry Bergholz, Feb. 9, 1969.

142. EW to Harry Bergholz, March 25, 1970.

143. EW, review of Peter Gay's "Weimar Culture," *Spectator*, May 23, 1969, p. 690. She noted parallels between late Weimar and "our times."

144. EW to Leonard Woolf, Aug. 26, 1965, Leonard Woolf papers.

145. EW, *Europe of the Dictators*, p. 247.

146. Letter from Prof. Sally Marks to Geoffrey Field, Jan. 10, 2016.

147. EW to Leonard Woolf, Nov. 22, 1960. Leonard Woolf died in August 1969.

148. EW to C.H. Rolph, March 18, 1971; C.H. Rolph to EW, April 19, 1971; EW to C.H. Rolph, May 7, 1971, C.H. Rolph papers.

149. "Feared She was Going Blind: Historian's Suicide," *Westminster & Pimlico News*, July 16, 1971, p. 6. Report on the inquest at Westminster.

150. EW's friend Heather Brigstocke was her executor and beneficiary. Her estate was valued at £64,472 (net duty/taxes paid of £17,021), i.e. about £47,000. I would guess that a sizable portion of the estate consisted of her house at 41 Moore Street, whose

estimated value had risen considerably since she purchased it in 1951. Baroness Brigstocke and her family lived in the house on Moore Street for several years.

151. Ian F.D. Morrow, *International Affairs*, 44, 3 (July 1968), p. 504.

152. Not only in the national press, but in regional papers in, for example, Belfast, Nottingham, and Leicester.

153. Cyril Connolly, *Enemies of Promise* (New York, 1983 edition of the 1938 book), p. 94.

154. M. Frank, *Expelling the Germans. British Opinion and Post-1945 Population Transfer in Context* (Oxford, 2007), p. 1.

155. For example: Eagle Glassheim, *Cleansing the Czech Borderlands: Migration, Environment and Health in the Former Sudetenland* (Pittsburgh, 2016).

156. Lucian M. Ashworth, "Czechs and Germans in the Twenty Years' Crisis: Mackinder, Carr and Wiskemann on Central and Eastern Europe after the Peace," *Journal of International Relations and Development* 24, 4 (2021), pp. 848–865. Working from the ground up, so to speak, from a detailed analysis of the Bohemian provinces and their politics, "she [EW] comes to conclusions that can be applied to ideas of world order." Recent studies of borderlands include: Omer Bartov, *Tales from the Borderlands: Making and Unmaking the Galician Past* (New Haven, 2022); Astrid Eckert, *West Germany and the Iron Curtain: Environment, Economy and Culture in the Borderlands* (Oxford, 2019).

157. Three women on this list have not been mentioned earlier. Dorothy Pickles (1903–94) was an authority on French politics and author of more than a dozen books who studied at Leeds, LSE, and the Sorbonne and worked in MOI during the war. After Oxford, Phyllis Auty (1910–98) studied in Hamburg in 1933 and switched from medieval to contemporary history. She worked for the Oxford University Extra-Mural Studies department and during the war was recruited by the BBC and then the Foreign Office's Political Intelligence Department. She became a specialist on the Balkans, and her publications include the first major biography of Tito; she taught at London University and ended her career as Professor of Modern History at Simon Fraser University in Canada. Violet Connolly (1899–1988) was an expert on Soviet Affairs. After University College, Dublin, she worked for the League of Nations in Paris and the Institute of Current Affairs at Harvard and in Geneva, She was also a researcher at Chatham House from 1932 under A.J. Toynbee, joined the Foreign Office in 1939, and became head of the Soviet Affairs section of the Foreign Office Research Department; she was also in the 1950s an economic attaché to the British embassy in Moscow and wrote numerous books on Soviet affairs and Soviet economic policy in Asia.

158. Franca Magnani, *Eine italienische Familie* (Munich, 1993), p. 283.

159. R.W., "Elizabeth Wiskemann: Guidance to Young," *Times*, July 15, 1971, p. 18.

160. *History Today*, Aug. 1, 1971, obituary notice.

161. *Times*, July 11, 1971, p. 14.

162. Letter ("A Friend," anon.) to the *Times*, July 9, 1971, p. 14. Anne Sebba, *Battling for News. The Rise of the Woman Reporter* (London, 1995), p. 147, cites Lord Arran's memorial address for EW, Golders Green, October 21, 1971.

Books by Elizabeth Wiskemann

Czechs and Germans. A Study of the Struggle in the Historic Provinces of Bohemia and Moravia (Royal Institute of International Affairs, Oxford University Press, Oxford, 1938), translated into Czech.

Undeclared War (Constable and Oxford University Press, New York, 1939) also published as *Prologue to War* (1940).

Italy (Geoffrey Cumberlege, Oxford University Press, London, New York, Toronto, 1947)

The Rome-Berlin Axis: A History of the Relations Between Hitler and Mussolini (Oxford University Press, New York and London, 1949), translated into French.

Germany's Eastern Neighbours. Problems Relating to the Oder-Neisse Line and the Czech Frontier Regions (Oxford University Press, London, New York, Toronto, 1956).

A Great Swiss Newspaper: The Story of the Neue Zürcher Zeitung (Oxford University Press, London, New York, Toronto, 1959).

Europe of the Dictators 1919–1945 (Fontana, Harper & Row, New York, 1966), translated into Spanish, Hebrew.

The Europe I Saw (Collins, MacMillan, St Martin's Press, London and New York, 1968), translated into German.

Fascism in Italy: Its Development and Influence (MacMillan, St. Martin's Press, London and New York, 1969).

Italy since 1945 (MacMillan, St. Martin's Press, London and New York, 1971).

Sections of Books

Reginald Robert Betts (ed.), *Central and South-East Europe 1945–1948* (Royal Institute of International Affairs, London, 1950), section: Hungary.

A.J. and V.M. Toynbee (eds.) *Hitler's Europe* (1954), section: "The Italian Resistance."

Survey of International Affairs 1939–46 (ed. A.J. and V.M. Toynbee): The Realignment of Europe (Oxford University Press and Royal Institute of International Affairs, London and New York1955), section: Czechoslovakia.

Jethro Bithell (ed.) *A Companion to German Studies* (Methuen, London, 1955), section: "German History from 1937–1952."

Survey of International Affairs 1939–46 (ed. A.J. and V.M. Toynbee): The Initial Triumph of the Axis: The Subjugation of Eastern Europe (Oxford University press and Royal Institute of International Affairs, London, 1958), sections: Partitioned Czechoslovakia 1939–1945; Hungary, Rumania and Bulgaria 1941–1944; Partitioned Yugoslavia 1941–1945; Albania 1941–1945.

Wolfgang Leonhard, *The Kremlin since Stalin* (Praeger, Westport, CT, 1962), translated by Elizabeth Wiskemann and Marian Jackson.

Milton Gendel (ed.), *An Illustrated History of Italy* (McGraw Hill, Weidenfeld a& Nicolson, New York and London, 1966), section "Modern Italy: 1870 to the Present."

The New Cambridge Modern History XII: The Shifting Balance of World Forces, edited by C.L. Mowat (Cambridge University Press, Cambridge, 1968), section: "Chapter 16: Germany, Italy and Eastern Europe."

H. Krausnick, H. Buchheim, M. Broszat, and H.-A. Jacobsen, *Anatomy of the S.S. State* (Collins, London, 1968), Introduction by Elizabeth Wiskemann. Translated by Marion Jackson, Richard Barry, and Dorothy Long.

Archival Sources

United Kingdom and Eire

The National Archives, Kew, Richmond, FO 898/256, FO 898/257 Political Warfare Executive papers.

Julian Bell papers, Kings College, Cambridge University, [Charleston papers].

BBC Written Archives, Caversham.

Helen Violet Bonham Carter papers, Bodleian Library, Oxford.

William Clark papers, Bodleian Library, Oxford.

Chattoo and Windus Ltd. Archive, University of Reading.

Chatham House [Royal Institute of International Affairs], London.

W.S. Churchill papers, Churchill College, Cambridge.

J.G. Crowther papers, The Keep, University of Sussex.

Sir William Deakin papers, Churchill College, Cambridge.

Gerald Duckworth and Co. Archive, Special Collections, Senate House Library, London.

University of Edinburgh, Special Collections, Edinburgh.

G.E.R. Gedye papers, Imperial War Museum, London.

Imperial War Museum, Sound Archives, London.

Stanislaw Kot papers, Polish Institute and Sikorski Museum, London.

Lady Margaret Hall, Oxford (EW bequest).

Sir Sean Lester papers, University College, Dublin.

Manchester Guardian Archive. Editors' Correspondence Files (W.P. Crozier, A.P. Wadsworth, A. Hetherington) F.A. Voigt and Elizabeth Wiskemann correspondence. John Rylands Library, Manchester.

Kingsley Martin papers, The Keep, University of Sussex.

New Statesman Archive, The Keep, University of Sussex.

Sir Clifford Norton papers, Imperial War Museum, London.

Observer Archive, Guardian News and Media Archive, London.

J.H. Plumb papers, Cambridge University Library.

Sir Michael Redgrave papers, Victoria and Albert Museum, London.

C.H. Rolph papers, The Keep, University of Sussex.

Sir Frank Russell papers, Imperial War Museum, London.

Cecil Jackson Sprigge papers, Special Collections, University of Reading.

Dame Lucy Sutherland papers, Bodleian Library, Oxford.

Anthony Thwaite papers ("The *Listener*"), Brotherton Library, Leeds University.

Julian O. Trevelyan papers, Trinity College, Cambridge University.

Hugh Trevor-Roper papers (Lord Dacre of Glanton), Bodleian Library, Oxford.

Sir John Wheeler-Bennett papers, St. Antony's College, Oxford.

Wiener Library, London, Wiskemann correspondence 1955–63.

Martin Wight papers, London School of Economics.

Elizabeth Wiskemann–Harry Bergholz letters, Newnham College, Cambridge University.

Leonard Woolf papers, The Keep, University of Sussex.

Italy

Guglielmo Alberti papers, Centro Studi Generazioni e Luoghi Archivi, Biella, Italy.

Bernard Berenson papers, I Tatti, Florence.

Piero Calamandrei papers, Istituto storico Toscana della Resistenza e dell'età contemporanea, Florence.
Luigi Einaudi papers, Fondazione Luigi Einaudi, Turin.

Germany, Switzerland, Netherlands

Bayerische Politische Polizei [Fa 119/2], Institut für Zeitgeschichte, Munich.
Christoph Bernoulli Nachlass, Universitätsbibliothek, Basel.
Joseph Breitbach Nachlass, Deutsches Literaturarchiv, Marbach am Neckar.
Carl Jacob Burckhardt Nachlass, Universitätsbibliothek, Basel.
Adolf Freudenberg Nachlass, Institut für Zeitgeschichte, Munich.
Ger Van Roon papers, Institut für Zeitgeschichte, Munich.
Paul Kluke papers, Hausarchiv, Institut für Zeitgeschichte, Munich.
Theodor Heuss Nachlass, Bundesarchiv, Koblenz.
Arnold Künzli Nachlass, Schweizerisches Literaturarchiv, Bern.
Golo Mann Nachlass, Schweizerisches Literaturarchiv, Bern.
Emil and Emmie Oprecht Nachlasse, Zentralbibliothek, Zurich.
H. Straumann Nachlass, Zentralbibliothek, Zurich.
Nederlands Instituut voor Oorlogsdocumentatie, Amsterdam (455 J. van Borssum-Buisman, Wiskemann file, "The Swiss Road").

United States

Max Ascoli papers, Howard Gotlieb Archival Research Center, Boston University.
Hamilton Fish Armstrong papers, Princeton University Library.
Allen Dulles papers, Princeton University Library.
Constantine FitzGibbon papers, Harry Ransom Center, Texas.
Richard Hughes papers, Lilley Library, Indiana University, Bloomington.
The Nation Archive, Houghton Library, Harvard University.
The National Archives, Washington, OSS papers [RG 226, Entry 210, Box 362. WN#13703].
PEN Archive, McFarlin Library, University of Tulsa, Oklahoma.
Alan Pryce-Jones papers, Beinecke Rare Book and Manuscript Library, Yale University.
St. Martin's Press Archive, Boxes 368, 587, Hay Library, Brown University, Rhode Island.
Christopher Sykes papers, Georgetown University, Washington, DC.
Rebecca West papers, Beinecke Rare Book and Manuscript Library, Yale University.

Index

Note: Please note that the abbreviation 'n' refers to endnotes. In the some of the subheadings under Wiskemann, Elizabeth, chronological order has been used, rather than alphabetical.

For the benefit of digital users, indexed terms that span two pages (e.g., 52–53) may, on occasion, appear on only one of those pages.

post-war 173–5, 182, 189, 218–19, 224,
      229–30
relationship with Nazi Germany 58–60, 62–3,
      69, 74, 76–8, 173
Czechs and Germans (Wiskemann) 60–2, 65–75,
      78, 191, 194, 228–9

Daily Express 27, 110–11, 146–7, 180–1
Daily Herald 36, 185
Daily Telegraph 27, 73
Dalton, Hugh 33, 42–3, 62–3, 65, 95, 98,
      110–11, 262n.95
Daniels, H.V. 258n.25
Dansey, Colonel Claude 83–4, 95–6, 116–17,
      128, 262n.89
Danzig (Poland) 45–6, 54–6, 78, 81–2, 94–5
Da Silva, Vieira 18–19
Das Schwarze Korps 46–7
Davies, Hugh Sykes 15–16
Davies, John Langdon 74–5
Dawson, Geoffrey 45–6, 101–2
Deakin, F. William 118–19, 212, 223–4, 234n.24
De Benedetti, Giulio 161–2
De Gasperi, Alcide 124–5, 162–8, 179
De Jonge, Louis 196–7
Dell, Robert 247n.19
Delmer, Denis Sefton 27, 110–11, 146–8, 180–1
Delogu, Giuseppe 120–1, 209–10
Delzell, Charles 222
Denmark 73–4, 85–6
"Der Kaufmann von Berlin" (Mehring) 19–20
Der Mann ohne Eigenschaften (Musil) 34–5
Der S.S. Staat (Kogon) 154, 177–8
Déry, Tibor 175–6
Deutscher Heimatbund (Germany) 179–80
Deutscher, Isaac 205
Deutsche Volkswirt 32
DGFP see *Documents on German Foreign Policy*
Die Grosse Politik 194–6
Die Pfeffermühle (political cabaret) 258n.22
Die Verbrecher ("Les criminels") (Bruckner)
      19–20
Dirks, Walter 177–8
"Disorder and Early Sorrow" (Mann) 19–20
Dobb, Phyllis 238n.53
Documents on German Foreign Policy, 1918–45
      (ed. Lambert) 8
Documents on German Foreign Policy
      (DGFP) 194–7, 204, 294n.178
Dohnanyi, Hand Von 129, 133–4
Dollfuss, Engelbert ("Tom Thumb") 35–8, 51–2
Dollmann, Eugen 136–7
Domodossola Republic (Sept/Oct 1944) 125–6
Donovan, William 112

Doren, Irita van 94–5
Douglas, R.M. 184–5
'Drang nach Osten'('Drive to the East') 51–6,
      58–61, 63, 65–9
   EW's writings on 69–74, 76–9, 81–2
Dreigroschenoper (Brecht) 178
Drtina, Prokop 154–5
Dubois, Pierre 265n.132
Düby, Oscar and Erika 208–9, 226–7, 276n.118,
      280n.180
Duckworth (publishers) 75–6
Dulles, Allen 3–4, 100, 125–6, 152–3
   German Opposition 136–7, 149
   intelligence officer in Switzerland 112–14,
      121, 127–8, 130–1
   recruitment of German agent 111, 128
   working relationship with EW 114–19,
      121–4, 127, 134, 139, 141, 151, 154,
      230–1, 269n.30
Dulles, John Foster 112–13
Duroselle, J.B. 295n.192, 296n.19

East Anglia, University of 212
Eastern Europe see Central and Eastern Europe
Ebbutt, Norman 2–3, 41, 45–7, 239n.68
   Czechoslovakia 55–7
   EW's mentor 26–8, 31–2
Eckert, Astrid 194, 196–7, 294n.178
Economic Consequences of the Peace (Keynes) 42
Economist, The 4, 71, 158, 162, 171–2, 282n.8
Eden, Sir Anthony 55–8, 98, 124–5, 132–3, 136,
      143–4, 149
Edinburgh University 5, 198, 201–5,
      210–11, 231
EH see Electra House (Department of
      Propaganda in Enemy Countries)
Eichmann, Adolf 140, 142–3, 215–16
Einaudi, Luigi 162–3, 221–2, 271n.48
Einheitsfront (anti-Nazi 'unity front') 41–2
Einsatzgruppen 139–40
Electra House (Department of Propaganda in
      Enemy Countries) (EH) 257n.7
Eliot, T.S. 239n.56
"Elizabeth Wiskemann and the Sudeten
      Question" (Cornwall) 234n.23
Elton, Geoffrey 218
Empson, William 15–17, 21, 237nn.24,28
Enabling Act (Germany) (1933) 33
Encounter 134–5, 215–16
Equalization of Burdens Law (*Lastenausgleich*)
      (1952) (West Germany) 187–8
Ernst, Max 18–19
Ethiopia 38–9, 43–4, 51, 71
Europa Verlag (publishers) 86